The Secession of Quebec and the Future of Canada

The Secession of Quebec and the Future of Canada

ROBERT A. YOUNG

Published with
The Institute of Intergovernmental Relations
Queen's University, Kingston
by
McGill-Queen's University Press
Montreal & Kingston • London • Buffalo

© Institute of Intergovernmental Relations 1995
ISBN 0-7735-1315-9 (cloth)
ISBN 0-7735-1316-7 (paper)

Legal deposit first quarter 1995
Bibliothèque nationale du Québec

Printed in Canada on acid-free paper

Publication of this book has been assisted by a grant
from the J.B. Smallman and Spencer Memorial Fund,
University of Western Ontario.

McGill-Queen's University Press is grateful to the
Canada Council for support of its publishing program.

Canadian Cataloguing in Publication Data

Young, Robert Andrew
  The secession of Quebec and the future of Canada

  Includes bibliographical references and index.
  ISBN 0-7735-1315-9 (bound) –
  ISBN 0-7735-1316-7 (pbk.)

  1. Canada – Forecasting. 2. Canada – Politics and
  government – 1993 –   . 3. Quebec (Province) –
  Politics and government – 1985 –   . 4. Quebec
  (Province) – History – Autonomy and independence
  movements. 5. Canada – Economic conditions – 1991 –
  6. Economic forecasting – Canada. I. Queen's University (Kingston, Ont.). Institute of Intergovernmental
  Relations. II. Title.

  JL27.5.Y68 1995 971.064'8 C95-900044-5

For my parents, Katharine and Gordon Young
and for J.R. Mallory

Contents

Tables and Figures

Abbreviations

BQ	Bloc québécois
CA1867	Constitution Act, 1867
CA1982	Constitution Act, 1982
CSIS	Canadian Security Intelligence Service
CDP	Civic Democratic Party
CF	Civic Forum
COR	Confederation of Regions Party
EU	European Union
FTA	Canada – U.S. Free Trade Agreement
GATT	General Agreement on Tariffs and Trade
GDP	gross domestic product
IJC	International Joint Commission
IMF	International Monetary Fund
JCC-QS	Joint Committee on Canada-Quebec Separation
MDS	Movement for a Democratic Slovakia
MFN	most favoured nation
NAFTA	North American Free Trade Agreement
NATO	North Atlantic Treaty Organization
NORAD	North American Aerospace Defence Command
NTB	non-tariff barrier
PAP	People's Action Party
PAV	Public Against Violence
PQ	Parti québécois
ROC	rest of Canada
SNP	Slovak National Party
UDI	unilateral declaration of independence

Foreword

The Institute of Intergovernmental Relations at Queen's University has a mandate to undertake research and to stimulate debate about federalism in Canada and abroad. The events of recent years have shown that Quebec secession is an option that must be taken seriously in our research agenda. In our view a full discussion of scenarios about the future of Canada and Quebec can provide Canadians with the means of making more informed judgments about alternative options.

We are pleased to co-publish Professor Robert A. Young's study on the secession of Quebec and the future of Canada. The research for this study was undertaken partly through the auspices of the institute since 1991, and the institute's involvement was supported in part by the CRB Foundation. The publication of this work does not imply that Professor Young's analysis or conclusions reflect the opinions of the Institute of Intergovernmental Relations, Queen's University, the CRB Foundation, or any of our sponsors. They are the responsibility of the author alone.

This work is comprehensive. It provides a thorough review of the existing literature on potential Quebec independence; a fresh analysis of comparative cases of peaceful secession; and a comprehensive assessment of constitutional options for Canada without Quebec. Yet the greater part of the author's work consists of his original contribution of the most detailed set of scenarios yet published on how the transition to sovereignty might occur and the implications of the separation for the long-term future of both Canada and Quebec.

We both expect and welcome debate about this analysis and its conclusions. The institute is confident that the author's work is balanced and scholarly, but we know that everyone will not agree with his findings. We trust that the study will provoke further examination of the assumptions of those who propose and those who oppose Quebec secession.

In bringing this project to completion, the institute would like to acknowledge the valuable partnership of McGill-Queen's University Press, and in particular of Philip Cercone and Joan McGilvray. We are grateful for the intitial support given to the institute by the CRB Foundation and its executive director, Tom Axworthy. I would like to thank the two external readers who provided editorial advice to the author, and the institute's Executive Committee for its continued support for this venture. For their role in moving the manuscript through the publication process with speed and efficiency, I wish to thank Patti Candido, Mary Kennedy, and Alice McLafferty at the institute and Mark Howes and Judy Burns at the publication unit of the School of Policy Studies, Queen's University. Finally and most importantly I would like to express our debt to Bob Young for this and other contributions to the institute's work.

Douglas M. Brown
Executive Director
Institute of Intergovernmental Relations
Queen's University
November, 1994

Acknowledgments

This study has been some time in the making. It was begun when I was a visiting fellow at the Institute of Intergovernmental Relations and the School of Policy Studies at Queen's University. For extending the offer to spend this happy and interesting year, I am grateful to the Executive Committee of the institute and Tom Courchene, who was director of the school at the time. I also appreciated the friendship and help of Doug Brown, now executive director of the institute. I would not have started on this work, or finished it, had it not been for encouragement by Doug Purvis.

In writing this book, as ever, I have enjoyed the help of many colleagues and friends. They have engaged in discussions about its components, lent books, invited me to give papers, read sections, offered advice, and provided the support that is essential for completing such an endeavour. Some, as well, have been remarkably tolerant. I wish to thank the following people: Don Abelson, Randy Ames, Tom Axworthy, Keith Banting, André Blais, Paul Boothe, David Cameron, Cris de Clercy, Édouard Cloutier, Andrew Cooper, Tom Courchene, Stéphane Dion, Philippe Faucher, Tom Flanagan, Alain-G. Gagnon, Al Heineicke, Michael Keating, David Laidler, Peter Leslie, John McDougall, Rob Martin, John Meisel, Henry Milner, Peter Neary, Sid Noel, Al O'Brien, Andrew Sancton, Hugh Segal, Jan Trimble, Richard Vernon, Ronald Watts, Marty Westmacott, Ron Wintrobe, and Ron Wonnacott. I am especially grateful to those who read all or parts of the draft manuscript. For comments and criticism, I also thank participants in sessions at the meetings of the Canadian Political Science Association, the Public Choice Society, and the European Public Choice Society, as well as those who attended seminars or lectures sponsored by the University of Waterloo, McGill University, McMaster University, the Alberta Treasury and the University of Alberta, 3-M Canada, the Centre de recherche en développement économique at l'Université de Montréal, and the Political Economy Research Group at the University of Western Ontario. I especially appreciate Peter Neary's steady help. All faults are mine, of course.

For research assistance, I am obliged to Daniel Bonin, Dwight Herperger, Cristine de Clercy, Allison Bramwell, and Andrew Goldstein. For secretarial help I thank Patti Candido and Helen Drokin; as well, Yvonne Adams provided great support, and also supervised a sometimes harried typist. I echo Doug Brown's thanks to the Queen's staff.

Carlotta Lemieux did fine editing under unusually hard conditions. It was a pleasure to have her counsel and encouragement, and I am grateful for the many improvements she made in this book.

I am also grateful to Philip Cercone and Joan McGilvray for their interest in this work and their efforts to expedite it.

My research would not have been possible without the support of Queen's University and the University of Western Ontario, and especially the Social Sciences and Humanities Research Council of Canada.

The Secession of Quebec and the Future of Canada

Introduction

This book may be about Canada's future, and Quebec's. It is written on the assumption that a majority of Quebecers could vote for sovereignty, despite the risks associated with choosing this option, and that separation would then occur. My purpose is to assess what the long-term future of Canada would be in the event of Quebec's secession and also to explore the political and economic relationships that would exist between Canada and Quebec.

This is no easy task, for three main reasons. First, the whole debate about Quebec sovereignty is charged with precisely such predictions. Partisans of both federalism and sovereignty construct and deploy alternative futures, aiming to influence the expectations and behaviour of citizens. This makes many extant analyses more suspect than is usual in the social sciences. As well, scenarios always depend on a host of assumptions about citizens' and governments' behaviour, and since the secession of Quebec would be a monumental and unprecedented event, there is much scope for disagreement about these assumptions, even among reasonable and dispassionate analysts.

Second, all the central questions that must be addressed are interrelated, both conceptually and temporally. This study will focus on three main issues: the characteristics and constitutional structure of Canada after a Quebec secession, the longer-term future of the Canadian system in the absence of Quebec, and the institutional relationships, both economic and political, that might be established between Canada and an independent Quebec. Obviously these issues are related. To take a simple example, a Canada that had become highly centralized would be unlikely to form a close political relationship with Quebec; conversely, proposals to form a close economic association with Quebec could cause Canada to fragment. It is feasible to lay out all the possible structural alternatives for Quebec and Canada, but these interactive effects bedevil predictions, even when one is guided by theories about how political and social forces, economic features, and political institutions are related. Moreover, even simple guiding propositions, such as that there is a close relationship between levels of economic and political integration, are contestable. More seriously, such analyses are static.

This is the third problem. A basic contention of this study is that the outcomes of secessions are path-dependent. This is simply to say that the long-term results depend on how events unfold. In part, this is because big decisions are taken in the course of secessions, and they are searing experiences. It is also because institutional structures are established during the separation process, both within and between the seceding state and the pre-existing ("predecessor") state. These institutions have enduring effects, but what exactly is established depends on how the separation takes place. Generally, political scientists will agree that basic geographic, economic, and sociocultural factors shape political decisions and the design of institutions. But there is no mechanistic determinism here. The underlying conditions and the institutional and policy results are loosely coupled, or weakly correlated. While the structural factors may set some bounds on the range of possible results, the outcomes actually reached are contingent on historical events. In an event as momentous as a secession, the underlying factors can change too, and this is yet another reason why making predictions about the future of Canada and Quebec after a separation requires a close analysis of how the transition to a new order would take place.

Predicting history – the course of a Quebec secession – is more difficult than examining Canada's economic and social structures and deciding how the country would evolve in the absence of Quebec. But if political actors do possess a lot of autonomy in instances of secession, then the effort cannot be avoided. The approach taken in this study is to rely, first, on the efforts of other scholars who have analysed the economic, legal, and political issues raised by Quebec's possible separation from Canada. Then, in order to flesh out the pure politics of the event, much attention will be devoted to the experience of other countries where secession has occurred – but only peacefully.

As this qualification suggests, this study has been guided by the view that a Quebec secession would not result in organized violence.

It is assumed that the sovereignty of Quebec would clearly be preferred by the Quebec electorate, and that this expressed preference would be accepted by the rest of Canada. These are important assumptions, and they are probed at several junctures. They rest in turn on certain preconditions, and there is much to indicate, both in comparative experience and in Canada, that these conditions might not be met. But these assumptions set limits on the scope of this study, effectively restricting it to the analysis of a peaceful secession. By peaceful, I do not mean one without conflict or even sporadic violence and disorder, but one in which state-sanctioned violence does not take place.

The study proceeds as follows. In part 1 are described the broad institutional outcomes that are possible after Quebec's secession. First, there is a brief survey of what Canada would look like without Quebec, both as a whole and in its internal characteristics. Then the major institutional alternatives are laid out for the constitution of Canada and for the political and economic relationships that could exist between Canada and a sovereign Quebec. This is followed by an analysis of a fundamental issue in the debate about separation – the relationship between economic and political integration. Then there is a brief survey of the structural forces conducive to centralization and decentralization in a new Canadian constitution, and to more or less integration between the two states.

Part 2 concerns the transition to sovereignty. Why this is important is the subject of the first chapter. The next one summarizes existing studies of the economic, legal, and political issues raised by Quebec secession, and these show clearly that the process of the transition would largely determine the long-term outcomes of secession. Although politics would drive events and produce the important results, analysts disagree fundamentally about what the process of separation would look like. So we turn to comparative experience, investigating other cases of peaceful secession. The purpose here is to find general patterns in the political processes that have occurred in such cases, and these are described and explained. A separate chapter presents in greater detail a noteworthy recent secession, the breakup of the Czech and Slovak Federal Republic. This case differs in a few ways from the other instances of peaceful secession because it was marked by political polarization between the Czechs and Slovaks, but the generalizations derived elsewhere still apply to it very well.

In part 3, all this material is brought to bear on Canada and Quebec. First, the politics and strategies involved in a referendum on sovereignty are analysed. Then, assuming a sovereigntist victory, the process of the separation is described. While this account is informed by studies of Canada and Quebec, its guiding framework consists of the generalizations that were derived from the comparative analysis. Here the study concentrates on how the disengagement would take place, how the crucial issues would be resolved through negotiations, how Canada would reconstitute itself, and what institutional relationships would be established between the two states. After this description, another scenario is sketched, one that features a gradual polarization between Quebec and the rest of Canada, and the earlier predictions are modified appropriately. In part 4, conclusions are reached about the long-term results of the secession of Quebec from Canada, and the study is briefly summarized.

Readers who want a more detailed guide to the arguments made here might choose to read the summary chapter first. As well, since other studies have canvassed the institutional arrangements that could be found in Canada after a Quebec secession, readers familiar with this material might wish to move directly to the chapters on the transition. There, some readers will find more than they ever wanted to know about other secessions, and especially about the breakup of Czechoslovakia, but their perseverance will be rewarded by discovering a pattern of peaceful secession that is remarkably uniform and robust.

In part 3, the tone of the study changes, and the separation of Quebec from Canada is described in definite terms and tenses. This is done for a purpose. The transition process laid out there is the best prediction that I am able to make about what would take place. On the assumption that Quebec will separate – a possibility that I do not welcome now, having completed this study, but one that justifies this whole work – the transition, in my view, will take place as described. Of course, this view may be wrong. It would be surprising if readers agreed with it entirely. As for events that may occur while the book is in press, readers may gauge whether and how they have affected this account.

Finally, the use of appellations should be clarified. If Quebec secedes and what is left of Canada continues as a sovereign country, that entity will surely be called Canada. At times in this book, "Canada" means precisely that. However, since Canada currently includes Quebec, clarity demands that another term be available to describe Canada outside Quebec (as, at times, does style). Here this entity is called ROC (rest of Canada), an acronym that is as irritating as it is common, because the alternatives – Canada without Quebec, English Canada – are hardly less irritating and are more cumbersome. Also, as the reader will see, the results of this study buttress, more or less, the connotations of coherence and stability that ROC carries with it.

The Grand Alternatives

CHAPTER ONE

Canada without Quebec

At the outset, it is appropriate to grasp what Canada would be like without Quebec. Most Canadians have contemplated this possibility, though they would do so much more intensely if a Quebec referendum on sovereignty were to produce a Yes vote; their views of the rest of Canada (ROC), including their deepest metaphoric conceptions of it, would then be important in determining what Canada would become. Here, however, the analysis begins with ROC's structural features. To make an initial assessment of whether Canada would be viable after a Quebec secession, it is necessary to survey briefly the country's demographic, economic, social, and political make-up. As well, some basic information about these features will later help in assessing how well various constitutional options would correspond with underlying cleavages or uniformities in the polity, and also in determining what characteristics would affect the ROC-Quebec relationship.

Table A1 presents some selected characteristics of Canada, Quebec, and ROC (see appendix). This is a summary view of what Canada would look like after a Quebec secession. Ignoring any movement of people resulting from secession as well as any new arrangements about citizenship, Canada would lose 6.9 million citizens, leaving ROC with 74.7 per cent of the current population. The loss of territory would be far less substantial, since ROC would retain 84.5 per cent of the area over which Canada now possesses sovereignty. Of course, the table does not reveal one outstanding feature of ROC – the complete physical separation of the Atlantic provinces from the rest of the territory.[1] The Atlantic exclave would amount to 6.5 per cent of ROC's territory (or 12.0 per cent of the land mass if one excludes the Yukon and Northwest Territories) and 11.3 per cent of the population. So one-tenth of ROC would be in noncontiguous territory, a feature perhaps more important psychologically than in other respects.

As with territory, the losses in most other dimensions would be less than the population loss. Gross domestic product (GDP), manufacturing output, and exports would all be higher on a per capita basis than they are in today's Canada. At present, the major federal revenue flows are higher per capita in ROC than in Canada as a whole. Only about one-tenth of chartered bank assets are not currently located in ROC, a consequence of the strength of Quebec's credit union movement. And although public investment is more heavily concentrated in Quebec, ROC attracts 80 per cent of private investment. ROC also receives a disproportionate share of new immigrants. As a country, it would be massively anglophone: people with French as their mother tongue would be outnumbered three to one by those with a "non-official" mother tongue, while the home language of 88 per cent of the population would be English. Finally, based on the last three federal election results, there would be no great changes in the distribution of political party support; obviously, though, the prospects of the New Democratic Party and the Reform Party would be relatively better in ROC than in Canada as it now exists.

Of at least equal significance is the internal composition of ROC, some dimensions of which are laid out in table A2 (see appendix). The central feature here is the relative weight of Ontario, which would account for 49 per cent of the population and well over one-half of manufacturing, exports, federal revenues, and new immigrants. Across the country, there are major differences in per capita GDP, with Alberta's being almost twice that of Prince Edward Island. Economically, the provinces fall into two tiers, Ontario, Alberta, and British Columbia being the "have" provinces. This distinction would be clearer in the future ROC than it is at present, since Quebec acts as a swing province (moderately "have not" but industrial). On the other hand, almost 78 per cent of ROC's population would be concentrated in the wealthier provinces. Hence, the cost of federal transfer programs (if they were continued) would decrease.[2]

The major economic cleavage in today's ROC is between Ontario's concentration of manufacturing (about 70 per cent of the ROC total) and the concentration of primary production and exports in the West (76 per cent of primary-sector exports). But the West is hardly homogeneous. Alberta and British Columbia attract more than their population share of investment, while the reverse is true of Manitoba and

Saskatchewan. British Columbia's percentage of manufacturing approximates its population share and outweighs its primary exports, while Alberta and Saskatchewan are much more oriented towards exports of grains and hydrocarbons (though manufacturing in the West is more resource based than it is in Ontario). It is also noteworthy that the western provinces' relative weight in the ROC economy is greater than in Canada's. They account for 38.7 per cent of GDP in ROC, but only 29.7 per cent in Canada as a whole.

In most other dimensions, provincial characteristics are roughly in line with population, though one potentially important exception is language. From Ontario westward, as a result of the location choices of immigrants and the large number of First Nations people, the proportion of those with "non-official" mother tongues is very much higher than in Atlantic Canada. Francophones are heavily concentrated in New Brunswick, Ontario, and Manitoba: 81.4 per cent of the ROC inhabitants whose mother tongue is French live in these three provinces. Of those in ROC who speak only French in the home, 84.8 per cent are in Ontario and New Brunswick. In these two provinces there are about 718,000 people whose mother tongue is French (which compares with the 623,000 in Quebec whose mother tongue is English).

Second, there are substantial interprovincial differences in political preferences. Third parties fare poorly in the Atlantic provinces, both federally and provincially. In recent federal elections, Alberta has been exceptional, first in its massive support for the Progressive Conservatives and then in the very heavy swing to the Reform Party. On the other hand, there are surprising political similarities across the provinces of ROC. Excluding Alberta and the northern territories, the PC share of the vote in 1984 ranged from 42 to 58 per cent, and it declined across the country in 1988 to a narrow range of 35 to 42 per cent. With the exception of Atlantic Canada, it ranged between only 11 and 18 per cent in 1993. Even the Reform vote in British Columbia was only 16 per cent higher than in Ontario. These are not large variations on general trends. In provincial elections, the same three major parties – the PC, Liberals, and NDP – have regularly captured almost 100 per cent of the vote (with the current exceptions of COR in New Brunswick and Social Credit in British Columbia), and nowhere is any one of them irrelevant. All the provincial systems are competitive, and the players are basically the same. It is always possible to focus on the differences between, say, two-party dominance in Atlantic Canada, the NDP's strength in Saskatchewan and British Columbia, and Alberta's history of one-party rule; but the similarities in ROC are at least as striking, especially when compared with other federations where long-standing regional parties are common,

Table 1
Distribution of Gross Provincial and Regional Output by Destination, Canada, 1989

	Origin of Output				
Destination	Atlantic	Quebec	Ontario	West/North	Canada
Foreign	15.3%	12.9%	16.4%	15.5%	
Atlantic	75.0	2.0	1.8	0.3	
Quebec	4.0	71.9	5.6	1.7	
Ontario	3.7	9.7	70.3	5.0	
West/North	1.9	3.5	6.0	77.5	
Value ($ billions)	57.6	228.8	459.8	298.4	1044.6

Source: Statistics Canada Daily, cat. 11-001E, 24 August 1993.

Table 2
Distribution of Provincial and Regional Manufacturing and Primary-Sector Output by Destination, Canada, 1989

	Origin of Output				
Destination	Atlantic	Quebec	Ontario	West/North	Canada
Foreign	37.5%	26.5%	33.6%	33.7%	
Atlantic	46.6	3.5	2.4	0.4	
Quebec	7.3	46.4	8.3	2.6	
Ontario	6.1	17.7	47.6	8.8	
West/North	2.5	5.9	8.0	54.4	
Value ($ billions)	18.9	88.6	186.3	107.8	401.6

Source: Statistics Canada Daily, cat. 11-001E, 24 August 1993.

and also compared with Canada's current political system, to which Quebec contributes a considerable degree of heterogeneity.

It is also useful to consider briefly the economic linkages between the existing regions of Canada. Gross figures are laid out in tables 1 and 2. The former shows, for instance, that in 1989 some 15.3 per cent of total output in the Atlantic region was exported to foreign countries, while 75.0 per cent was consumed in the region. Focusing first on ROC, the overall image is one of loose interconnection. Ontario sends only 7.8 per cent of total output to the Atlantic provinces and to the West and North, while the West/North region sends only 5.3 per cent to the rest of ROC. In every case, exports abroad outweigh sales to the rest of ROC. But the regional figures for Atlantic Canada and the West count shipments to other provinces as intraregional consumption, and a large proportion of gross regional product consists of services that are not exportable. Table 2 concentrates on the primary and secondary sectors, where interregional flows are much more significant. Once more, though, the total value of production exported is greater than the amount traded between regions.

The tables also provide information about ROC-Quebec links. For each of the three regions of ROC, inter-ROC trade is greater than regional trade with Quebec. But the same pattern is not true of Quebec, which exports to ROC 15.2 per cent of its total output and 27.1 per cent of primary- and secondary-sector output, quantities that exceed its foreign exports. Some volumes of ROC-Quebec trade are very important, however. In 1989, Ontario made sales of $25.7 billion to Quebec, while the reverse flow was $22.2 billion, for a total of $47.9 billion. In the existing configuration of Canada, this is the most important regional trading nexus. Still, the total trade between Ontario and the West/North region, at $42.5 billion, is a very close second.[3]

From this very brief survey, a few conclusions can be drawn. First, on paper it appears that Canada would be a viable economic entity without Quebec. As a nation, it would be considerably more homogeneous than it is now, culturally, linguistically, and politically. Although interregional economic linkages are outweighed in today's ROC by each region's foreign trade, the volume of business transacted across the country is very large and is considerably greater than it is with Quebec. Finally, Ontario would be economically dominant in the future ROC. On the other hand, the relative importance of the western provinces and of "outer Canada" generally would increase substantially compared with the situation today, in which Ontario and Quebec together comprise the central-Canadian bloc. All these features, though, are only the skeleton on which a new Canadian constitution would be fitted in the event of a Quebec separation. They leave open many alternatives.

CHAPTER TWO

Canada's Constitutional Options

If Quebec secedes, ROC could reconstitute itself in a variety of ways. Here, the major alternatives are described. These range from a much more centralized structure right through to total fragmentation of the country. Even though all these possibilities have been the subject of some discussion, it is important to survey them briefly. While this is a straightforward exercise, even a casual acquaintance with the existing literature shows that there is no consensus among analysts about what configuration is likely or what would be desirable.[1]

The first constitutional alternative is the status quo. Canada – as it would continue to be called after Quebec's secession – could retain a constitution very similar to its current one. This option will be analysed in much more detail later, because it is the most probable outcome; suffice it to say here that Quebec could be excised from the existing constitution rather neatly. The major objections to this alternative are procedural and substantive. Given that there is considerable discontent with the existing constitution (as shown by the demands made by a wide range of interests during the negotiation of the Charlottetown Accord), under many scenarios of Quebec secession there would be strong pressure to make a variety of other amendments when the constitution was opened for review. Moreover, many observers believe that notions of popular sovereignty have so infused Canadian politics that no constitutional amendment would be possible without broad participation in the process and popular ratification of the result; hence, changes to the status quo would be essential. Depending on how the transition to Quebec sovereignty occurred, however, both these procedural considerations could be met or obviated.

The major substantive objection to fitting ROC within the existing constitution is that Ontario would dominate the truncated federation. This is a special problem for the West. As Archer put it long ago, "The bargaining over national policies of the new Canada would be hard and sharp, [and] unless the West were sure of some means of countering Ontario's economic, financial, and political power, it would consider going its own way."[2] This problem rests on the sense that Ontario and the western provinces have economic interests that conflict to some extent, and that westerners' sense of regional solidarity has heightened even as their suspicions about central-Canadian dominance have been reinforced by such measures as the National Energy Program and the awarding of the CF-18 maintenance contract to Quebec firms. These are genuine issues. But the absence of Quebec would alter the political dynamics that exist under the present constitution. In its decentralist pressures, Quebec has been an ally of Alberta and British Columbia, and has contributed to increasing provincial autonomy, in the sense of freedom from the policy constraints and intrusions of Ottawa. But when western representatives have sought positive federal policies to advance their region's interests – when the West Wants In – Quebec, as a large element of central Canada, has helped stymie them. It is also worth noting again that the West is not homogeneous. In particular, the governments of Manitoba and Saskatchewan have traditionally supported a central government powerful enough to redistribute income to their citizens. As well, there are considerable differences in attitudes among citizens within and between the western provinces, as well as a substantial general affection for "Canada" as such. So the constitutional status quo might prevail, in the absence of Quebec, insofar as it can be maintained without that province.

On the spectrum of possible constitutional alternatives, one extreme position is that ROC become a unitary state. Free of Quebec, English Canada would reconstitute itself in non-federal form. Advocates of this solution favour it as promoting a strong internal common market, eliminating administrative duplication, and providing economies of scale in service delivery.[3] Moreover, the problem of Ontario's dominance would be resolved, or, more precisely, dissolved. On the other hand, there would still have to be an extensive, decentralized bureaucracy to deliver services. And many analysts argue that for most government functions, economies of scale are reached at the regional or provincial level, except in the smallest provinces.[4] The unitary solution also ignores the real diversity of preferences and sense of provincial identification that exists in ROC, even if this reality is to some extent the residue of past provincial policy. As well, in eliminating the negative effects of intergovernmental competition, both among provinces and between provinces and Ottawa, the unitary solution would also terminate the benefits of this competition, which include policy innovation, efficiency, responsiveness, and the opportunity for citizens and firms to participate in various political arenas.[5]

Of course, a unitary state could be combined with a system of administrative regions, to which various powers could be delegated. But this alternative weakens the argument that unitarism would promote economic efficiency: small administrative units with any power at all could balkanize the economic union and fragment social policy rather effectively. In either form, this alternative also encounters a serious practical problem. Under the existing constitution, amendments require the approval of provincial governments. It is conceivable that Quebec's separation could produce large shifts of public opinion in all provinces in favour of radical centralization or could result in alternative constitutional mechanisms, such as a constituent assembly, which could force through amendments to create a new, unitary constitution; it is also possible that the constitutional order could break down entirely, with only a central government re-emerging. Short of such events, however, eliminating federalism would depend on "the willingness of the provinces to acquiesce in their own demise," and this is improbable.[6]

The next alternative is that ROC would become more centralized. The federal structure would remain, but the central government would acquire greater powers. Often underlying this suggestion is the view that Quebec's presence in the federation has impeded an outcome that is the natural consequence of ROC's cultural, social, and economic coherence. As Kwavnick has argued, "Quebec nationalism is legitimate. Canadian nationalism is illegitimate. That, in a nutshell, is the price of satisfying Québécois nationalism within Confederation."[7] Without Quebec, the central government would more accurately reflect, and more vigorously promote, English-Canadian unity.[8]

Which powers should be transferred? In some variants, Ottawa would acquire more control over social and cultural policy, the areas most subject in the past to Quebec's decentralizing influence. Health, job training, higher education, and even social assistance might be transferred to the central government. Other analysts maintain that Ottawa should be equipped with more substantial powers of economic management. Apart from the transfer of specific heads of power found in section 92 of the Constitution Act, 1867, the central government might acquire new powers to prohibit provincial measures that create barriers within the economic union, and also to act creatively to strengthen the economy and to make it more efficient. Finally, Ottawa might acquire more explicit powers to make international agreements.

After a Quebec secession, more centralization might well be the outcome in Canada. But these proposed constitutional changes raise several problems. First is the fact that transfers of jurisdiction would increase uncertainty. Shifting heads of powers and inscribing new powers in the constitution would entail substantial administrative rearrangements, and how the new powers would evolve when exercised in practice would be unpredictable. In the midst of a secession crisis, Canadians might not be willing to risk such changes. Second is the likely opposition of provincial governments: greater federal powers of economic management have been resisted, particularly in the West, because they could easily justify "integrative" measures such as the National Energy Program. Third, transfers to the centre make more acute the problem of representation at the centre: further changes would be necessary in order to reduce Ontario's dominance in Ottawa. One possibility here would be to increase the number of units in the federation by creating the provinces of Labrador, Acadie, Metro Toronto, Niagara, Southwestern Ontario, and so on, and then limiting their sovereignty to a few matters such as education. This has theoretical attractions for those who see large units as impeding flexibility in federal systems, but the practical difficulties of drawing boundaries, negotiating the new division of powers, and securing provincial assent would be substantial. Submitting to division would also be risky for Ontarians, because it would not be evident that the new federation would be viable, whereas the province could be a viable country in its present form.

A final problem with the centralization alternative is that it suggests stronger government at a time when Canadian public opinion has shifted to favour less state intervention than there was, say, in the 1960s, and when governments generally are perceived as less legitimate than they were. As shown by the support for the Reform Party and for expenditure restraint, this sentiment is particularly strong in the West. On the other hand, the momentous issues raised by Quebec secession, and the immense uncertainty that would very likely prevail if Quebecers proceeded along this course, might produce support in ROC for a stronger government in Ottawa. Whether such support would culminate in a formal constitutional change to centralize power, given the difficulties with this option, is quite another matter.

Moving past the constitutional status quo, the next alternative is that ROC would become more decentralized. This could occur, first, by involving the provincial governments more fully in decisions taken at the centre, so that what Ottawa does would better reflect regional preferences. One mechanism for increasing intrastate federalism along these lines would involve a new body, whose members would be appointed by the provincial governments (as described in the Quebec Liberal Party's 1980 proposal for a Federal Council, or in Ottawa's 1991 proposal to create a Council of the Federation to oversee the exercise of some central-government powers). But adding a third chamber would be unwieldy, and as reaction to the 1991 federal proposal showed, it is an unpopular idea. Another possible device is Senate reform. Insofar as the public does not favour abolishing the Senate altogether, it aligns with the western demand for a triple-E Senate (elected, equal, and effective). Such a Senate would greatly increase the relative power of the Atlantic provinces as well as the West. More deeply, it raises the question of how senators would balance the representation of regional, provincial-government, and partisan policy preferences. In any case, while Senate reform would diminish Ontario's representation in one chamber, it would not solve the problem of the province's predominance in the House of Commons.

The most likely form in which decentralization would occur is through the transfer of powers to the provincial order of government. This option has been extensively canvassed in recent years.[9] The provinces might gain exclusive or primary jurisdiction in job training, unemployment insurance, health, immigration, culture, tourism, forestry and mining, recreation, higher education, housing, the environment, energy, and municipal affairs. Tax bases could be transferred too, and the central government's regulatory and spending powers in other policy areas could be constrained. Other transfers and checks on central power might further increase the relative capacity of the provincial order of government.

This decentralist option has the advantage that fewer decisions would be taken in Ottawa, so the issue of representation at the centre would be less salient. Arguably, decentralization would result in a closer matching of government services and policies with local preferences, and in greater accountability as well.[10] The immediate disadvantages concern the costs of concentrating power in provincial governments. In some of the functions now delivered or coordinated by Ottawa, economies of scale could not be attained at the provincial level, and duplication in administration could impose extra costs on citizens. A more substantial danger is that provincial policies would tend over time to fragment the Canadian economy. Interprovincial competition can be creative and efficiency enhancing, but it can also reduce overall welfare when measures impede the free flow of goods, services, capital, and labour. There is also the possibility of competitive deregulation in areas such as the environment, and avoiding such destructive competition might require a central authority that was capable of acting as an umpire or monitor. Conceivably, though, new mechanisms of interprovincial consultation could serve the same purpose, as they did in the recent agreement to reduce interprovincial trade barriers.

It is not only in the economic realm that such disadvantages emerge. Increasingly it is becoming clear that social policy is fundamental to economic success as well as to social justice. For example, without a sound set of programs in education, job training, social assistance, and unemployment insurance, not only will labour markets operate inefficiently but the overall tax burden will be excessive. There is a case to be made that such programs should be integrated at the provincial level. But without effective coordination, there is a lot of potential for inefficiency. First, population mobility might be reduced. Second, individual provincial governments would have little incentive to provide programs that had large externalities, such as higher education and support for research and development. Finally, if redistribution within the federation decreased along with the central government's powers, there would be less money for social spending precisely where it was most needed and could be most productive – in the "have not" provinces.

This leads to a final consideration about the decentralization alternative. If, in the medium term, it resulted in less interprovincial mobility and redistribution through Ottawa, then it might represent a slippery slope towards fragmentation. Many scholars believe that there is a strong relationship between economic and political integration: the more integrated regional economies are, the more probable and necessary it is that common political mechanisms with a democratic base actually manage the economic space; conversely, economic disintegration entails a decreasing sense of community, less willingness to redistribute, and political fragmentation. As Harris and Purvis argue, "the alternative vision of Canada offered by many with a substantially decentralized political system, and most important powers residing at the provincial level will result in an increasingly economically fragmented and balkanized economic situation, which will inevitably undermine most national institutions including the concept of national citizenship, and ultimately the political union we now think of as Canada."[11] This is a proposition that is widely held. But the underlying theory – that levels of economic and political integration are highly correlated – requires further analysis. It is relevant in connection with both the long-term structure of Canada and Quebec-Canada relations, and is taken up below.

Before proceeding further along the range of decentralist options, it is appropriate to consider a "rebalanced" ROC, in which a new division of powers would strengthen the central government in some respects and the provinces in others. In essence, Quebec's secession would provide ROC with an opportunity to modernize the constitution. The nature of rebalancing, however, is open to question. Often, a large distinction is made between social and economic policy. Some would argue that "the main basis of unity in a Canada without Quebec is cultural and social, and that the real basis of diversity is economic."[12] In this view, the federation should be rebalanced so that the central government maintains the Canada-wide social programs that bind all citizens into a "sharing community," while the provincial governments acquire greater powers of economic management. The opposite rebalancing option is that Ottawa increase its economic powers while the provinces attain greater control over social programs. The rationale here is that the economic union requires central management, whereas social programs should be delivered by the governments that most closely represent regional preferences in matters such as health, education, and social assistance.

Some problems with both possibilities have already been traced in the above discussion of centralization and decentralization, but there are two practical difficulties that should be stressed. First, if social powers were centralized and programs made more uniform, the wealthier provinces would have to be prepared to redistribute the fruits of their economic success, and they might not be willing to do so if the economic union tended to fragment over time. Second, if economic powers were centralized, the provincial governments would risk becoming mere administrative organs of Ottawa, unless tax bases also were transferred and there was provision for greater provincial participation in central-government policy making. In either case, rebalancing might reduce the extent to which economic and social policy could be coordinated.

A variant on rebalancing is to allow for more constitutional flexibility in ROC. Several devices have been suggested. Provinces could be allowed to opt in to central-government programs, as provided for in section 94 of the Constitution Act, 1867, which allows the Parliament of Canada to legislate in the areas of property and civil rights in Ontario, Nova Scotia, and New Brunswick; such laws take effect in a province only when enacted by the provincial legislature. Another device would be to allow provinces to opt out of central-government laws or spending programs, with compensation. Provision could also be made for the interdelegation of powers between the provincial and central governments. And the range of concurrent powers could be broadened, so that bilateral federal-provincial agreements, or federal-regional agreements, could effectively determine policy in more areas. All such devices would have two advantages. They would allow for asymmetry in Canada, and they would provide for a measure of flexibility that could be desirable given the uncertainties attendant on Quebec's secession. If it is unpredictable how intergovernmental relations would evolve over the long term, such constitutional arrangements could be useful. The disadvantage of such devices, of course, is that they could lead to a "checkerboard federalism," in which federal powers and programs would be quite different in the various provinces.

Returning to the decentralist options, another alternative is that ROC would be reconstituted as a collection of regions rather than provinces. In one version, the regions would have powers roughly like those of the provinces; in another, their jurisdictional scope would be considerably enlarged. A regional reconstitution has several advantages. The units would be more similar in size and resources, some economies of scale in service provision could be realized, and the advantages of intergovernmental competition could be retained to some extent. But the difficulties are obvious. There would still be substantial variations in power: the population of Atlantic Canada is only 24 per cent of Ontario's. More important, the regions are not homogeneous in interests or preferences. There is little community of interest between Newfoundland and Prince Edward Island, for instance, and agricultural issues on the prairies are largely irrelevant to British Columbians. As two keen analysts of western Canada have concluded, "there is significant economic diversity among the four provinces. These intraregional differences are probably sufficiently large that many of the problems that currently confound federal-provincial relations would remain and perhaps be even more serious" within a western region.[13] Moreover, there is little evidence of major regional differences in Canadians' sense of national identification or in their preference for particular constitutional outcomes.[14] As well, it would be difficult to determine the regional boundaries, especially in the West. Finally, regional governments would submerge some minorities, such as the Acadians and the residents of the Yukon and Northwest Territories.

The decentralist variant of a regional reconfiguration involves very substantial transfers of power to the regions. All of the above practical problems remain, and in addition this solution possesses the general advantages and disadvantages of a decentralization to the provincial governments. An issue that becomes more acute, though, is whether redistribution, which presumably would become greater within regions, would still occur across regional boundaries.[15]

A more extreme solution would be confederation. Here, the provinces (or regions or some combination of the two) would attain sovereignty; then powers would be delegated to central authorities, whose functions would be very circumscribed. They might include defence, justice, some aspects of foreign relations, monetary policy, and some regulatory powers over the economy. Such a configuration would probably follow failed attempts to reconstitute ROC in some more centralized form, and the secession of one or more units from the federation. In a confederal arrangement, "Canada" would cease to exist as a subject of international law. Much has been written about the erosion of state sovereignty through international agreements and the complex of forces commonly called globalization, and in practice these assessments have some validity. But sovereignty remains the fundamental organizing principle of the international community of states, and it must have a single legal locus. In a confederal reconstitution, that locus would be the provincial or regional governments.

The advantages of confederation are similar to those often propounded by sovereigntists in Quebec. The central authority would be restricted to a very few essential functions. There would be an end to duplication and waste in the provision of government services. Policy making in the regions could be integrated across a much wider range of social and economic programs. Rather than being subject to national policies that are inevitably the result of compromise and are often slow to be adapted to new conditions, their citizens and firms would enjoy policies tailored to their distinct interests and preferences, and they might be more successful competitors in the continental and global economies. As small sovereign states, these new units' economic vulnerability would be limited by international agreements that secured access to foreign markets.

But there are disadvantages to confederal outcomes. If the new states were admitted to the General Agreement on Tariffs and Trade (GATT), the Canada–U.S. Free Trade Agreement (FTA), and the North American Free Trade Agreement (NAFTA), their policy autonomy would be constrained by rules that currently do not apply to substate governments. Their international negotiating power would be less, even collectively, than Canada's is today. Some units would be very weak economically, and in the absence of substantial redistribution, people's living standards would plummet. Moreover, since regions and provinces tend to be economically specialized, the economic performance of these new states would be more volatile and more vulnerable to economic shocks; and if regional policies fragmented the economic union, there would be welfare losses for all.[16] These disadvantages could be circumvented, but the principal way of doing so would be by delegating power to the confederal authorities.

This raises a central problem of confederations. They require a decision rule for making common policy, and the more policy is to be decided collectively, the more crucial are the rules through which it is made. There are three broad alternatives that would be available to a confederal Canada. The first is the population principle. Either through a directly elected legislative body or through proportional voting, the constituent states would have power proportional to their populations. This raises the familiar problem of dominance by the larger provinces, especially Ontario, and it would be more acute in the confederal arrangement since there would probably not be a second legislative chamber based on equality of the states. On the other hand, since the common functions would be more limited than in a true federation, the problem would be diminished, and there could be some mechanisms put in place to protect minorities, such as super-majority voting requirements. The opposite decision rule is that each constituent unit has equal weight. This is akin to many formal procedures in the international realm, such as voting in the General Assembly of the United Nations. The problem is that wealthy and populous states can be outvoted by coalitions of the smaller units. Somewhere between these alternatives lies the third possibility – systems of weighted voting, such as that employed in the Council of Ministers of the European Community. The problem here, of course, is deciding how to weight the various members' votes.

Whatever the decision rule, confederations are notoriously unstable. When constituent states are sovereign, collective decisions are not readily enforceable, and members often have recourse to retaliation or to negotiations that are likely to be seen as unfair because of the threat of retaliation. Neither of these is conducive to stability. Second, if the central authorities are delegated powers sufficient to overcome the disadvantages of independent policy making by the states, then, whatever the decision rule employed, it is very probable that a majority in some state will perceive itself to be permanently disadvantaged by the confederal arrangement and will withdraw its delegation of power. In short, the problem of confederations is secession. Finally, confederal arrangements must include transfers of funds or taxation powers. Assuming that the sovereign states emerging from ROC would be unwilling to alienate tax bases, the central authority would be dependent on allocations. If Canada's national debt had not been divided among the constituent units (a course that would cause immense difficulties for the fiscally weaker states) and if debt management therefore remained a function of the central authority, confidence in the confederation would be low: "A confederation that inherited the debits of Canada while depending for its assets on grants from its members would have a very shaky financial and political basis."[17]

At the extreme of the decentralist possibilities for Canada is its complete fragmentation into provinces or regions. There would be no common institutions or "national" policies short of the dispute-settlement mechanisms and provisions for policy harmonization that exist under GATT and NAFTA (assuming that the units were admitted to these agreements), though provinces or groups of provinces could engage in treaties of various kinds. Overall, this alternative would entail very substantial welfare losses, until – and unless – the units could make bilateral and multilateral arrangements between themselves or with other countries about defence, labour mobility, and the currency, to name only the most significant matters. On the other hand, some provinces or regions could make net gains as independent states; this might be true of Ontario and also of an Alberta–British Columbia union.[18] Calculations of such "gains," however, tend to ignore the costs of the transition to independence. Furthermore, the inhabitants of the weaker provinces undoubtedly would suffer under any conceivable scenario of the fragmentation of ROC.

That is why this alternative is often coupled with the suggestion that a fragmented ROC would sooner or later join the United States. Some provinces or regions might be forced to opt for this course almost immediately; others might maintain their independence longer. Obviously, maintaining any degree of constitutional unity in ROC would become much more problematic if individual provinces or regions joined the United States. The only exception might be the defection of the Atlantic region, for a Canada stretching from the Ottawa River to Vancouver Island might be sustainable. Yet it seems likely that the psychological blow to people in the remaining provinces would be substantial; more seriously, if a large component of "outer Canada" left ROC, the problem of Ontario dominance in the remainder would be accentuated.

This last scenario illustrates a difficulty about union with the United States, for the Atlantic region is arguably the least desirable potential addition to that country. Would the United States agree to absorb it or any other part of ROC? From official statements and from the opinions of experienced American observers of Canada, it is evident that the United States' preferred option is that Canada remain intact. Were Quebec to secede, it is most likely that the U.S. government would be a force for stability and the quick resolution of uncertainty. American firms already have access to Canadian markets and investment opportunities under the FTA and NAFTA, so there is little to be gained by exercising direct control of this country. And ROC's absorption would entail some evident disadvantages for the United States: the event would not be uncontested, for a significant proportion of Canadians harbour anti-American sentiments, and they would make unwilling citizens; the ROC debt would presumably have to be absorbed along with the territory; and, most significantly perhaps, the admission of another 21 million citizens in several new states could change the balance of political power in the republic (though some Democrats might favour this tectonic change). On the other hand, it might be possible to extend to the provinces associate status such as Puerto Rico now has. In geopolitical terms, the United States would gain through a land link to Alaska, control of the Arctic, and ownership of unalienated crown land. So if ROC showed tendencies towards fragmentation, the uncertainties that would prevail might make Americans more willing to absorb the remnants of the country. (This would be especially disadvantageous for the citizens of some provinces; for while none would have much influence within the American system, all, under the U.S. constitution, would lose control of their energy revenues.)[19] Annexation by the United States would of course end the separate existence of Canada, and many of its citizens would be dismayed to become Americans. But as Bill Lederman has noted, "there are worse fates possible in the modern world."[20]

One other long-term constitutional option for Canada remains to be considered – a union, federal or confederal, between Ontario and Quebec. This possibility would emerge if Quebec seceded and ROC was unable to reconstitute itself as a functioning state.[21] An Ontario-Quebec federation would have a population of 17 million people and a gross domestic product almost two-thirds that of present-day Canada. It would be a powerful international actor. The two states are contiguous and share the Great Lakes–St Lawrence system. They are strongly integrated by flows of commerce and investment, and since the economies are relatively similar, it could be easier to agree on common trade and economic policies than it is in Canada now or would be between Canada and Quebec after secession. And since the positions of linguistic minorities in the two units are relatively symmetrical, a federation-wide language policy and system of minority rights might be agreed.

Despite this community of interest, however, an Ontario-Quebec union would face, even more acutely, many of the problems discussed about ROC. First, economically, Ontario has a much larger stake in ROC than in Quebec, not only in terms of trade but also with respect to the ownership of firms.[22] More important, if a new constitution allocated substantial powers to a central government, this bipartite system would produce either dominance or *immobilisme*. Where interests were seen to conflict, Ontario would always predominate under the principle of representation by population; on the other hand, if equality was the decision rule, either in a common legislature or a second chamber, Ontario's population could be frustrated by a minority within the new country.[23] As well, the extent of redistribution within the union would probably not be great. As the wealthier component, Ontario would face a continuing stream of transfers out of the province; and assuming that the new union was formed as a consequence of Quebec's original secession, Ontario citizens would not be likely to support much redistribution to Quebecers. Hence, some important advantages of integration, such as mutual insurance against economic shocks and the capture of social-policy externalities, would not accrue within this union. Indeed, the benefits of union for Ontario would be at least as great in most conceivable versions of a reconstituted ROC.

To this point, our discussion of ROC's constitution has focused exclusively on the division of powers and the degree of centralization that would obtain in the country. But these are not the only important issues that would arise in reconfiguring a Canada without Quebec, for the current constitution has provisions about many other matters. In all probability, many aspects of a ROC constitution would remain unchanged. For example, it is hard to imagine that the parliamentary system would be jettisoned by Canada if Quebec separated. But Canada would face three contentious issues: language rights (including minority-language education rights), Aboriginal rights, and equalization and regional development. Of course, the occasion of creating a new constitution for ROC might elicit demands from many quarters for all sorts of changes to other parts of the constitution, notably the Charter of Rights and Freedoms, but the above three are likely to be the most pressing issues.[24]

The decisions about equalization would depend on how centralized ROC was. If a federal authority retained independent taxing power and the capacity to manage a national economy, then provisions committing Parliament and the provincial legislatures to promote equal opportunities, to reduce regional disparities, and to provide services of reasonable quality to all Canadians would probably be maintained. But ROC would not be likely to remain a "sharing community" to the extent that Canada is now if most powers over economic and social policy were devolved to the provinces or regions.

In today's Canada, francophones make up about 25 per cent of the population; in ROC they would amount to less than 5 per cent, and outside Quebec there is a significant trend towards their assimilation into the anglophone community. After a Quebec secession, it is doubtful that the full range of francophone language rights would survive in ROC as a whole, though these rights might remain unimpaired at the provincial level in New Brunswick and perhaps in Ontario. But like so much else about ROC's reconstitution, the precise outcome would depend on how the process of Quebec secession took place, and also on the arrangements that would be negotiated with Quebec.

As for Aboriginal rights, Quebec's secession would provide another opportunity to inscribe in Canada's constitution the inherent right to self-government that First Nations leaders have sought for over a decade. There is considerable sympathy in English Canada for embedding this right, though sentiment is not unmixed and the land claims associated with self-government vary considerably across the country in scope and status. In a highly decentralized ROC, it is not obvious that rights for Aboriginal peoples would be clarified and strengthened even if they did remain uniform across the country. In a confederal or fragmented ROC, both Aboriginal and other rights could differ significantly in the various component units; and if elements of Canada were absorbed into the United States, the American regime of limited tribal self-government presumably would apply here.

In summary, if Quebec secedes, Canadians will face a long menu of constitutional options. Each has, and will have, its advocates. Moreover, the criteria of evaluation can differ. Here, the analysis has relied on some standard foundations: whether governments could deliver services efficiently while being politically accountable; whether they would be fiscally sustainable; whether decision making would be effective or stalemated; and whether citizens' national, regional, and provincial loyalties could underpin particular distributions of power and redistributions of money. While other criteria could be deployed, these seem the most general.

As well, this very preliminary analysis has begun to highlight some interregional and interprovincial cleavages. It is hard not to regard the Atlantic provinces as minor players in the great debates about Canada's future which Quebec secession would unleash, even though their inhabitants could have most at stake. The region is economically vulnerable, and its governments have traditionally supported a central government sufficiently powerful to redistribute income towards it, as have governments in Manitoba and Saskatchewan. As for the West, no observer can ignore the historic sense of oppression and neglect which now, as economic and ideological differences continue to divide it from central Canada, has produced strong demands for both autonomy and a more powerful voice in national affairs. Much less attention has been devoted to Ontario, the invisible province, despite its fiscal problems, its position as paymaster of the federation, and its links with Quebec. In thinking about provinces and regions, it is easy to fall prey to anthropomorphic stereotypes and to regard whole units as distinct and homogeneous.[25] But these regional and interprovincial cleavages and characteristics will re-emerge later.

Here, some attention was also paid to issues of process. This is crucial. It is one exercise to describe the grand alternative structures that Canada could adopt if Quebec separates; it is quite another matter to achieve any one of them. How Canadians try to "get there" –

how they choose collectively the form of a new country – may well determine where they get. The same is even truer of the relationships that might be established between Canada and a sovereign Quebec, a subject to which we now turn.

CHAPTER THREE

Economic Relations
between Canada and Quebec

At present, ROC and Quebec are joined in an economic union, one with a degree of integration that surpasses what has been achieved in the European Union and in some other federations. There is very broad agreement among analysts and political actors that maintaining a common economic space is desirable on efficiency grounds. Even among Quebec sovereigntists, there is very little opposition to this proposition.[1] But if Quebec secedes, there will be several possible long-term economic relationships that could operate between Canada and Quebec. The degree of integration ranges from an economic union similar to that which currently exists, right through to zero – to the relationship between any two sovereign states. In addition, it should be remembered that Canada is a monetary union with a single currency and one central bank. Apart from economic integration – though related to it – are the options about currency and monetary policy that could be realized by Canada and a sovereign Quebec. (These are surveyed in the next chapter.)

The degree of economic integration that would exist after a separation will be determined by four factors. First is the nature of ROC itself. If Canada fragments, for instance, the chances of re-establishing a full economic union will be reduced. The second factor is, as ever, the nature of the separation process. There may be broad agreement that maintaining the economic union would be rational, in terms of minimizing dislocation and economic uncertainty, but this does not mean that this outcome is inevitable. The postsecession trading and economic regime might be linked in the separation negotiations to thorny issues such as division of the debt and the treatment of minorities, with suboptimal outcomes. Or negotiators from either side might adopt a noncooperative stance, either because of domestic political considerations or as a part of a long-term strategy to win concessions later, with the result that the economic arrangements established would fall far short of a full economic union. Third, outside actors and opportunities will play a role. There will be some pressure on both Canada and Quebec to maintain a high level of integration in order to avoid disrupting existing treaty structures or threatening the profitability of foreign investment here. For instance, one American observer has concluded that the United States might offer the two states continuing membership in the G-7, provided they maintained economic integration at the level of a customs union at least.[2] Finally, what long-term economic structures can be established will be a function of what political and institutional arrangements are essential to make them work. There is a common view that higher degrees of economic integration require closer political integration in order to be functional and stable. This proposition will be taken up in more detail below, but it is certainly relevant to a separation process that will fundamentally redefine political communities and produce new institutions of government.

Since the various economic structures that could be established between Canada and a sovereign Quebec have been well canvassed,[3] the review here will be brief, concentrating on the advantages and disadvantages, mainly economic, of each level of integration. It should be noted at the outset that these structures are ideal types: they are nowhere found in pure form, and many variations upon them can be imagined. Still, they are the major structural alternatives. Second, this survey assumes, generally, that ROC itself would continue to operate as an integrated economy after Quebec's secession.

The fullest economic integration is found in an economic union. This is characterized by both negative and positive integration. The former refers to measures that prevent the erection of barriers to the movement of goods, services, and factors of production; rules prohibit states from discriminating against other states, mainly by establishing the principle of "national treatment." Under this regime, governments cannot treat foreign products and services and factors of production – capital and labour – differently from their domestic counterparts. Positive integration, in contrast, refers to measures that actively facilitate the flow of factors in the economic space and promote the overall efficiency of the unit. They include a broad array of policies: common external barriers that encourage trade to take place within the economic space; a wide range of standard laws and regulations, uniformly enforced, in areas such as taxation, competition, weights and measures, consumer protection and bankruptcy; efficient, large-scale provision of public services and growth-promoting infrastructure; and adjustment assistance. Many of these policies have the effect of homogenizing the framework within which competition occurs, or, more technically, of eliminating non-tariff barriers to trade (which include subsidies of various forms). Others enforce a uniform conduct of behaviour on firms and public authorities. While the economic union is integrated internally, of course it has a unique external commercial policy. Finally, economic unions normally have some programs for regional stabilization and redistribution, in part because the common currency that usually characterizes them prevents the component states from devaluing a currency to absorb economic shocks.

Some gains from an economic union arise from size and factor mobility. Firms can take advantage of scale economies and they can specialize, and there are also dynamic gains because of the competitive environment and the flow of information and innovation. Some of these effects are present as well in less integrated arrangements, such as free trade areas. The unique gains of the union arise because the common regulatory environment minimizes the costs of making transactions and acquiring information. Not only does this make production more efficient and adjustment smoother, but it heightens the trade diversion effects that occur even within free trade areas, for there is a tendency to do business within the union. As well, the member states individually have economies that are more specialized and volatile than the whole; hence, they pool risks in the union, with factor mobility and interregional transfers cushioning the adjustment to economic shocks. The stabilization and interregional transfer systems also protect the economy from making wasteful permanent adjustments to temporary shocks. At the same time, by allowing similar services to be provided by subnational units, these transfers provide a more homogeneous environment for business while allowing human capital to be developed in the poorer regions. A final advantage of an economic union is that it has greater bargaining power in international negotiations.[4]

The Canadian economic union has many of these features.[5] Goods, services, and factors of production flow relatively freely within it. The federal government has established a common regulatory framework for many sectors, and provides uniform enforcement of competition policy and many product standards. Tax systems are highly harmonized, especially on the corporate side. As Stanley Hartt has stressed, an elaborate network of provincial "comity" laws facilitates the conduct of business across provincial borders.[6] So do provincial regulatory regimes, which are fairly well harmonized (trucking, labour), or under which cooperation has been possible (securities). Although there are some substantial interprovincial barriers to the flow of some goods and services and people, and although the central government has caused large distortions in interregional prices through fiscal and regulatory policy, as well as impeding adjustment in the interregional labour market, the Canadian economic union is highly integrated. It clearly is a more homogeneous economic space than Europe, even after the Maastricht treaty.[7]

If the economic union could be preserved in the event of Quebec's secession, there would be advantages to each side. Since the status quo would prevail, uncertainty about commerce and investment would be minimized. Transaction costs would remain at current levels, and learning costs would not rise. Opportunities for specialization and mobility would still exist, and adjustment would occur as at present.

In the standard analysis, the major disadvantage for Quebec would be the amount of potential policy autonomy that would be forgone. One of the major thrusts of the sovereigntist argument is that an independent Quebec would control the levers of economic development and growth. In an economic union, however, vast areas of policy have to be standardized. This was highlighted by the secretariat of the Bélanger-Campeau Commission (the Commission on the Political and Constitutional Future of Quebec). The secretariat noted the desirability of uniformity or harmonization in the following areas: banking regulation, competition policy, patents, intellectual property, transportation regulation, taxation, telecommunications, postal services, weights and measures, standards, and bankruptcy.[8] Coordination with Canada in all these areas would minimize the losses associated with sovereignty, but it would inhibit Quebec from making the economic gains the sovereigntists believe will be possible when Quebec achieves policy autonomy.

Another problem for Quebec is that federal transfers would end. The sovereign state would collect all taxes within its borders but would receive no more payments from Canada. The estimates of the Economic Council, in a sanguine study of secession's effects on government budgets, imply that even if an economic association were to be maintained with Canada, the Government of Quebec would have to raise the total tax burden on its citizens by 3.3 per cent of GDP in order to provide current levels of government services.[9] (The other provinces would be able to reduce taxes.) More serious in the long run would be the elimination of one buffer – transfers – against external economic shocks. Finally, because there are no barriers to labour mobility in an economic union, in order to retain immigrants Quebec would, as currently, have to provide an environment at least as attractive as ROC's. One of the great advantages of sovereignty is that Quebec could hold immigrants simply by being more attractive than the home country or other possible receiving countries, but labour mobility in an economic union would eliminate this benefit.

On the Canadian side, these problems would be mirrored. Both the federal and provincial governments would have their policy autonomy constrained by the decision-making rules necessary to operate a formal economic union. And any supranational body that had regulatory powers, let alone the capacity to spend, would be capable of introducing interregional price distortions, just as Ottawa has done in the past.

A customs union is the next qualitative step down in the degree of economic integration, but somewhere between it and an economic union is a common market, the characteristics of which have often been taken from the European Community or other specific entities. A common market allows for relatively free factor flows within it, this being assured primarily by negative constraints against the erection of barriers between the component states. Core elements such as commercial law, competition policy, weights and measures, and standards are uniform, but there is less regulation by a central decision-making authority than there is in an economic union. Instead, member states rely more heavily on "mutual recognition" of each others' regulations; that is, they accept the other states' regulatory frameworks as being equivalent to their own. There is some harmonization of taxation and social entitlements, but redistribution and regional transfers normally are far smaller than in an economic union, and indeed they may be nonexistent. A common market thus preserves many of the gains realized within an economic union. The difference is a matter of degree. There are larger transaction and information costs, and further economic losses because non-tariff barriers cannot be authoritatively policed by a central authority or by mutual agreement between the states.

A customs union is quite different. Here, the level of integration is substantially lower. The defining feature is that the states comprising it have common external tariffs, along with a single system of quotas and other non-tariff border measures. Commercial policy, in the form of contingent protection against surging or unfairly subsidized imports (through safeguards, anti-dumping measures, and countervailing-duty measures) must be conducted jointly. Although the states may have very different domestic policy environments, they act as an economic unit *vis-à-vis* third parties.

The economic losses incurred through sinking to this level of integration are substantial. Transaction and information costs are much greater because the internal policy environment is not uniform. On such matters as product standards there is some pressure towards standardization because of the uniform treatment of third-country products, but these effects are dwarfed by the lack of regulatory harmonization. Nothing in a customs union prevents the member states from erecting non-tariff barriers in the form of subsidies, discriminatory procurement practices, or uncoordinated taxation systems. These can cause trade disputes and the application of protectionist measures within the customs union itself. There is no guarantee of capital mobility within a customs union, and labour mobility can be constricted severely, to become a privilege rather than a right. Because labour cannot move, trade in services is inhibited (as it can also be by regulation). Moreover, the economy's capacity for adjustment through migration is much reduced, at the same time as inter-regional transfers are not available for temporary stabilization.

The great advantage of a customs union over the next level of integration, a free trade area, is that there is no need to have border posts between the countries to monitor trade. Because of the common tariff and commercial policy, there is no possibility that imports can enter a high-tariff country through the low-tariff partner; hence, there is no need for agreements about domestic value-added to imports, or for certificates of origin or other cumbersome border procedures that inhibit trade and economic efficiency. Of course, if labour mobility is restricted, or if immigration policy is not coordinated, border posts will still be necessary to verify personal identification, but costly constraints on the trade of goods need not exist.

If, after separation, Canada and Quebec were to agree to integrate only at the level of a customs union, the economic losses on each side would be significant. Still, a customs union would be more advantageous than lesser forms of integration. Trade between the two countries would remain relatively free, without the application of border controls. As well, the unit would maintain its external weight in trade negotiations. However much less efficient the internal economy might be, it would be represented as a bloc internationally. A customs union also would ease a sovereign Quebec's entry into GATT, because the existing structure of tariffs and quotas would not be changed. More important, maintaining integration at this level would simplify re-negotiation of the FTA and NAFTA, because tariff schedules would not be altered, there would be a single authority for commercial policy, and the entire market would remain open on the same terms to American and Mexican trading partners.

But a customs union would raise difficult issues. The current structure of protection in Canada represents a compromise between sectoral interests that are regionally based. Foreign trade in textiles, clothing, and footwear is diverted from Canada in favour of domestic producers that are disproportionately concentrated in Quebec, while Ontario benefits from the Quebec market for automotive and electrical equipment, to name only two examples. Trade protection also involves the agricultural marketing boards and the internal division of production quotas. As well, Canada maintains quantitative restrictions on certain products and commodities, notably under the Multifiber Agreement; their levels and allocations would have to be negotiated.

The general problem of a customs union would be agreeing on a decision rule for setting external tariffs and quotas. In some respects, Quebec would be better placed if the current trade-negotiation arrangements were maintained, because all the provinces are involved and there is opportunity for logrolling and coalition formation among them. But if a ROC trade position were to be decided before discussions with Quebec commenced, the alternative rules would again be parity (unacceptable to Canada) or proportionality (unacceptable to Quebec). Similar difficulties would arise in negotiations with third parties, when concessions and trade-offs have to be made. How would a joint delegation operate? Finally, to run a customs union, the two countries would require some bilateral authority to enforce the common commercial law. Designing this institution could prove difficult, and the differential regional effects of its decisions could bring its legitimacy into question.

The next level of economic integration is the free trade area. Here, countries agree to eliminate barriers to trade in goods and perhaps services, outlawing mutual tariffs, quotas, border taxes, and some trade-inhibiting regulations. But each maintains its independent commercial policies towards third parties. Hence, border controls remain to enforce rules of origin and to police value-added requirements. Free trade areas allow firms to benefit from economies of scale and specialization, and they establish a more competitive environment, which may produce dynamic gains. There may also be positive benefits from trade diversion. But compared with an economic union, the remaining obstacles and the lack of regulatory harmonization increase costs and reduce productive efficiency. Moreover, since there are no guarantees of factor mobility, the avenues of adjustment are limited.

It is possible that Canada and Quebec could negotiate a free trade agreement after separation. But Canada is already a signatory of the FTA and NAFTA. The free trade option should be considered first in this context, because it is possible that Quebec would be admitted to these agreements and that Canada would continue to adhere to them. If these conditions were met, a third trade agreement between Canada and Quebec might be superfluous.

The FTA provides that tariffs between the United States and Canada will be phased out by 1998. Hence, tariff-free trade between Canada and Quebec would be assured by then (and each side could agree not to impose any tariffs in the meantime). But the FTA is far more than a simple agreement to remove barriers. While the operative principle in multilateral trade, for instance, is most-favoured-nation (MFN) status, meaning that all signatories must be granted the same tariff treatment as the most favoured one, the underlying principle of the FTA is national treatment; that is, goods from the other country (with some exceptions) must not be subject to rules or taxes that are not applied to domestic products. Beyond this, the FTA removes many barriers to trade in services, especially in banking and telecommunications, and facilitates service trade by allowing some labour mobility (temporary access to work is allowed for some occupations). It provides for capital mobility by guaranteeing foreign firms the right of establishment (and by restricting the screening of take-overs of domestic firms). It provides for energy sharing, and it incorporates the Auto Pact, a 1966 agreement that contains guarantees about the level of automobile production to be maintained in Canada. It also commits the signatories to some regulatory harmonization, especially about customs procedures, and to mutual recognition of some standards. It establishes special mechanisms for settling bilateral disputes, while maintaining intact each country's trade laws. Finally, it envisages closer integration through consultations about agriculture and subsidies, and ultimately about competition policy. NAFTA has not affected this basic structure. It builds upon it and extends it. There are some special provisions for each country, some new agreements about environmental and labour standards, and some modifications to the dispute-resolution mechanisms. In a few areas the FTA continues to prevail, but NAFTA has largely superseded the earlier treaty, incorporating its main provisions.[10] Unlike the FTA, though, NAFTA does have explicit provisions about the accession of any new members to the agreement: the existing signatories must agree to their joining the treaty.

The advantages for Canada and Quebec of retaining this structure are considerable. Simply enough, it would preserve the status quo with respect to the most important foreign trading partner of each country, and it would provide mutual market access under familiar rules, so the business environment would be predictable. Beyond this, western Canada would keep its FTA gains, including lower tariffs and the energy provisions, Ontario would retain the Auto Pact, and Quebec would maintain access to the U.S. market.

There are disadvantages, however. Since the FTA has no explicit purchase on external tariffs, border controls would be necessary between Canada and Quebec. As well, trade between the two countries would be subject to domestic commercial law, and contingent protection measures could be applied to goods moving across the border. (It is worth noting that under the FTA there is little access to the courts for private parties: trade disputes are interstate disputes.) More important, economic integration would be profoundly weakened. If the provisions of the FTA, for example, were to become the operative rules between Canada and Quebec governing the financial services sector, massive readjustments would be necessary and the current integrated capital market would become much less efficient. Finally, the overall negotiating position of Canada as it now exists would be weakened *vis-à-vis* the United States and other partners, simply because each of the new countries would be smaller economically.

Both Canada and Quebec would face risks in the free trade context, and these would exist whether or not they agreed to maintain between them a higher level of integration than the FTA represents. The risk for Canada is that the United States would consider the separation to represent a fundamental change in circumstances, such that bilateral trade agreements would have to be renegotiated. The United States could use this opportunity to open sections of the FTA that have been irritants in the past, including those on culture and agriculture. The risk for Quebec would be higher. If Quebec entered the FTA and the NAFTA as a sovereign signatory, it would no longer enjoy the protected status of a subnational unit.[11] These trade agreements were designed to bind national governments, and their purchase on provincial governments has been much less. Government procurement provisions, for example, apply to national purchasing entities and not to provincial ones, and the chapter on financial services specifically excludes provincially constituted financial institutions. As a sovereign state, Quebec would become exposed to treaty disciplines in these and other important areas of policy, including culture, subsidies, agriculture, standards, and investment. The last might be particularly sensitive, for Quebec would have to pass new legislation to prevent some foreign take-overs. Even if the United States did not take the opportunity to negotiate new constraints, the existing treaty provisions would restrict Quebec's policy autonomy much more than they currently do.[12]

The final level of economic integration would be that existing under multilateral treaties, primarily GATT. It is possible that the separation would cause the FTA and NAFTA to cease to apply with their current scope. This could occur if the U.S. administration or Congress refused to modify the agreements to admit Quebec, or if they insisted on renegotiating sections with Canada; it could also happen if anti-FTA sentiment in the truncated Canada was sufficient to cause the agreements to be abrogated. The treaties might then cease to apply to Canada, Quebec, or both countries. Hence, there could be no continental arrangement covering Canada-Quebec trade and economic relations. This result could also occur if Canada itself fragmented, or, more generally, if it proved impossible to negotiate any framework trade agreement between the separating countries.

In this case, Canada-Quebec trade would be covered by multilateral accords, primarily GATT, to which both parties would be signatories. This result would entail very substantial economic disintegration. Each country would have most-favoured-nation status *vis-à-vis* the other, but there would be tariff barriers to trade between them, at an average level (for all goods) of about 2 per cent.[13] As a result, the agricultural marketing system would break down, and the service trade could be much inhibited. Of course, GATT imposes some constraints on the member states – in such areas as procurement, intellectual property, and contingent protection measures – but there are many loopholes that allow trade-distorting policies to exist, and the procedures for settling disputes are weak and cumbersome relative to those in the FTA. Disintegrating the Canada-Quebec economy to the GATT level would entail very heavy losses.

To this point, the analysis has assumed that Canada-Quebec economic relations would be governed by a general framework agreement. That is, there would be a formal treaty like the FTA or the Treaty of Rome that would lay out the joint objectives of the two countries, state the principles governing the various dimensions of the relationship (trade, investment, mobility, and so on), enumerate the rights and obligations of the parties, and establish some mechanisms for consultation, management, joint decision making, and dispute resolution. Thus, the level of economic integration to be maintained would flow from a comprehensive and legally binding international treaty.

But there are other ways to proceed. The first is to negotiate separate treaties covering particular economic sectors or other dimensions of the relationship. For example, Canada and Quebec could reach agreements in transportation, banking and financial institutions, securities markets, or agriculture, and this could be accomplished without any comprehensive economic accord. Similarly, limited treaties could establish a regime for capital or labour mobility. There could be a free-standing treaty providing for a general dispute-resolution mechanism, perhaps in the form of arbitration procedures or a supranational judicial body.

There are some advantages to this approach. The two sides would not have to reach a comprehensive agreement that would lock each into a fixed level of integration; thorny issues could be set aside, in the short term at least, and sectoral accords might be reached more quickly than a global treaty; some economic losses through disintegration would be avoided; and, in theory, limited agreements could be reached with provinces or regions. But there are also disadvantages to this approach. While certain "islands" of integration would be maintained, considerable uncertainty would surround the rest of the economy; there would be costs to reducing integration in non-treaty areas, and economic agents would have to adjust behaviour at the boundaries of particular sectors or dimensions of trade; furthermore, it is not evident how such agreements would be articulated with the FTA and NAFTA if Canada and Quebec stayed party to these treaties; finally, there would remain the basic problem of establishing mechanisms and decision rules to govern change in the regulation of these sectors.

The second noncomprehensive way to achieve some level of economic integration would involve no treaties whatsoever. It is voluntary harmonization. Presumably it would be done primarily by Quebec, the smaller economy. Harmonization could be accomplished by Quebec simply adopting Canadian legislation as its own law. In bankruptcy or product labelling or corporate taxation, for example, the Quebec regulatory environment could be made identical to the Canadian one. When Canada changed regulations, so could Quebec. Beyond this, Quebec could simply abjure unilaterally from erecting other barriers to trade.[14] The advantage of such a policy is that much of the economic union could be maintained, simply because the business environment would be identical on each side of the border. As well, it would require little if any formal negotiation to achieve. Change in legislation by Quebec could be incremental as the economic situation evolved.

For Canada, the disadvantage of this strategy would be that the existing arrangements would not be secure; Quebec could alter its legislation at any time, so creating new obstacles to trade. But there would be even greater disadvantages for Quebec. Simply enough, its government would have no control over Canadian policy, and its firms would have no avenues of participation in Canadian decisions. Canada could change policy according to domestic events and the impact of external shocks on its economy (including its trade relations with Quebec), and the alterations might not be appropriate for Quebec.

Moreover, mirror legislation is not sufficient to maintain economic integration at the level of a common market or economic union. Formal agreements are essential for government action to be effective across borders. Agricultural marketing arrangements and telecommunications regulation provide obvious examples. Similarly, in the securities industry, while it is possible that Quebec could mirror Ontario regulations about the content of prospectuses or the disclosure of insider trading, active cooperation would be necessary for clearing accounts between exchanges. In short, although unilateral harmonization could be an effective method of achieving uniformity in the regulatory environment in the two states, it is passive. It cannot provide for the positive action necessary to maintain high levels of economic integration. Hence, there would be substantial costs of disintegration without some Canada-Quebec treaties that would bind governments and require cooperation. There would also be costs associated with Quebec's duplication of institutions, such as those necessary to enforce competition policy or register patents, though such costs would be incurred at any level of integration less than the current economic union.

CHAPTER FOUR

The Currency and Monetary Policy

Another aspect of Canada-Quebec economic relations concerns monetary policy and the currency. Here there is a very large set of possible arrangements, in theory.[1] Generally speaking, currency matters are somewhat independent of the level of integration that exists in economic and commercial relations: it is possible to have a common currency even without a free trade agreement. This can be done through a currency board or simply by the adoption of another currency, as in Panama's use of the American dollar. Similarly, the European Union and NAFTA show that it is possible to have a common market or a free trade agreement without a common currency.

Several core considerations would bear on Canada-Quebec currency arrangements. First are the basic macro- and microeconomic functions of monetary policy. Monetary policy establishes the long-term rate of inflation. As well, a separate currency allows for adjustment to economic shocks, such as a drop in demand for a country's exports, because changes in the exchange rate alter real domestic prices, so adjustment need not be borne directly by decreases in employment or nominal wages. Finally, monetary policy may affect economic growth; while the view that monetary expansion can reduce unemployment is now a minority one among experts, it certainly continues to be heard, and there is much more support for the argument that achieving perfect price stability rather than acceptable inflation rates can cause long-term economic damage.[2] In short, control of a currency remains a policy tool, and this would be important to the governments of both Canada and Quebec.

A second consideration is the cost of having separate currencies. This creates transaction and accounting costs when trade or capital movements take place. There are also costs incurred for the risk associated with holding any currency. For users of money, this involves efforts to hedge against inflation and devaluation; for citizens and governments, it involves paying interest rate premiums. If confidence in the currency declines, the perceived risk of holding it rises, and so do the premium costs. When governments attempt to implant a new currency, establishing its credibility is exceedingly difficult, and this imposes large premium costs. Further costs can be incurred in the underlying economy if the central bank must prove itself to investors and demonstrate more discipline than would be expected of the managers of a long-accepted currency. Consequently, although the costs of establishing confidence in a new Quebec currency would be short term, they could be very large.

The third general consideration is how monetary policy and currency issues mesh with other elements of the political and economic systems. Having a separate currency and an independent monetary policy allows governments to adopt a distinct stance on inflation. As for adjustment, ideally a common currency should be used within a relatively homogeneous economy. Otherwise, different regions will have different monetary-policy (and exchange-rate) needs, and this can cause regional tension, as it often has in Canada – for example, when inflationary pressures in Ontario are fought by an interest rate policy that impedes recovery in Atlantic Canada.[3]

Generally speaking, there are many avenues of adjustment in an economy. They include fiscal policy, capital mobility, labour migration, protectionist measures, wage and price changes, unemployment, and transfers into a region for stabilization and structural adjustment. In a sovereign Quebec, however, some of these mechanisms would cease to exist, others could be prohibited by trade agreements, and some would simply be politically unpalatable for any government. It is possible that the adjustment possibilities offered by a separate currency would be attractive to Quebec.[4] This could be the case whether or not monetary policy ultimately has any long-term purchase on any real economic factors other than the rate of inflation. As regional conflicts over monetary policy demonstrate, citizens believe these policy choices make a difference.

Monetary policy is also related to fiscal policy. Government deficits affect expectations about inflation, because they increase the temptation of governments to increase the money supply so that inflation will increase revenues and reduce the real cost of debt repayment. Hence, lenders have less confidence in the currency's value, and they demand a premium rate of interest. At the same time, the cost of government borrowing is affected by monetary policy, which may be set in part by exchange-rate considerations. For both reasons, there should ideally be some harmonization of monetary and fiscal policy within a currency area, including the fiscal policies of states or provinces. (An alternative view is that markets will enforce discipline on the borrowing practices of the various states, but this may take some time: coordination is more sure, if it is possible.)

Finally, currency and monetary-policy issues mesh with the institutions of the financial system. If capital markets are well integrated across an economic space, there need be less concern with the regional impact of monetary policy, because flows of funds through financial institutions help adjustment.[5] As well, it is within financial institutions that the transaction and accounting costs of separate currencies are registered. Beyond this, institutional failure can cause a loss of confidence in a currency and lead to devaluation or higher interest rates; conversely, a severe loss of confidence can cause runs on a country's banks. In these extreme circumstances, a country's central bank can act as a lender of last resort to prop up the financial system; and if there is a serious flight of capital from a country, it is through its power over financial institutions that the government can institute foreign-exchange controls.

Bearing these considerations in mind, the Canada-Quebec currency options can be assessed. There are four basic possibilities: Quebec could (1) establish a separate currency with a floating exchange rate; (2) establish a currency and peg the rate to the Canadian dollar or the U.S. dollar; (3) keep using the Canadian dollar, either without or with a voice in monetary policy; or (4) use the U.S. dollar.[6]

A separate currency would provide a sovereign Quebec with policy autonomy and the opportunity for independent adjustment, once its credibility was established. But in the long term, there would be losses from greater transaction and accounting costs, caused by the need to convert accounts of commerical and financial transactions. It has been estimated that these costs would range from $0.5 billion to $1.0 billion per year.[7] On the other hand, the Quebec Central Bank, which would have to be established, would reap perhaps $0.5 billion per year in seigniorage: this is the financial benefit that authorities derive from issuing currency, largely in the form of not paying interest on the liability represented by notes and coins.[8] Such considerations would be dwarfed, however, by the short-term costs imposed by the lack of credibility of the new currency. Anticipating economic uncertainty in Quebec, and perhaps economic decline, many people and firms would avoid the new currency, seeking to keep their assets in harder money. International investors would have to be encouraged to hold it, through interest rate premiums, and this would take place, probably, when the economic shocks of sovereignty would be diminishing the tax base, when federal transfers would end, and when Quebec would assume some new obligation for central-government debt. Not only would it be much more expensive for Quebec to borrow, but runs on financial institutions could also occur. Without special assistance from Canada or abroad, Quebec could be hard pressed to defend its financial system, even if it took its share of the $9 billion in Bank of Canada foreign-currency reserves. It is well understood in Quebec that the benefits of establishing a separate currency would be long term, but the short-term costs of introducing it would be very large.[9]

There would be costs to Canada, too, if Quebec opted for a new, separate currency. These would include transaction and accounting costs on exchanges across the border and the loss of about one-quarter of the Bank of Canada's seigniorage. More seriously, there could be speculative pressures against the Canadian dollar until it was clear that this currency would continue to be viable. These pressures would be fought with higher interest rates.

As one alternative, Quebec could establish its own currency and peg it to the Canadian dollar. This would entail many of the same long-term costs of maintaining a separate currency as well as the big up-front costs of establishing confidence in it. Yet this option has no benefits in the form of policy autonomy. Its currency fixed, Quebec would have to accept whatever monetary policy the Canadian authorities chose, along with the consequent exchange rate *vis-à-vis* third countries. This would only accentuate the problems of setting the initial exchange rate and maintaining its credibility. Unless the currency was backed fully with Canadian dollars, speculative pressures in either direction could force revaluation. It has been suggested that Quebec could manage an internal devaluation in conjunction with a fully backed currency, and gain a competitive edge in exporting.[10] But this reduction in real wages and assets would demand a degree of popular support that a newly sovereign government might not command. If Quebec pegged a new currency to the Canadian dollar, Canada would experience speculative pressures as well, stemming from uncertainty about whether Quebec would maintain the arrangement or whether it would move towards an independent, floating currency, with the implications this move would have for the survival of the Canadian dollar, the payment by Quebec of its share of the debt, and the Canadian financial system's stability.

Pegging a separate currency to the U.S. dollar is generally considered a less advantageous option for Quebec. The short-term costs would be at least as great, and transaction and accounting costs would be larger, given the relative volumes of Quebec's trade with the two countries. It would also set up another obstacle to continuing an integrated Canada-Quebec financial system. Yet there could be some advantages for Quebec in this arrangement. Since debt considerations rather than trade convenience might be paramount, pegging to the U.S. dollar, which is more widely used in capital markets than the Canadian dollar, could seem desirable. Moreover, although the transaction and accounting costs of converting currency into American dollars would be onerous, at least the routines are familiar. Finally, trade diversion away from Canada and towards the south would occur if the economic union was significantly weakened after secession, and linking the currency to the U.S. dollar would represent an acknowledgement of this fact, an anticipation of the trend, and a symbolic commitment to Quebec's North American future. It should be recognized that this arrangement would impose large costs on Canada. These would consist, naturally, of transaction and accounting costs on exchanges with Quebec. More important would be the uncertainty about whether the Canadian dollar could continue to float independently. Some economists have argued that if Quebec were to make this choice, Canada might well have to do the same.[11] And if Canada fragmented or decentralized radically, this is a likely outcome: either the country as a whole or each of the provinces or regions would become a "taker" of monetary policy set in Washington. Even if this political result did not occur, the costs of fixing the Canadian to the American currency would include a long-term loss of flexibility and autonomy and short-term speculative pressures against the arrangement.

Economists tend to agree that the optimum resolution of the currency issue is that Quebec and Canada maintain the monetary union. This would allow the financial system to operate with minimal disruption, it would save costs on cross-border transactions, and Quebec would not have to bear the burden of establishing a new currency's credibility. In one version of this basic arrangement, the two countries would cooperate. Quebec would establish a central bank, and management of monetary policy would be vested either in the Bank of Canada – with representation from the Bank of Quebec – or in a new, joint, supranational authority. And Quebec would be entitled to a share of seigniorage. Even in this cooperative arrangement, however, there could be disadvantages for Quebec. If its government's voice in monetary policy was proportional to its GDP or population, its representatives would be permanently in a minority. Essentially it would be a policy taker, while monetary policy would be set according to conditions in Canada. Consequently, Quebec's particular adjustment needs would have to be accommodated by other policy instruments. On the other hand, Canada would be unlikely to accept an arrangement by which representation in the monetary authority was based on national equality. Even proportionality would make the peripheral provinces regard the arrangement with distrust: the configuration of the monetary authority would raise old suspicions about a cabal of central-Canadian industrial and financial interests dictating interest and exchange rates.[12] Another problem for Canada is that it would have no control over Quebec's fiscal deficits, nor could it affect Quebec's response to balance-of-payments deficits with the United States. If Quebec were to run either type of deficit, Canadian foreign-exchange reserves could erode, or Canadian interest rates could rise, or both, because of Quebec's trade and fiscal problems. Finally, there could be speculation that the arrangement would not be stable and that Quebec, sooner or later, would have to introduce its own currency.[13] Such speculation could produce pressure on the Canadian dollar, runs on Quebec banks, and, ultimately, a decision by Quebec authorities to establish a new currency in order to stabilize the situation.[14]

In the second variant of this arrangement, there would be no supranational monetary authority, nor would Quebec's central bank have representation in the Bank of Canada. Quebec would use the Canadian dollar, and it would be a pure policy taker. This possibility is generally advanced as a default option should no agreement be possible about joint control of monetary policy. Even with a breakdown of relations, this would be a feasible option, because Canada would not be able to stop Quebec from using its currency, except through draconian measures to stifle the flow of banknotes into the country, and possibly by restricting Quebec firms' access to the Canadian payments system – measures that would be very costly to Canada. This arrangement might satisfy post-separation sentiment in Canada, but Quebec's lack of autonomy and even of influence in such an important policy area could prove politically uncomfortable for the government of the new country. Ultimately, the Bank of Canada would be responsible to the minister of finance of Canada, and the minister would have no incentive, after secession, to take account of conditions in Quebec, except insofar as they might have second-order consequences for the Canadian economy. If Quebec encountered deficit or balance-of-payments problems, there would be adverse consequences for Canada; more important, the domestic pressure in Quebec to withdraw from the arrangement and establish a separate currency could become overwhelming. Realizing this, holders and potential holders of Canadian-dollar assets would be even more likely to demand risk premiums and to speculate against the currency than they would if Quebec participated in setting monetary policy in the currency union.

The final option is that Quebec simply adopt the U.S. currency as its own. This possibility has been little analysed relative to the others.[15] Obviously, this alternative would increase transaction and accounting costs, but far less so than the imposition of a new Quebec currency pegged to the American dollar. It would strain the Canadian payments and financial systems, but these are well habituated to dealing in American currency. The credibility problems would be reduced almost to zero, because Quebec would be declaring itself to be permanently a policy taker, prepared to accept the American inflation rate and to adjust through other means to differential shocks. The Quebec authorities would encounter much less resistance by individuals and firms to a forced conversion of their accounts into the world's most familiar currency than to a conversion into "dollards" or "quebucks." It would be essential to secure a supply of dollars, of course, but this would require minimal cooperation from the United States. By using the U.S. dollar directly, rather than merely pegging a separate currency to it, Quebec would declare even more strongly a practical detachment from Canada and a symbolic commitment to the continental future: "Toutefois, l'utilisation de la monnaie américaine par un Québec souverain pourrait être envisagée compte tenu de la tendance à la hausse des échanges commerciaux et financiers entre le Québec et les États-Unis. En plus, l'utilisation de la monnaie américaine éviterait des problèmes conflictuels avec le Canada."[16] In short, using the U.S. dollar would be a viable and potentially attractive option for a sovereign Quebec.

This alternative would be costly and awkward for Canada, however. Dealings with Quebec would involve new transaction and accounting costs, and Canada would lose the seigniorage on one-quarter of its currency. Much more seriously, the credibility of the Canadian dollar itself would be threatened. Could it continue to function as an independent, floating currency? There would be speculative pressure against it, risk premiums to be paid, and possibily a liquidity crisis.[17] This could force the Bank of Canada to fix the dollar in relation to the U.S. dollar or, in the longer term, to declare the U.S. currency to be legal tender (or even the sole legal tender) in the country. In that case, Canada would lose the benefits of seigniorage, of access to the Bank of Canada as a lender of last resort, and of the adjustment mechanism of a floating currency: it would also have to accept the U.S. inflation rate. Certainly, such a currency union with the United States would have some offsetting benefits – prices could be more stable, and the costs of doing business would be reduced.[18] But Canadians would forfeit an important real and psychological degree of national autonomy at a time when their collective future was already uncertain enough.

CHAPTER FIVE

Political Relations between Canada and Quebec

If Quebec secedes, the event will represent a huge political rupture. There will be a fundamental schism in the political community that is now Canada, even – and perhaps especially – if ROC accepts the development and even if separation takes place constitutionally.

Nevertheless, many prognosticators expect that some new set of political institutions would be established between the sovereign countries of Canada and Quebec. As in the economic realm, in theory there is a wide range of possibilities open. The dimension along which they vary is that of political integration. If the two states were to become highly integrated, joint political superstructures would be established between them. At the extreme, there could be legislative, executive, and judicial institutions in which substantial power would reside, almost like the current federation. Weaker integration, by degrees, would see no legislatures, then no executive bodies, and then no joint mechanisms to settle disputes. At the extreme of nonintegration, relations would be conducted by international negotiation, as between any two sovereign states, with no institutions governing the relationship other than those existing under general international law or the particular regimes to which both countries adhere (such as GATT and other treaties and conventions).

What the result would be, after secession, depends on several factors. One is the internal composition of Canada; that is, how ROC reconstitutes itself. Paradoxically, a very decentralized or confederal Canada might accommodate itself more readily to political integration with Quebec than a centralized country would. Another factor is the level of economic integration that is to obtain between the countries. A third is how the transition to Quebec sovereignty occurs. Not only will the process of the separation establish precedents about interstate political relations, but decisions will be taken during the transition about the shape of Canada and about what supranational political institutions, if any, are to be established between ROC and Quebec. Over the long term, the political relationship between the two countries will also be determined by deeper social and economic forces that tend towards centralization or decentralization (though these will be acting on the structures established at the time of the separation).

The most highly integrated arrangements would involve a central authority with substantial functions. These would be laid out in a separate constitution, one that could take the form of a treaty between the two states. The areas of jurisdiction often suggested for common political control include defence, the currency and monetary policy, tariffs and commercial policy, the environment, international relations, and some state enterprises; and sometimes it is proposed that all residents will have a common citizenship. Such an arrangement would require a jointly elected legislature, an executive, and a judiciary. One elaborate example of these proposals is Resnick's "Canada-Quebec Union," which would be an "ensemble" or "condominium" of the two states and peoples.[1] The joint legislature would be composed of Canadian senators (who would be elected, and on the basis of greater provincial equality than now exists) and directly elected Quebec representatives. Quebec's number of representatives would be proportional to its population share. Ministers would be members of Parliament or members of the National Assembly. The joint prime minister would be the prime minister of Canada or of Quebec, while the head of state would be chosen, on a rotating basis, by the Canadian Parliament or by both the National Assembly and the directly elected Quebec representatives. The "Union" government would have some taxation powers; there would be a constitutional court; the separate constitutions of Canada and Quebec would each recognize minority rights; and the central organs would function bilingually. With some variations, this scheme is representative of several proposals for sovereignty-association.[2]

Such arrangements would have several benefits. Despite a separation, a good deal of the existing order would be retained. In particular, a Union government would be capable of managing an integrated economic space. The scheme would avoid disputes – potentially, very acrimonious ones – about difficult practical matters such as the debt and about symbolically charged issues such as citizenship. At the same time, there could be sufficient disengagement for the separate national projects of Quebec and Canada to be realized by the two communities.

But there are many drawbacks to such arrangements, for both Canada and Quebec. One is their sheer institutional complexity. If Canada did not entirely fragment in the process of secession but retained a central government similar to the current one, it would acquire yet another level of government, leaving its citizens to be served by a minimum of four, and in most cases five, governments. Also, devising new, untried institutions would introduce an element of uncertainty into a political context that was already unstable. The structures of the European Union, often taken as a model for such proposals, have evolved gradually over a period of four decades. As well, the allocation of functions would raise problems, even if it could be agreed what core areas of jurisdiction should rest with the Union. It is impossible to divide jurisdiction cleanly. At the margin, programs and regulations in any functional area spill over into others. The environmental regulation of rivers, for example, intersects with control over timber harvesting and fishing. Similarly, even if there was clear Union authority to negotiate trade agreements, these would reach back into domestic policies about agriculture, investment, and even labour relations. This is a generic problem within federations, of course, but established federations have evolved administrative arrangements and legal precedents that clarify responsibilities. In the case of Canada-Quebec, all this would have to develop, and there is much potential for friction, delay, and legal uncertainty.

There are other practical problems with Union proposals. One is how policy would be implemented. Either the central state would command a substantial bureaucracy, or, more likely, it would depend on the separate Canadian and Quebec governments to enforce laws and regulations. In the latter case, there would be scope for opportunistic "slippage" – the lax implementation of unpopular or costly policies. Accountability would be a related problem in such an arrangement, since the responsibility for decisions could not be clearly attributed. As well, partisan conflict probably would hinder government effectiveness and also would cause animosity between the units. If Canada had a right-wing government, for instance, but the Union was dominated by a left-wing coalition anchored by a Quebec bloc, there would clearly be potential for conflict; and if either was a minority government, the system would be even less effective. Of course, federations sometimes produce such results. The difference in sovereignty-association arrangements is that blame is targeted at the other national unit.

But would the other state be "national"? Some union proposals are extremely vague about where sovereignty is located. Ultimately, it must lie either in the central state or in the national units. If the centre was sovereign, Quebecers would be denied the symbolic attributes of independence such as citizenship and a distinct foreign presence, and they would be a permanent minority within the new state. But if the national states were sovereign, there would be no secure base for the central government; so when disagreement became sharp, representatives could be withdrawn, tax revenues withheld, debt payments stopped, and treaties broken.

This raises the related issue of how a Union state would be established. Resnick proposes that a constituent assembly be held with representatives elected from ROC only, on the approval of the federal government and at least six of the nine provinces. This body would consider the constitution of Canada and also, in conjunction with its Quebec counterpart, the Union arrangements. Ratification would take place by a referendum. This, of course, entirely ignores the constitution's existing procedures, which require amendments to be passed through Parliament and through most, perhaps all, provincial legislatures. More important, it seems to suppose that the Union could emerge while Canada's sovereignty and constitutional continuity remained intact. But this is simply to say that secession has not taken place; and this is to fudge the issue. Either constitutional amendment produces a Union government or Quebec becomes a sovereign country (while the rest of Canada remains one). In the first case, the new system would simply be a change to a highly asymmetrical form of federalism, and there could be no significance to any "basic document" agreed by ROC and Quebec, because the constitution would remain the basic law.[3] In the second case, the new complex of political institutions would result from negotiations between ROC and Quebec, either after separation or in anticipation of it. Then the arrangements would be enshrined in a treaty between sovereign states, after "Canada," as it was, had ceased to exist. As has been clear in other cases, secession means that a sovereign political community is fractured. Future relations are conducted on an international basis, even if treaties establish new political institutions.[4]

If a treaty created a highly integrated political union, a fundamental problem would be how to share power at the centre, in the common institutions. There are only two possible principles, and neither would be likely to produce satisfactory or stable results. In some proposals, representation in common legislatures or executive bodies would be on the basis of population. This is a basic democratic principle that rests ultimately on the proposition that people are equal;

hence, "one person, one vote." With majority voting, however, the Quebec representatives would always face the prospect of being in the minority. In an integrated union, partisan and ideological considerations might allow for transnational governments, since divisions on issues would cut across national lines. But Quebec representatives could always be outvoted by those from ROC, a possibility that would be likely to materialize precisely when the stakes in some issue were very high and the national interests of the two communities were opposed. Even if matters never came to such a climax, the slow accretion of decisions that could be portrayed as unfavourable to Quebec would provide an incentive for politicians to contest the foundations of the system.

The other possible decision rule is equality, or parity between the national communities. But if equality was the basis of representation, the citizens of Canada would face the prospect, on issues vital to them, of being immobilized by Quebec's opposition.[5] This would be intolerable, on both practical and democratic grounds. Possibly worse would be a series of decisions against the interests of an important component of ROC, which passed because a solid Quebec bloc combined with a minority of Canadian representatives. There are devices to prevent such outcomes – for example, supermajority voting – but they are complex and they inhibit decisive state action. The basic problem would remain. While a sovereign Quebec would find the proportionality principle threatening and unacceptable, Canada would never submit to parity in decision making over important areas of policy. One simple illustration of this is the negative reaction in ROC to the Charlottetown Accord's relatively modest guarantee to Quebec of 25 per cent of the House of Commons seats.[6] Parity in a common legislature would be regarded as even more undemocratic.

A lesser degree of political integration would find two independent states making joint decisions over a few policy fields through coordinated legislatures and executives. The basic model is that of joint parliamentary or ministerial delegations. In the East African Common Services Organization, for example, a legislative body was elected from the legislatures of Kenya, Uganda, and Tanganyika, and there was a small executive composed of the prime ministers and a few ministers from each country. The sovereign states cooperated in some specific matters: the post office, railways, a malaria institute, and so on. Most departments were self-financing, though the organization received 6 per cent of customs duties and 40 per cent of the profit tax. The common legislature passed laws that were not binding on the national parliaments but were recommendations.[7]

Austria and Hungary also operated a system of parliamentary delegations between 1867 and 1917. Each parliament elected sixty representatives to yearly sessions that were held in alternating capitals. If the delegations approved the common budget, it was binding on the national parliaments. The delegations and parliaments negotiated decennial agreements covering tariffs, the central bank and the currency, the quota of common expenses to be paid by each country, and joint railroads; these required approval by each country's parliament. There were three common ministers, responsible for foreign relations, the military, and common finance; they reported to the emperor of Austria, who was also king of Hungary, and who therefore chose and coordinated the three separate ministries.[8]

Similar proposals have been advanced for Canada and a sovereign Quebec. Dauphin and Slosar, for example, have outlined a Canada-Quebec treaty on the economic union. According to this treaty, the union would be capped by a council composed of ministers from the two countries. Assisted by committees of experts and a secretariat, the council would prepare legislation to be presented to the national parliaments. There would also be common management of such sectors as communications, the fisheries, and agricultural marketing, as well as an arbitration commission. This commission would not be able to make binding decisions, however, and the decision rule in the council would be parity.[9]

A system of delegations would have some benefits. It would allow for joint control of common functions that have economies of scale, and also of those with large externalities. And because measures would be approved by elected representatives, policies would have the legitimacy of popular sanction, if only indirectly. But there are many drawbacks to a system that is essentially confederal. As noted above, even with carefully delimited areas of jurisdiction, the central policies inevitably would spill over into areas reserved for national governments. The centre would remain dependent on national governments for implementation. More important, the centre would lack an independent financial base, relying ultimately on transfers from the constituent sovereign states. If the joint delegations could pass binding legislation, it would be difficult to hold any representatives responsible, and this is objectionable on democratic grounds.[10] But if the measures were not binding, obstruction and delay would certainly occur. The Austria-Hungary arrangement was plagued by extended conflicts about tariff levels, the currency, relative numbers of military conscripts, and the language of the armed forces. Confederal arrangements are unstable because in the areas of joint jurisdiction there is no central authority with an independent base of political support. The East African Common Services Organization fell apart in discord, and the Austria-Hungary arrangement survived, shakily, only because of the personal authority of the emperor-king.

Bipartite confederal arrangements are especially vulnerable. The principle of representation is national equality. This means that the larger unit must surrender authority over significant policy areas to the veto power of the smaller partner, an arrangement certain to cause disaffection in democracies.[11] Financing the common activities raises analogous problems. Since power is divided, so, arguably, should the contributions be split equally.[12] Such proposals are not well received by the smaller unit, because the benefits of common activities are said to flow disproportionately to the larger partner. These basic problems are less tractable in bipartite confederations because there is no room for coalition building and there is less opportunity for compromise. If there are more units, with multiple cleavages dividing them, shifting coalitions can form on different issues, and conflicts of interest are much less stark. Arguably, a confederal arrangement joining Quebec with sovereign Canadian provinces or regions would be more stable than a bipartite one, but even then the basic problems would remain: the centre cannot bind the sovereign parts; all parties have an effective veto on fundamental issues, so delay and conflict are inevitable; and at the same time, the units cannot fully enjoy the policy autonomy and symbolic independence of sovereignty. For these reasons, confederations are notoriously short-lived.

A lower level of political integration is found where powers are delegated by sovereign states to bodies that have regulatory or administrative authority. These can be special-purpose agencies with narrow mandates, or ones equipped with substantial powers over a range of policy areas. An example of the latter is the European Commission as it operated before the recent movement towards a single market and greater political integration. An example of the former is the joint boards that operated facilities such as railways and airlines in Central Africa after the federation there failed.[13] Regulatory bodies and administrative agencies can have a variety of governance structures. Members can be politicians or not, they can be delegates of the national governments or they can be selected for their neutrality (sometimes by the other delegate-members), and representation can be equal or weighted. The defining feature is that the agencies have the power, delegated jointly by the states involved, to make rules or to manage organizations delivering services.

This device is a most flexible one. Such agencies can maintain common functions by providing services, and they can create harmonized policy in certain fields by issuing directives. Free to organize functions efficiently or to regulate according to the conditions and requirements of the sectors supervised, the agencies may transcend politics, or at least be shielded from national political pressures. Finally, these special-purpose agencies often can be largely self-supporting, especially since regulation as a governing instrument requires little expenditure; hence, the contentious flows of funds that support supranational expenditure programs are avoided.

But such authorities have their drawbacks and limitations. On the regulatory side, implementation typically depends entirely on national bureaucracies. In the end, sovereign states control the application of directives on their territory, and if rules are circumvented or ignored, there are no sanctions available beyond those at the disposal of any state in the international community, including retaliation and terminating the agreement. Second, there is the perennial problem of representation. To the extent that the agency's functions are significant, this is an important matter to governments. There must be a decision rule within the agency, and this, as ever, can be parity or proportionality. "Neutral" members can moderate this problem, but when functions are important, governments generally are unwilling to confer much power on unaccountable delegates.

A related difficulty is the lack of responsibility of special agencies, whose operations and decisions can affect firms and individuals deeply. They are obviously creatures of the state(s) and consequently cannot be depoliticized. Unfavourable decisions and unsatisfactory rules inevitably will be contested in the national political arenas. In Europe, for example, the Commission's broad authority has given rise to the "democratic deficit" – the perceived inadequacy of popular control over regulatory decisions. Popular discontent with supranational agencies is a function of democratic expectations (or, inversely, of deference), of sensitivity to foreign control or influence, and of the scope and depth of regulatory intervention. When functions are limited or directives are not binding on national states, the democratic-deficit problem is moderated, and when the agencies' activities are narrowly focused and are accompanied by opportunities for participation and appeal, international political disputes are less probable. But this suggests that the scope for common Canada-Quebec special agencies would be rather limited. They might operate in segmented, technical areas such as weights and measures, or they might provide particular services such as ice breaking, but they could not handle the scope of regulation involved in maintaining a common market or controlling pollution, let alone the responsibility of managing foreign affairs or the military.

A lower level of integration involves judicial or quasi-judicial bodies to resolve disputes. By treaty, countries commit to having disagreements over certain matters referred to a supranational body that holds hearings and reaches decisions, which may be binding or not. This dispute-resolution device is essentially negative: the thrust of the judicial institutions is to determine whether existing obligations have been met rather than to create new ones. But these mechanisms do have the advantage of extricating disputes from normal political processes, if only for a time, and they can therefore deflect retaliation and escalation. Also, the quasi-judicial bodies can take on an "apolitical" mantle more convincingly than regulatory agencies that make positive decisions, and thus the democratic-deficit problem is less acute. In Canada, for example, citizens generally accept Supreme Court decisions with little protest, even when these sweepingly create new law; and the lack of much public pressure for even an indirect role in appointing judges contrasts sharply with the strong demands to participate in constitutional negotiations or to have governments use instruments of direct democracy such as the referendum.

However, the disadvantages of dispute-resolution mechanisms could outweigh the advantages. In the first place, decisions must be taken about whether the bodies will be permanent, like the World Court, or whether they will be set up as panels on an ad hoc basis to deal with particular disputes. There must also be agreement about the rules of procedure, such as standing, evidence, subpoena powers, and appeals. More substantially, there must be a definition of the matters over which the judicial bodies will have some jurisdiction. This presupposes that a set of rights and mutual obligations, in the form of a treaty, has already been agreed on by the countries involved. In general, governments are reluctant to alienate authority over such vital domestic matters as defence, policing, culture, minority rights, and research and development, and consequently dispute-resolution procedures are normally restricted to the economic realm. Governments are even more reluctant to surrender sovereign power and to establish judicial bodies that can reach binding decisions. Thus, appeals may be allowed to national courts. And since sovereignty cannot be alienated permanently, the parties can always disregard the decisions of the judicial bodies even if they have powers of binding arbitration, if the stakes are high enough. Retaliation is then the only recourse.

In quasi-judicial bodies, the standard basis of representation is parity (often with the two sets of national representatives agreeing on further, neutral members). Parity on such bodies is less problematic than in legislatures, executives, or special agencies. Since the purpose of the bodies is to decide legal issues arising from existing obligations, their procedure is based on the adversarial presentation of cases, and their argumentation is technical and jurisprudential. The underlying principle is to determine what is fair, not what is expedient. Nevertheless, some resistance to parity can generally be anticipated in the citizenry of the larger state, especially when binding decisions are taken about important matters. A similar qualification applies to the democratic-deficit argument: acceptance of judicial decisions is a function of their legitimacy, which in turn depends on their reputation for fairness, and this takes some time to establish. In Canada, Supreme Court decisions are accepted not only because of the court's long history (and its political perspicacity) but also because of its national character. But joint Canada-Quebec judicial institutions would have neither an established reputation nor a national character.

For all these reasons, judicial and quasi-judicial institutions would have a limited range of application in the case of a Quebec secession. Dispute-settlement mechanisms could only be established to oversee matters about which agreements had already been reached between Canada and Quebec. They would probably not be accorded the power to make binding decisions, and their legitimacy would be fragile. The scope of matters in their purview would be restricted, with the most likely field of application being the economy. And here it is worth noting that if Quebec were to accede to the FTA and NAFTA, the dispute-settlement mechanisms already established under these treaties might well be adequate to deal with many economic disagreements between the two countries.

A more tenuous level of political integration involves the creation of advisory and consultative mechanisms. Joint advisory bodies can be mandated to investigate developments and problems in some policy field, and to make recommendations about the appropriate national or joint responses. This is a flexible device that can serve as a neutral source of information and suggestions. Advisory bodies can be elaborate and permanent, like the International Joint Commission of Canada and the United States, or they can be established as required. Although their policy recommendations are not binding, they can have considerable weight when they are based on credible research, expert analysis of problems, broad public participation, and a realistic appreciation of the constraints on national governments.

There are few drawbacks to such bodies. One, of course, is that they have no power other than the force of analysis and suasion: this tends to cause their effects to be felt only in the longer term. They can also prove embarrassing to governments by highlighting flawed policy and neglected problems, and support can always be withdrawn from them. Finally, there is the matter of cost, and of dividing it between two countries that have comparable interests in the policy area but different sized populations and revenues. Despite these difficulties, it is possible that Canada and Quebec would establish advisory bodies in some areas, such as securities regulation and the environment, if no higher level of political integration was reached, provided that common interests were recognized at the outset of the new relationship.

An even weaker level of political integration is reached when national governments have no mutual obligations other than to consult each other regularly. Consultation can occur between ministers, legislatures, regulatory authorities, and even judiciaries. It can be required by treaties or arranged through official or quasi-governmental organizations. Consultation forces decision makers from each state at least to confront the other's agenda, and it can promote mutual understanding and informal cooperation, but it offers no certainty of joint or coordinated action.

The final level of political integration is one in which integration is null: relations between Canada and Quebec would be like those obtaining between any two states in the international arena. There would be no bilateral institutions linking the two communities; instead, the "normal procedures of international law and diplomacy" would govern their relations.[14] These relations would be state-to-state. Of course, the two countries would share membership in existing international organizations. Each would participate in the United Nations, the International Monetary Fund, and many other organizations, and these regimes would impose constraints on the bilateral relationship. But there would be no bilateral political integration. The results of interstate negotiations could be pragmatic agreements to take particular actions, or they could be formal treaties establishing certain rights and obligations. But there would be no general decision rules, and cooperation would take place only when each side judged an arrangement to be in its national interest. The advantage of such an outcome is that full political autonomy would be attained. The disadvantage, of course, is that mechanisms to make collective, binding decisions about matters of common interest would not exist.

Which level of political integration would exist between Canada and Quebec in the long run would depend on the relative strength of structural forces conducive to centralization and decentralization. It would also depend on Canada's internal structure: a system of parliamentary delegations or a set of powerful executive agencies would be unlikely to emerge if the secession left a coherent ROC confronting Quebec about whether parity or proportionality would be the rule in joint decision making. The process of the transition would also be crucial. Not only would the procedures for arranging the secession establish precedents about political relationships, but high levels of mutual hostility at the mass level would limit the degree of political integration that the leaders could arrange. The reason is simple: citizens of neither side would accept infringements on their autonomy imposed by the need to compromise with the other: "In the first place, giving the common institutions any degree of independent authority would be perceived by certain Québécois as giving the rest of Canada a veto power or at least avenues of intervention in fields vital to the building of the Quebec nation. In the rest of Canada, conversely, some might argue that to have Quebec leave is bad enough, but to see imposed on the remainder of the country yet another level of bureaucracy through which Quebecers can meddle indirectly in its affairs, would be intolerable."[15]

On the other hand, there may be material benefits associated with different levels of political integration. These would arise if political integration was necessarily associated with economic integration. Less abstractly, although public sentiment in the two states might dictate that there should be little political integration between them, it might be that high levels of economic integration, with their attendant benefits, can only be achieved or sustained when a political superstructure of common institutions is in place, and this could moderate pressures towards political disengagement. Similarly, secession might produce a weak political superstructure, or none at all, and this might place a ceiling on the level of economic integration that could be maintained in the long run, thereby increasing the costs of separation. This issue merits a short analysis.

CHAPTER SIX

Does Economic Integration Require Political Association?

The preceding chapters have laid out the various levels of economic and political integration that are possible between sovereign states. Whether there is a connection or correlation between these dimensions is a highly abstract question, but one with a lot of practical significance. After a Quebec secession, many sovereigntists maintain, economic integration between Canada and Quebec would continue at a high level, that of a common market or an economic union. So the economic disruption caused by the political act of achieving sovereignty would be minimal. Sovereigntists also often envisage that some joint institutions would be established to manage the common economic space, and generally these represent a low level of political integration – quasi-judicial bodies, special agencies, or executive councils of ministers.

Most English-Canadian analysts agree that the level of political integration would be at least this low, because the rupture of secession would make it unlikely that the two countries would agree to vest much power in common legislative or executive bodies. But they tend to assume that there is a close relationship between economic and political integration, and so the lack of joint institutions inevitably would limit the degree of economic integration that would be sustainable between the two countries. As a result, sovereignty would bring economic loss, compared to what would have been attained in the present economic union. This is an important anti-sovereigntist argument. As the following quotations illustrate, it is also widespread:

- "A customs union, a common market, or an economic union, let alone a monetary union, are impractical because they all require a significant degree of political integration."[1]
- "However, to some extent there is a relationship between economic integration and political integration; as one moves from a free trade agreement to a customs union to a common market to an economic union, the required extent of political integration also increases. A free trade agreement, for example, requires only a dispute settlement mechanism, while a common market requires some policy coordination and an economic union requires more extensive policy coordination (especially if it is accompanied by a monetary union) as well as a central government with sufficient powers to enforce citizenship rights. This relationship between political and economic union will, for example, therefore constrain the options available under the banner of sovereignty-association; that banner misleadingly suggests that the degree of political integration (sovereignty) can be chosen independently of the degree of economic integration (association)."[2]
- "The key point is that maintaining a customs union requires some minimal degree of political union, because of the divergence in regional interests. Conversely, the rupture of the Canadian political union seems to almost inevitably imply dismantling of the Canadian customs union."[3]
- "The choices in the economic and political realms are not unrelated, however. The political institutions must be compatible with the chosen degree of economic interdependence."[4]
- "Indeed, one of the great lessons of recent European experience is that economic union cannot be achieved without a significant degree of political union, probably crossing the threshold from confederalism to federalism. It is utterly unrealistic to imagine that the even wider economic purposes envisioned for 'economic association' between Quebec and CWQ [Canada without Quebec] could be achieved while breaking apart the existing political union."[5]
- "As we shall see, each time one moves from a lesser to a greater degree of integration, an increasing proportion of the economic powers of the nation states must be delegated to supranational institutions."[6]
- "The existing Canadian customs union has evolved over years in response to the shifting balance of regional and sectoral economic and political forces. It would be highly unrealistic to expect it to persist if political ties between Quebec and Canada were ruptured. Its continuation requires a federal government for resolving

disputes. There can be no economic union without a political union."[7]

In the same vein, Courchene agrees that an economic union requires central institutions with enough power to compel member states to act in certain policy areas, and he asks, "Why would Quebec risk its economic future by becoming independent only to immediately hand back to the confederal superstructure much of – and in some areas more than – the 'sovereignty' that it gained?" Once more, the assumption is that an economic and monetary union would require that substantial power reside in a joint "legal and administrative superstructure."[8] Such propositions are denied by Quebec sovereigntists, of course. In the words of the Parti québécois, "En accédant à la souveraineté, le Québec coupera bien entendu le lien politique avec le régime fédéral, mais dans l'intérêt du Québec et du Canada, de nombreux liens à caractère économique seront maintenus."[9]

The conclusion that economic and political integration are correlated rests on several axioms. Four seem to be critical. First, only some economic gains can be delivered through negative integration; that is, through rules against barriers to the movement of goods, services, labour, and capital. Further gains require positive integration – uniform regulations and active measures to facilitate the flow of factors in the economic space and to increase economic efficiency within it. Second, positive integration is best assured through a central authority, because there are few incentives for politicians governing separate states to reach cooperative agreements. Third, in democracies, citizens are reluctant to accept laws and regulations that emanate from authorities that are foreign or are otherwise impervious to democratic political control. Fourth, redistribution outside the boundaries of a "sharing community" is politically impossible. Apart from these general axioms, there is some tendency to overstate the economic benefits of greater political integration, because the policies of an ideal central authority are sometimes contrasted with the costs imposed by noncooperation between real states.

One argument for the link between political and economic integration is that higher levels of the latter, such as a free trade zone or a common market, require removing not only tariffs but also non-tariff barriers to trade (NTBs). To allow fair competition and greater efficiency, the economic space must be relatively homogeneous. Many NTBs are subtle. They include subsidies to domestic firms, discriminatory government procurement, and regulations about such matters as investment and product standards, as well as the regulatory frameworks of such sectors as transportation, communications, and banking. To remove NTBs, the argument runs, there must be an authoritative enforcement mechanism to settle disputes about unfair trade and to determine whether national policies are acceptable. Naturally, this requires a framework treaty. More effective is a single central authority, such as the European Commission, that can enact uniform regulations and codes of conduct so that the constitutent states' practices become standardized.

But levelling the competitive playing field may not require such a high degree of political integration. If national policies are broadly similar in effect, constituent governments can extend "mutual recognition" of each other's policies, accepting them as equivalent. In the Canada–U.S. Free Trade Agreement, for example, each country agreed to provide for the accreditation of the other's testing facilities and inspection agencies.[10] When practices are not similar, one state may choose to harmonize regulations voluntarily, a choice that depends on how much inconvenience and economic loss is being caused by noncongruence. As well, unfair NTBs can be attacked, within the framework of an overarching treaty, by dispute-settlement mechanisms. As in the FTA and NAFTA, treaties can impose constraints in areas such as government procurement, agricultural regulations, and foreign investment controls, and disputes about whether regulations have been unfairly applied or are in conflict with the goals of the treaty can be settled by quasi-judicial bodies. Such processes, however, are slow, are bound by precedent, and produce zero-sum decisions in favour of one side or the other. The constraints they impose are legalistic and administrative, and hence inflexible.[11] There is less scope for creative compromise than exists within an integrated political system. But such compromises can also be suggested by joint advisory bodies, a very low level of political integration, and they can also be struck by politicians even when interstate consultations are infrequent. The question is whether those politicians have an incentive to compromise.

Another argument focuses on trade policy. Any level of economic integration beyond a free trade zone requires a common commercial policy. Minimally, this means that the cooperating states must agree on a tariff schedule and on common quotas in special sectors, for example, agriculture, textiles, and footwear. They must also be capable of joint action in trade disputes with third parties, and of negotiating multilateral agreements as a unit, one that is able to bargain coherently and strategically within a complex set of international coalitions. Finally, commercial policy has spread from simple matters of tariffs and quotas to wider issues such as investment, subsidies, intellectual property, and the environment, so the domestic impact

of trade agreements also has broadened, along with its political ramifications.

The basic requirements of a common commercial policy may be
met more effectively and at less cost by a single central authority
that has executive and perhaps legislative powers. The large consultative apparatus associated with trade negotiations need not be du-
plicated. Decisions may be reached more quickly within a single
government than when their implications must be gauged separately
in two or more communities before being aggregated by negotiation
into one common position. As the scope of commercial policy broadens, so does the complexity of the trade-offs to be made between
domestic interests, and so too do these theoretical advantages of a
single political authority. But of course much depends on how different the economic interests of the constituent states are, for the regional politics of trade arise from international agreements that create
benefits and losses that are concentrated regionally. Two states could
readily agree on a common commercial policy if their economies were
identical – but they never are identical. A single authority also has
the capacity to assuage the "losers" from the new policy; that is, it
can extend assistance to those bearing costs, by means of regional
funds, retraining programs, and adjustment subsidies. Thus, the losers are cross-subsidized by the beneficiaries of the new trade policy.

These arguments are not watertight, however. The commercial policy
of a customs union can be set by joint parliamentary delegations or
through ministerial meetings. Intergovernmental negotiations may
then be slower and more complex. But they can still result in a common position; indeed, the difficulty of agreeing can increase leverage in negotiations with others.[12] Obviously, the decision rule is
important. If policy is not set by a single authority, where the rule is
consensus within a responsible executive and a majority vote in the
legislature, it must be parity or proportionality. But both are unsatisfactory when the states differ considerably in size. If each state insisted on positions that benefited its interests at the expense of the
other, nothing would result under parity, and the smaller side would
always lose under proportionality. The problem is that interregional
trade-offs cannot be made under a strict decision rule. But in a customs union, which always is also a free trade area, interests in each
state are interdependent, in complex ways. So an alternative is for
there to be no formal decision rules and for negotiations to continue
(including, informally, with trading partners) until agreement is
reached. Relative power need not be formalized. While such processes
would be complex and time consuming, they could moderate politi-

cal resentment, because precise responsibility could not be assigned by the losers.

What really counts in commercial policy is being able to implement or "sell" the new rules. At the extreme, in theory, one state could simply adopt the trade policies set by its partner(s) in the customs union, as long as domestic public opinion was willing to accept the outcome. This could depend on the cohesiveness of the citizenry, the organization of interests, and also the adjustment mechanisms available. In theory, again, it is possible that one state's losses could be compensated by transfers from the other, even without much political integration. If not, the individual states could design adjustment programs; cross-subsidization across borders is not essential.

Another argument holds that economic integration at the level of a common market or economic union requires a very high degree of regulatory harmonization. Some relevant regulations are purely domestic; others, such as competition policy, span the states in the union. There must also be a standard system of commercial law, or agreements that circumvent legal gaps and incompatibilities. Tax structures should be comparable if not identical, especially on the corporate side. Finally, for positive integration there must be provisions for infrastructural efficiency, either through regulation (as in telecommunications and transport) or through direct provision of installations. All of this is facilitated by a single authority.

But can similar results be achieved by independent states at a low level of political integration? Clearly, a substantial part of the regulatory framework governing commerce can be made homogeneous by voluntary harmonization, which needs no contact whatsoever between states, let alone a common legislature and executive. All that is required is that the state which does most of the harmonizing has a government capable of resisting domestic pressures to legislate more favourable or suitable measures.

If economies are interdependent, governments have an incentive to negotiate changes to laws and regulations jointly. One problem in their doing so is delay, because of conflicting interests, and this can be costly in a period of rapid change. But single central authorities also can have difficulty in accommodating regional interests quickly. More serious is the argument that interstate agreements would represent the lowest common denominator – if agreements could be reached at all. Fundamentally, this argument for political integration distinguishes those who believe that sovereign states can and eventually will make mutually beneficial common policy from those who do not. The first position assumes that cooperation to enact economically efficient policies results from the pressure of people and firms who seek the gains that are not possible because of discordant policies. Along these lines, one analyst described Canada's legislation facilitating commerce as "the reflection of a spontaneous order shaped by the requirements of trade and the needs of the economic agents, and this order exists whether or not Quebec remains part of the Canadian federation."[13] But of course there is much in history to warn that institutions providing mutual gains might not arise spontaneously. GATT, to name the most obvious example, has developed very gradually, and it was established after a destructive period of beggar-thy-neighbour trade policies. One theoretical reason to expect low levels of international cooperation is that states may be motivated not by the prospect of making absolute gains but by considerations of relative gains: even though both sides might benefit from cooperation, this might be refused if one side would benefit more.[14]

More generally, suboptimal outcomes can be attributed to political incentives, under conditions of intergovernmental competition. This competition can be horizontal, between states, or vertical, between states and the central authority. Some analysts see intergovernmental competition as fruitful, because it stimulates innovation and efficiency; horizontally, this can occur because governments must be responsive when mobile factors are free to move to the other jurisdictions. Others see horizontal competition as potentially destructive, since governments can adopt policies that impose costs on other states, and they can fail to make agreements in the best interests of the whole union, simply because they are responsive only to domestic constituencies. For example, if some potential change in procurement rules or transport regulation would benefit 80 per cent of the people in one state but only 40 per cent in the other, it would not be adopted, because the second state would not agree. But if there was a central authority, under majority rule, the change would be made. Further, the argument runs that governments tend to be more responsive to those threatened by change, because these groups have a stronger incentive to organize and lobby for protection than those who would benefit from a new, efficient policy.[15] So, for example, some regulatory change might benefit 80 per cent of the people in one state and only 60 per cent in the other, but if the losers were more powerfully organized in the second state, the change might still not be agreed. If there were common political institutions, all the potential "winners" would be more likely to prevail over the losers (and there might be more opportunity for redistribution to mollify the losers). In this view, economic efficiency cannot be maximized without a central "monitor."[16]

But there are other monitors that exist besides a central government. For instance, there is currently little coordination of the provincial governments' fiscal policy stances within the Canadian federation, and arguably it is the financial markets that monitor these in the end. Moreover, there are costs to having a central authority, since it can be exercised at the expense of policy innovation and administrative efficiency. More important, there is no guarantee that a central authority will enact economically efficient policies. Certainly, in Canada, the federal government has legislated and spent in ways that have distorted interregional prices and thus tended to fragment the economic union.[17] In short, a central authority also has incentives to respond to regional constituencies.

Still, the absence of a central monitor will sometimes lead to destructive competition between states, and potentially efficient agreements will not be reached. But perhaps the central authority need not involve political integration at the level of a common executive or legislature. One obvious possibility is a joint advisory body, which could gather information, investigate problems in the economic union, and suggest policies to improve its operation. Another is a dispute-settlement mechanism, or a trade and regulatory tribunal. The latter has more power but faces several practical obstacles. First, with little legitimacy at the outset, quasi-judicial bodies must slowly build their credibility as impartial monitors. Second, to maintain high levels of economic integration, their purview must be very broad: states have to agree on a comprehensive and detailed treaty, one reaching far beyond a free trade agreement. If the judicial mechanism is not to be purely negative, but is to be empowered to require action as well as forbidding particular measures, then the treaty must also include common goals agreed by the states, goals that are amenable to judicial interpretation. Third, judicial bodies are not well equipped to act as program designers so as to provide positive direction when states fail to meet their commitments or adhere to the union's goals.[18] But they are capable of declaring regulations and policies to be inadequate and to need redesigning. Even so, judicial bodies must act with more reserve than a central political authority, for decisions requiring sweeping policy changes could make the democratic-deficit problem acute. In the end, without a positive central authority, there is no mechanism to compel states to reach agreements that strengthen the economic union. But this is also true whenever subnational governments have any areas of sovereign economic jurisdiction.

Some aspects of positive economic integration are particularly difficult for politically independent states to achieve. In the first place, a common infrastructure requires joint action. This can involve regulation of common services and the direct provision of facilities that increase economic integration and efficiency. While many such matters can be delegated to special-purpose agencies, they cannot be depoliticized. How serious a problem this is depends on the sensitivities about decisions over which there is no direct democratic control. Such agencies also require agreement on decision rules, staffing, and funding responsibilities, and this may be difficult to achieve when only a few states are involved.

Another area where simple harmonization is not enough is the legal framework of commerce. Parallel domestic rules about such matters as bankruptcy and competition policy and the enforcement of court orders will not suffice to maintain high levels of economic integration. There must be scope for the extraterritorial enforcement of legislation. It is feasible, for instance, to have identical bankruptcy laws, but if a firm in one state goes bankrupt, there can be no authority over its assets in the other without some treaty providing for this. The same is true for taxation and many areas of corporate law. Similarly, in the securities industry, mirroring another state's regulations does not guarantee active cooperation. Again, fully harmonized competition policy requires one state to submit the pricing practices of its domestically based transnational firms to the scrutiny of competition authorities that are based in the other jurisdiction. Although some of these problems can be circumvented by requiring that all corporate activity in the other states be conducted through subsidiaries, this reduces economic integration and increases transaction costs. It also raises the problem of transfer pricing in the case of unfair competition – or fraud in the case of bankruptcy – and therefore simply pushes the extraterritoriality issue back one stage. Alternatively, authority over such matters can be allocated by treaty to a joint body, either regulatory or judicial. In this case, the states have to agree on a decision rule within the body, and its legitimacy will be contested to the extent that its decisions allocate costs and benefits differentially among the component units. Nevertheless, the rather arcane matters involved in competition policy and many other areas, and the uniform interests of dominant businesses in a legal system that integrates the economic space, might help insulate such bodies from domestic political forces.

Finally, it is worth noting that the whole problem of cooperatively achieving positive integration is reduced when governments favour less state management of the economy: "Economic integration is, however, not only the result of international agreements. It is also the spontaneous outcome of the market mechanism in the absence of obstacles to the movement of commodities, people, capital, and enterprise. But widespread government interference in the market mechanism has made it necessary to coordinate national policies if they are not to have a disintegrating effect on the economies on which they operate."[19] If market forces are allowed to prevail in the economic space, less coordinated policy will be required, and negative measures to restrict discrimination may suffice. Of course, if the governments of the states have different orientations towards this basic issue, the probability of maintaining high levels of economic integration is much reduced. The whole framework of the economy will tend to differ in the two states, and the less interventionist government will constantly oppose the distortions introduced by the other state.

Another case for the link between economic and political integration concerns social policy. One prong of this argument is that the traditional instruments of economic management – tariffs, subsidies, regulation, and public enterprises – have become constrained by international agreements or by the state's fiscal incapacity. Growth now depends on human capital formation and rapid economic adjustment, which require sound and integrated social-policy design.[20] Separate states may not achieve economies of scale in providing some social and educational services, and if people are mobile the constituent units may undersupply some services, such as specialized job training. Hence, there must be a central authority with spending or regulatory powers in these areas. Another prong of this argument is that differences in social policy can produce unfair competition within a common economic space. If one state provides few social entitlements, for example, or has weak laws about workplace safety or the right to unionize, its products are cheaper, unfairly. Furthermore, wide social-policy variations among the states in a union are inefficient, because firms move to less productive locations in order to access disadvantaged workers and lax regulations, and people are drawn to move by lower taxes or higher benefits ("net fiscal benefits") rather than by market wages.[21]

At the extreme, some of these arguments favour a highly centralized or unitary state. But there can be advantages to social-policy differentiation, in the form of competitive efficiency and innovation, that offset the market distortions it creates. As well, much social-policy harmonization can be achieved without a common political authority that has some jurisdiction in these fields or is capable of spending to enforce uniformity. Minimum standards can be agreed on through treaties or through a basic charter of social entitlements, like the European Social Charter.[22] This would require only a dispute-resolution mechanism for enforcement.

Despite all these options, there are two areas of socio-economic policy in an economic union that appear unattainable without high levels of political integration. The first concerns personal mobility. One dimension of this is immigration into the economic space. National governments tend to guard jealously their right to control immigration into the community. It is possible that separate states could harmonize their immigration requirements and procedures or that immigration could be managed jointly under a treaty; but this is a highly sensitive issue in every country, one that is difficult to manage without the public being able to express its views democratically and to hold accountable the political executive that is responsible for the policy. Internal migration is at least as sensitive. An economic union can be most efficient when there is free movement within the economic space, but this means that individuals must receive the equivalent of "national treatment" status – the right to work and to receive social benefits and domestic constitutional protections in any jurisdiction. In theory, this status could be extended mutually by treaty, but the benefits expected to flow from it would then have to be comparable. More important, these are basic entitlements of citizenship itself. They help to define the community. It is unlikely that they could be extended without some political expression of a common identity, particularly an elected legislature.

The other policy area where high levels of political integration seem imperative is redistribution. In integrated economies, interregional transfers are necessary for efficiency. They allow states to offer comparable social-policy packages and so reduce inefficient migration (though this involves no extra cost when migration is restricted anyway). They also ease structural adjustment to external economic shocks that distribute costs and benefits on a regional basis, and adjustment to common policies that have the same effect. Redistribution can prevent adjustment that is inefficient because the shocks are temporary (such as a trade war in grains). It acts as a mutual insurance system within the union. And when policies in the union create inequality or threaten to do so, the resistance of regional coalitions can be overcome when some of the net benefits of the policy change can be redistributed to them. So redistribution can increase the economic efficiency of the union.

Does this sharing require common political institutions? It would appear so. The notion that one citizenry should be taxed in order to provide transfers to another government is generally unacceptable.

It is difficult enough to tax for foreign aid to desperately impover-
ished countries; governments could not tax in order to make transfers to the partners in the economic union. Redistribution on any
significant scale can only take place within the confines of a political
community and through a common government with an independent electoral base. Questions of redistribution are quintessentially
political ones: they cannot be hived off to neutral commissions or
groups of experts. Only politicians can make the necessary trade-offs,
based on their own reading of public opinion and electoral accountability. If transfers were made without such a common government,
the citizens in each state would certainly resist, not only on grounds
of material self-interest but because transfers would violate basic democratic principles. As well, it is improbable that the separate states
would be willing to compensate their own domestic losers from a
common policy when they were numerous, perhaps a majority, and
when the beneficiaries were beyond the reach of taxation; instead,
the state's government would have a strong incentive to oppose the
policy.

The economic significance of these limitations depends, of course,
on the real contribution of interregional transfers to the economy.
The basis of such allocative decisions is their political efficiency, which
may not correspond with economic efficiency. Indeed, there are persistent arguments that the Canadian economy has suffered from excessive interregional redistribution. Transfers have impeded
adjustment, have added to the fiscal burden, and have reduced competitiveness.[23] Nevertheless, if redistribution can strengthen an economic union, and if common political institutions are essential for
this function as well as for allowing individual mobility, then there
clearly is a ceiling on the level of economic integration that can be
achieved without them.

A final consideration concerns monetary policy and currency. Based
on the evolution of the European Union, it is sometimes argued that
a common monetary authority cannot be sustained without deepening political integration. But the experience of currency boards and
the existence of countries where the American dollar is used speak
against this suggestion. In fact, many economists are persuaded that
monetary policy affects nothing except inflation levels in the long
run, and they use this to argue for isolating central banks from political influence. In any case, one state in an economic union obviously could be a pure monetary-policy taker. Equally obviously, if
the population of that state did not believe in the neutrality of monetary policy, or if short-term shocks were not appropriately adjusted,
there would have to be a strong political consensus that the costs of

accepting another state's policy were outweighed by other benefits of the economic union or by other benefits of sovereignty.

The overall conclusion here is that there is only a weak link between economic and political integration. Particular levels of economic integration can be achieved within a variety of institutional frameworks. Indeed, it is easy to neglect the full range of political institutions through which economic arrangements can be made and managed. These include voluntary harmonization, consultations and the use of expert advisory bodies, standard international negotiations that produce treaties, quasi-judicial mechanisms to settle disputes, special-purpose regulatory and administrative bodies, and joint delegations, as well as common legislatures and executives. Even this list omits non-official mechanisms that can promote harmonization, such as the Scandinavian Inter-Parliamentary Union and the Uniform Law Movement in the United States.

One can classify the broad functions of government with respect to economic integration. Judicial and quasi-judicial bodies have the advantage of some insulation from normal political pressures and lend themselves to formal parity in representation. They can achieve negative integration by outlawing discrimination, and they may have some ability to promote positive integration by ruling against measures that are uncoordinated or are not in the spirit of treaties. Regulatory and special-purpose bodies can also achieve positive measures, though if their activities are very intrusive, the problem of democratic accountability will arise. Allocative functions cannot be sustained in the absence of a common political authority with an independent democratic base; this expresses the existence of an underlying sharing community that constitutes a political union. Without such central institutions, the highest levels of economic integration cannot be attained.

To sum up, high degrees of economic integration can be achieved more quickly, flexibly, effectively, and efficiently by a central authority with an independent democratic base than by the separate or co-operative action of sovereign states – in principle. These advantages are not inevitably realized, because internal conflict and the political incentives in place may produce stasis or economically inefficient policies. It is not inconceivable that fairly high levels of economic integration could be maintained through voluntary harmonization, though this will require a government capable of resisting domestic pressures to establish a separate regulatory regime. Nor is it impossible that more positive measures could result from the joint action of the constituent states, though there is much to suggest that this will occur only when there are clear mutual gains to be realized and when functions can be hived off to quasi-judicial or regulatory bodies that can gradually establish their legitimacy. Generally, the political incentives within two states that do not share a common legislature and executive are purely domestic, so the separate governmental calculations of costs and benefits are necessarily partial. This would inhibit some cooperative solutions, though there will still be incentives to promote economic integration when economic interests are interdependent.

What does all this suggest about the effects of a sudden drop in the level of political integration? First, there would be an immediate decline in economic integration because cross-border mobility and redistribution would end. Positive integration brought about by a joint legislature's spending throughout the economic space would also cease. The size of these losses to the whole economy or any part of it would depend on how important mobility had been as an avenue of adjustment and how economically efficient transfers and other expenditures had been.

Beyond this, the effects are less certain. A drop in political integration is rather different from that normally contemplated in analyses of economic and political unions, most of which focus on increasing integration. Generally, economic integration is the desired end, and political nonintegration is an obstacle to it, largely because the separate constituencies of governments resist particular measures or a general surrender of authority. But this situation may not be symmetrical with a decrease in political integration.[24] For instance, if two governments tentatively agreed on a change of regulations that increased efficiency in the common economic space but created a set of losing interests in one state, these interests could block the change; they could also stir resistance to laws derived from "outside" the democratic polity. But when the regulation is already in place, there exists a political and economic equilibrium. People and firms have already adjusted to it, and no losers are created by leaving it in place. Of course, some domestic interests might mobilize to promote a change that would benefit them, or economic shocks might provide an incentive for change; and if some state(s) in the union made policy changes, the other governments would have to decide whether to follow suit or not. But these pressures are different from, and probably less powerful than, those that inhibit governments from departing from the status quo in order to enter new integrative arrangements.

Over the longer run, the separate governments, responsive to different domestic constituencies and subject to different external economic influences, would tend to enact distinct policies, thereby decreasing the level of economic integration. The propensity to do this would be a function of the extent of economic interdependence, which would decline as political integration eroded, thus producing less incentive for cooperation, and so on. But much could depend on the institutions still in existence. We have seen that central political institutions can play a powerful role in maintaining an integrated economic space. Except for redistribution and mobility, a joint legislature and responsible executive are not, in theory, essential to maintain high levels of economic integration. Still, replacement mechanisms would have to be established to substitute for the roles played by central authorities. These could include, as described above, a dispute-settlement mechanism about economic regulation, an advisory body on the economic union, and agencies to manage common infrastructure and assure extraterritorial legal enforcement. Treaties also would be required to provide for mutual recognition of regulations, the general goals of the union, and social entitlements.

In theory, such a framework could maintain economic integration at a relatively high level, but in fact its long-term effectiveness would depend on the willingness of citizens to accept rules over which they had no direct democratic control (or, conversely, on the ability of politicians to explain the rules as necessary). The initial question, of course, is whether such a framework would be established in the first place. This would depend on the attitudes of citizens and the incentives facing governments at the time of the change.

To return to Canada and Quebec, this implies that the process of the transition to sovereignty requires careful, detailed analysis. The political atmosphere of the time and the decisions taken during the event would have enduring consequences. How the secession took place would help determine the degree of political integration that would exist between Canada and Quebec and, not quite independently, the level of economic integration that would be maintained between them. This in turn would determine in part how costly the separation would be. First, however, it is necessary to examine briefly the underlying factors that are conducive to centralization and decentralization in a political system. These, too, would help determine the degree of integration that would obtain between Quebec and ROC, and also the long-term configuration of Canada itself.

CHAPTER SEVEN

Determinants of Centralization and Decentralization

If Quebec secedes, Canada could take on any one of a variety of constitutional forms. As discussed earlier, it could reconstitute itself anywhere along the continuum from highly centralized (or unitary) to highly decentralized (or fragmented). The alternatives are clear. Here, our subject is the underlying factors that help determine the degree of centralization in any political unit. The basic idea is that institutions are shaped by societal characteristics.[1] In theory, constitutions should accommodate the socio-economic features of the polity; in practice, the structural characteristics give rise to currents of opinion and political forces that influence the creation of constitutions. These underlying factors are relevant both to the constitutional make-up of Canada and to the degree of economic and political integration that would exist between Canada and an independent Quebec. For example, if ROC was more homogeneous culturally than Canada is now, then, other things remaining equal, this would be conducive to a constitution more centralized than the current one. Similarly, if Canada and Quebec had very different economic and trade interests, this would restrict the level of political integration of the post-secession institutions that the two countries would establish.

Structural factors shape constitutions in two ways. First, they have an impact at the time of their creation, both because they help give rise to the political forces at play and because those engaged in writing constitutions take them into account. Second, the characteristics of the polity are always in flux, however gradually, and this evolution will create pressure for constitutional change. Our interest here is in the first relationship rather than in long-term evolution. This is justified because in assessing ROC's constitutional make-up and the level of integration between Canada and Quebec, the most important determinant will be the conditions at the time of the separation. In part, this is because secessions are such monumental events that some "underlying" characteristics can change during their course. As well, there is more room for disagreement about how these factors are evolving than about their current nature. Some analysts see global economic and technological change eroding Canada's east-west economic links and integrating Canadian regions economically and culturally with the United States.[2] All this is conducive to decentralization over the long run. But others focus on ROC's prospects for cultural, ideological, and economic coherence.[3] At the time of a separation, political actors would operate "in the shadow of the future," as they see it, but this is indeterminate, and the first issue to settle is how structural characteristics would affect institutional design during the secession.[4]

The analysis here will be brief. This is certainly not because of a shortage of factors. To explain the degree of centralization written into constitutions, scholars have invoked a very large number of geographic, social, economic, institutional, and political characteristics. Moreover, these elements are interrelated. As one analyst of stability in federal states put it, almost despairingly, "there is a complex interplay among all the variables."[5] Theories of centralization and decentralization also differ in the relative emphasis placed on these factors and about the nature of their interrelationships. Nevertheless, there are several comprehensive surveys of the factors that shape the initial form of federal states and of those that determine their evolution and stability. This discussion relies on them,[6] but it treats the subject only briefly because structural characteristics would not strictly determine the constitutional outcome in Canada (or the degree of integration that would exist between Canada and Quebec). To anticipate, the analysis shows that there are few very strong pressures towards either centralization or decentralization in ROC and that those that do exist point in contradictory directions. Beyond this, analysts have shown that when institutions are being established, both structural and conjunctural factors are important in determining their form. If Quebec secedes, the conjunctural factors will be crucial. In short, the underlying characteristics of the polity would leave much latitude for political choice.

The most comprehensive surveys of the determinants of federal structures have been made by Ronald Watts. These address the factors that promote more or less centralization when federal constitutions are created and those determining their later evolution and stability. The first set of factors is laid out in table 3.[7] The top panel lists those conducive to a centralized union, while the bottom panel contains those that tend towards regional autonomy. For the most part, the second are mirror images of the first, but some deserve separate discussion. The table also scores the strength of each factor. Most of the factors are structural characteristics, relatively immutable, but others (denoted by "C") are conjunctural, meaning that their force and direction depend on the events of the time. The factors are presented both for Canada (as it would exist without Quebec), and for Canada-Quebec integration after secession. The qualitative analysis here can be supplemented by reference to the data in tables A1 and A2, as well as to the discussion of ROC's characteristics in chapter 1.

Taking the structural factors first, an important one is the prospect of economic advantage. In deciding, after secession, whether and how to maintain the Canadian federation, economic considerations would weigh heavily. In the Canadian economic union as it exists, there are large trade flows, considerable corporate integration, and much labour mobility. There is also scope for positive integration by the central government, through the judicial system, federal regulation and spending on infrastructure, and redistribution. These considerations would be a force for maintaining the economic union in Canada along with a central government capable of managing it.

On the other hand, regional economic interests are diverse, a factor conducive to decentralization. The Atlantic provinces are weakly linked by trade to the rest of Canada. But their residents and governments have an overwhelming interest in continued federal direct spending and transfers. In 1990 net federal transfers to these provinces ranged from 20 per cent of provincial GDP in New Brunswick to 36 per cent in Prince Edward Island.[8] The major economic divergence in ROC is between the West and Ontario. Insofar as their resource-based and manufacturing economies are complementary, much of the historical legacy is one of central-Canadian domination, through tariffs to protect manufacturing in Ontario and Quebec, and through "positively" integrating measures such as the Canadian Pacific Railway and the National Energy Program. Nevertheless, there is no inherent conflict of economic interest between these regions. Because of the extreme fluctuations of the resource-based western economy, it is recognized that the economic union provides substantial benefits in the form of mutual insurance, stabilization, and labour mobility; without these, price volatility would directly affect wages and employment. Also important is the power of Canada in international negotiations. The West alone probably could not have matched Canada's success in disputes with the United States about potash and lumber.[9]

Table 3
Factors Conducive to Centralization and Decentralization

I		UNION	Canada	Canada-Quebec
C^1	1	Desire for independence/external threat	XX^2	OO^3
	2	Economic advantage:		
		(i) scale and complementarity	X	X
		(ii) positive economic integration	X	$-^4$
C		(iii) unified interest groups	X	O
	3	Administrative efficiency	X	–
	4	External relations:		
		(i) defence	X	X
		(ii) diplomacy	X	O
		(iii) trade	–	–
	5	Ethnic and cultural homogeneity	X	O
	6	Geographic contiguity	OO	X
	7	Historical political association	X	X
	8	Similar political and social institutions	X	–
C	9	Political leadership	X	OO
	10	Successful models of federalism	X	O
C	11	American/international policy	X	X
	12	Sense of common citizenship	X	OO

II		AUTONOMY		
C	1	Fear of domination after independence	OO	OO
	2	Diverse economic interests:		
		(i) regional specialization	O	–
		(ii) inequality	O	–
	3	Administrative convenience:		
		(i) regional homogeneity	–	O
		(ii) effectiveness	O	O
	4	Conflicting external relations:		
		(i) defence	X	X
		(ii) diplomacy	X	O
		(iii) trade	O	–
	5	Ethnic and cultural diversity	X	O
	6	Geographic dispersion	O	–
	7	Historical identity	–	O
	8	Dissimilarities:		
		(i) political and social institutions	X	–
		(ii) ideologies	O	O
C	9	Regional political leadership	O	OO
	10	Models of autonomy	O	O
C	11	American/international policy	X	X
	12	Sense of regional identity	O	OO·

Notes: [1] Conjunctural factors, whose force and direction depend on the events of the time

[2] X signifies tendencies towards centralization

[3] O signifies tendencies towards decentralization

[4] A dash means neutral

Still on the decentralization side, it is true that considerable regional inequality would exist in ROC; in fact, without Quebec, disparities would be more obvious. This is normally a factor conducive to demands for autonomy, but in Canada these demands would not arise from poorer provinces concerned about economic domination or exploitation; on the contrary, the pressure for decentralization could emanate from wealthier provinces that were no longer prepared to subsidize the poorer regions. On the other hand, as noted above, the burden of redistributive programs would be lessened if Quebec had seceded.

The next factor is administrative efficiency. There are obviously some gains to be realized when a central government has substantial powers with respect to defence, foreign affairs, taxation, justice, standards and patents, and other common services. This especially benefits the smaller provinces. But most provinces fully realize economies of scale in services such as elementary and secondary education, and there are strong arguments for provincial administration of many other functions. More responsive to local interests and preferences and quicker in decision making, the provinces can also compete in program design and delivery, and this stimulates innovation and efficiency.

In foreign affairs, there are evident advantages to a strong federal role. There is no interregional disagreement with the country's well-defined role in North American and NATO defence or with its peacekeeping functions. The same is true of diplomacy. Trade is another matter. Although the major interprovincial disagreements about the FTA and NAFTA have now been decided, there remain substantial differences in the direction of trade flows. British Columbia is orienting towards the Pacific Rim economies, including that of the northwestern United States; Alberta's major flow of output is into the United States, as is Ontario's; and the Atlantic region is heavily dependent on foreign markets. In fact, every region sells more abroad than it sells within ROC. This produces some trade policy differences, as in the east-west split in the GATT negotiations about supply management in agriculture. Once more, though, the major divisive issues, both in North America and in GATT, have been settled, and there is a common structural interest in a central government that is capable of negotiating internationally and protecting domestic interests in trade disputes, especially when the provinces can still be integrated into international bargaining frameworks or left free to make international arrangements of their own.

There is no doubt that Canada without Quebec would be more homogeneous ethnically and culturally than at present. With respect to language, the data in table A1 make this clear. Beyond simple demographics are the cultural elements of a national character. According to Charles Taylor's analysis, ROC would share several elements of a common identity: the fact that English Canadians are united by a sense of being different and less violent than Americans; a commitment to the collective provision of public goods and to regional equality; an endorsement of multiculturalism; and a strong support for the Canadian Charter of Rights and Freedoms.[10] At present, these values conflict with some of those widely shared in Quebec. In particular, the desire to preserve Quebec's autonomy and to ensure its cultural survival contradict ROC's insistence on regional equality, multiculturalism, and the Charter. The removal of this conflict would be conducive to a more centralized ROC constitution.

However, Canada would become geographically discontiguous, a factor that normally works strongly in the opposite direction. In Canada's case, though, this factor might be more psychological than real. As Watts points out, transportation and communications facilities can be more important than sheer geography. Moreover, the Atlantic provinces are economically dependent and have traditionally supported a strong central government that is able to direct equalization and other transfers to the region.[11] Although Quebec secession would lead to greater intraregional cooperation in Atlantic Canada, as the threat of it already has done, it would not weaken the region's adherence to Canada.[12] Nor should discontiguity in itself lead other citizens or governments to advocate decentralization. More generally, though, the geographic dispersion of the country's population is a factor against centralization, as it always has been.

The Canadian provinces have a long historical association within the present federation. This is an inertial force for continued unity, and it would especially be so in the absence of the province that has most resisted great national efforts – in the two world wars – and also has most strenuously demanded structural changes in the federal association. On the other hand, the adherence of the western provinces to the federation is relatively recent and is still marked by their former neocolonial status, which was apparently reasserted by Ottawa's resource policies in the 1970s and 1980s. The effects of these historical grievances cannot be ignored, even though they have been somewhat mitigated by the constitutional amendments of 1982 and by less interventionist central governments since 1984.

The Canadian provinces also have very similar political and social institutions. The basic political institutions, administrative structures and traditions, and legal systems are all marked by only minor variations. Less formally, the political party systems are basically alike, and the national party system remains an integrating force. On the other hand, it can be argued that there have emerged significant ideological cleavages between the West and the rest of Canada, focused on the populism and belief in direct democracy that have swept the West in the past and are now concentrated in, though not restricted to, the Reform Party. This ideology includes a mistrust of strong central government, and to the extent that it is a regional phenomenon, it must be counted as a force against centralization.

For most Canadians, the present constitutional system represents a satisfactory model of federalism. Opinion has varied over time, affected by the incumbent government's performance, but there is little evidence of the strong and pervasive dissatisfaction with the federal system that exists in Quebec.[13] However, there are also strong models of provincial autonomy and decentralization in Canada, particularly in the West. Governments in British Columbia and especially in Alberta have supported Quebec demands for greater provincial powers, and the core western requirement for constitutional change has become a triple-E Senate. While the pervasiveness of decentralist "province building" has been overstated somewhat (though it obviously applies to Alberta), there are clear models of provincial autonomy that conflict with the existing distribution of powers. Some have argued that Ontario, traditionally supportive of a strong central government, could also take a more autonomist position as a consequence of fiscal restraint, shifting trade flows, and the failure to have its interests adequately represented in federal policy.[14]

Finally, there is the underlying sense of common citizenship, a factor stressed not by Watts but by Hicks and others.[15] Undoubtedly, there is in the population a substantial reservoir of identification with Canada as such, though there is also a strong identification with regions and provinces. Donna Dasko, summarizing a decade of Environics polls, notes a decline in the propensity to identify with Canada more than with one's own province. Between 1980 and 1991, the proportion who did so dropped from 62 to 53 per cent, the biggest drop being in Quebec. The percentages identifying most with Canada at the end of this period were 69 per cent in Ontario, 57 per cent in the West, and 49 per cent in the Atlantic region.[16] Of course, this mixed loyalty is characteristic of federations.[17] It underpins a system where power is divided on a regional basis. These deep loyalties are enduring, but as the change noted by Environics shows, they do move with events. So this factor is conjunctural to some extent, and it would certainly be so if Quebec seceded, for the issue at the time of Canada's reconstitution would be how strongly people identified with Canada-without-Quebec, not with Canada as it exists today. How citizens actually felt would not become apparent until the event occurred. For example, some English Canadians take pride in the cultural duality of the country: Quebec's distinctiveness is a characteristic that strengthens their identification with Canada. So if Quebec separated, one of the foundations of their sense of community and citizenship would be lost. For others, Quebec's distinctiveness is irritating and an impediment to their identification with the country as a whole, and therefore its "departure" would permit a greater attachment to ROC. The relative size of these two groups is impossible to estimate, but if irritation with Quebec is stronger in the West than elsewhere, that region's identification with the country should increase with separation.

Beyond this, the sense of common citizenship can be affected by momentous events. National solidarity during the crisis of war is an obvious example. This implies that the balance between national and regional identities, so important because it sets parameters to the actions of political élites, may be strongly influenced by how the process of Quebec secession occurs. A sense of crisis could lend support to centralizing forces. As Roger Gibbins put it,

If Quebec remains in Canada, the likely drift of constitutional evolution will be towards the concentration of the instruments of governance within Quebec and the fragmentation of the same outside Quebec. However, if Quebec should leave, there may be strong incentives for Canadians to reconstruct an effective national government for the rest of the country. In this case, the dynamics of reconstruction could result in a more centralized federal state in which Ottawa, and not the provinces, would be empowered to address the concerns of the new political agenda ... At the very least we should expect a period of assertive nationalism as Canadians try to redefine their new country and national community; the classic Canadian search for a national identity would come back with a vengeance.[18]

Of course, if this search failed, the sense of crisis could lend support for decentralist or secessionist alternatives in Canada. Or this could happen earlier. In Gordon Gibson's view, rallying to Ottawa would be to respond to the siren call of national solidarity. If English Canadians gathered in a constituent assembly and contemplated where their interests and loyalties lay, the result could well be "a vastly pruned back central authority, amounting to little more than a vehicle for international continuity and a service bureau for the provinces."[19]

This leads to the more obviously conjunctural factors denoted in table 3. Historically, the desire for independence and the presence of an external threat have often been critical in the decision to form federations and in determining the degree to which power is vested in the central authority. Centralization can be a response to an external threat. The obvious candidate, as in 1867, is the United States. While anti-Americanism has declined in Canada over the past two decades, there is strong public sentiment that Canada should remain independent of the United States, and thus the fear of fragmentation and absorption would support centralization. As Léon Dion, an astute observer of Canadians, put it, English Canada has been unable to accept decentralization because of "la peur de son propre éclatement" [the fear of itself busting apart].[20] But more important would be the immediate threat that Quebec secession would pose to Canadians in the form of economic loss and uncertainty. In the course of a separation, Quebec could come to be seen as a foreign, dangerous entity. Both dynamics could support resolute action from the centre. Consequently, the secession could leave a residue of centralism, one that might even be inscribed in the constitution of a reformed Canada. In opposition to this tendency, however, could be the decentralizing fear of domination within the federation. The cause would be the power of Ontario in the new Canada. The Atlantic region would have few options but to accept this, albeit grudgingly. The real concern would be in the West, where many citizens distrust central Canada and Ottawa, and would resist a federal government with strong powers if it was dominated by Ontario. The relative balance of these forces would depend on the sense of crisis generated at the time of secession, as well as on the other conjunctural factors.

When constitutions are created, organized interests play an important role. Thus, if Quebec seceded, many groups would seek constitutional changes, though only a few would be most concerned with the distribution of power within Canada. These groups would probably stress the advantages of continued economic union and the need for central power. Many business, labour, and other organizations are federal in structure, but most business associations are unitary.[21] Some of the most important business groups are organized primarily in English Canada, having only weak confederal links, if any, with their Quebec counterparts. The same is true of labour organizations, and their advocacy of strong central power, or at least of maintaining the economic union in ROC, would be buttressed by their declining ties to American unions and their concentration in the public and para-public sectors.

Political leadership would be a crucial conjunctural factor. At the creation of the federations surveyed by Watts and others, it is clear that politicians had considerable autonomy, within the complex of structural forces, to design institutional arrangements. Leadership would also be important because structural characteristics are open to differing interpretations at any particular time, and so political discourse shapes, to some extent, the salience of factors such as regional economic specialization, ethnic homogeneity, and even geographic contiguity. Thomas Berger provides a good example of the "spin" that articulate leaders can apply to such factors:

With Quebec gone, will Canada be a Pakistan of North America, with the Maritimes inevitably breaking away, as Bangladesh did from Pakistan? Such comparisons are trivial. A better one would be the United States, which is a Pakistan of North America: it has forty-eight contiguous states, and Alaska with Canada's land mass in between (not to mention Hawaii). Alaska shows no sign of leaving the Union because of the distance it lies from the lower forty-eight. I lived in Alaska for two years in the mid-1980s. Alaskans, like Canadians, believe they have good reasons to remain where and as they are.[22]

In ROC, there are strong national parties focused on the central government, and with an interest in its perpetuation. In the event of a secession, there certainly would be leaders arguing for a federation at least as centralized as the current one. But there are also powerful regional spokesmen, especially in the West, who are prepared to articulate the vision of a decentralized Canada or one with stronger regional representation in central institutions, and who perhaps are even prepared to advocate secession. Similarly, there is Ontario leadership that is ready to protect the interests of the province, whether these are said to lie in a more or less centralized federalism or even in some separate arrangement with Quebec. In the abstract, leadership's effects are unpredictable, but at a time of profound uncertainty, constitutional and otherwise, it would be crucial in determining the constitutional make-up of a new Canada.

Finally, there is the attitude of foreign powers. Most important by far is the United States. This country can be counted on to support a united Canada. It would also support a ROC at least as centralized as Canada is now, and the attitude of other foreign states and international organizations would be similar. The reason is simple: "If secession occurs, foreign governments have two unknowns to deal with: the newly seceded government, and either a weakened old regime or an unpredictable new one which displaces it. All these possibilities portend disruption and instability in international relations and strengthen the inclination of foreign governments to support central regimes."[23] The same holds true for foreign attitudes towards the integrity of the states that emerge from the separation.

This concludes the analysis of the factors conducive to centralization and decentralization in a new constitution for ROC. Table 3 also displays the direction and strength of structural and conjunctural factors that would bear on the degree of centralization – or political integration, to adopt the terminology used earlier – between Canada and Quebec. Each one need not be discussed here. But it is evident that there are far fewer characteristics conducive to integration than would be operative within ROC. Most notable among the structural factors are the more limited opportunities for positive economic integration, the diplomatic differences in foreign policy, the lack of social and political homogeneity, and the possible dissimilarities in political institutions and ideology; as well, there are few successful models of strong integration between two sovereign states, and the sense of "regional" identification in each unit would be very strong. The conjunctural factors are even more heavily weighted against close integration. With secession, the other unit would represent a potential threat, to autonomy on Quebec's side and integrity on ROC's, and to economic well-being on both sides. The act of separation, by definition, would fracture any existing sense of common citizenship. Political leadership might be oriented towards maintaining the existing degree of integration, but the strongest political incentives would be towards safeguarding the interests of the respective states. The conjuncture – the process of the transition to sovereignty – needs closer investigation, but clearly the structural factors are not conducive to a high degree of political integration between Canada and an independent Quebec.

The conclusions here are straightforward. The underlying characteristics of ROC alone are more compatible with centralization than are those of Canada as it is currently composed. One major structural problem would be the geographic isolation of the Atlantic provinces. Much more significant would be the incipient suspicion between the West, especially Alberta and British Columbia, and an Ontario that might be capable of dominating the federation. Geographic, economic, political, and ideological cleavages overlap to some extent along this divide. Of course, it is not entirely evident that if Quebec seceded, Ontarians or their leaders would support a federation centralized even to the existing extent. In any event, while most underlying factors are conducive to centralization, there are countervailing propensities towards regional autonomy along almost every dimension. So these factors in themselves could hardly determine the shape of the institutional arrangements that would be put in place if Quebec seceded. This means that the conjunctural factors would be crucial. The main ones are the exercise of political leadership and the extent to which secession and the uncertainty it creates would be perceived as threats that could be countered only through the determined wielding of central power.

This brief analysis suggests once again that the internal make-up of Canada, as well as the relations likely to obtain between Canada and an independent Quebec, can only be understood by a close study of the transition to Quebec sovereignty. The institutional outcomes of the secession will be shaped largely by the process through which it occurs, by the events and decisions involved in this momentous development, rather than by the deeper geographic, economic, social, and cultural characteristics of the two countries.

PART TWO

The Transition
to Sovereignty

For reasons suggested in the preceding part of this study, in order to predict the future of Canada and the shape of Canada-Quebec relations, one has to comprehend the process of separation. The first chapter of this part explains why this is so. Then the analysis turns to other studies of Quebec secession, surveying the existing literature in order to reach some tentative conclusions about what might take place in the course of a separation of Quebec from Canada. But these are inconclusive and contradictory. So we proceed to comparative analysis of other secessions. Here, the focus is almost exclusively on cases where secession has occurred peacefully. From the analysis of the few relevant cases, we draw some generalizations about how the process of separation takes place. The pattern of peaceful secession seems to hold true, uniformly. But it should be stressed now that the pattern is composed of mere empirical generalizations. They define a process that has occurred when peaceful secession has happened in the past – that is all. No claim can be made that this pattern constitutes a theory of peaceful secession, that any set of generalizations is more important than the others, that any one is a necessary or sufficient condition of peaceful secession, or that the pattern will be found in future separations. Still, the regularity is striking. Consequently, the generalizations are used in part 3 as the framework for analysing the Canada-Quebec case. Before that is done, the last chapter of this part considers another case, the separation of Slovakia and the Czech Republic. This is the most recent instance of secession that could have much relevance for Canada. In the Czech-Slovak case, the generalizations reached from comparative analysis are, for the most part, borne out, but there are also some interesting variations, and these are analysed in some detail. The point of all this groundwork is to allow a detailed assessment of how the transition to Quebec sovereignty would occur. But why is this so crucial?

CHAPTER EIGHT

Why the Transition Is Important

One purpose of this study is to predict what ROC would become if Quebec secedes – but there is a wide range of institutional configurations that Canada could take on. Another purpose is to predict what economic and political relations would exist between Canada and a sovereign Quebec – but there are many alternative levels of integration that could be established. Each of these various arrangements has its advantages and disadvantages, theoretically, but each also has its partisans and predictors. There is a simple reason for this: no one knows what will happen if Quebec secedes. And yet no one can know what will become of Canada and Quebec unless they understand the process of getting there. The transition to sovereignty would determine long-term outcomes. There are several good reasons to believe this.

In the view of most scholars, there exist underlying structural characteristics in any country that are conducive to creating a more or less centralized constitution. But these would not determine the outcomes of a Quebec-Canada separation, for they tend in contradictory directions; geography, for example, dictates a decentralized Canada, while social and cultural homogeneity would support a more centralized system. This means that there is no overwhelming pressure towards one or another option.

Anyway, such factors are never quite determining of constitutional and institutional outcomes. Within the constraints they appear to impose, there still exists a range of alternatives. Even if the factors were unidirectional, so that they would appear to rule out extreme outcomes such as a fragmented Canada or a Canada-Quebec federation, analysts could still imagine some trajectory of events that would produce the extremes. This is because the underlying factors are subject to interpretation. Analysts disagree about their relative importance, so that some would regard a geographically divided Canada as quite unsustainable while others would portray noncontiguity as irrelevant. As well, the very nature of these factors is open to debate. In one theory, Canada-Quebec relations would depend mainly on the degree of cultural distinctiveness between the two states; but some analysts find little that separates the communities except for language, while others regard each as a "global society," sharply defined by a distinctive and all-pervasive cultural viewpoint.[1] When it is realized that all citizens of the two states are "analysts," it becomes clear that interpreting and defining the underlying characteristics, their direction, and their relative influence is a matter of political debate. The outcome of that debate is not predetermined.

This is all the more true because many factors are conjunctural. Geography may be eminently predictable, but public attitudes towards the other community, the position taken by organized interests, and the stance of foreign powers are far less certain. So is the process of the event. For instance, one possibility for a post-secession Canada is that existing provincial boundaries would be changed, to form regional units or many small provinces. One can identify forces conducive to each outcome, but as Maureen Covell has pointed out, the results would depend on how the transition was negotiated: "Scenarios that envisage the elimination of the provinces are less likely to emerge from a negotiation process dominated by provincial governments than from a process in which they are absent."[2] To understand the outcome of the separation, it is essential to comprehend what form these conjunctural factors would assume and how they would evolve under the pressure of events.

Secessions offer huge scope for political debate and leadership. It has long been recognized that political leaders and governments have some autonomy from socio-economic forces and their attendant political expressions, even in democracies. When these forces are contradictory, that autonomy increases.[3] Beyond this, secessions are not times of normal politics. The system is changing, profoundly. There is a high degree of uncertainty about the future and about where people's interests lie. The normally settled relationship between socio-economic interests and their political expression is much attenuated, if not quite eliminated. At least in the short term, this may open up more room for both public debate and the determined exercise of political leadership.

Secession is not politics as usual. It is an historic event. In any society, it is unprecedented, and in the Canadian case it would be doubly extraordinary because there has never been a secession in an advanced, industrial, capitalist democracy.[4] By definition, an historic event is one in which the past is a feeble guide, the future is radically uncertain, and decisions taken in the present have great consequences. As it unfolds, the event is sweeping enough to affect profoundly the economy, society, and polity in ways that are interrelated. Deep economic uncertainty, for example, has political ramifications; social unrest or the creation of new political institutions has economic consequences. This means that the transition to sovereignty must be studied in close detail. The forces at play and the interrelations between them must be seized in their historical specificity. As Wood put it, secession "is less aptly understood as a condition than a process."[5]

The long-term structure of Canada and the relations that would exist between Canada and a sovereign Quebec are a function of what happens in the transition. They are path-dependent. After a period of turbulence and uncertainty, a new equilibrium will be established, and this will depend on the choices made during the transition.[6] This result is not merely a matter of normal historical change or evolution, in the sense that a particular condition would not exist without its antecedents, although it is true that big decisions are made when states are breaking up. During a secession, choices are also made about institutional structures. This is inescapable, for the existing institutions have been challenged or demolished. Once established, structures have enduring effects. Institutions channel peoples' interactions, shape expectations, and embody, more or less explicitly, particular norms and values.[7] So they have some independent weight in producing policy outcomes and determining the long-term evolution of the system. Institutions help shape the underlying societies from which emanate future political demands.[8] This is another reason why the outcomes of a secession depend on the process through which it occurs.

So the events marking the secession and the conditions within which it takes place set the atmosphere for taking crucial decisions. In making these decisions, despite the constraints of cultural and socio-economic factors, there is considerable leeway for political debate and political leadership. The decisions set other events in train, sometimes momentously. They produce new institutions, ones that have concrete effects in themselves, as evolving complexes of political forces are channelled through them to produce new outcomes. In the end, the system may settle into a relatively stable equilibrium, and underlying factors such as social homogeneity and geography may exert their marginal pressures on its evolution. But the equilibrium that is reached after the secession is only one of many that are possible. Which one results is dependent on the transition, so this must be analysed closely, using the insights of other analysts and the experience of other countries.

CHAPTER NINE

Other Studies of the Transition to Quebec Sovereignty

INTRODUCTION

This study is guided by the view that a Quebec secession would be peaceful. That is, there would be no state-sanctioned use of military force against the citizens or armed forces of other states. There might be violent unrest and armed forces might be deployed, but there would be no massive repression or civil war. These parameters apparently render inapplicable much comparative experience from cases where secession succeeded or failed only after long attempts to suppress it or through a civil war, as in Switzerland, the United States, Ireland, Katanga, Biafra, Bangladesh, Sri Lanka, and so on. We assume a peaceful separation in which the Quebec electorate expresses a clear preference for sovereignty, and Canada agrees that Quebec will become a sovereign state. Thus, it might not seem necessary to deal directly with some basic problems normally attendant on the formation of new states, such as the legitimacy of the secessionist claim and the matter of international recognition when sovereignty is contested.[1] Nor might it seem useful to consider the potential for military conflict between Canada and Quebec, or to contemplate possible Canadian efforts either to reassert control over the portions of the province that were added in 1898 and 1912 or to assist subsecessionist movements in Quebec, though these topics recently have attracted the attention of some commentators.[2] Despite our guiding assumptions, however, these issues must be addressed. Any survey of other studies has to include them, and a comprehensive analysis of Quebec's secession and Canada's future cannot ignore extreme possibilities. But this does not invalidate our assumptions. As will be shown, it is the very potential that extreme possibilities could materialize that would lead to our assumptions being met in reality. Yet it is essential to be aware of the conditions under which our guiding assumptions would be true.

Existing analyses of the process of Quebec secession fall into four groups. First and most numerous are studies of the economic costs and benefits of independence. Some of these take into account the political climate surrounding the secession, but economists' tools are not well suited to this task; nevertheless, the economic costs of separation would depend primarily on the politics of the process. A second group of studies explores the legal issues surrounding secession. These are helpful in laying out the alternative ways through which the transition to sovereignty can occur, in gauging the legal armaments at the disposal of the parties to the secession, and in highlighting particularly difficult issues. Despite the complexity of legal argument, however, the critical matters are political in the end, and a third type of study lays out contrasting scenarios to which the course of political events might correspond. These are useful in isolating the critical variables that would shape the broad course of the transition. Finally, there are studies of the detailed politicial processes through which secession might occur and of the institutional arrangements which might be established at the time. These help serve as a foundation for further predictions.

ECONOMIC STUDIES

Most economic studies of Quebec secession make a sharp distinction between the province's long-term prospects as a sovereign state and the economic impact of the transition to sovereignty. Debate about the long run hinges less on Quebec's resource endowment and industrial base than on how the country would be inserted into the international economy, including its relations with Canada, and on whether government policy and the sociocultural fabric of the new state would more surely promote growth and facilitate adjustment than is possible at present within the federal system. In the optimistic view, a cohesive, flexible Quebec, with a loyal business class and state policies tailored to its needs, outward looking and with access to markets assured through international trade regimes, would fare better than it currently does.[3] In the pessimistic view, either Quebec would fail to gain adequate access to international markets, or its sociocultural endowment would fail to produce economic growth, or the effects of the transition to sovereignty would hobble its long-run prospects.

One study sensitive to both alternatives was conducted by the Economic Council of Canada before the last round of constitutional talks. The council explored five structural options: the status quo, moderate decentralization, extensive decentralization, a confederation of regions, and sovereignty-association. The last included an economic union, with Canada and Quebec coordinating external trade, transportation and communications, and monetary policy. It was assumed that equalization payments would end and that there would be no other transfers either explicit or through programs such as housing. As well, Quebec would assume 22 per cent of the federal debt. Using a sophisticated computer model of the interregional economy, the Economic Council found that Quebec's GDP would decline under the sovereignty-association structure, by 1.4 to 3.5 per cent.[4] However, the council could not build into this model any estimate of the dynamic gains that it admitted might result in a sovereign Quebec from a "better business and political climate," such as a possible social contract between economic partners.[5] Equally important, the council described a range of costs associated with the transition to a new constitutional order, but it could not quantify them: the results "do not take into consideration the path of adjustment or the transition costs that may be incurred in going from one situation to another."[6]

Focusing on the transition, however, one finds unanimous agreement among economists that secession would impose short-term economic costs on both Canada and Quebec. Transition costs comprise three elements: transaction costs, fiscal costs, and uncertainty. Transaction costs include the governmental resources devoted to negotiating new arrangements, and to transferring programs, revenue sources, and public servants, as well as the substantial costs to firms and citizens of learning about and accommodating themselves to the new arrangements. Not all transaction costs would show up as measurable losses in GDP. Grady assesses the cost of "institutional restructuring" as "large" for both Quebec and Canada (meaning over 1 per cent of GDP, or over $1.5 billion for Quebec and $5 billion for Canada).[7] This loose estimate is probably high on the Canadian side, but not necessarily so. Fortin, in contrast, estimates the costs of reorganizing the Quebec state at only $600 million over two years.[8]

Fiscal costs are the costs of higher taxes to provide the services that are now provided to Quebecers by the federal government (net of their current taxes paid to Ottawa). Much economic analysis of the transition has centred not on the economy per se but on government finances. This may have been caused by the provocative and exhaustive study of the subject by the secretariat of the Bélanger-Campeau Commission.[9] Or it may be that public finances are apparently more calculable (when assumptions about shocks to the tax base are restricted), since the largest part of the change would result from Quebec's taking responsibility for some precisely measurable share of Canada's national debt. In any case, under its sovereignty-association assumptions, the Economic Council estimated that the tax burden on Quebecers would rise by 3.3 per cent of GDP (to 41.8 per cent).[10] John McCallum has provided a useful compendium of such estimates, which shows the deficit of a sovereign Quebec as lying in the $10 billion to $22 billion range; he also updates the moderate $13 billion figure of Pierre Fortin to show that it would have reached $17 billion in 1992–93.[11] Even ignoring other borrowing for Hydro-Quebec and for retiring some of Quebec's share of the national debt, this deficit would amount to 10 per cent of GDP and would require a severe austerity program starting right after the attainment of sovereignty.[12] Côté predicts that spending cuts of $8 billion would be necessary, which, combined with real shocks and uncertainty in financial markets, would cause an economic "implosion" beyond the experience of industrial countries.[13] Pierre Fortin, under far more optimistic assumptions, still finds that spending cuts of $3 billion would be necessary to get Quebec's deficit/GDP ratio into line.[14]

The third set of transition costs is caused by uncertainty. This simply means that when conditions change, economic actors have less confidence in their expectations about the future. Doing what they have been doing appears more risky, so they are less likely to continue doing it. This applies to individuals deciding whether to move, firms deciding where to invest and to place orders, creditors deciding where to make loans, and all other economic activity. The Economic Council, for example, focused on financial markets and argued that borrowers would pay extra during the transition, because lenders would worry more about (1) political risk, or uncertainty over the impact of political and institutional change on public policies, (2) default risk, because of uncertainty about the creditworthiness of the emerging states, and (3) currency risk, arising from uncertainty about future exchange rates.[15] These premiums could impose significant increases in borrowing costs for governments, firms, and individuals. But the effects of uncertainty are potentially very much wider, involving migration, savings propensities, firms' decisions about sources of inputs and market outlets, and investment decisions.

Estimation of uncertainty costs is difficult. This problem confronted economists at the Royal Bank, who argued that "the things that cannot be measured accurately in the current debate are the things that will have the most important influence on the economic consequences of disunity."[16] Many assessments of the impact of uncertainty are fragmentary. André Raynauld provides data on head-office relocation and outmigration from Quebec, and these seem to suggest that a significant effect was caused by the 1980 referendum; actual secession would presumably have a larger impact.[17] McCallum and Green concentrate on the effects of the transition in Quebec. They assume that unemployment would be higher than its base level over a five-year transition period by 1.0, 2.0, 2.0, 1.5, and 1.0 per cent: this would imply GDP drops of 1.5, 3.0, 3.0, 2.3, and 1.5 per cent below the base level.[18] Moreover, outmigration of 2.7 per cent of the population would depress the tax base by perhaps 3.5 per cent. These authors also assume an interest rate premium on government debt of between 0.8 and 1.6 per cent over the five-year period.[19] Were this to hold across the economy, the long-run effect of the premiums alone would be a loss of between 1.2 and 2.4 per cent of Quebec's GDP.[20]

In the Royal Bank study the major factor in the calculations was "the deterioration of the investment climate that would accompany a fragmented Canada."[21] The key assumption was that a 15 per cent decline in investment would occur over the two years following a breakup (in 1993). With investment growth at 2.5 per cent per year thereafter, real GDP growth over the 1990–2000 period would be 1 per cent per year, instead of 3 per cent in a united Canada. As a result, in 2000, per capita income would be $22,200 rather than $26,100, real GDP would be 17.8 per cent less than it would have been, and the unemployment rate would be in the range of 10–15 per cent instead of 7–11 per cent.[22] The income gap between Canada and the United States would widen considerably, and the emigration rate could double, with enduring effects. The study did not directly quantify several important parameters, such as breaking the monetary union, division of the national debt, and the repercussions of both on government finances, but its treatment of the investment climate appears to have been based on the assumption of a currency breakup, disruptions in existing trade agreements, and a fragmented Canada in which fiscal policy could not be coordinated and interregional transfers would be much reduced if not ended. These are very strong assumptions, but if such developments did occur, they would surely contribute to uncertainty and a big drop in investment. The Royal Bank "deliberately ignored" the regional distribution of economic costs, but it did warn that "the potential for economic disaster is real and it should not be ignored by assuming or hoping unrealistically that a country can be dismantled without acrimony, dissent and economic antagonism."[23]

Patrick Grady has attempted the fullest accounting of the transition's effects on GDP. Many of these depend on political arrangements, but even excluding the most questionable of these, the short-run costs to Quebec arising from the loss of federal transfers, larger public debt charges, net outmigration, the "confidence-induced output loss," and institutional restructuring add up to at least 7.4 per cent of GDP.[24] For Canada, the same factors produce a loss of at least 1.9 per cent of GDP. Under some assumptions about trade, the short-run costs could be 10 and 5 per cent of GDP respectively. These estimates have drawn polite fire from economists more sympathetic to sovereignty.[25] But the only counter-argument is that reason will prevail and the transition will be smooth; certainly, no one else has tried to compile a full accounting based on clearly stated assumptions. And Grady's figures accord with the looser estimates of Marcel Côté, who examines real shocks as well as those consequent upon government negotiating positions and policy.[26]

Most analyses find that transition costs will be substantial. They are also likely to be significant over the long term, because they can have permanent effects. Using the concept of path-dependence, for example, McCallum and Green describe how initial shocks can lead to second-order consequences and to an "unraveling process" through which the economy of an independent Quebec might sink to a much lower long-run equilibrium position. Lower investment and higher taxes cause unemployment and outmigration, which cause lower tax bases, less investment, less employment, and so on.[27] Similarly, the Royal Bank study suggested that decreased investment would result in obsolescent plants and skills, and a long-term lack of competitiveness. Such hypotheses are contested, largely on the grounds that in the long run secession would produce a more dynamic, cohesive, and flexible Quebec economy.[28] Short of the event occurring, these competing theories cannot be tested. But if the second, optimistic view is correct, it could be quite rational for Quebecers to choose the short-term losses that produce long-term gains.

Let us assume that a Quebec that became sovereign in 1996 could achieve, within three years, an extra 1 per cent per year growth in GDP beyond what it would have attained as part of Canada. Then, even if Quebec lost 8 per cent of potential GDP over these three transition years, all the loss would be recovered by about 2008, and real gains would be made subsequently. At normal discount rates, it would be quite sensible for Quebecers to choose sovereignty, accepting the transition costs in order to achieve long-term growth. However, if it took six years to get onto the faster-growth trajectory, and if 20 per cent of GDP growth was sacrificed in the interim, then Quebec would not recover lost ground until around 2023. Quebecers would have to value future income – or some non-economic benefits of sovereignty – very highly indeed to make such a choice.

The longer and more severe the economic loss associated with the transition, the less attractive is the option, even assuming that the fundamentals favouring higher growth – the features known as Quebec's "atouts" – operate in the first place and do not erode in the interim.[29] Of course, the same applies to Canada. In the view of two leading Alberta economists, "instability and uncertainty are the enemies of investment. The Alberta economy is very capital intensive, highly dependent on foreign capital, and very sensitive to interest rates. As a result, it could be seriously affected by higher interest rates or disruptions to capital flows that are almost a certainty, at least for a period of time, if Québec separated."[30] Moreover, such transitional phenomena could have enduring structural effects.[31]

The economic studies show that the transition is crucial. The economic costs could be large and enduring. What is most important, however, is that only a small proportion of the transition costs are *fixed* or inevitable. The rest are *variable*, in that they depend directly on the process of secession and the attitudes of the parties as expressed politically.

The fixed transition costs include some minimum level of transaction costs, for negotiating, for restructuring the states, and for learning and adaptation by firms and individuals. For Quebec, they also include the fiscal pressure of assuming full program responsibilities and some portion of the national debt. In an event as remarkable and unpredictable as the secession of part of an advanced industrial country, some degree of uncertainty is inevitable – and costly. But the bulk of the cost of transition is variable. Most costs depend on politics. They depend on whether, and how, the two sides could reach agreements about how to manage the secession and post-separation issues. Transaction costs would swell if there were no cooperation about the transferring of public servants and programs and jurisdictions. Imagine, for example, how difficult it would be for Quebec to set up an unemployment insurance program if the names and work histories of current UI recipients were not made available by Canada. The costs would also rise if negotiations were prolonged. Second, arrangements made about public finances could leave Quebec with higher or lower fiscal costs. And by far the largest impact of how the disengagement occurred would be on uncertainty, which is a function of the level of conflict, the gravity of the issues left unresolved, and the time that passes without settlement. If Quebecers were to choose to secede, and if the two sides were noncooperative so that understandings were not soon reached about such fundamental matters as citizenship, the national debt, the currency and monetary policy, taxation, and trade treaties, then interest rates would have to rise sharply in order to stop capital flight, stock markets would decline, the dollar would come under pressure, and investment would drop. The financial system could be severely tested. But if these matters were settled quickly and definitively, uncertainty would soon be relieved and economic agents would adjust to the new order. If negotiations reached a stalemate or crumbled, transition costs could become very high indeed. However extreme it seems to be in the context of the suffering induced by the recent recession – a matter of a 2 per cent decline in GDP – and however unlikely it appears in the light of sovereigntist optimism that cooperation must prevail, Grady's estimate of 10 and 5 per cent GDP drops in Quebec and Canada, respectively, is surely within the realm of possibility. The economic stakes are very high.[32] What counts in determining them is the level of variable transition costs, and this cannot be estimated economically, for it depends directly on the politics of the transition process.

THE LEGALITIES OF QUEBEC SECESSION

The transition to Quebec sovereignty could happen quickly or slowly. It could be precipitated by a referendum vote in favour of sovereignty or by the Quebec National Assembly adopting various resolutions. In either case, the event would represent a sharp break with the existing order, one from which no return would be likely. Once Quebecers authoritatively declared that they wished no longer to remain in Canada, they could no longer appeal to other Canadians as fellow citizens, as members of the same political community, and if Canadians accepted the decision to secede they would thenceforth seek arrangements that served only their own interests.[33] But it is essential to understand that until secession occurs in law, Quebec will remain within the constitutional order of Canada as a province. The basic law with all its obligations and rights will continue to apply on Quebec territory.

At the level of constitutional law, a Quebec referendum result in favour of sovereignty would have no binding effect. However overwhelming and undeniable the expression of popular will, the instrument for its formal pronouncement must be Quebec's National Assembly.[34] Through actions of the assembly, secession can be accomplished in two ways – constitutionally and unconstitutionally.[35]

This distinction is absolutely critical. The constitutional route would begin with the assembly passing a resolution stating Quebec's intent to secede, probably within a specified time period. Separation would occur through making appropriate amendments to the Constitution Acts (as is discussed in much greater detail in chapter 14, below). When these amendments had been properly ratified by the provincial legislatures and Parliament, and proclaimed by the governor general, Quebec would become a sovereign state. It would proclaim its own separate constitution, and the Constitution Acts of Canada would no longer apply to Quebec. This would be a constitutional secession.

An unconstitutional secession would begin with a unilateral declaration of independence (UDI), passed by the National Assembly. This is a very serious act. A UDI would declare that only Quebec law prevails on Quebec territory. Since the Constitution Acts would not have been amended, Canada's constitution would conflict with the assembly's declaration, and by so declaring independence Quebec would "step outside" the existing constitutional order. Some analysts suggest that in domestic Canadian law, even an outright declaration of Quebec independence would have the legal status of a proposed constitutional amendment, which would then be disposed of according to the amending procedures laid out in part 5 of the Constitution Act, 1982.[36] But a UDI would be much more serious in reality. As Peter Leslie argues, it would represent a fundamental repudiation of the Canadian constitution and would create a sharp legal discontinuity, "of which the consequences are unknowable, but presumably vast, tumultuous, and economically devastating."[37] In a situation of legal discontinuity, "all established rules and procedures no longer apply," which is why a UDI could be so hazardous. It would throw the issue of secession into the arena of international law. This law is also relevant to discussions of Quebec's "right" to secede, which would colour the politics of the transition even were secession to occur constitutionally, and it therefore requires some exploration.

There has now been considerable analysis of Quebec's right to self-determination and secession, and of how a UDI would be received in the international community.[38] One immediate conclusion that can be drawn from this literature is that there is no consensus about the fundamental legal principles at stake; nor is there much agreement about how certain principles would apply to the case of Quebec secession. On the one extreme is the position expressed by Daniel Turp – that a referendum result in favour of sovereignty is effectively determinative, since it would directly express the collective will of people to define themselves as Quebecers and sovereign.

On the other extreme is the firm rejection of such subjectivist definitions of nationhood and statehood, with the implication, drawn most
severely by Stephen Scott, that a nonconstitutional secession subverts
Canadian law and is therefore a revolutionary act, one to be suppressed because it "is the duty of the Parliament and government of
Canada to enforce and defend the constitution and laws – and therefore the territorial integrity – of Canada against its enemies, whether
foreign or domestic."[39] There is a kernel of truth in each of these views.
There is some legality as well: international law, unfortunately, supports both views and settles no questions about Quebec secession.

Those who assert that Quebec legally may secede unilaterally try
to establish three propositions: Quebecers are a people, as a people
they have the right to self-determination, and this right allows sovereign self-government, by secession if necessary. There is no agreement on the first proposition, because there is no legal consensus
about what constitutes a "people." One approach is to rely on objective definitions based on language, race, ethnicity, religion, or some
other ascriptive characteristic. Brossard, for example, argues the case
that French Canadians constitute a people and then manages to transfer
the rights of "le peuple canadien-français" to the "peuple québécois."[40]
But when a definition of the people is based at least in part on ascriptive
criteria, like Brossard's, it encounters the problem that the distribution of the people is not coterminous with existing borders.[41] If the
Québécois are a people with collective rights, these rights can hardly
be denied to other peoples living within the territory of Quebec, such
as the First Nations.

Another approach relies on subjective definitions, according to which
the people defines itself by its collective will. Turp, among others,
argues for a subjectivist definition of Quebecers, beyond observable
commonalities in language, culture, or religion: "Le vouloir-vivre
collectif contribue davantage encore à l'affirmation de cette qualité
de peuple."[42] This sort of definition appears to allow all inhabitants
of a bordered territory to constitute a people, thus avoiding
subsecessionist movements by minorities. But the problem remains:
there may be minorities within Quebec which are not only objec-
tively different in terms of language, ethnicity, or race but which also
may not share the "vouloir-vivre collectif."

Assuming nevertheless that the Québécois are a people, do they
have a right to self-determination? Again, opinions diverge widely.
In favour, one can cite declarations of the General Assembly of the
United Nations, along with international human rights covenants,
to the effect that "all peoples have the right to self-determination."[43]
There is also the precedent of the 1980 referendum, which was to

permit the Quebec government to negotiate sovereignty-association, along with numerous motions and Acts of the Quebec National Assembly which show that Quebecers have claimed the right to self-determination. For example, the preamble to Bill 150 authorizing the 1992 referendum stated that "Quebecers are free to assume their own destiny, to determine their political status and to assure their economic, social and cultural development."[44] These acts have not been resisted by the federal authorities. Indeed, the right was recognized implicitly by the Pepin-Robarts task force on Canadian unity and explicitly by the Progressive Conservative Party of Canada.[45] Yet in terms of international law, the situation is not at all clear-cut. There are powerful arguments that self-determination is a right that generally has been accorded by the international community only to peoples inhabiting existing states or to colonized peoples in "non-metropolitan" areas; hence, "there is simply no basis for a claim that Québec is a self-determination unit at international law."[46]

Even if the inhabitants of Quebec do have the right of self-determination, whether they have the further right of secession is also contested. Some international human rights covenants prescribe that peoples have a right to "freely determine their political status and freely ensure their economic, social and cultural development."[47] On the other hand, metropolitan states have taken a dim view of the anarchic consequences that could flow from an unfettered translation of rights to self-determination into rights of secession. Apart from colonial non-self-governing countries undergoing a struggle for independence, states rely on the 1970 Declaration of Principles of International Law concerning Friendly Relations and Cooperation among States in Accordance with the Charter of the United Nations, which holds that "nothing in the foregoing paragraphs shall be construed as authorizing or encouraging any action that would dismember or impair, totally or in part, the territorial integrity or political unity of sovereign and independent States conducting themselves in compliance with the principle of equal rights and self-determination of peoples as described above, and thus possessed of a government representing the whole people belonging to the territory without distinction as to race, creed, or colour."[48]

What this means is that the question hinges on whether the "people" in question is so repressed within a state that the "principle of equal rights and self-determination of peoples" has been denied. If a government is repressive, the people may be justified in seceding. One sovereigntist line of reasoning on this point is to argue that Quebecers are colonized. Brossard admits that this would be a hard case to make legally, but he does try to present evidence that the proposition may be true, beyond the "décor juridique" (legal façade) of equal rights, representative democracy, and so on.[49] Turp takes another line on this issue. He argues that the right to self-determination has been violated domestically in Canada by the imposition of the Constitution Act in 1982 and the rejection of the Meech Lake Accord. He then relies on the precedents about Quebecers' right to self-determination, and the convention that supposedly exists to this effect, to argue, in a logic breathtaking in its tautological compactness, that the refusal to recognize a UDI as valid would constitute an oppressive negation of the right to self-determination. The refusal would therefore license that same self-determination to be exercised in secession through a UDI:

Qui plus est, le refus de donner effet à la convention constitutionnelle autorisant l'accession du Québec à la souveraineté s'avérerait une atteinte grave au principe démocratique et permettrait de conclure que l'État canadien ne se conduit dès lors pas en conformité avec le droit à l'autodétermination de Québec et que le people québécois dispose dès lors d'un droit à l'autodétermination sur le plan international, y compris le droit de sécession, et ce en conformité avec la Charte des Nations Unies telle qu'interprétée par la Déclaration sur les relations amicales.[50]

Contrary to this line of reasoning, other jurists cleave to the basic position that a noncolonized people has no positive right to self-determination in the form of secession. As Williams puts it, "There seemingly is no rule of international law which actually makes secession illegal, but neither is there a right to secede in a metropolitan context."[51]

The uncertainty of the law about secession is significant for three reasons. First, if Quebec has no broadly recognized right to secede in domestic or international law, it means that in the case of a UDI there can be no assertion of a fundamental right "which trumps any competing claims or entitlements."[52] The legal issues are fundamentally contestable. Further, in the case of a nonconstitutional secession, if the law is not definitive, there must be recourse to two basic criteria for accession to statehood: recognition by other sovereign states, and the capacity to exert effective control over the territory claimed. These matters are worth examining briefly, despite the third conclusion – that in the case of Quebec secession, Canada's position is the determining factor. Even though there is no clear legal obligation to do so, its acceptance of Quebec sovereignty would clear away most fundamental legal issues.

The question of recognition of claims to sovereignty by a seceding state raises issues of both domestic and international law. Domestically, it is clear that only the Government of Canada has the authority to grant or deny recognition to new states. Recognition is accomplished through an executive certificate, which the courts recognize as definitive.[53] Recognition is therefore a political act, one with the important consequence that any acts or proclamations of an unrecognized state will not be made effective by Canadian courts. To repeat, it is within the power of the Canadian federal government to grant or withhold recognition of other states.

The international legal dimension would be critical if Quebec opted to secede through a UDI. Recognition by other countries would admit it to the international community of sovereign states. Legally, the requirements for recognition are straightforward – a permanent population, a defined territory, a functioning government, and so on. In practice, however, recognition is political, and whether the international community accepts secessionist claims has depended on a variety of factors. The probability of recognition is higher when (1) the seceding state is territorially anomalous within the existing state, as East Pakistan was; (2) the territory is well defined and the inhabitants homogeneous in objective characteristics such as language; (3) a strong and democratically expressed popular will supports secession; (4) the secessionists have attempted to work peacefully within the existing order to have their grievances resolved; (5) there is oppression to the extent of gross human rights violations and a lack of physical security; and (6) the impact of secession on the rest of the country is small.[54] Magisterially, Buchheit reduces these factors to two: the internal merits of the claim (unity, oppression, and so on), and the degree of disruption secession would cause internationally.[55]

Recognition is acknowledged even by legal scholars to involve political decisions about national self-interest. This is why Morton has remarked that the United Nations' doctrine on self-determination can be explained as "political expediency flavored with opportune moral outrage."[56] Recognition is a matter of power and *realpolitik* rather than law. In the case of a Quebec UDI, the stance of major international actors, especially the United States, France, and the European Union, would be critical. The EU would be unlikely to grant quick recognition to Quebec, partly because of its experience with the former Yugoslavia. Sovereigntists, among them Louise Beaudoin of the Parti québécois, often look towards France for recognition: "Par ailleurs, la France, leader historique du monde francophone et membre permanent du Conseil de sécurité, est l'État qui, plus qu'aucun autre, aura la légitimité et le poids nécessaire pour enclencher, le moment venu, le processus même de la reconnaissance internationale du Québec et l'aider à devenir progressivement irréversible."[57] While this statement acknowledges the political nature of recognition, it is somewhat optimistic about the French position. France fears its own internal secessionist movements; it has a large stake in Canada; and if Canada fragmented, the power of the United States could increase in absolute terms, a prospect that French governments have not recently tended to welcome.[58]

The United States itself would have more weight in influencing other states to recognize Quebec or not. The U.S. position on Quebec sovereignty has been one of strict nonintervention, with a pronounced tilt in favour of Canadian unity: it would not encourage trends that could lead to the balkanization of Canada.[59] Were Quebecers clearly to opt for sovereignty, the United States would favour cooperation between Quebec and Canada, and, as discussed below, negotiations between the United States, Canada, and the seceding Quebec would be inevitable. Even so, a pro-sovereignty referendum vote (or, presumably, a legislative declaration of intent to secede) would find the United States reluctant to take precipitous action out of respect for Canadian sovereignty; it would await the onset if not the outcome of negotiations. Similarly, although a UDI, or a breakdown in negotiations followed by a UDI, would force the Americans to decide pragmatically on an approach, there would probably be no quick recognition if the secession was contested. The United States has a "very conservative policy about the recognition of states based on the control of national territory."[60]

Overall, other countries have more invested in Canada than in Quebec and more to lose (at least in the medium term) either by offending the Canadian government through recognizing Quebec or by acting in any way that might help precipitate the fragmentation of Canada. However, if Canada recognized Quebec's sovereignty, even in principle, other states could proceed to deal officially with the secessionist province. This could occur even before the full measure of sovereign power was transferred to Quebec.[61] The same is probably true with respect to arranging for a seat in the United Nations. Much would depend on how the two entities were conducting themselves at the time, as well as on the factors governing recognition discussed above. But Quebec's rapid admission to the United Nations would be unlikely if the Canadian government firmly opposed it.

What all this means is that the key to Quebec's recognition internationally is in Canada's hands. If Canada accepts Quebec sovereignty, so will other states. This is why Beaudoin and Vallée call Canada the "seul adversaire déterminant" (only determining adversary).[62] Its recognition of Quebec would be quickly and automatically followed by that of most other states. It is equally evident, though, that if Canada were to withhold this recognition determinedly, Quebec would not soon accede to membership in the international community. Eventually it could do so, but only by fulfilling the other criterion of statehood – effective control of the territory in question. Again, Canada would be the critical actor: "As for effective control, the attainment of that control is measured by the emergent State's ability to defeat its competitors. As the Canadian government is the only contender claiming international personality over the territory of Québec, the issue resolves itself into which of the two, Québec or Canada, can be said to effectively control that territory."[63]

This is where a contested UDI leads ultimately, despite all the intervening thickets of legal argument – back to the kernel of empirical truth in Professor Scott's extreme position.[64] A contested secession leads to a contest of national will, possibly through forceful means. All the legal arguments bend before force and will. As Turp proclaimed, "Devant le désir de liberté des peoples, le Droit n'a jamais constitué un obstacle décisif."[65] And as the Bélanger-Campeau Commission clearly put this alternative, in a remarkably calm fashion: "Failing such an agreement, Québec would have to secede unilaterally, on the basis of an unequivocal, clearly expressed will among Quebecers to do so. The success of such a procedure would reside in the ability of Québec's political institutions to implement and maintain exclusive public authority over its territory. Under international law, other States would have to recognize Québec as a sovereign state."[66]

So a UDI can lead right through the law to a contest of force.[67] This prospect, ultimately, is why states negotiate secession and accomplish it through constitutional means. The abyss of repression or civil war is too awful to contemplate. But then so are the intermediate steps. If Canada and Quebec did not achieve a peaceful secession, one step towards conflict would be a UDI followed by a refusal to recognize Quebec's sovereignty over its territory. Similarly, a refusal to accept a referendum result could push Quebec to declare a UDI. This would plunge the two parties into deep legal uncertainty, and there is no obvious point where disagreement need cease. On the other hand, if Canada recognized Quebec's claim, an enormous amount of legal dispute, political conflict, and economic uncertainty would be avoided. Acceptance of Quebec's decision would immediately cut through the entire legal morass that we have just traversed. Such acceptance is a rare event in history, and it would represent an enormous benefit for the fledgling state of Quebec. In the view of Quebec sovereigntists flush with a pro-secession referendum vote, this might be a benefit that was only just and due, but it would be a major benefit nonetheless.

Even with recognition, however, other legal problems would remain to be resolved. Undoubtedly, the thorniest issue concerns the Aboriginal population of Quebec. Natives insist that they are peoples with full rights to self-determination and a claim to sovereign rule over their lands. They too could be "contenders" with a claim to international personality over their historical lands in Quebec. The Grand Council of the Crees, for example, has declared repeatedly that the imposition of Quebec sovereignty over their nation would be resisted, precisely on this basis of competing sovereignty.[68] Quebec First Nations have asserted that they have the right to choose whether to secede from Quebec and remain in Canada.[69] These Aboriginal peoples might well hold referendums of their own to bolster their claim to self-determination and secession. There is also the special case of the James Bay Cree and the Inuit and Naskapi, who are signatories with Canada and Quebec to the James Bay and Northern Quebec Agreement and the Northeastern Quebec Agreement. Beyond their general claim to self-determination, the Cree argue that Quebec secession would abrogate an agreement through which Quebec committed itself "in perpetuity to a constitutionally-entrenched federalist relationship with the Crees and Canada concerning Cree territory and Cree rights."[70]

While there might be considerable public sympathy in Canada for this position, it will be shown below that the Government of Canada would not be legally constrained to respond to such appeals; nor would Canada need to be bound by the Aboriginal peoples' desires if it chose to amend the constitution so as to transfer authority over Quebec's Native peoples to the government of the new state. (The politics of such a move are, of course, another matter.) As for self-determination and secession by First Nations, Finkelstein and Vegh make short work of this claim. First, there is a rule of international law, stemming from the case of Southern Rhodesia, that prevents the creation of states where the principle of self-determination would be violated because internal minorities (or majorities) would be repressed. However, repression comparable to that suffered by black Africans in Rhodesia cannot, and presumably could not, be demonstrated in the case of Aboriginal peoples in Quebec.[71] Second, the Cree have no stronger claim to statehood against Quebec than they now have against Canada. Lastly, there is in international law no right of indigenous peoples to self-determination.[72]

But this might be too quick. Buchanan argues that the status of the northern Quebec agreements would be affected by secession. It is unclear whether they would be voided, but if they were, the Native territorial rights extinguished by them could be renewed. In any event, alteration of the agreements could lead Ottawa to insist that a satisfactory resolution of the status of Aboriginal peoples must be a condition of a negotiated secession.[73]

The Aboriginal claims would be a legal lever to contest Quebec's sovereignty over the northern territories appended to it in 1898 and 1912. This is a complex and explosive issue. There is some support for the argument that the territories were appended to Quebec as a province and would revert to Canada if Quebec's status was changed.[74] But a strong opinion by international jurists has supported the opinion that Quebec could secede with its borders intact and that no minorities or inhabitants of border regions have a similar right.[75] This opinion is contestable, of course.[76] But the Aboriginal claim adds an extra dimension to the northern boundary question. Kent McNeil has presented the case that the border extensions are disputable because the Hudson's Bay Company never had sovereignty over Aboriginals in the region and therefore could not legally have transferred the territory to Canada in the first place. But McNeil admits that Canada did control the territory and that it cleared up some jurisdictional problems in 1933 (even if these measures reflected a "colonial attitude"). More important, if this argument were to be accepted, it could equally apply to all the rest of the lands ceded by the Hudson's Bay Company.[77] This illustrates the general dilemma that accepting the broad Aboriginal claim to self-determination and secession in Quebec would open the rest of Canada to precisely the same claims.

Still, even Turp admits that Quebec's Native people have the right of self-determination under the same criteria he applies to Quebecers, and he suggests that competing territorial claims might require international arbitration.[78] Further, it is obvious that there is strong international public opinion in support of indigenous people's rights, and that law in this area may evolve rapidly. Hence, Beaudoin and Vallée suggest that the Aboriginal people's status might have to become the subject of a tripartite accord, the principles of which would apply uniformly to all of what is now Canada, even though Quebec would by then have become sovereign. This is one solution to what obviously would be a critical issue. And it is a political one.

The legal rights of others are also an issue. Some anglophone communities might claim the right of secession from an independent Quebec in order to preserve their Canadian rights and citizenship.[79]

But there is no right in international law for secession when minorities in metropolitan states have not been oppressed. The linguistic and other rights that Quebec would write into its own constitution would be relevant here, as they would be with respect to Aboriginal peoples. These might be more generous than the existing regime of rights in Quebec.[80]

Another hard legal issue is citizenship. Here, it is clear that the domestic law of each state prevails. Therefore, the laws of a sovereign Quebec could extend Quebec citizenship to all residents, including perhaps landed immigrants and people born in Quebec but resident elsewhere.[81] It could also allow dual citizenship for those wishing to retain their Canadian citizenship. In the context of Quebec secession, Canada could also allow dual citizenship; alternatively, it could legally force people to reject their Quebec citizenship as a condition of retaining their Canadian citizenship.[82] *In extremis*, the Canadian constitution and the Citizenship Act could be amended to require Quebecers who wished to remain Canadians to emigrate from the sovereign state of Quebec and reside in Canada. The law here is quite open, and citizenship clearly is a delicate and potentially explosive matter.

Another legal issue concerns the assets and liabilities of Canada. Here the law seems quite clear. As the seceding state, Quebec is entitled to all public property situated on its territory; Canada has the right to possess all assets on its territory and those under its control (which are generally movables, mainly financial assets but also items such as databases).[83] The issue of the national debt is complicated by the 1983 Vienna Convention on Succession of States in Respect of State Property, Archives, and Debts. This would impose an obligation on Quebec to assume an "equitable proportion" of the debt in the absence of any agreement about its division. However, the convention has been ratified by no state, and it does not reflect customary international law, which holds that responsibility for national debts remains entirely with the predecessor state – in this case, Canada.[84]

The last thorny legal issue is the right of Quebec to succeed to treaties of which Canada is a signatory (or, alternatively, to refuse to be bound by them). Canada is a signatory to hundreds of multilateral treaties and conventions and to more than a thousand bilateral treaties, including more than two hundred with the United States alone. These cover a vast range of matters, from international trade to extradition and to North American defence. In general, treaty succession is still governed by customary international law, whereby obligations and rights do not automatically devolve to seceding states.[85] The exceptions include boundary treaties, localized treaties governing matters such as fishing rights, and some multilateral conventions (where the new presence would be insufficiently disruptive to require formal agreement by the other parties). An important example of a localized treaty that would very likely survive is the St Lawrence Seaway Agreement, whereby Quebec would have to offer navigation rights to the United States and Canada.

Trade agreements would be particularly important for a sovereign Quebec. It could accede to GATT through negotiations, under article 33, though this is a long, complex, and expensive process.[86] Alternatively, Canada could sponsor Quebec's membership, under article 26 (5)c, a process that is undoubtedly simpler and faster. In a short study for the Bélanger-Campeau Commission, Ivan Bernier argued that no declaration of sponsorship is now necessary, but he admitted that if Canada opposed secession, an uncertain legal situation would make the contracting parties unlikely to accept Quebec's membership quickly.[87] Even if Quebec were to accede to GATT, it is important to note that Canada could legally impose duties on imports from the new state (and vice versa), along with quotas on agricultural products. Each party would have to accord MFN status to the other's products. But much room for discrimination would exist – as in government procurement – and normal laws about countervail, anti-dumping, and safeguards would still be in force.

The case of the Canada–U.S. Free Trade Agreement (FTA) is less clear-cut. Canada would automatically succeed to the treaty unless the United States maintained that the absence of Quebec materially changed the benefits it expected under the agreement and sought to reopen negotiations with Canada. Quebec's accession to the FTA raises several considerations. First, it would have no legal right to be admitted: this would be a political decision to be settled by negotiations between Canada, Quebec, and the United States. Second, the FTA has been very largely superseded by the trilateral North American Free Trade Agreement (NAFTA), which includes Mexico. There is a great deal of overlap between the two agreements, but NAFTA takes priority over the FTA. In a few areas not covered by the trilateral treaty, such as the cultural industries, the FTA prevails, but the bulk of the benefits of market access now is assured by NAFTA.[88] And NAFTA, unlike the FTA, provides a legal mechanism for the entry of new members: they may be admitted into the agreement "if the NAFTA countries agree."[89] More precisely, the agreement states that a country or group of countries may be admitted "subject to such terms and conditions as may be agreed between such country or countries and the Commission." The commission comprises cabinet-level representatives of the three parties, and implements and supervises the agreement. It establishes its own rules and procedures, and it operates on the unanimity principle: "All decisions of the Commission shall be taken by consensus, except as the Commission may otherwise agree."[90] *De jure*, this would appear to confer on Canada a veto power over the admission of Quebec to the treaty that guarantees favourable access to its most important foreign market. *De facto*, of course, strong American desires to avoid economic distress and political unrest and to see Quebec remain part of the North American economic space could lead to pressure on Canada to approve terms for Quebec's admission. Nevertheless, that admission would in no way be legally guaranteed or automatic, and the American response to a Quebec request would be conditioned by the attitude of Canada towards Quebec sovereignty in general and by Quebec-Canada economic relations in particular.

Although the legal questions surrounding Quebec sovereignty are many and complex, they can be succinctly summarized. First and most important, secession can be legally accomplished by amending Canada's constitution so that it no longer applies to Quebec. Second, a unilateral declaration of Quebec independence would be a nonconstitutional rupture in the basic law that would lead to fundamentally contestable arguments about Quebecers' status as a people, their right to self-determination, and whether their political condition justifies secession. There is no legal stopping point on this path. Third, the international law about secession boils down to *realpolitik*. International recognition of the new state, ultimately, is decisive. Recognition is a political matter, and the crucial factor that would determine the position of other states, in the short and medium term, would be Canada's stance. If Canada recognizes the secession, many fundamental legal issues will be settled. If Canada accepts Quebec's borders and does not contest its territorial control, the matter will be decided, for all practical purposes. As for the other issues between the two states, neither side has an overwhelming legal advantage. In law, Canada could seize all movable national assets and prevent Quebec from joining NAFTA; in law, Quebec could renounce its share of the national debt and accede to GATT without Canada's support. In reality, however, these issues could be settled efficiently only through negotiations. If they were not so resolved, there is nothing in domestic or international law to prevent secession from entailing real conflict and immense costs of transition, costs far beyond the calculations, if not the imaginations, of economists.

POLITICAL SCENARIOS

Political processes will determine the size of the economic costs of the transition to Quebec independence. Politics also will determine whether the process of secession is cast on the treacherous waters of international law. Realizing this, political scientists have proposed some contrasting scenarios of the politics of the transition. The strategy of depicting extreme alternatives is useful to define the outer limits of speculation and to isolate some of the factors that will shape the course of events.[91]

In the case of Quebec's secession, the classic statement of the grand alternatives was presented by Richard Simeon.[92] His optimistic scenario corresponds to the one often outlined by sovereigntists: "The decision to separate is made in an orderly, legitimate fashion; it is broadly accepted as fair by the governments and people of English Canada, as well as by Quebecers themselves; the referendum vote is followed by correct and polite discussion of how to carry out the transfer of sovereignty, convey to Quebec the required powers, draw up the plans for association, and place the final seal of legitimacy on the agreement."[93]

The pessimistic extreme contrasts with this on every front: it envisages "the refusal of English Canada to accept a referendum result, followed by increasing hostility and tension, strong appeals from federalist Quebecers to 'save us,' and a general pattern of mutually reinforcing tension leading to a spiral of escalation beyond anyone's control, culminating either in official repression or in civil disorder of the type which has convulsed Northern Ireland. This scenario also contemplates armed intervention from outside, massive economic collapse, and indefinite chaos."[94]

This Manichean presentation depicts two scenarios which certainly are conceivable. However much sovereigntists may protest the contemplation of the pessimistic possibility, it exists, and it is simply incongruous, at best, that some nationalist scholars in Quebec cite precedents from the arbitration commission of the Peace Conference on Yugoslavia to support claims for a sovereign Quebec's territorial integrity, while others reject as terrorism and blackmail any suggestion that the Yugoslavian tragedy could in any way be relevant to Canada.[95] However repugnant the pessimistic scenario is, it is supported by a considerable body of comparative and historical experience.[96] Contested and violent secessions are far more common than peaceful ones. Consequently, if Quebec is to secede, the important thing about the pessimistic scenario is understanding the conditions that could produce it so as to know how to act in order that it can be avoided.

According to Simeon, there are four basic conditions that would determine the broad political path of the transition. First, Quebec's decision must be seen as legitimate, as corresponding to broadly held democratic norms. To be accepted by Canadians, a referendum result in favour of sovereignty must follow a fair campaign fought around an unbiased question, which produces a clear majority. Alternatively, a government passing a declaration of intent to secede through the National Assembly should have a clear and recent mandate, and strong support in the legislature.

Second is the shock that secession would cause Canadians. However it was accomplished, the declaration of intent to secede would represent a sharp break. It would occur at a single instant – when the results of the referendum or the National Assembly vote were announced – and theoretically it would be preventable until that moment. Although English Canadians have become familiar with the possibility of Quebec secession, the actual event would have a huge symbolic impact. Canadians' reaction to this would vary, according to each individual's sense of national identification, but for most people there would be a shock or, as Simeon put it, "a blow," to their conception of Canada. It is this psychological shock that could trigger behaviour contrary to their immediate material interests. In essence, the problem of the sovereigntists, if they wish to avoid large transition costs, "is to arrange the birth of Québec without convincing English Canadians that their own country is doomed in the process."[97] As David Bell has insightfully shown, leadership in deploying symbols and metaphors would be important here. A metaphor of Canada as a family or a business partnership, for example, presages far less damage and acrimony than the metaphor of divorce.[98]

Simeon's third factor is the intentions and actions of the Quebec authorities. Animosity and resistance to secession would rise if Quebec pursued social and economic policies that threatened the fundamental values or interests of Canadians. These could include oppression of linguistic or ethnic minorities and a determinedly statist or autarkic economic stance. As well, Quebec élites, like those in Canada, would need sufficient unity and authority to "restrain their more extremist followers" if moderation was to prevail.[99]

Finally, Canada's actions would affect Quebecers. Threats of repression or of economic sanctions could produce greater militance and resentment in Quebec, especially in a hot referendum campaign that produced a close decision. A refusal to accept a decision that was widely regarded in the province as legitimate would lead to a breakdown of relations. As well, intervention in aid of minorities could produce severe conflict, and intransigence in negotiations could fuel radicalism in Quebec and a drift towards the pessimistic scenario.

These political scenarios suggest once more that the costs of the transition to sovereignty could be very high indeed. The most important factor in mitigating those costs is that Canada accept the basic premise that Quebec will become a sovereign, independent state. For this to occur readily, Quebec's intent to secede must be made through a legitimate and democratic process, the Canadian public must be led to accept that outcome, and Quebec's economic and social policies must be moderate. If these conditions held, the politics of the transition would tend to be such that massive social and economic dislocations would be avoided.

In the pessimistic scenario, costs would not be limited to Quebec. Indeed, the predominant view in ROC that Quebec's losses would exceed those of Canada actually presumes a relatively smooth transition, or at least a Canada coherent enough to protect its own interests in the bilateral negotiations. But the pessimistic scenario could involve very large Canadian losses if a breakdown in political order occurred, or if ROC became ungovernable as political leadership and unity failed.

Finally, scenario sketching is useful not only to specify the preconditions for a peaceful secession but also because political leaders and citizens must be conscious of these possibilities. Any pessimistic depictions of the dangers lurking down the path of secession are decried by sovereigntists as fear-mongering and blackmail. Yet their own predictions that Canadian leaders will be cooperative in the project of secession depends entirely on the assumption that these same leaders will be aware of the dangers and will seek to avoid the damage that is a real possibility during the transition and beyond.

STUDIES OF THE MECHANICS OF THE TRANSITION

Much has been written about the economic consequences of Quebec secession and about the legal issues surrounding the event. Both, in the end, boil down to politics. The analyses of political scenarios make this clear in an extreme fashion. Yet relatively little has been written about how the transition would be managed or about how the political dynamics of the event would unfold. There is a growing and useful literature about some issues that would have to be dealt with politically in the event of secession, such as division of the national debt and maintaining the St Lawrence Seaway.[100] And there is a respectable body of work about the long-term implications of the various political and economic arrangements that might be adopted after or in the course of the separation. But there is little close analysis of the political modalities of the transition.

A noteworthy piece by Banting provides some insight into the problem. He points out that if there was a substantial vote for secession, Quebec would emerge with self-confidence, a sense of direction (based on years of contemplating the option), and, most important, with its institutions intact and unquestioned. In Canada, however, the mood would combine resentment against Quebec with "collective psychological disorientation" as people realized that the national project was terminated.[101] Canadians outside Quebec have not contemplated an alternative project to maintaining the existing system. More seriously, they would possess no stable political institutions. Banting envisages the formation of a multiparty coalition government in the event of a declaration by Quebec of its intent to secede. An election would be desirable, since the coalition would be "weak," but obviously there would be no constitutional way to prevent Quebec from electing MPs. Even if a government was formed that was not dependent on Quebec support, it would face challenges to its legitimacy as the negotiator with Quebec. The provincial premiers, representing the "stable component" of the system, would "undoubtedly claim to speak for the country."[102] If the legitimacy of all established leaders were suspect, perhaps through their manifest failure to resolve a secessionist crisis or to win a referendum, demands would arise for the convening of a constituent assembly to redesign the constitution. "A period of political instability would be inevitable."[103] In Banting's view, Canada might hold together in the long run, or it could fragment. The outcome would depend on the politics of the transition.

In a very different analysis, one that paints Quebec secession in a favourable light, Bercuson and Cooper assume that both Quebec and Canada would emerge "internally more united" from the decision to disengage.[104] In their view, the Quebec National Assembly would declare itself the government of a sovereign Quebec. Then the Government of Canada would immediately grant *de facto* recognition. This would allow Canada to have "dealings" with the emergent state and would presage a period of negotiations. The interlocutor on the Canadian side would be the federal government. Somehow, a new government would be formed, one presumably not dependent on the support of the seventy-five Quebec members of Parliament.[105] No election would be held: calling one would not be "prudent." Instead, the federal government would appoint negotiators to deal with Quebec, and it would consult closely with the provinces and other "interested parties." After a set of negotiations through which Quebec would be stripped of what was Rupert's Land and the entire South Shore of the St Lawrence, Canada would adopt a new constitution. This would make the federation indissoluble, enshrine a true economic union, recognize popular sovereignty over governments, abolish all collective rights, eliminate bilingualism and multiculturalism and support for separate schools, erase the notwithstanding clause, and institute a genuine triple-E Senate.[106] How this reconstitution would take place is not explained by Bercuson and Cooper.

Obviously, there is room for substantial disagreement about how the mechanics of the separation would occur. Some analysts are quite vague about what would happen. Jonathan Lemco, for example, has provided lengthy accounts of possible political developments and of the issues surrounding the national debt and the currency, but he can make no precise predictions about outcomes: "There is no certainty that the rest of Canada will accept a sovereign Quebec. Nor is it clear that the rest of Canada will pursue relations with Quebec. Indeed, the rest of Canada might itself be restructured, forcing endless haggling with the resulting uncertainty. The negotiations for dividing Canada's assets and liabilities could be especially complicated."[107] He does, however, list an abundance of important questions about how the politics of the transition would take place.[108]

To this emerging debate, Quebec sovereigntists have contributed very little. Although huge energies have been devoted to analysing the legal and economic issues around secession, there is little published work on how the transition might unfold. The Parti québécois has been almost mute. Its 1991 program committed a PQ government to pass through the National Assembly a declaration of Quebec's will to secede. Then the government would seek to negotiate (with the federal government) a timetable and mechanisms for the orderly transfer of powers to the province, along with a division of federal assets and debts, and an economic association that would establish, by treaty, some joint management bodies. At the same time, a commission would be preparing a new constitution for Quebec, through wide consultations, as well as proposing mechanisms for the legal shift from the federal constitutional regime to one of sovereignty. Then a referendum on both sovereignty and the constitution would be "l'acte de naissance du Québec souverain."[109]

Other documents amplify this only slightly. One insists that Quebec seeks "une transition sans soubresauts" (a transition without jolts), and sketchily lays out favoured positions about citizenship, rights, immigration, assets and debts, crown corporations, a monetary union, and Quebec's army and public servants.[110] The assumption remains that these will all be negotiated with the federal government. And Canada, it is claimed, cannot refuse to negotiate, because Quebec will be proceeding democratically and, more important, because Canada has a clear interest in these matters. Not to negotiate would be "contre toute logique" (against all logic). If Canada refused nevertheless, a referendum could approve the declaration of sovereignty, and then negotiations certainly would take place.[111] A more recent manifesto repeats the basic negotiation-referendum process but also suggests that Quebec would adopt a minimally changed constitution and would declare that all federal laws continue to apply until amended. The PQ advocates maintaining the economic and monetary union "as it now exists," and suggests that a treaty of association could provide for a council of ministers, a secretariat, a tribunal, and specialized commissions. Once more, a harmony of interests is assumed to support the negotiations.[112] Once more, there is no consideration of what Canada's position might be, of the timetable for the negotiations, of their economic and political context, or of the possibility that Ottawa alone might not be capable of negotiating the terms of separation.

Much more work on secession has been done by official commissions in Quebec – the Bélanger-Campeau Commission (Commission on the Political and Constitutional Future of Quebec) and the National Assembly's Committee to Examine Matters Relating to the Accession of Quebec to Sovereignty. Each conducted hearings, received many briefs, and commissioned a lot of research. But the great bulk of this work concerns legal and economic issues about Quebec's sovereignty and viability. It largely ignores the process of secession, and it is blind to the political dynamics in ROC; in fact, it is studiously apolitical. As noted above, the Bélanger-Campeau Commission contemplated a constitutional or unilateral secession – in two paragraphs. Most of its report dealt with matters of substance, such as accession to treaties and the public finances, rather than questions of process. About the latter, the commission said only that "sovereignty poses the problem of managing in an orderly fashion a change implemented on the basis of free choice. Successfully managing any change hinges upon a thorough knowledge of the ins and outs of the issue at hand."[113] In all of the commission's voluminous background studies, there is no detailed analysis of how the transition would occur, of opinion in ROC, or of the politics of secession.[114]

The more recent National Assembly committee report followed much the same lines, albeit in greater detail. It discussed the legalities of the important issues – citizenship, Aboriginal peoples, and borders – and it summarized much research about the transfer of public servants, currency, the financial sector, economic performance, and the public finances. When agreements with Canada would be necessary or desirable, this was mentioned, but there was no sustained consideration of whether or how these could be reached. This issue surfaced only in connection with negotiating economic arrangements between Quebec and Canada, which could be difficult because of acrimony, Ottawa's lack of negotiating capacity, and the limited time available. Obviously, the committee was split about whether Quebec-Canada relations after a secession would preclude cooperation:

Various observers have mentioned the possibility that Canada-Québec relations would be acrimonious when Québec acceded to sovereignty. Such a situation could very well hinder the conclusion of a treaty, although it has been suggested that reciprocal economic interests, especially those of Québec and Ontario, are such than [sic] an agreement to preserve the essence of the economic space would necessarily (and fairly promptly) be concluded. The Committee was unable to settle this issue.[115]

As for the process of secession itself, the committee was confused. Secession could occur with Canada's consent. It seems this would involve a bilateral agreement that the separation would be "orderly," followed by a constitutional amendment. But such an amendment is said to be "unlikely"; instead, were "the federal and provincial governments to consent to Quebec's secession, the decision would probably be political in nature."[116] Somehow, this consent could be "formal and detailed," or else in the form of a unilateral declaration, or simply "implicit"; all of this is terribly vague. Sovereignty could also be attained through a Quebec UDI. Here, at least, the report is quite clear in describing the legal difficulties that would ensue, principally that "uncertainty might persist among Quebecers about which body of law prevails."[117]

No such reticence and understatement mark one recent treatment of the politics of the transition. Lansing Lamont has presented a docu-drama account of a Quebec secession in some detail. Highly coloured, the prediction is based on an explosive combination of existing forces – the anglophone minority, Aboriginal peoples, and a variety of military units – along with economic uncertainty and "fiercely contested negotiations" about debt, assets, territory, and the currency.[118] Here, Parliament rejects recommendations that the country be decentralized, and it also rejects asymmetrical federalism along the lines of the Meech Lake Accord. The National Assembly approves a declaration of independence, to be ratified by a referendum that passes by a large majority. The assembly then takes five months to pass a new constitution. Two more months are needed to assemble Quebec and Canadian negotiating teams (their composition is unspecified), and after nine months of tedious and inconclusive meetings, negotiations break down over the currency issue. The provincial governments begin to cut back services to francophones, and anglophone rights are restricted in Quebec. The federal government moves to secure its assets in Quebec; then Quebec cuts off services to federal installations, and in turn Ottawa mobilizes army units to protect its property and Canadian citizens. Riots break out in Montreal and in smaller centres. The Mohawks at Akwesasne erupt and are suppressed in serious fighting; in sympathy, the Cree sabotage the dam and generators at La Grande 2. Although the forces of order hold together, they are stretched too thinly, and the United States sends a division north to help restore calm. In the meantime, a meltdown takes place on currency and financial markets. Under these pressures, the two sides settle quickly. Canada recognizes Quebec's sovereignty. Quebec assumes 25 per cent of the debt and uses the Canadian dollar with no participation in making monetary policy, and Canada retains some vestigal control over transport facilities in the province. The First Nations settle for something less than full sovereignty. The U.S. refuses Quebec admission to NAFTA, and the economy shrinks. In the rest of Canada, central power weakens. ROC tries to reconstitute itself as a grouping of regions, but this fails. The country fragments as provinces opt to join the United States, which admits them, not without grave misgivings.[119]

This is lurid stuff, but it is detailed, and there is a logic to it.[120] Lamont's account depends at every turn on questionable assumptions about public opinion, leadership, and the potential for escalation. As he admits, the study is "an informed surmise of what could happen in the worst circumstances."[121] But the author has some experience in Canadian affairs and has access to official and quasi-official American thinking about Quebec separation. He reports that "in the autumn of Canada's 125th year there was near consensus among knowledgeable American diplomats that Quebec would eventually go and that Canada's odds for survival were poor."[122]

Not all the pessimistic accounts are docu-dramas. Patrick Monahan, a veteran constitutional observer and adviser, has argued that separation from Canada could be "far more complicated, costly and acrimonious than Quebecers had been led to expect."[123] He argues first that a constitutional secession would require the unanimous consent of Parliament and all ten provinces. The other route is a UDI, which Canada could accept or challenge. Were a referendum to pass, Monahan believes that Canada might not negotiate with Quebec: it might not have the legitimacy to do so; the provinces and Aboriginal peoples and other groups would demand to participate; and there is no "authoritative, obvious or politically legitimate process that might lead to the creation of an interlocutor" for Quebec.[124] Stalemate would result. Even if there were negotiations, they would very likely fail. First, Monahan claims that the "terms of any deal" would require unanimous provincial consent, which would not be forthcoming. Second, the secession negotiations would become entangled with ROC's reconstitution and the demands of various provinces and special interests. Third, the issues are simply too complex and divisive – especially how to apportion the national debt. Canada would remain responsible for the whole liability during a long transition period, and neither side would agree on how to eliminate the risk of Quebec's defaulting or how to pay the extra risk premiums that would be incurred. If there were an agreement with Quebec, both it and the constitutional amendment would require ratification by referendum in every province and would in all probability be defeated somewhere, so Quebec would not be able to secede constitutionally. If Quebec were then to take the UDI option, Canada would resist until agreement on the debt was reached. Domestic opinion in ROC would favour forcing Quebec to return to negotiation. Then there "inevitably" would ensue a "struggle for supremacy between the Canadian and Quebec governments in relation to Quebec territory," which would cause immense economic damage.[125]

Another recent study also focuses on the relationship between ROC's post-referendum politics and the process of Quebec secession. Prepared by Gordon Gibson, a former leader of the B.C. Liberal Party, it is remarkable for its detailed account of some transition issues and its occasional strategic insight. An activist, Gibson has taken on the mission of organizing grassroots movements towards a constituent assembly to reform the constitution ("Plan C") so as to avoid the adverse effects of secession that emerge from his own description of the event ("Plan B," for Breakup).[126]

After a Yes victory, the leaders of Quebec and Canada would issue reassurances that external obligations would be met and that all Canadian laws would continue to apply in Quebec. If Canada accepted the result, a negotiating team would be established; this might be the existing Government of Canada, a new one formed after an election, or a federal-provincial committee (though there are difficulties with each alternative).[127] The "deal" with Quebec might be ratified by Parliament or by Parliament and the provinces (under a version of the general constitutional amending formula), or by a referendum, for Gibson assumes that a negotiated settlement with Quebec would need "constitutional validation."[128] The stabilization and negotiation period would be one year.

The major issues to be settled with Quebec are fivefold. First, Canada would have an obligation to ensure that Quebec provide guarantees for rights for Aboriginal and anglophone minorities, which, he assumes, is in Quebec's interest in any case. Then Quebec's borders would be accepted, including the Labrador boundary drawn in 1927. Some cooperative trade arrangments would be reached, along with one about currency (and in both matters, Gibson claims, ROC has bargaining leverage). Finally, the debt issue, critical for foreign confidence, would be resolved by ROC's insisting that Quebec assume about 25 per cent of the total, as justified by its proportion of the population.

In Gibson's view, the more important task for ROC would be its reconstitution. With the shock of a Yes vote, the whole country would be "up for review," as he believes it should be.[129] He assumes that this process would take place at the same time as the negotiations with Quebec and that there would be both the time and the inclination to engage in fundamental questioning of all alternative structures. Much of Ottawa's legitimacy would have been lost, and the role of the provinces would have become predominant: Alberta and British Columbia would insist on thorough change to ROC's constitution. The mechanism for redefining ROC could be the First Ministers' Conference, but since the governments in place would have no mandate to reconstitute the country and since any agreement would have to pass a referendum, it would be better to convoke a constituent assembly.[130] This would include representatives of provincial governments, the "residual Ottawa," and interest groups, but the voting members would be specially elected (ten per province). The assembly would pass constitutional provisions through provincial unanimity (a majority of the voting members from each province), and the new constitution would be ratified by a referendum in each province. In this whole process of negotiation, the richer provinces would be dominant, and they would favour radical decentralization. Thus, the outcome could be a fragmented ROC, or one in which the central government retained very few powers, acting only as a "service organization" for the highly autonomous provinces.[131] It is evident that the cost of this whole exercise would be great, even if it were to succeed. So to avoid the costs of a breakup, Gibson's "Plan C" envisages a radically decentralized country, almost a confederation. This might be attractive enough to Quebecers for a secession to be avoided, but how it could be implemented before a Quebec referendum is problematic.[132]

Others have argued that such exercises in wholesale constitutional design are unlikely in the event of Quebec secession. Maureen Covell notes the bitterness, the crisis of legitimacy, and the deep constitutional uncertainty that would very likely exist in Canada. These phenomena could lead to demands for a constituent assembly, but this would be very difficult to arrange. Who would decide on the method of selection or election of the members of such a body? If the Constitution Acts had not somehow been declared inoperative, what authority would the assembly possess? Such a constitutional conference would function effectively "only under conditions of extreme disruption such that both the federal and provincial governments were unable to operate as they are supposed to."[133] But would this happen? Covell maintains that the provincial governments' relative position would be strengthened by a move towards secession by Quebec. Yet Ottawa would be able to retain some authority. First, a negotiator would be needed; second, issues would have to be settled quickly. While the federal government might be discredited by its failure to prevent secession, a "unity backlash" could even lead Canadians to support its efforts in order to preserve "what remains of the nation."[134]

The group involved in the York University Constitutional Reform Project have also published some reflections on the secession process. They suggest that Canada should recognize a clear and democratically expressed Quebec sentiment in favour of secession. The federal government, however, could not alone undertake negotiations, because the provinces, the territories, and the Aboriginal peoples have a right to be consulted. So a negotiating authority should be established, with representation from all these parties, to "oversee" negotiations about Quebec's secession.[135] The negotiating authority would be briefed on the negotiations and consulted about them, but its role would be advisory only, because any agreement with Quebec would have to be ratified by Parliament and the provincial legislatures, "in accordance with the amending formula."[136] (This assumes, of course, that arrangements negotiated with Quebec – economic, political, or both – would be constitutional matters, requiring formal constitutional amendment.) The negotiating authority should be consulted even about the recognition of Quebec's claim to sovereignty, despite the time delays and the fact that recognition is a prerogative of the federal government. The reason, essentially, is to ensure that those affected by the decision are involved in making it, if only in a consultative manner: "We believe that some type of joint Negotiating Authority is required for political as well as strictly legal reasons. It will be essential that there be a high degree of public legitimacy and acceptance of the negotiating process. We believe that this legitimacy can only be assured if all the relevant actors and interests are involved in the process from the very beginning."[137]

The York group also discussed several of the issues to be negotiated. Territory is the most problematic. Some members felt that opening up the border question would immediately ruin any prospect of an amicable solution; however, the majority, who were concerned mostly about the Aboriginal peoples and other geographically concentrated minorities, took the position that such groups must have the right to express democratically their choice of community and state.[138] Insofar as the Aboriginals are concerned, one proposal was that a Canada-Quebec protocol should ensure that the same constitutional rights to self-government obtain in each country. As in the suggestion of Beaudoin and Vallée, this would remove the border issue from that of how this crucial minority is treated. With respect to the national debt, the York group favoured division on an equal per capita basis.

Finally, there remains to be considered the most detailed and practical depiction of the secession process, as laid out by Hugh Thorburn in 1977.[139] This analyst recognized that the transition to sovereignty would be much eased if talks could be opened before the event occurred, though he thought this improbable. Nevertheless, Thorburn presents an optimistic scenario, which envisages a disengagement that occurs "as quickly and harmoniously as possible."[140] The key to this is an agreement on separation, which would be a framework document laying out the terms of the settlement, the timetable of events through the transition period, and the date for the proclamation of the separate existence of the two states.

Like others, Thorburn expects that the federal authorities would be weakened by their failure to prevent secession. Since an election might centre on whether or not to recognize an independent Quebec, and since Quebecers could not be prevented from voting under the existing constitution, a "crisis coalition" government would be formed. This would include representatives of the opposition parties. Then, Thorburn presumes, negotiations would open at a conference that was attended also by provincial representatives, and the participants would agree here on the general terms of the separation agreement.

In the transition period, the agreement would be implemented under the supervision of a "joint control commission" with equal representation from the governments of Canada and Quebec, under a neutral, presumably foreign, chair.[141] This commission would function throughout the disengagement period, which could last one year. Thorburn surveys the issues to be dealt with in the separation agreement and the disengagement. In general, his solutions assume that there would be bilateral management of the secession by temporary or permanent joint agencies, on which Canada and Quebec would have equal representation. The first problem would be the boundary, though it would probably remain intact. Next would be the army. As in the case of federal civil servants, Thorburn favours allowing the members of the military free choice about which state to serve. Remustering should be done right at the start of the transition period, since the forces might be needed to maintain order. A joint Quebec-Canada army council, reporting to the joint control commission, would direct the forces of both countries. Next, citizens would require guarantees of their freedom and security, including civil, property, and language rights. More generally, Thorburn assumes that existing federal laws would continue in force in Quebec until changed by the National Assembly. The debt would be split on a per capita basis. Quebec would retain all immovable assets in the province, while some other assets (including CN, Air Canada, the Seaway and the Port of Montreal) would be run by cooperative state organizations. Other issues about debt and assets would be determined by a joint financial settlement commission, again with equal representation and a neutral chair. Depending on longer-term prospects for economic cooperation, the common currency might be maintained, along with free access between Atlantic Canada and the rest of the country. If cooperation seemed unlikely, the agreement would provide for a transition to a new currency for Quebec, and for minimizing the border controls with Ontario and New Brunswick. Finally, Quebec Aboriginals would require some guarantees, especially about the language of schooling; otherwise, Ottawa's obligations would be transferred to the crown in right of Quebec. Last, and only after these negotiations had been concluded, Canada would design for itself a new constitution, from which Quebec would be absent.

There is a good deal of calm sense in this analysis. Nevertheless, it is substantially at odds with the expectations of other scholars on some important points. Indeed, this brief survey of studies of the politics of the transition shows a striking lack of consensus about questions that would critically determine the outcome of negotiations with Quebec and the way in which ROC would be reconstituted. There is profound uncertainty – or disagreement – about several basic issues. When would negotiations begin? Who would negotiate with Quebec? What would the public mood be like? Would power flow to Ottawa or to the provinces in the event of a secession? Would an election be held? Would the Canadian constitution be amended, and how could this occur? How would the disengagement be managed, and how would particular issues be resolved? How long would the whole process take? It is clear that these are crucial questions. The economic costs and benefits of secession would depend mainly on how the process took place, and the law would only be a tool in the politics of the event. In order to guide our analysis of the transition, further work is needed. One fruitful way to proceed is through comparative analysis, which might produce lessons applicable to the separation of Quebec from Canada. So it is to other cases of secession that we now turn.

CHAPTER TEN

The Comparative Politics
of Peaceful Secession

INTRODUCTION

On the assumption that Quebec secedes, analysis of the long-term future of Canada shows that many configurations are possible, and there are many kinds of economic and political relationships that could be established between the two countries. Structural factors show no overwhelming tendency towards any outcome, and they could be outweighed in any case by the events of the separation itself. But although studies of the transition to Quebec sovereignty show that the economic stakes could be very high, the legal arguments are indeterminate, and the outcome of the transition would depend on the politics of the event. Yet here again there is a wide range of predictions about how the secession would occur. Since the literature on the Canada-Quebec case provides no clear guidance, one solution is to turn to comparative experience. How has secession taken place elsewhere? What characteristics have marked the politics of the event? Does the process of peaceful secession conform to a pattern that can serve as a guide to predict what could happen in Canada? These questions require comparative political analysis.[1]

Recently, the phenomenon of secession has attracted much attention from scholars working within a variety of theoretical perspectives. Spurred by events in the former USSR, specialists in comparative politics have returned to classic questions about nationalism and state viability;[2] studies of the legal and moral issues around secession have begun to proliferate;[3] political economists have engaged a process that lends itself well to calculation and strategic games;[4] and theories both deductive and inductive are emerging about the causes and process of secession.[5] Secession has become a hot topic.

But the purpose here is more pragmatic and straightforward than that of most other current studies. It is to arrive at empirical generalizations about the politics of secession. Such generalizations are simply features of the political process that are commonly found when states separate peacefully. The objective is not to investigate the causes or consequences of secession; nor is it to formulate theories about the relations between economic and social factors and political events; nor is it to predict when and how particular secessionist movements may achieve their ends. The aim is simply to explore how secessions have occurred in the past and to search for general patterns in the political dynamics.

If peaceful secessions do follow a pattern, this can help predict how the process would unfold in other cases. But of course every country and every secessionist movement is different, and this is precisely what renders predictions about each case unreliable. Such predictions are also contestable, not least because those making them often have attachments or commitments to one side or another in secessionist struggles. So any evidence from comparative experience that suggests how the process might occur should be welcome to those who want to know what would happen in any particular case, such as the secession of Quebec from Canada. Of course the separation of Quebec would be a unique event. Not only do Canada and Quebec have a distinct history, geography, and so on, but there has never been a case of secession in an advanced, capitalist, democratic country. Canadians and Quebecers would themselves have to determine how the process of disengagement would occur and what would be the dimensions of their subsequent relationship.

This does not mean that other cases are irrelevant. If there are general features in the political dynamics of peaceful secession – if politicians and citizens do tend to behave in certain ways – these can only be isolated by comparative analysis. Working through induction, it is possible to discern such features: cases of peaceful secession have indeed been marked by a particular pattern. Here, thirteen generalizations about the politics of peaceful secession are discussed. They appear to be robust and reliable. As a consequence, these characteristics will be used in part 3 to form the framework for analysing how Quebec's secession would take place.

Before proceeding to elaborate the generalizations in more detail, the limitations of this survey should be noted. The most serious is that there are few cases to be considered. Most attention is devoted to only three – the secession of Singapore from Malaysia in 1965, of Hungary from Austria in 1867, and of Norway from Sweden in 1905. There is a handful of other cases to which some reference can be made, but these are mainly breakups of short-lived colonial federations, countries outfitted by the receding British Empire with generic (or "neoclassical") federal systems that did not long endure.[6] This small sample also ignores contemporary secessions from the former Soviet Union, not because withdrawal from a Communist empire is less relevant than some of the cases explored here, but because time and linguistic constraints have not allowed reliable information to be gathered. On the other hand, the breakup of the Czech and Slovak Federal Republic is of greater interest, because it is recent and because it involved a functioning democracy in a modern, industrial, highly integrated country. This case is treated separately, in the following chapter. Although its politics largely corresponded to the basic pattern described here, which increases confidence in its generality, the separation was also marked by political polarization, a phenomenon that could occur in Canada and therefore deserves fuller exploration.

Another limitation is that the survey covers only cases of peaceful secession. Contested secessions are excluded. This is not because those cases are irrelevant; on the contrary, useful lessons and analogies have been drawn from them.[7] Moreover, contested secessions are far more numerous than peaceful ones. Bookman, for example, examines thirty-seven secessionist movements, most of which emerged after World War II (the exceptions being Northern Ireland, Ukraine, and the Kurds) and only twelve of which were peaceful: six in the USSR (where the central state was collapsing), three in Europe (Catalonia, Lombardy, and Scotland), Tibet (where Chinese repression is pervasive enough to prevent any mass resistance, peaceful or not), and Puerto Rico and Quebec. The other movements were violent, or they resulted in civil war.[8] However, contested secessions fall into a different class than the one that is of interest here. For our purposes, it may be more fruitful to examine cases of "success" and to look for patterns in the transitions, rather than focusing on instances of repression, government breakdown, or civil war in the hope of discovering salutary lessons. So how has peaceful secession occurred in the past? What features have characterized the process?

THE PATTERN OF PEACEFUL SECESSION

There is little point in summarizing all the generalizations here, but the overall pattern is clear enough. After long and fundamental disputes, partisan realignments or external shocks cause one state to make an authoritative declaration of intent to end the union (or federation). This is accepted in principle by the other government, a move that obviously distinguishes peaceful from contested secessions, since the only alternative is to attempt violent repression.[9] Negotiations inevitably follow, and they are fast, limited to big issues, constrained by foreign powers, and conducted by small teams to which broad authority is delegated. Throughout this process, the two sides polarize, and there are substantial pressures to maintain national solidarity. Peaceful secessions occur constitutionally and involve minimal changes to the existing constitutional order(s). But policies in the new states soon begin to diverge, and some friction continues, as is normal between interdependent sovereign entities.

Secession Follows Protracted Constitutional and Political Disputes

While the event of secession is always abrupt, cases of peaceful secession have capped long periods of disagreement between the constituent units of a federation or empire. In a sense, secession results from an impasse about an important matter of principle, even though this may be only one of many irritants or one that becomes important as the symbolic focus of deeper autonomist yearnings.

In 1867, Hungary and Austria were separated through the Ausgleich (Compromise), which was finally sealed when it was accepted by the Austrian Reichstat on 21 December.[10] This agreement provided a durable arrangement for the coexistence of territories that had been united but had been riven by fundamental conflict for almost two decades. As part of the 1848 revolutions that swept Europe, Hungary had achieved first a separate ministry responsible to the national diet (legislature) and then had declared formal independence in April 1849. This revolt was crushed by the Russians, who returned the errant state to the Austrian emperor. After a period of authoritarian rule in the 1850s, a brief flirtation with a decentralized structure was followed in 1861 with a centralized, bicameral system. This the Hungarians boycotted for some years in a struggle for greater autonomy, and their local diets generally refused to raise taxes or military recruits for the imperial authorities. In April 1865, Francis Deák and other Hungarian moderates published a program for reform that envisaged a largely autonomous country, and the emperor encouraged discussions to be held with Hungarian leaders because the central authorities were weakened by the boycott and by rapidly rising debt.[11] In early 1866 a new Hungarian diet was called, and it worked out a program for negotiations. But these became serious only towards the end of the year, after Austria was defeated by the Prussians at Sadowa and the Treaty of Prague dissolved the Germanic Confederation, essentially removing Austria from the Germanic system and making an internal reordering highly advisable.[12]

A second case is that of Norway-Sweden. Norway, a Danish possession, was united with Sweden under King Karl XIII in 1814. While each country maintained separate citizenships, ministries, civil services, and courts, and while there was no joint legislature (formally), there were important joint and common functions. The king appointed each of the ministries, he could veto legislation, and, most critically, he conducted war and foreign policy. Despite the fact that Sweden's main economic links were with Germany while Norway's were with England, there was substantial economic integration. A common coinage was introduced in 1875, and joint tariff laws prevailed after 1825. Although the tariffs covered only a few items, they were a cause of continuing dispute, for Sweden sought to increase protection towards the end of the century; but since no agreement could be reached, these joint tariff laws lapsed in 1897.[13] On the other hand, there were no serious economic disputes between the countries at the time of the separation.

Meanwhile, deeper political integration was resisted, mainly by Norway. An 1850s plan for a confederal legislature failed, and Norway also blocked moves towards closer cooperation in 1871, causing much bitterness.[14] As under the Austro-Hungarian Ausgleich, it was the common royal prerogative that ensured some internal policy harmonization, through the veto power and the authority to select ministries. More important in an era of very limited government, the crown's control over war and foreign policy enabled the countries to operate as a unit on the international stage, and although such an arrangement was not envisaged in the Riksakt (the Act of Union), the king was working through a joint council for diplomacy and foreign affairs by the late nineteenth century.[15] Nevertheless, growing nationalism and liberal demands for a fully responsible government led to the secession.

The immediate issue of contention was the Norwegian demand for a separate consular service. This brought the countries near to war in 1895. Further negotiations over the issue opened in 1902, and the stakes escalated in a bitter election campaign in Norway, which was won by the Conservatives, who then had one last chance to find a negotiated solution.[16] In February 1905, however, inadequate Swedish proposals were refused by the Norwegians, and in March a coalition government was formed in Norway; then a consular bill was passed in the knowledge that the king would veto it and precipitate a crisis.

A third case, the secession of Singapore from Malaysia on 9 August 1965, was remarkable for the speed with which it was accomplished. But the final, very brief negotiations put the seal on a disengagement that was motivated by acrimony on several fronts, for discord had been growing almost since the formation of Malaysia in September 1963. Although this federation was very young and in part was a contrivance of British imperial withdrawal, its origins stretched back some years: the sovereign Federation of Malaya had been formed in August 1957, building on the four-state Federated Malay States (1895) and the Federation of Malaya Agreement (1948). More important, under colonial rule, Singapore and the Malay states had been governed as an economic unit since the nineteenth century; the common Malayan dollar, for instance, had been issued by a currency board since 1906.[17] And although the (British-led) defence cooperation between the colonies had been interrupted by World War II, it had been close since 1951.

In this case, there were disputes about central-bank arrangements, which were protracted and tense and were unresolved at the time of secession.[18] As well, Singapore, which had supported the federation in part to gain fuller access to the Malayan market, was disappointed by the slow progress towards the goal of a full common market, which was enshrined in the 1963 constitution.[19] Other causes of friction included the distribution of tax revenues in the federation, economic favouritism towards the Borneo territories (Sabah and Sarawak), and Singaporean underrepresentation in Parliament and the cabinet (a consequence of the asymmetrical powers that Singapore possessed under the constitution).[20] All these were aggravated by an undeclared war with Indonesia – the Confrontation – which put pressure on expenditures and led to the imposition of emergency-power rule.[21]

The major incompatability between the units, however, concerned race and the deep ideology that was to underpin the federal political system. The accession of Singapore (80 per cent Chinese) to the federation posed a threat not only to the special privileges of the Malays (who became a minority overall) but also to the communitarian system through which the country traditionally had been governed. This was a system of élite accommodation between racial groups, which had largely been achieved within the alliance between the United Malay National Organization and the Malayan Chinese Association (UMNO-MCA, known as the Alliance). The Indian community, about 10 per cent of the population, was also incorporated into this system. But communitarianism was challenged by Lee Kuan Yew of Singapore through his People's Action Party (PAP), which advanced an ideology of progressivism, individualism, and pluralism, under the slogan of a "Malaysian Malaysia."[22] While the long-standing conflict was expressed through partisan competition, it went to the cultural and systemic foundations of the federation. PAP swept the 1963 elections in Singapore and then contested the 1964 elections on the mainland, albeit with little success. Undeterred, Lee Kuan Yew continued in 1965 to press for noncommunal equality and spearheaded the Malaysian Solidarity Convention to fight the Alliance, targeting the sensitive states of Sabah and Sarawak.[23] In the summer of 1965 there were serious race riots in Singapore, but even before this manifest unrest, it seems, the Tunku Abdul Rahman, prime minister of Malaysia, had concluded that Singapore's secession would be desirable for Malaysian stability.[24]

The Secessor State Declares Its Intent to Withdraw

This event happens abruptly. It can be a collective decision or a personal one, but it is registered at a precise moment in time. For example, the Jamaican referendum of September 1961 was immediately followed by a declaration that Jamaica would quit the Federation of the West Indies. In the case of Singapore, the situation was reversed: the Malaysian leader consulted his inner cabinet about Singapore's exit in July 1965 and declared his decision to the government of Singapore upon his return to Kuala Lumpur on 5 August. The announcement that Singapore would leave the federation was made in the legislature on 9 August.

In the case of Austria-Hungary, the Hungarian diet drew up and approved a program for independence in early 1866. But war with Prussia was declared the following day. In July 1866, after the empire's stunning defeats, Deák, the leader of the Hungarian moderates, met the emperor and in a famous interview was asked what Hungary wanted now that the realm was so weakened. He replied, "No more after Sadowa than before."[25]

In the Norwegian case, the declaration took two forms. The first was a Storting vote in favour of the principle of dissolving the union, passed under the new coalition government in March 1905. Then the consular bill was passed in May, and it was duly vetoed, whereupon the Norwegian ministry resigned. The final act came on 7 June, when the Storting passed a resolution authorizing the ministry to continue as the government and to exercise the authority granted to the king under the constitution; it also dissolved the union.[26] This resolution passed unanimously.

The Predecessor State Accepts the Principle of Secession:
Negotiations Follow

This is a truism, *ex post facto*, but it reflects the most profound decision on the part of the leadership of the predecessor state – to accept
that secession will occur. In the cases examined here, it was a bitter
and very difficult decision. But the decision makes the fundamental
difference between peaceful secessions and those that are violent.
This immense concession then sets in train all that follows, and the
first item, obviously, is negotiations.

In the case of the breakup of colonial federations, it was the imperial power that generally had to accept that secession would occur.
In late 1962, for instance, Britain recognized the right of Nyasaland
(later Malawi) to secede from the Central African Federation; this
led directly to a similar demand by Northern Rhodesia and to the
Victoria Falls Conference in June 1963. Similarly, the British government accepted both the Jamaican referendum result and the decision
of Trinidad to seek its own independence.[27] In Malaysia-Singapore,
the normal situation was reversed. It was Lee Kuan Yew who had to
swallow the bitter pill presented by Malaysia and to negotiate as best
as possible around the terms of secession which were presented to
him and his colleagues.[28] The acceptance in Austria-Hungary was
through the emperor, who had come to the conclusion that the weakened realm could be salvaged only by placating the Magyars through
recognizing the principle of Hungarian independence. After his meeting with Deák, negotiations were opened.

Acceptance was most difficult in Sweden, where the populace as
well as the government and the king were deeply shocked by the
Storting's vote to sever the union. Yet on the same day, despite some
ministers' advocacy of war, the cabinet decided to proceed peacefully. This decision was confirmed by an extraordinary meeting of
all party leaders the following day. Negotiation represented the only
viable course of action, because Norwegian opinion was solid for
sovereignty, war would be ruinous, and the Great Powers would isolate
Sweden if it tried to maintain the union forceably. Even Conservative newspapers declared that, after the Storting vote, the union had
become "devoid of value for Sweden and therefore the use of force
was unthinkable."[29]

Secession Is a Momentous, Galvanizing Event

Despite contemporary slogans such as the "velvet divorce" or the
rupture tranquille, even peaceful secessions are times of much dis-

ruption and uncertainty. They mark profound changes in the relations between peoples and between states, and this is fully recognized at the time. Secession opens new possibilities and closes off
options, and it does so in a compressed time period in which the
actors and the arguments and choices are known to have big long-term
consequences. Even peaceful separations are marked by considerable ferment.

There are always changes at the élite level. In the Hungarian case,
for example, new leadership emerged in the moderate party during
the early transition (in the person of Count Andrássy), and in Austria the minister-president resigned in some confusion after the major elements of the Ausgleich had been agreed. Coalitions formed
and reformed in both Norway and Sweden. As will be discussed below, the internal politics and policies of the defederating units change
a great deal, reflecting the turmoil of the transition.

There is also considerable mass unrest and excitement. In Singapore,
racial tension and conflict continued after secession; in Austria, the
Czechs and other minorities saw new opportunities for autonomy
during the uncertainty of 1866–67, a prospect that led to external
appeals to Russia and internal agitation by Prussia;[30] and in
Norway-Sweden, secession was marked by huge public demonstrations in both countries, much chauvinism and tension, and the mobilization of defensive forces even as the negotiations about
disengagement were taking place.[31]

The Government Is Broadened and Strengthened on Each Side:
There Is a Premium on Solidarity

In order to undertake fundamental constitutional change, the governments of both the predecessor and the seceding state are strengthened. As will be discussed below, attention is focused on the immediate
need to reach a settlement rather than on other constitutional matters. Hence, it is the leaders in place who assume responsibility for
negotiating secession. And in non-bipartite cases, it is the central
government that negotiates. In the extreme case – Malaysia-Singapore
– the state governments (including Sabah and Sarawak, which had
entered the expanded federation with Singapore) were not even informed about the secession arrangements.[32]

For their part, the national governments seek to augment their
authority by broadening their bases of support. This occurs both in
the period leading to the declaration of intent to secede and in the
transitional period of negotiations. In Hungary, for example, the platform of demands that issued from the diet in 1866 was forged by a

special committee of 67 members, representing all factions, and by a strong executive committee of 15 members. In Singapore and Malaysia, PAP and the Alliance, respectively, had overwhelming majorities, so broadening was not necessary. But in Norway and Sweden, where the transition was particularly tense, this process was very evident.

In Norway there was a tremendous premium on solidarity in the spring of 1905 as the crisis developed. This is not to say that partisan considerations were entirely forgotten, for the radical Venstre party pressed a hard line on the consular issue. That matter decided, however, Norwegian politicians submerged their differences. A special committee of the Storting was established, and it took much initiative. Then a new coalition government was formed with broad representation, and until the 7 June vote and during the subsequent negotiations, this ministry relied heavily on the committee.[33] In Sweden, after the vote, an extraordinary committee of the Riksdag was formed, and it helped frame the national response to the Norwegian declaration, which consisted of a set of conditions to govern the secession. Then, in July, a coalition cabinet was assembled. Since this cabinet included the opposition Liberals, it had a much broader composition than any preceding Swedish government.[34]

The crisis of secession, then, unites each side politically. And the sides polarize. These effects are undoubtedly less thoroughgoing than what occurs in contested secessions, when war entirely divides the states and forces internal unity. Nevertheless, those responsible for negotiations seek truly national support by submerging partisan and ideological differences for the duration of the crisis. And this effect is not confined to political élites. The plebiscite about secession forced upon the Norwegians by the Swedes as a precondition of negotiations carried by 367,149 to 184.[35] Such a margin could never have been achieved six months earlier. The process of secession, or the crisis of the transition, itself generates internal unity on each side.

The Negotiations Involve Few Participants

Some cases examined here involve quasi-democracies characterized by a limited franchise and deference to regal or charismatic leaders. Nevertheless, it still is striking that the negotiating teams have been very small, and this is the more remarkable when this feature is combined with the broadening of support discussed above. But the paradox vanishes when one realizes that the teams incorporate the strongest leaders of all factions and that the same solidarity that arises from the national dimension of the crisis permits the delegation of substantial power to a very few representatives.

In Singapore-Malaysia, only the prime ministers were involved, aided by a few key members of their cabinets.[36] In East Africa (where a projected federation collapsed), just as the Nairobi Declaration had been the product of the anticolonial leaders from each state, so were the failed negotiations about federation conducted by them. In Austria-Hungary, the predecessor state was effectively represented by the minister of foreign affairs, Baron Ferdinand Beust, who was appointed in November 1866 and who alone conducted the serious negotiations, which began in January 1867. In the case of Norway and Sweden, one immediate and critical issue to be settled was whether Norway should invite a member of the Swedish royal house (the Bernadottes) to take the throne; secret negotiations undertaken by one man produced a solution – Prince Carl of Denmark – within a month (though confirmation was delayed until after the main negotiations were through, because the election of a king had implications for international recognition).[37] The main negotiations about secession and its terms, conducted at the Karlstad Conference, involved Norwegian and Swedish delegations of only four members each.

The Separation Is Accomplished Quickly

Negotiations about secession are not protracted. When a unit breaks up peacefully, the two sides disengage quickly, and the negotiations concern a relatively short list of items that are settled in principle. Singapore-Malaysia is the extreme case. The Tunku Abdul Rahman returned from London to Kuala Lumpur on 5 August 1965 and summoned Lee Kuan Yew in order to present him with the separation agreement, which was signed on 7 August and was passed through the legislature on 9 August, effective immediately.[38] The Victoria Falls Conference that dissolved the federation of Rhodesia and Nyasaland took place in less than a week in June–July 1963; the federation was terminated formally in December of that same year. The Jamaican referendum in favour of secession took place in mid-September 1961, and the Federation of the West Indies was wound up in May 1962. The Karlstad Conference opened on 31 August 1905, and negotiations were completed on 22 September; the Storting then approved the arrangements on 30 September, the Riksdag legislated the abrogation of the Act of Union on 16 October, the king abdicated, and on 18 November the Storting unanimously elected Prince Carl of Denmark as Haakon VII.

The content of negotiations, of course, is primarily about the terms and conditions of disengagement. Even when it is not limited to this and when the framework for future relationships is also being established, events still move quickly. In the Austria-Hungary case, a complex set of institutions was established under the Ausgleich. While these were patterned on the Hungarian proposal of 1866, serious negotiations began only in January 1867. By mid-February the Hungarian constitution was restored, along with a responsible ministry, and Hungary approved the Ausgleich on 29 May. In Austria, approval was delayed by an election and by the insistence that all financial arrangements be finalized; nevertheless, the Reichstat enacted the Compromise on 21 December 1867. Thus, the institutional structure of what Lloyd George called this "ramshackle realm" was settled within a year.

Foreign Powers Play an Important Role

This generalization holds in every case. The dissolution of the new Commonwealth federations was crucially dependent on Great Britain's approval of terms, and also on the probabilities of international recognition. In Malaysia-Singapore, the Confrontation with Indonesia made precipitous action more possible (and more necessary, from Malaysia's standpoint). But Indonesia also offered potential new markets to Singapore, which quickly assumed a friendlier stance towards it; in fact, after Singapore withdrew from the Combined Defence Council in March 1966, Indonesia aimed to establish normal relations with the new state.[39] Meanwhile, despite Singapore's moves towards both nonalignment and a new relationship with the United States, its partners in the existing Anglo-Malayan Defence Agreement insisted that it continue to cooperate in defence with Malaysia.[40]

In Austria-Hungary, the threatened international position of the empire was an underlying cause of disengagement. In the longer term, relations with Germany (through the 1879 Dual Alliance against Russia) also helped maintain the newly established confederal system of the Ausgleich. This system mitigated the fear of absorption into Germany of the inhabitants of Cisleithania (especially the minorities) while diminishing the threat posed to the Magyars by the southern Slavs.[41] More generally, the secession was peaceful and the new arrangement worked because outside powers – Germany, Turkey, and Russia – each could pose as an ally of some internal minorities and therefore presented threats to others.[42]

Norway-Sweden provides more examples. As the consular crisis mounted, the Norwegians immediately understood how important would be international recognition of their new state. This underlay both a vigorous public relations campaign among the Great Powers and the decision to continue a monarchical system (with a Bernadotte as king, if necessary).[43] As well, fear of outside intervention in Scandinavia certainly helped lead both sides towards compromise when, even during the Karlstad Conference, each country contemplated war.[44]

The Settlement Involves a Relatively Short List of Items

In cases of peaceful secession, negotiations centre on a few significant matters. This certainly is not a sufficient condition for a quick resolution of the crisis, but it does appear to be a general feature of these secessions. The two parties settle the most pressing issues in framework agreements and leave other matters and details to be worked out later.

The Singapore-Malaysia separation agreement, for instance, has only eight articles. It recognizes Singapore's sovereignty, commits the parties to a treaty on external defence and mutual assistance (spelling out four principles which mainly confer military rights on Malaysia), establishes the principle of economic cooperation, repeals the economic union provisions of the 1963 constitution, and releases Malaysia from its guarantees of Singapore's debt. In the case of Norway and Sweden, the Swedes imposed the prenegotiation condition of a plebiscite to sound Norwegian opinion. The actual negotiations concerned only: (1) Sweden's demand that the recently built Norwegian forts along the frontier be razed; (2) the establishment of a 10-kilometre neutral zone along the border; (3) guarantees for the unimpeded migration of the Lapps; (4) equal rights for transit and access to transfrontier watercourses (for railroads and water for log drives); and (5) a general arbitration treaty to govern future disputes between the two countries.[45]

Finally, in the case of Austria-Hungary, the negotiations concerned not only the principles of disengagement – the restoration of the Hungarian constitution, a fully responsible ministry, and the coronation of Franz Joseph as king of Hungary – but also the mechanisms for future coordination. These were complex, involving a small number of common ministers, decennial agreements about each state's contributions to the common expenses and about the common tariff schedule, and a confederal system of "delegations" from each state to approve annual budgets. But much of this was left to be fleshed out in subsequent discussions and later practice. Hungary approved the arrangement even before the first fixing of tax contributions had been made.

The Secession Is Accomplished Constitutionally

Peaceful secessions, without exception, are achieved through established legal processes. Even such fundamental constitutional change occurs constitutionally. There is no legal rupture of the type associated with unilateral declarations of independence. Basically, this is a straightforward consequence of the predecessor state accepting the principle that secession will occur.

In Austria-Hungary, the restoration of the Hungarian constitution was effected through a royal letter, and the Ausgleich was properly passed by the diet. Similarly, the Austrian diet amended the 1861 constitution to bring it into conformity with the new arrangement, and these changes to fundamental laws were duly sanctioned by the emperor. In the case of Norway-Sweden, established rules prevailed as the Act of Union was abrogated by the two legislatures, the king abdicated from his Norwegian throne, and the new king was properly elected and crowned. In Singapore-Malaysia, although it took the Malaysian legislature only three hours to do so, the constitutional amendment that eliminated Singapore from the federation was passed by the required two-thirds majority.[46] The generalization also holds for the new colonial federations that broke up: each failure was "marked by a constitutional act, like federation itself."[47] Even in the case of Iceland's separation from Denmark, in 1944 in the midst of war, when the Nazis controlled Denmark and the British were in Iceland, the matter was accomplished constitutionally. Iceland invoked a clause in the Act of Union that allowed for unilateral termination of the Act, and the decision was confirmed, as required, by a national plebiscite.[48]

There Are No Other Substantial Constitutional
Changes in Either State

This is a rather surprising fact, for one might anticipate that such a fundamental change as secession might either force or allow for other constitutional alterations. But this is not the case. The reasons appear to be twofold. The predecessor state and the seceding state especially seek stability, the first for damage control and the other for international credibility. Second, for the significant policy changes which each state generally does undertake, constitutional amendment is not a prerequisite.

In any event, there are some limited exceptions. In some short-lived colonial federations, the exit of one state – Jamaica, Nyasaland – led to the collapse of the rest of the federation. In Austria-Hungary, much of the drive for the new arrangements came from ethnic tension, not only between the two major ethnic groups but also between each group and internal minorities. Hungary's Magyar majority was well served by the traditional constitution, and no post-secession change occurred there. But in Austria, secession was accompanied by a vigorous debate about the degree of centralization that should obtain within the realm, with the non-Germanic minorities pressing the case for local autonomy. In the end, constitutional changes were enacted to confer the residual power on the regional diets.[49] But provincial legislation still required the emperor's approval, and the crown also appointed the provincial governors and the presidents of the regional diets; moreover, in 1873, direct elections to the central parliament replaced indirect election by those diets, thus further weakening their power. There were policy changes, however. In Hungary, the separation allowed the continuance and heightening of social conservatism, including a firm policy of Magyar supremacy that was pursued in the linguistic and educational fields. In Austria, in contrast, the German-speaking Liberal Party introduced important social and economic reforms.[50]

In Malaysia, there were post-secession constitutional changes associated with ethnic issues, which had been made acute by Singapore's both joining and leaving the federation. In 1967, Malay became the sole official language, except in Sabah and Sarawak. But this had been due to happen in any event under the 1957 constitution.[51] Further, in response to sectarian violence, discussion of racial issues was outlawed between 1969 and 1971, under constitutionally invoked emergency powers. For its part, Singapore established a constitutional commission in March 1966. But there was no change until 1969, and this was minor: the Presidential Council was established to advise on legislation and to scrutinize it. Again, while there was no constitutional change directly associated with secession, there was considerable policy change. Malaysia moved to diminish internal economic barriers. Singapore did much more. Under the slogan "Survival," the government moved towards *dirigisme*, towards the construction of a "tightly organized society," with national service, new labour legislation attractive to investors, and a general stance favouring order and economic growth.[52]

In the case of Norway-Sweden, policy changed in Sweden as the Liberals came to power in late 1905. But there was no constitutional change after secession. Norway provides a clear example of how secessionist states avoid unnecessary constitutional change, for its leaders decided to retain the monarchy so as not to offend the European powers (a choice ratified by plebiscite) and even extended an invitation to a son of the very monarch whose abdication would be occasioned by secession. There was no change in the form of government, for three main reasons: to avoid a constitutional crisis simultaneous with secession, to placate Swedish rage, and to attain quicker international recognition. Subsequently, Norway moved on several policy fronts to become one of the most liberal states in the world, but apart from an extension of the franchise, this did not involve internal constitutional restructuring.

Policies in the Two States Soon Begin to Diverge

In Austria-Hungary, secession produced two sovereign states. But in contrast to the other cases, it was accompanied by new institutions for coordination. The keystone of the system was the monarch, Franz Joseph, who was emperor of Austria and king of Hungary, and who chose separate ministries in each country as well as special, common ministers for foreign relations, the military, and the joint finances to support these functions. This structure was successful in maintaining a common defence, monetary, and tariff structure until the dual monarchy collapsed during World War I. But there was tremendous friction between the two states, and this grew over time. The tariff negotiations broke down in 1897; only Austrian tolerance permitted agreement on the level of financial contributions; and the Hungarians sought more influence over the national bank and the army. Moreover, domestic policies on minorities and religious matters began to diverge shortly after the Ausgleich was enacted; indeed, secession had come about in part to allow autonomy in these matters.

In Norway-Sweden, although domestic policies diverged along broad ideological lines, there was some coordination. It took place within the Scandinavian framework and was accomplished through informal mechanisms such as the Scandinavian Inter-Parliamentary Union (established in 1907), the Nordic Societies (established in 1919), and many voluntary associations.[53] In this, the common foreign policy of neutrality and isolation helped, as did the stabilizing presence of Denmark (and the later participation of Iceland and Finland). After the separation, the two (and three) countries sometimes passed parallel legislation, such as the Marriage Law of 1921–25, but this simply continued a tradition dating back to the monetary convention of the 1870s and the Bank Drafts Act of 1880.[54] Lindgren argues that the union of Norway and Sweden "itself formed a barrier" and that its dissolution "opened the way for an integration impossible under pre-1905 conditions."[55] But it would not do to overstate this case. The two countries never signed a mutual defence treaty, Norway enjoyed a Great Power guarantee of its borders, and the kings did not meet until 1914. The development of genuinely integrative institutions awaited the formation of the Nordic Council in 1951.[56]

The countries of the colonial federations did not tend to harmonize policies upon dissolution. In Central Africa, economic integration had been deepened considerably in the federation era, and existing trade patterns did continue, even with the renegade state of Southern Rhodesia.[57] But this was a consequence of Zambia's abject dependence on Rhodesian coal and hydroelectric power for its copper industry. Apart from this, integration eroded, notably when Malawi and Zambia issued their own currencies in 1963. Similarly, in East Africa, even though Tanganyika, Zanzibar, Kenya, and Uganda had an even longer history of cooperation – with a postal union dating from 1911, a customs union from 1917, and a common currency from 1920 – these soon deteriorated after the projected federation failed. By 1965 Tanzania was imposing quotas on Kenyan goods, and the currency union was fractured in 1966. Generally, economic policies came to diverge sharply, and there were also military tensions between the former partners.[58]

Singapore-Malaysia provides a striking instance of policy divergence. Article 6 of the separation agreement provided for cooperation in economic affairs and the establishment of joint committees and councils to promote it; but within a week of the secession, Singapore restricted imports of 187 manufactured goods from Malaysia. Malaysia retaliated. By October, the governments had agreed to revert to the status quo ante; but when Malaysia announced that it would work towards an internal common market within the federation, Singapore reimposed tariffs. It then established a system of work permits for non-citizens, and Malaysia set up immigration controls.[59] Despite some later relaxation of these measures, Singapore's foreign-labour policy was dictated exclusively by its domestic interests.[60] Further divisive measures followed. In 1967 the currency union was ended; Singapore withdrew from the Combined Defence Council, and there was little cooperation in this area; and Singapore was even thrown out of the Associated Chinese Chambers of Commerce in Malaysia.[61] There were no prime ministerial visits until the early 1970s.[62] As a consequence of nation-building policies on both sides, economic integration was weakened. In 1964 Malay Peninsula imports from or via Singapore were 37 per cent of the total, and exports were 28 per cent. This dropped to 9 and 20 per cent by 1975.[63] Although the federation itself had been short-lived, its breakup led to the erosion of an economy that had been becoming more integrated for decades.

Secession Is Irrevocable

There has never been a case of reunification after secession. Fundamentally, this is because of two factors. First, the whole project of the seceding state is to acquire more autonomy. The exercise of these greater powers would be compromised by integrative arrangements. More important, though, are the effects of the transition itself. The process of secession marks both élites and masses. It affects them profoundly. Not only is there the psychic break, with the recognition that the community is fractured, but there is also the internal solidarity forged in the process of disengagement. Unity on each side develops through the crisis and is built by a collective concentration on the "other." Hence, each community is solidified through the transition process, and even where there is not great animosity between the two citizenries, the crisis forges separate identities and interests that cannot subsequently be subsumed in a new union. As Watts delicately put it, "whenever secession has occurred, it has inevitably been accompanied by sharp political controversies which are not easily forgotten ... The resentments aroused by the circumstances occurring at the time of separation have tended to persist and to discourage the subsequent creation of a looser form of association between the territories concerned."[64]

CONCLUSION

There is little to add to this bare account of how peaceful secessions take place. Perhaps it is appropriate to emphasize, though, that these generalizations are quite robust. They hold true more or less (and mostly more) in circumstances separated by geography, culture, time, and degrees of democracy. It is also worth emphasizing that the process of the transition helps determine the long-term outcomes of the separation. In uncertain and unprecedented times, political leaders have considerable scope for taking decisions that have lasting consequences. By far the largest decision taken in the cases reviewed here was that the secession would not be contested. As well, choices are made about institutional arrangements, both domestically and between the two states, and these structures have enduring effects. Finally, it seems that this set of empirical generalizations is universal enough to form the framework for analysing the politics of how Quebec would secede from Canada. First, however, it will be useful to examine in greater detail one further case – the separation of Slovakia and the Czech Republic.

CHAPTER ELEVEN

The Breakup of Czechoslovakia

One recent case of peaceful secession deserves some special attention. This is the end of the Czech and Slovak Federal Republic, which occurred when the new sovereign states of Slovakia and the Czech Republic came into being on 1 January 1993. Comparative analysis could extend further, to the emergence of new states from the former Soviet Union and Yugoslavia, but some of these secessions were violent, and others were a consequence of the collapse of the central state. The Czech-Slovak separation had neither of these features. It is therefore the most recent case of peaceful secession, and it is the only one ever to have taken place in a modern, highly integrated, industrial economy, where there was also a full democracy, albeit a nascent and turbulent one.

The Czech-Slovak case, naturally, has many unique features. The country was in quite a different position from Canada, as well as from the other cases examined here. Nevertheless, most of the empirical generalizations found to characterize peaceful secessions also hold true for Czechoslovakia. This testifies to their robustness, validity, and potential application to a Quebec secession from Canada. On the other hand, there are certain noteworthy variations in the Czech-Slovak separation. These occurred, essentially, because this separation was the climax of a gradual process of polarization, one in which partisan forces in each unit found it politically profitable to engage in mutual antagonism, to emphasize conflict and disagreement, and ultimately to effect the breakup of the federation.[1]

BACKGROUND

Czechoslovakia was formed in 1920 out of the residue of World War I and the collapse of the Austro-Hungarian Empire. By this union, the Czechs were able to escape Austrian dominance while the Slovaks, who had never been considered an "historic" or self-governing people, were freed from Hungarian control. Within the new state, however, the Slovaks experienced a persistent sense of domination by Prague, and nationalist movements resisted the "Czechoslovakianism" of the early leaders as a Czech imposition.[2] One nationalist, conservative, and Roman Catholic party seized power in 1938 and declared independence with Hitler's support in 1939, just one day before Germany completely occupied the Czech lands. The Slovak fascist state under Jozef Tiso lasted until 1945.

After the Communist putsch in 1947–48, the country was run in a centralized fashion, both economically and politically. As part of the liberalization of the Dubcek government, a federal constitution was adopted in 1969. This created Czech and Slovak national councils, with separate executives and some legislative power, but after Soviet intervention and "normalization," Czechoslovakia was highly centralized for the next two decades.[3] Economic growth was rapid, especially in Slovakia, and more Slovaks entered both their national bureaucracy and the federal bureaucracy.

In late 1989, anti-regime demonstrations culminated in the Velvet Revolution. This was led by the large umbrella organizations, Civic Forum (CF), represented by Vaclav Havel, a noted dissident and playwright, and its Slovak counterpart, the Public Against Violence (PAV). In short order, the Communist government was swept away, Havel was elected president, and the reformers began the task of reshaping the system.[4] Through all of this, the state institutions remained intact. The Federal Assembly consisted of the House of the People (150 members, with 99 from the Czech Republic and 51 from Slovakia), and the House of Nations (75 members from each republic, sitting in separate chambers), both elected by proportional representation. The assembly chose the president, who selected a prime minister capable of assembling a government. Constitutional changes required a three-fifths majority in each of the three chambers. At the republic level, the structures were similar, except that the national councils were unicameral (with 150 members in Slovakia and 200 in the Czech Republic).

The first free elections were held in June 1990, and they produced a convincing victory for the CF-PAV coalition. This took 170 of the 300 Federal Assembly seats, and Civic Forum also won a clear majority in the Czech National Council. In the Slovak National Council,

PAV took 48 seats and formed a coalition government with the Christian Democratic Movement in Slovakia. Apart from the Communists, the other parties represented federally were ethnic and nationalist, and, ominously, the CF-PAV coalition did not gain control of the Slovak chamber of the House of Nations, which had to approve constitutional amendments.[5]

The renewed government continued to confront the huge challenges facing the country. One was coping with the political residue of the Communist regime. At the same time as democratization unleashed an efflorescence of political activity, the Communist past and questions about collaborators lent at times a sinister air to political competition in the country. There was as well the task of completely overhauling the administrative and legal structures of the state. Through 1990–91, new laws reformed the army, the educational system, the civil and penal codes, and the state administration.[6] The constitution was amended several times, and it was to be entirely rewritten; the republics were also to equip themselves with constitutions. Further, Czechoslovakia had to reposition itself internationally, negotiating an exit from the ebbing Eastern Bloc and affiliating with Western countries as well as with the World Bank, the International Monetary Fund, the Council of Europe, and the European Community (of which it became an associate member). Finally, the government undertook a rapid transformation towards a market economy, a program involving new laws about property rights, price controls, subsidies, foreign investment, trade relations, and the privatization of state companies.[7] While there was consensus about the need for transformation, there was hard debate about its speed and its differential regional impact. Slovak nationalists objected to rapid decontrol of prices and to subsidy cuts, and argued that some policies were unsuitable to their country's heavy industry, which was geared to the East Bloc.[8] But there were strong free-marketers in the federal cabinet, including Vaclav Klaus, the minister of finance. They pushed rapid reform, even though polls showed in 1991 that far fewer Slovaks than Czechs were satisfied with their economic situation, that few Slovaks thought the central government treated them fairly, and that a majority of Slovaks favoured gradualism in economic liberalization.[9] These attitudes provided fertile ground for nationalist critics of the federal system.

POLARIZATION

The most striking overall feature of the Czech-Slovak separation was political polarization. This is a process of growing mutual hostility between two communities, accompanied by a sense among members of each that their interests are distinct and can only be met through separation. This phenomenon was driven largely by politicians, but it was manifest in public opinion. After the June 1990 elections, when constitutional revision came onto the political agenda, a poll found that only 6 per cent of the population (5 per cent of Czechs and 8 per cent of Slovaks) favoured dividing the country into two independent states. The responses broke down as shown in table 4.[10] Hence, 72 per cent of Czechs and 57 per cent of Slovaks favoured a federation. The ill-defined "confederal" option, which was often vaguely associated with sovereignty, attracted twice as much support in Slovakia as in the Czech Republic, but it was still a minority position.

By July 1992, at the time of the next elections, 3 per cent of Czechs favoured confederation and 16 per cent wanted two independent states; on the Slovak side the figures were 30 and 16 per cent. But by September 1992, the Institute for Public Opinion Research reported that 46 per cent of Czechs favoured a split and 45 per cent were opposed; the Slovak figures were 41 and 46 per cent. While the two polls did not ask identical questions, public opinion clearly had shifted towards separation in both republics, and especially in the Czech lands, both before and after the elections. More important, over 80 per cent of both Czechs and Slovaks agreed in September that the separation was inevitable.[11] By October 1992, Czech opinion had hardened further: 37 per cent of Slovak respondents thought the separation was necessary, compared with 56 per cent in Bohemia and 43 per cent in Moravia.[12]

These data show the effects of polarization as the republics moved towards separation. But the process was a gradual one. It was marked, first, by the opening of extreme nationalist positions in Slovakia. This was done in part by the Slovak National Party (SNP), which moved to clearly advocate independence after its unexpected success in the 1990 elections. Less weighty groups of intellectuals and radicals also played an important part in making a series of nationalist thrusts between 1990 and 1992. The parties of the left, for their own purposes, were neutral on the national dimension or else supportive, and the centrist parties were pulled towards nationalist positions or were split. They were in the awkward position of having to decide whether to condemn the extreme manifestations of sentiments which, they perceived, most Slovaks shared in muted form.

The first crisis was over the very name of the state, in early 1990. During the "hyphen controversy," Slovak deputies insisted on a formulation that would not echo the domineering Czechoslovakianism of the past; hence the choice of the Czech and Slovak Federal Repub-

Table 4
Constitutional Preferences in the Czech and Slovak Federal Republic, June 1990

Preference	Throughout Czechoslovakia	Czech Republic	Slovak Republic
Common state with large powers vested in central government	33%	42%	16%
Common state with large powers vested in Czech and Slovak national governments	34	30	41
Confederation	21	16	30
Two completely independent states	6	5	8
Do not know or other alternatives	6	7	5

lic. More serious was a language crisis in September 1990, when nationalists demanded that Slovak become the sole official language and that minority rights be restricted (measures directed mainly against the Hungarian, not the Czech, minority). Amidst street demonstrations, hunger strikes, and university boycotts, a more moderate law was passed, but it still made Slovak the official language, limited non-Slovak official communications, and eliminated official bilingual signs.[13] In March 1991 another crisis erupted when intellectuals and the SNP published the Declaration of the Sovereignty of Slovakia, which envisaged full independence, asserting that Slovak laws would take precedence over federal ones and that the country would endow itself with a separate army, currency, and foreign policy before signing a treaty on a common state with the Czech Republic. The radicals urged the National Council to approve the declaration.[14]

In this context, symbolic acts acquired great significance, even when they were carried out by very few people. Within a week of the declaration's appearance, a crowd of a few thousand dedicated a cross on Tiso's grave. The next day, five thousand people gathered in the Slovak National Uprising Square in Bratislava to hear a recording of Tiso's speech proclaiming Slovakia's independence fifty-two years before. Unexpectedly, and apparently by happenstance, President Havel turned up at the rally, only to be jostled, spat upon, and shouted down with jeers of "Judas" and "Go back to Prague." Even before this, the government of the Czech Republic had reacted to the pro-Tiso events: a formal statement on 13 March declared, "We have always understood 14 March, and continue to do so, to mean that at that time Slovakia found itself in a difficult situation in which, under duress, it chose the lesser of two evils. If, tomorrow, we were to be persuaded that our understanding was incorrect, this could not fail to affect our attitudes toward Slovak politics."[15]

Polarization was accelerated when the great anti-Communist political movements fragmented. After Vaclav Klaus became chairman of Civic Forum (CF) in October 1990, some right-leaning deputies formed a separate club within the organization. At a January 1991 congress of CF, Klaus and his allies pushed through a resolution to create a party from the movement: members of all groups allied within CF would have to join the party directly. Some groups left, but others formed the Civic Movement, retaining the old, loose organizational form, while Klaus's group soon became the Civic Democratic Party (CDP), a normal, right-of-centre political party with a strong emphasis on economic reform.

In Slovakia, the Public Against Violence (PAV) also split. This was caused by Vladimir Meciar, the premier. In February 1991 he attempted to become chairman of PAV, to make it a formal party, and to emphasize the nationalistic elements of its platform, but members rejected these initiatives. Amidst accusations about his use of police information to blackmail ministers, Meciar and fourteen others walked out of an emergency PAV council meeting on 5 March, in the midst of the developing nationalist crisis.[16] Meciar's new group, the Movement for a Democratic Slovakia (MDS), emerged as a separate party, with seventeen federal deputies in its caucus. Meciar was removed as premier, but forming the MDS was a strategic move, given the intense constitutional negotiations that were underway in the spring of 1991. The Slovak Christian Democrats had advocated that a "state treaty" between the two republics precede and underpin the new federal constitution. Since the Slovak Communists resisted a strong central government that could drive rapid reform, and since the SNP was overtly sovereigntist, this meant that three major parties with a total of 75 of the 150 National Council seats favoured a confederal approach to redesigning the common state. By breaking from the federalists and splitting PAV, Meciar could hope to capture nationalist support and take the lead of this imminent majority, for his MDS was more moderate than the SNP, it was less tarnished than the Communists, and it was more coherent than the Christian Democrats.

The polarization around the constitutional issue was focused by Klaus and Meciar. Conflict about the basic form of the state was politically profitable for each of them. On 14 March the constituent committee of Meciar's new group had advocated a federation created "from below" by the republics as a stage in building a "sovereign and democratic Slovak Republic."[17] Then, after losing the premiership, Meciar was in the ideal situation of being able to criticize federal government policies while not taking any responsibility for them, and he could well position his MDS on the constitutional front by advocating both sovereignty and a vague confederal form of association between the republics. In September 1991, for instance, he rejected the compromise outcome of talks between the presidiums of the two National Councils, declaring that Slovakia should adopt its own constitution because "the time has come for the Slovak Republic to demand its right to self-determination and achieve sovereignty."[18] As the Christian Democrats and the loose remnants of PAV suffered internal tensions by having to take responsibility for fundamental decisions, Meciar gained the upper hand: by January 1992, the MDS had the support of 30 per cent of Slovaks, while the Communists were at 16 per cent and the Christian Democratic Movement had only 13 per cent.[19]

On the Czech side, confronting radical Slovak thrusts, government incoherence, and delay of economic reform, there was partisan advantage to be won by taking a firm position on the constitution. Czech public opinion strongly favoured the continuation of a federation, with substantial powers for the central government. Federalist forces were dominant within both the government of the Czech Republic, led by Petr Pithart of the Civic Movement, and the federal coalition government, led by Marian Calfa of PAV. The government of the Czech Republic generally took a pragmatic and conciliatory line on constitutional matters through 1990 and early 1991, and on the federal front, the negotiations in 1991 over the "state treaty" between the two republics were effectively led by Havel and leaders of the federal coalition. However, soon after the formation of the Civic Democratic Party (CDP), Klaus and his party rejected the notion of a state treaty, stood against having the republics ratify the federal constitution, and declared that only a "functional" federation would be acceptable to Czechs.[20] In short, he advocated the status quo or an even more centralized federation. When the federal government in November 1991 listed its own minimal requirements for the common state – including, notably, the unity of the economy with respect to currency, tariffs, economic laws, and macroeconomic regulation – Czech premier Pithart made a conciliatory address to the Slovaks. This was roundly condemned by Klaus as offering too many concessions and leaving the door open to confederalism. Klaus's line was clear and hard. He stood squarely against unrealistic Slovak demands and damaging delays in settling economic and constitutional issues. By the end of 1991, right-wing and centralist parties were strongest in the Czech republic and Klaus's CDP had 20 per cent support, twice that of its nearest rival.[21]

In February 1992, an ad hoc commission established by the Czech and Slovak national councils finally reached agreement on a draft state treaty. But it was rejected three days later by the presidium of the Slovak National Council, because the government split over this agreement, which presumed the continued existence of the common state (four of the Christian Democratic Movement's presidium members voted against the treaty). In the wake of the vote, the Slovak National Council suspended further talks. The Christian-Democratic premier, Jan Carnogursky, had supported the treaty, but it was attacked by nationalist politicians, including Meciar, who declared it "a betrayal of the contemporary national movement," and said, "I am afraid that in order to be able to say that he has done something, Mr Carnogursky sacrificed the basic interests of the Slovak Republic, to be able to present a certain document that he was able to get through. This is not allowed."[22] The federal prime minister, Marian Calfa, declared that the separation of the Czech and Slovak republics had begun with that rejection, an historic move towards the breakup of the state: "In my view we have now set in motion a centrifugal process for the two parts of our common state – the Czech lands and Slovakia."[23]

Indeed this was true. Polarization increased in the time before the elections of 5–6 June 1992. Support drained from the centre and flowed to the political formations that had most staunchly defended autonomy for Slovakia, on the one hand, and a "functional" federation that could continue economic reforms, on the other. While not calling for complete independence during the campaign, Meciar did advocate a declaration of Slovak sovereignty, a Slovak constitution, and a president for Slovakia, as well as a separate central bank. Klaus's CDP and its right-wing allies rejected such measures, calling for a complete split if an effective central government could not be maintained because of Slovak intransigence.

The 1992 election results completed the polarization at the political level.[24] First, only two parties campaigned in both parts of Czechoslovakia. One was the extreme-right Republicans; the other was Klaus's CDP. Second, the existing federal political élite was massively rejected, for only 17 per cent of the Federal Assembly's deputies were re-elected. Klaus was the only cabinet member returned. Third, the centrist parties were eliminated as a force. The moderate successors to CF and PAV gained less than 5 per cent of the vote and no seats; the Slovak Christian Democrats received only 9 per cent; and while the Communist parties managed 14 per cent in each republic, the Social Democrats won less than 5 per cent in Slovakia and only 8 per cent in the Czech lands. Fourth, the victors were Klaus and Meciar. The CDP–Christian Democrat alliance took 34 per cent of the Czech vote, securing 48 of 150 seats in the House of the People and 37 of 75 in the Czech chamber of the House of Nations. Meciar's MDS took 34 per cent of the Slovak vote, winning 24 seats in the House of the People and 33 of the 75 seats in the Slovak chamber of the House of Nations. The MDS had allies in the 9 SNP deputies in the Slovak chamber and also in the 13 Communists, but even without them it could block any constitutional change at the federal level, as could Klaus's CDP. Of equal significance were the republic results. The CDP gained 30 per cent of the votes and 76 of the 200 seats in the Czech National Council, while Meciar's MDS took 38 per cent of the votes and 74 of the 150 Slovak National Council seats.[25] These results suggested, and initial discussions confirmed, that forming a federal government with any positive and coherent program would be impossible, since it would have to consist of Czech rightists and Slovak leftists and nationalists.

With polarization so complete, separation became more probable. Still, public opinion was far less extreme than the positions taken by the politicians. Party fragmentation and the disorganization of the centre had helped bring aggressively led, extreme formations to power in each republic. The main dynamic was one of mutual repulsion, or, more accurately, "mutually profitably antagonism." The evolution of this phenomenon is depicted in figure 1. First, as in panel (a), radicals open up new, extreme positions (such as publishing the Declaration of the Sovereignty of Slovakia or celebrating the Tiso state). This expands the parameters of discourse on the constitutional dimension, and in the absence of a strong countervailing defence of centralization or the status quo, the median opinion in Slovakia shifts towards separation. Equally important are the effects on the other populace – the Czechs. The median opinion there may not move much, but the range of opinion also broadens. A rejection by Czech leaders, not only of extremism but also of softer decentralist or confederal options (as in late 1991) then further shifts the Slovak median position. Antagonistic rejection by the Slovaks of the status quo or of apparently generous reform proposals then pushes Czech opinion further towards separation. In panel (d), which roughly corresponds to the situation after the June 1992 elections, Meciar's position is depicted as continuing to be more extreme than the median Slovak opinion, while Klaus has shifted from being more centralist than the median Czech to being much more inclined towards separation. At this point, each leader is attempting to move his domestic opinion towards the extreme position. He does so by interpreting the moves of the other as showing there is no more reasonable alternative than the extreme one that he favours. Meanwhile, difficult negotiations, insults, flat rejections, and threats all help consolidate each leader's domestic opinion while pushing the other's domestic constituency towards the position he advocates. Antagonism between the leaders is beneficial to each of them as opinion polarizes and consolidates.

Figure 1: POLARIZATION OF CONSTITUTIONAL OPINION

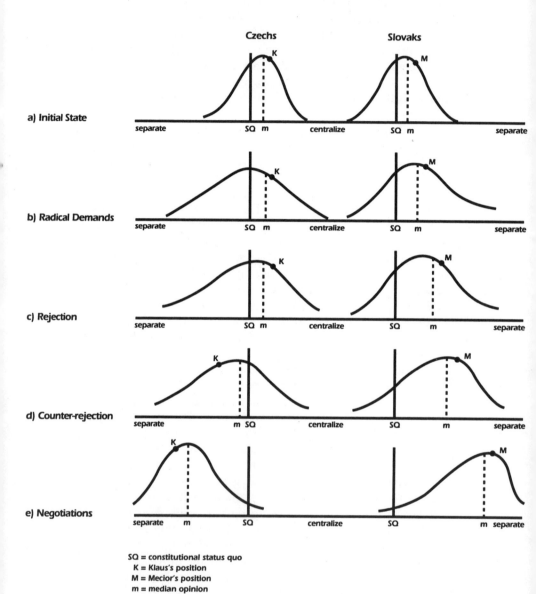

SQ = constitutional status quo
K = Klaus's position
M = Mecior's position
m = median opinion

Polarization continued after the elections. Klaus and Meciar, along with key party leaders, met on 9, 11, and 17 June. Klaus claimed that Meciar wanted not a common state but an "economic and defence community," which the CDP would reject: "It is clear that our Slovak partner doesn't want a common state. For Mr Meciar the federation is over, and we are accepting this position more and more."[26] The CDP apparently did propose a looser federation, but Meciar's party insisted that the republics be sovereign in international law, and Klaus rejected this. Meciar told the press that the Czech side presented the extreme options of a "single, centralist state or disintegration" and that Klaus had called a confederal union of two sovereign entities a "joke."[27] Hence, Meciar argued, the Czechs "say Slovakia has to make a unilateral step leading to the total disintegration" of the federation: "That is not what we want."[28] But Klaus would not accept a confederal solution – the creation of a "nonstandard entity" that would not be "functional."

Two weeks after the election, the sides reached a "political agreement" about the shape and program of the federal government. It would be a weak, caretaker government with no prominent leaders and with only ten portfolios, four of which would be wound down. The agreement contemplated the probability of separation by committing the two sides to good relations and a constitutional resolution of the situation, which was to be achieved by the republican national councils by 30 September.[29] This agreement was widely interpreted as the death-knell of the federal republic, especially as Klaus, who had been asked by Havel to form a federal government, announced that he would stand for premier of the Czech republic instead.

But public opinion had not yet moved enough. Many citizens still advocated a referendum to unblock the constitutional impasse, and so did Havel himself. And the leaders were cautious. As Klaus summed up the political agreement, "We are not pre-determining the result, our duty is to take part in the creation of a process which will make it possible to see this choice with clarity."[30] But the Slovak side continued to press, and the Czech leadership interpreted the next moves as provocative and irreversible.

First, Slovak deputies blocked the re-election of Havel as president. He was defeated in two rounds of voting and lost in the second only in the Slovak chamber of the House of Nations. It is possible that the CDP caused the re-election to fail by forcing a quick second vote so that there was no time to negotiate a compromise; but for public consumption Klaus stressed "the fact that Vaclav Havel was elected by Czech deputies but not by the Slovaks" and said that the

Czech people would "regard this as yet another step casting doubt on the common state."[31] Soon after this demonstration of conflict and paralysis at the centre, each national council approved government programs that presumed the federation would be dissolved. The Czech program declared that the government "must take all measures needed for the republic to be able to exist as an independent state."[32]

Then, on 17 July, the Slovak National Council finally passed the Declaration of Sovereignty. It was carried by 113 votes to 24, with 10 abstaining and 3 absent. The opponents were the Christian Democrats and the coalition representing the Hungarian minority (which was steadfastly against a separation that could threaten their rights). This was an intensely emotional event. Church bells pealed throughout the country, and crowds surged and celebrated in Bratislava. Meciar declared that the Slovaks had awaited the moment "for more than a thousand years."[33] In fact, the constitutional significance of the act was unclear, because the existing document already affirmed the right of each nation to self-determination. Meciar and the MDS argued that the declaration was a symbolic statement of this, rather than a binding, legal declaration of independence.

But it had consequences. Havel resigned within the hour. It was now too late for a referendum, he thought, and his powers were insufficient to allow him to defend the federation. Most important, the Slovaks were doing what he felt governments should not undertake – building "structures" before asking the citizens what they wanted.[34] His resignation and the declaration strengthened the Czechs' conviction that the separation would take place, and the presidium of the Czech National Council called for immediate talks on "a civilized dismantling of Czechoslovakia."[35]

These talks took place within a week, as Klaus and Meciar met again. Once more they acted as party leaders only, for accords would have to be approved by their governments and national councils and by the Federal Assembly. But now their "basic thesis" was "to attempt to achieve the legitimacy of the process of disintegration of the Federation."[36] They agreed to propose to the Federal Assembly by 30 September a draft constitutional amendment to dissolve the state and distribute its assets; the deadline for settling the constitutional impasse had become a deadline for agreeing on how to wind up the federation. The two republics were to negotiate treaties covering citizens' rights, foreign policy, defence, and a customs union. Working now on the assumption of "minimum common interests," the leaders could not agree on how to coordinate budgets and fiscal policy, which was seen as essential for maintaining a common currency, and so they could not settle the currency issue. Nevertheless, the process of separation was now in motion.

In August, though, there was evidence of some hesitation on the Slovak side when confederal proposals emanated from the MDS. But these were firmly rejected by the Czechs. Post-separation treaties would be preferable to a confederation as a means of ensuring cooperation. At the end of the month, another Klaus-Meciar summit reaffirmed the July agreements. It was decided that the federation would cease to exist on 1 January 1993, and a timetable was set for a "controlled transition to two separate states."[37] It was further agreed that a common currency would be maintained for an indefinite period, along with a joint army command; and that, to avoid future misunderstandings, the CDP and MDS caucuses would coordinate their strategies in the federal parliament.

The final move by the Slovak side then followed. On 1 September the National Council adopted a constitution for Slovakia. This was a "full" constitution. It provided that federal laws were valid only insofar as they did not contradict the constitution of Slovakia. In order to avoid a sharp rupture with the existing federal constitution, some clauses were to come into effect only in January 1993, but others, like those providing for a central bank and a customs service, could be operative as soon as the constitution took effect (which was to be 1 October). The formal signing took place in Bratislava Castle, after which Meciar and the SNP leader appeared on a balcony before wildly cheering crowds.

To the Czechs this was a grave step. As one parliamentary leader put it, "By adopting a full constitution, Slovakia has quit the federation, with all the possible consequences."[38] Indeed, as the public opinion polls reported above make clear, both the Czechs and the Slovaks had come to the same conclusion by the autumn of 1992. Polarization had proceeded so far that the separation was widely seen on both sides as desirable, and was even more widely regarded as inevitable.

THE EMPIRICAL GENERALIZATIONS
ABOUT PEACEFUL SECESSION

In most respects, the Czech-Slovak separation was characterized by the same features that have marked other instances of peaceful secession. As the process of polarization shows, however, there were noteworthy differences: there was no sharp, clear declaration by either side of its intent to secede, nor was there a corresponding acceptance of the principle; moreover, broad coalitions were not formed in each state to confront the national crisis. Each of these deviations from the general pattern merits exploration. They can be explained by the profound confusion and uncertainty that marked the re-emergence of democracy in Czechoslovakia, and the massive challenges facing its governments. More deeply, though, they were a consequence of the interplay of democracy and partisanship. Simply enough, there was not sufficient public support for separation. A referendum on sovereignty probably would not have carried in either republic until polarization had proceeded and the separation process was well advanced. No referendum was ever held. Instead, polarization took place because political formations were seeking profitable niches in a highly competitive system; then, in bilateral negotiations under high levels of uncertainty, the leaders could not reach a compromise settlement. Both Klaus and Meciar had been elected on clear platforms, and as it turned out neither could, or would, renounce his party's position.

The separatist initiative undoubtedly came first from Slovak leaders, but their moves were tentative. There was no authoritative declaration of an intent to secede until the full constitution was effective in October 1992. There were, instead, many near-declarations, and these were used as threats to win concessions in the constitutional negotiations. As early as November 1990, when an agreement on the new constitutional division of powers had been reached, Meciar and other Slovak leaders threatened to declare the supremacy of Slovak over federal laws, in order to deter changes to a strongly decentralizing amendment.[39] Then the Slovak government called for the state treaty between the two republics. This treaty would have built the common state on the foundation of two sovereign entities. Moreover, the federal constitution was to be adopted after the republican ones. To federalists, this threatened a serious constitutional discontinuity: neither republic was sovereign, so an interstate treaty could not be signed without violating the existing constitution whereby sovereignty resided in the federal state. Alternatively, the federation might have to be abolished before the treaty to recreate it was signed. This seemed absurd.

As constitutional negotiations continued through late 1991, the Slovak National Council toyed with passing the Declaration of Sovereignty, and Meciar and the MDS were already pressing for a full constitution to be adopted. But even the declaration could be read as a UDI that would create a constitutional rupture. A vote was postponed twice, in part because the Czech National Council had resolved that such a declaration would be an unconstitutional act, would represent secession, and would make the remaining republic the successor to the federal republic's international rights and obligations. Since Slovakia would be a renegade unit, it would have to seek international recognition and renegotiate treaties.Finally, the Slovak side rejected the draft state treaty, and negotiations ceased, dissolving into the hard 1992 election campaign. Then Meciar clearly advocated the declaration, a full constitution, and a president for Slovakia. After the election, and the uncompromising negotiations with Klaus and the CDP, these promises were kept.

The Czechs were slow to accept the principle of separation. It took time to appreciate the depth of the Slovak nationalism that emerged once the revolution made free expression possible, and it also took time for Czechs to be led to believe that these forces posed a greater threat to them than their own independence did, despite the costs of separation.

The long constitutional negotiations certainly were a source of frustration, both for citizens and for political leaders. Always there was a Slovak party ready to condemn as inadequate such arrangements as could be negotiated, and always, it seemed to the Czechs, this pulled the Slovak side to make new demands. The state treaty was particularly rich in ambiguity. To the Czech side it represented an agreement that would guide the drafting of the republican and federal constitutions. But Slovak politicians like Meciar could oscillate between interpreting the treaty as a way to wind down the central government to a minimal level or seeing it as a means to achieve sovereignty without taking risks, because the basic degree of interstate cooperation would have been established in advance.

Symbolic acts also provoked the Czechs. The hyphen controversy, language laws, celebrations of Tiso, disrespect for Havel – all were deeply offensive to many Czechs. At least as troublesome were the economic repercussions of constitutional and regional conflict. Allied with the left in both republics, the Slovak nationalists persistently delayed and modified the economic reforms which the CDP championed – reforms which appeared by the end of 1991 to have been remarkably effective and which Czechs increasingly came to support. Another irritant was the federal budget, to which the Czech contribution reportedly was ten times that of Slovakia. The eastern republic received about $300 million in subsidies in the first five months of 1991, and Czechs began to speak of the "money pipeline" flowing into Slovakia.[40] As Klaus and the CDP also stressed, the political uncertainty was impeding foreign investment. The country had fallen from the most attractive in Central Europe in 1991 to the level of Romania by mid-1992, and for a people anxious to join the Western market economies this was cause for serious concern.

There was also the threat of internal fragmentation. Autonomist parties in Moravia and Silesia were articulating regional aspirations and grievances. The issue was whether to develop as lands within the Czech Republic, which each was, or to demand recognition as a republic within a tripartite federation, the third element being Bohemia. Unrest in the regions produced several major demonstrations, and for a time the tripartite notion was disingenuously encouraged by the Slovak Christian Democrats. But if such a federation emerged from the constitutional morass and if Slovakia then seceded, the Czechs would be left in a difficult position.

Under all these influences, the Czechs moved to accept and prepare for separation. Republican leaders had left much initiative in the constitutional talks with the federal authorities and Vaclav Havel, but the president warned repeatedly about the possibility of secession and advocated a referendum to settle the issue. This helped force the Czechs to contemplate a future – and so to consider themselves in the present – as Czechs rather than as Czechoslovaks. On 10 March 1991, for example, in rejecting the Slovak proposal for a state treaty, Havel said (in words that could be read by the Slovaks as old-fashioned Czechoslovakianism) that there was "simply no Czech partner for such a treaty." At the same time, however, he declared, "The breakup of the state is an alternative we must think about seriously." Thinking about breakup inevitably forced the Czechs to look on their republican National Council as the counterpart of the secessionist Slovakia.[41]

This shift was assisted by power-sharing arrangements. Demanded by Slovakia, widened areas of jurisdiction were also conferred on the Czech Republic. Beyond this was a deeper dynamic. Czechoslovakia was a two-state federation, a bi-national union, so the secessionist state had a natural interlocutor in its Czech partner. As the republics assumed power and as polarization moved them towards separation, the central government could simply wither away. This is not true of many other federations, where the central government, not without difficulty in maintaining the cohesion of other states or provinces, must be the interlocutor of the secessionist state. Moreover, as the central government and legislature contain representatives from the potentially seceding state, they cannot readily acknowledge the possibility of fragmentation before it occurs, even to the point of commissioning reports and contemplating scenarios. But in the Czech-Slovak case, it was possible for the centre to become redundant as initiative, legitimacy, and negotiating power shifted to the two republics.

The Czech government did move. During the March 1991 crisis, the National Council established a commission under the premier to examine "alternative solutions for the arrangement of the state."[42] (In response, Meciar urged that Slovakia do the same thing.) At a meeting of the Czech National Council in May, scenarios for separation were discussed. The debate was not public, but the projections had been prepared under official sanction, and soon the Czech government had released a report on the economic implications of separation.[43]

More concrete action followed, in part because of the harder line taken by Klaus's CDP, which insisted that separation might be preferable to a federation that was not "functional." The Czechs pressed for a clear resolution of constitutional issues, and when the Slovak parliament debated the Declaration of Sovereignty in late 1991, the Czech National Council resolved that its passage would be unconstitutional and that if it was passed the Czech Republic would do whatever was necessary to "secure its own independent existence."[44] In early 1992 the government approved construction of an oil pipeline from Germany to Bohemia, thereby reducing its potential dependence on imports from Russia through Slovakia. When the Slovaks established a Ministry of International Affairs, the Czech Republic did too. The breakdown of negotiations over the state treaty, therefore, found a government that was increasingly familiar with the prospect of its own sovereignty.

The Czech people were not quite persuaded. But many did support Klaus. Although his campaign emphasized economic policy, he made it clear that the Czech Republic needed to become as coherent as Slovakia, rather than drifting in a pattern where "a Slovak representation is emancipating itself and a Czech representation considers itself a not so clearly defined part of the Czechoslovak federation."[45] The CDP's first priority, Klaus claimed, was "a reasonable common state," but he also said, "If there won't be a reasonable united state, a reasonable federation, it will be necessary to decide in a quick and intelligent manner on a different way."[46]

After the initial meetings with Meciar and the MDS, Klaus was quite prepared to declare deadlock and to move towards separation. The MDS considered a confederation to be a common state, but as the June "political agreement" put it, the CDP "does not consider a confederation of two republics as two subjects of international law to be a common state, but a union of two independent states."[47] The difference between the parties arose fundamentally from the fact that sovereignty is indivisible, and the CDP position was clear: it "prefers the constitutional separation of the current state to this confederation."[48]

After this momentous decision, Klaus formed the new Czech government. His decision to operate at the republic level was welcomed by Meciar as a "very wise step" that would lead to interrepublican cooperation "on a balanced principle."[49] The aim of the CDP government now was to build a strong Czech state and to transform the republic into a "normal, democratic European country."[50] This was still a more extreme goal than Czech public opinion would support, but polarization was soon increased by the Declaration of Sovereignty and Havel's resignation.

In subsequent negotiations, the Czech position was strong. The republican leadership was prepared to accept the consequences of separation. It declared, for example, that the Czech Republic would, if necessary, assume responsibility for the federation's whole foreign debt.[51] This eliminated uncertainty and also removed the possibility of having to compromise on other issues to induce the Slovaks to pay their share. Similarly, Klaus was now in a position to renege on agreements. In early September he announced that there would be no joint military command after all and that the armed forces would be split by the time of separation. As well, renewed confederal proposals in August and October were squelched by the government: confederation in any form simply was "not in the interest of the Czech Republic."[52] Now it was the Czech side that blocked proposals for a referendum. In 1991 the Slovak nationalists had done so to prevent having their negotiating position undercut by a vote in favour of the federation. In late 1992 the Czech government rejected demands for a referendum as futile attempts to buy time or delay economic reform. In the end, it was a Czech threat of unilateral action that drove the Federal Assembly to pass a constitutional amendment dissolving the federation.

In the Czech-Slovak case, one more generalization fails to hold fully, again because of the gradual process of polarization. On neither side did the government form a broad coalition in order to deal with the crisis and negotiate. Instead, Klaus and Meciar both formed narrow coalitions that were just capable of dominating their respective legislatures. Essentially, this was because their positions were more extreme than those of their domestic constituencies. Fully representative coalitions would not have supported the decisive steps towards separation that the leaders were prepared to take. On the other hand, as polarization proceeded after the governments took action, there was a tremendous premium on national solidarity. Politicians opposed to the breakup or its terms found that resistance would be strategically difficult, because their opposition would weaken the bargaining position of their "own" national side. As the separation proceeded and public opinion grew to accept it, partisan leaders could not blemish the national mantle that Klaus and Meciar had assumed.

In Slovakia, Meciar entered a coalition with the SNP and formed an unusually tight government on 24 June 1992, after the political agreement was made with Klaus. The cabinet had only fourteen members, reduced from twenty-three. It included twelve MDS deputies, one member of the SNP, and one independent (the general commanding the eastern military district). All were of Slovak nationality. Moreover, Meciar realigned the senior bureaucracy by recalling fifty-three deputy ministers who had served the previous government. Even more unusual was the composition of the National Council presidium, which had formal responsibility for choosing the government and setting the council's agenda (not to mention, later, negotiating with the Czechs). It had fifteen members: seven from the MDS, three from the Party of the Democratic Left (former Communists), two from the SNP, two from the Christian Democratic Movement, and one from the coalition of Hungarian parties. This meant that the MDS-SNP coalition had a 60 per cent presidium majority despite having taken just 45 per cent of the vote. Moreover, the chairman was an MDS member, and the three deputy chairmen were from the MDS, SNP, and Democratic Left, much to the dismay of the Christian Democrats and the Hungarians, who also found their deputies assigned to less important committees. The former prime minister, Jan Carnogursky, was voted off the Foreign Affairs Committee.[53]

In the Czech Republic, Klaus also formed a tight coalition. The core consisted of the CDP (nine members, controlling six of the nine economic portfolios) and the Christian Democratic Party (two members). Also represented were two other right and centre-right parties. This assemblage gave the government a very slim majority in the National Council – 105 of 200 seats. The major opposition parties were leftist, with a total of 67 seats: all the leftist parties favoured further efforts to save the federation. Klaus broke tradition by naming only one deputy prime minister, Jan Kalvoda of the Civic Democratic Alliance, who had taken a relatively hard line in previous constitutional talks. As for the National Council presidium, the ruling coalition again broke precedent by electing only its own members to the five major posts of chairman and deputy chairmen. Klaus also tried to exclude altogether the Communists and the extreme-right Republicans from the other seventeen positions on the presidium.[54]

As bilateral negotiations proceeded in the summer of 1992, it became apparent that opposition parties would have tactical and strategic difficulties. On the referendum issue, for example, the Czech Social Democrats and the Slovak Christian Democrats stood with the Communists in favour of a popular consultation (the public probably still favoured holding one). Yet if these parties had tried to hold out for a referendum by defeating federal laws that would amend the constitution to dissolve the federation, then Meciar and Klaus could well have decided to proceed unconstitutionally. Since this would have increased tension and disruption, to the detriment of all citizens, the more responsible opposition parties were forced to moderate their stance.

Beyond this tactical impotence was the solidaristic pressure not to undermine the emerging "national" interest. Meciar often made appeals of this kind. On introducing the Slovak constitution to the National Council, for instance, he said, "It is humiliating if the Slovak National Council deputies, for whom the interests of the Slovak Republic should be foremost, throw dirt on their own republic and their own constitutional situation."[55] The same pressure was evident on the Czech side in October 1992, when the Federal Assembly briefly supported a motion to draft a constitutional bill that would be essentially confederal, with a common president and legislature. Moved by the Czech Social Democrats, this resolution, surprisingly, was supported by Meciar's MDS deputies, and it passed (after many deputies had left the legislature). Klaus rejected it as totally unacceptable in principle and as a Slovak delaying tactic. The Czech opposition parties then quickly backed off when "the union proposal was seen by many Czechs as merely an effort to harm Klaus's bargaining position in the face of growing Slovak demands, thus damaging Czech interests."[56] Again in November, when the Federal Assembly was debating a bill to permit the federation to be wound up, the Czech opposition deputies were squeezed by Klaus's determination on the one hand and Havel's formal announcement that he would seek the Czech presidency on the other; the Social Democrats and the Liberal Social Union supported the bill, and it passed in the Czech chamber of the House of Nations.[57]

As an instance of peaceful secession, the Czech-Slovak case is unusual in that public opinion was against the separation for some time and continued to be divided in each republic even as negotiations were well underway. Hence, there were incentives for political forces within each state to oppose the leading pro-separation parties. This is also the only case to have occurred in a full democracy with a universal franchise, and where élites were constrained by public opinion both directly and indirectly through the widely publicized results of modern opinion polling. Nevertheless, democratic mechanisms had produced republican governments with mandates to settle the constitutional issue. These mandates were slender, especially in the Czech Republic, and it could certainly be argued that the leaders had not exhausted all means to reach agreement, but there was never any fundamental contestation of either government's legitimacy. The June elections, in effect, were like very narrow majorities in a referendum, and there is no democratic principle more profound than that the majority rules. In this case, narrow victories produced coherent, determined governments that could lever more widespread public support through the process of negotiation itself.

Once negotiations were underway, safeguarding each republic's interests – or claiming to do so – was the first priority for the leaders of the respective governments and, increasingly, for other members of the separating communities. Opposition parties could disagree about where these interests lay. The Czech left, for example, feared more rapid economic reform within a republic freed from the constraints of the Slovaks, and the Christian Democrats in Slovakia were apprehensive about the economic impact of separation. But with the breakup imminent, there was a strong interest in ensuring that it occurred smoothly. Hence, it could not be resisted at all costs. And overt disagreement with negotiating positions could not be long countenanced. These positions were those of one's republic, and to oppose them was to bolster the position of the "other," to undermine one's "own" government, and ultimately – since both leaderships had become committed to separation – to risk a chaotic split.

All the other empirical generalizations about peaceful secession remain true in the Czech-Slovak case.[58] The separation was preceded by a long and frustrating constitutional negotiation, one complicated by regionally articulated conflict about the pace of economic reform. When the secession was decided, the critical negotiations involved few participants. The initial meetings were between Klaus and Meciar and a few leading party members, only five on each side in July 1992, though once the parameters were set, the process broadened out somewhat, and it included full cabinets by late October when detailed treaties were being drawn up. The process was also fast. Critical decisions were taken within two weeks of the election, the basic framework for separation was set within another month, and it took only four more months to decide all post-secession arrangements, as well as to enact new republican constitutions and dissolve the federal state. The settlement involved few agreements, despite the very high degree of social, economic, and political integration between the two republics. A total of thirty-one separate treaties were signed, covering matters ranging from the common currency and the post-secession customs union to the mutual recognition of marriages. Foreign powers were crucial in the whole process. In particular, the European Community was not prepared to extend associate status to the two states unless the level of economic integration between them was no less than that prevailing in the community itself; this set a floor below which economic cooperation could not sink, and resulted directly in the customs union agreement.

The separation also followed the pattern in that it was effected constitutionally, though last-minute brinksmanship was necessary to convince the Federal Assembly to acquiesce and to pass an amendment dissolving the federation as of 1 January 1993. Each republic adopted a constitution in time for the separation, and these constitutions were very similar to the basic laws they superseded. The Slovaks founded their state on the principle of national citizenship rather than declaring it a civil society, and the Czechs inserted some minor devices to avoid deadlock; as well, each constitution slightly increased executive power relative to the legislature. But unchanged were the electoral system, size of the legislature, unicameralism (except in the Czech Republic), internal territorial divisions, and procedures for electing the president and amending the constitution.

Despite this continuity, the separation was a momentous event. Its progress was punctuated by demonstrations, strikes, boycotts, and mass petition campaigns, along with outpourings of nationalist celebration and substantial ill-feeling; and when the event occurred, people on both sides of the new border soberly realized that a fundamental break was taking place. The policies of the new states soon diverged: their foreign preoccupations differed, they treated minorities differently, there were continuing disputes about assets, the currency arrangement broke down, trade flows dropped precipitously, and controls went up at the border posts. Overall, relations remained cordial, but within a shrinking zone of mutual interest and in part because of the requirements of foreign powers. Finally, the secession was irrevocable: reunification of Slovakia and the Czech Republic as a sovereign state with a common legislature and executive is inconceivable.

CONCLUSION

The Czech-Slovak separation is a striking, instructive, and recent instance of peaceful secession. Overall, it conforms to the pattern that characterized other such cases, and this affirms that there are important commonalities in the process of peaceful secession. The differences that did emerge resulted from the peculiar development of polarization in an intensely competitive, fully democratic system, where there already existed a high degree of political, social, and economic dislocation and uncertainty.

Polarization certainly is a phenomenon that deserves further study in a comparative context. The Czech-Slovak case demonstrates how it can be advanced by partisan manoeuvring, how it can be politically profitable for each of the opposing factions, and how leaders can move public opinion, especially when they have access to state resources. Polarization also merits consideration in the Canadian context, and it is the focus of the discussion in chapter 15 of this study.

But we should not draw too many direct parallels between Czechoslovakia and Canada. First, the history of relations between the Czechs and the Slovaks was a very bitter one, marked especially by the traumatic events of World War II. Second, the Communist regime left a residue of suspicion and distrust that soured relations between many politicians, divided the population, and led many citizens to be cynical about politics in general. The Czechs and Slovaks also faced massive legal, administrative, and economic turmoil in the wake of the Communist collapse: they had to undertake nothing short of a complete reconstruction of the society. In this, there was a broad consensus that the country had no alternative but to modernize and westernize, and the great legitimacy of the anti-Communist movement helped carry the restructuring for a while; but when disagreement arose, accommodation was impeded by the institutions inherited by the young democracy. In particular, the rules governing constitutional amendments encouraged noncooperation, while the electoral system worked against centrist parties and also accentuated regional interests. In contrast to Czechoslovakia, Canada has a known constitutional and institutional framework. It retains strong and well-disciplined national parties. It has a central government that can control Parliament. And it is not a bipartite federation. The dynamic of polarization may be most applicable in such states, where legitimacy, power, and ultimately sovereignty can easily flow to two component units that are the natural interlocutors of each other, rather than in multistate federations. On the other hand, if polarization does occur in federations like Canada where one unit among many aims to secede, the process of finding a negotiating partner, and of arranging reasonable terms of disengagement, might be much more complex and uncertain than it was in the Czech-Slovak case.

PART THREE

The Dynamics of Quebec Secession

Let us summarize the argument to this point. First, Canada without Quebec would be a viable state. If Quebec seceded, the rest of Canada (ROC) could be reconstituted in many ways. The underlying features of the economy, society, and culture have both congruences and cleavages across provincial and regional boundaries, and so are not clearly conducive to either integration or fragmentation. The political process through which secession occurs and the structures established at that time would very much shape the long-term structure of ROC. So, too, would the kind of economic and political relationships established with the separated Quebec, and here again a wide variety of options is possible.

Turning to other studies of the secession process, drawn from a variety of disciplines, several conclusions emerge. The separation into two sovereign states could entail very heavy economic costs for people and firms in both states. By far the largest component of these costs, potentially, is the cost of the transition itself, which would be mainly determined by the politics of the event. Second, the legal framework around the phenomenon of secession, especially in metropolitan states, is quite indeterminate. Secession, simply enough, is successful when the sub-unit seeking to withdraw from the larger state can establish physical control of the territory and also gain recognition from member states of the international community. In Quebec's case, Canada is primordial on both counts: it is the only currently sovereign actor likely to resist Quebec's claims to territory, and if it does not do so, but instead recognizes Quebec's independence, other states will follow. Finally, studies of the potential politics of Quebec secession are quite diverse in their findings, with general scenarios ranging from relatively smooth disengagement to extreme political turmoil. Even so, they clarify some of the preconditions for a peaceful secession, and they also suggest some of the major points of contention that would emerge in bargaining between Canada and Quebec over the terms of disengagement and post-secession relations. The political studies, however, generally have little to say about how the detailed process of separation would occur, or else their conclusions are conflicting.

Hence, we turned to comparative experience. The focus here was on cases of peaceful secession, which, it should be stressed again, are far less numerous than instances of contested secession. Nevertheless, especially in democracies, there are a few cases of peaceful secession, and analysis of these reveals common patterns in the process. Our purpose now is to build on these empirical generalizations. In this part of the study, we assume that Quebec will secede, and our objective is to predict in some detail the process of the transition to an independent Quebec and a ROC of some form. Even this is filled with some uncertainty, however, because of the Czech-Slovak separation, which departed from the common pattern of peaceful secession: the process was gradual and political polarization was the main dynamic. After the application of the general pattern, therefore, the terrain of the transition will be revisited, briefly, to modify the initial depiction under conditions of polarization.

CHAPTER TWELVE

Getting to the Table

SECESSION FOLLOWS PROTRACTED CONSTITUTIONAL AND POLITICAL DISPUTES

Canada's constitution has been under negotiation for thirty years.[1] After repeated failure to reach agreement on amendments, it finally underwent fundamental change in 1982, when the Charter of Rights and Freedoms and the amending formula were added, without the approval of the Quebec National Assembly. To satisfy Quebec's core demands for change, in 1987 further amendments were proposed in the Meech Lake Accord, but this failed to pass in June 1990.[2] The Charlottetown Accord, agreed in 1992, broadened the scope of amendments, but it too failed, after defeat in referendums held in Canada and Quebec.[3] Thus, in the view of nationalist Quebecers, it has proved impossible to change the Canadian constitution so as to accommodate the distinct nature of Quebec.

This whole process has had several effects. First, having been exposed to "searing experience(s) of constitutional consciousness raising" and to the impact of the courts' Charter decisions, the populace has become more aware of the stakes involved in altering the fundamental law of the land.[4] Along with this has developed the expectation that the public, at least as represented by interest organizations, will participate in negotiating major change, and there is now a widespread presumption that amendments require popular approval. Third, existing institutions have been devalued. Thrown onto the bargaining table and almost replaced by negotiated alternatives, the constitution has been declared inadequate, yet it has not been super-seded by suitably renewed structures. Fourth, constitutional fatigue has set in. The Chrétien Liberals were able to capitalize on this senti-ment by promising in the 1993 election campaign to set constitutional matters aside. But the issue cannot be laid to rest, because of the Bloc québécois (BQ), which took fifty-four seats in that election, and the victory of the Parti québécois (PQ) in the September 1994 Quebec election. National unity has re-emerged as a compelling national prob-lem.[5]

In ROC, one result of this pressure is the desire for "closure" – for resolving constitutional disputes "once and for all." Expressed most fervently in the West, this sentiment is fuelled not only by fatigue with the issue and by deeper irritation with a Quebec that drives the national agenda, but also by the evident costs to all Canadians of constitutional uncertainty. The perception of these costs at the per-sonal level – higher interest rates, a weaker Canadian dollar – is also strong at the governmental level, where the effects of uncertainty exacerbate a fiscal crisis that has forced all governments to reduce services and to run large operating surpluses in order to meet inter-est charges; indeed, accompanying the constitutional malaise is a disaffection with governments that extract more in taxes than they provide in services. (In every region of the country except Ontario, a majority of respondents to an Environics poll felt that their province did not receive its fair share of federal spending.)[6] Finally, in ROC, as intellectuals have come to recognize the impending threat posed by Quebec secession, there has developed an existential concern about its future. The perception that Canada will have to reconstitute itself if Quebec attains sovereignty, and the absence of a consensus about what arrangements would then be possible and desirable, add to the profound constitutional uncertainty that exists in the country because of protracted and fundamental disputes over its basic law.

These factors operate in Quebec as well. The importance of the constitution has been driven home there not only by continual nego-tiations but also by the referendum of 1980, the constitutional "coup" of 1982, and by the Meech and Charlottetown attempts to provide wider powers to the provincial government, to recognize Quebec's distinct status, and to protect its special interests through a constitu-tional veto and through guaranteed representation in central institu-tions. The Supreme Court decision overturning sections of the popular Charter of the French Language demonstrated constitutional vulner-ability to the extent that the federalist Bourassa government felt com-pelled to override the ruling.[7] At the same time, potential constitutional gains have not been realized. No constitutional expansion of provincial powers has been won, nor has the province achieved special protection or guarantees. The constitutional status quo remains, at a time when opinion in ROC appears to be shifting from a dualist conception of Canada towards one based on individual rights and equality of the provinces.

Constitutional fatigue is also evident in Quebec. On the one hand is the sense that negotiations have not achieved any result and cannot do so, and that in this impasse only a vote for secession can produce change and security and the opportunity for the global society to develop; on the other is the sense that constitutional wrangling should cease because it wastes energy and exacerbates economic problems. Although the Bloc québécois won fifty-four seats in the 1993 election and although its core vote was sovereigntist, it is worth noting that the federal Liberal Party, which stood explicitly against reopening the constitution, still took 33.0 per cent of the Quebec vote (while the Progressive Conservatives took another 13.6 per cent). A particular constitutional fatigue exists, too, among sovereigntists, many of whom came to the movement as young people in the late 1960s. Among many in this generation is the sense that the last chance for independence – their last chance – is imminent.

The constitutional debate in Quebec will occur in the context of a fiscal crisis that will exacerbate deep cleavages over the province's options. Governments have been compelled to compress spending. In the 1992–93 fiscal year, Quebec government revenues were $35.5 billion, budgetary expenditures were $40.5 billion, and interest payments on the total debt reached $4.77 billion, or about 13.4 per cent of revenues.[8] Meanwhile, unemployment has been stubbornly above the Canadian average. The burden of government has been alleviated only marginally by net inflows from Ottawa for equalization and unemployment insurance. These economic and budgetary conditions feed directly into the constitutional debate, for federalists maintain that separation is too costly and risky an option, while sovereigntists argue that the inefficiencies of the federal system and the incapacity of Quebec to manage its own economy have created the crisis in government finances and slow economic growth.

Public opinion about constitutional options has been thoroughly charted in Quebec,[9] and several elements are clear. First, the electorate is rather evenly divided on the issue. Analysts often distinguish among committed sovereigntists, committed federalists, and moderate nationalists. The last occupy the centre of the constitutional dimension and are the "swing voters." During the 1992 Charlottetown referendum campaign, for instance, one team of researchers found 39 per cent of the electorate to be "firm" sovereigntists, 8 per cent to be "diffident" sovereigntists, and 15 per cent to be non-francophone and federalist; the 38 per cent who were non-sovereigntist francophones were "clearly on the battleground."[10] Another team used an eleven-category scale to categorize francophone Quebecers in 1991; they found 29 per cent firmly in favour of independence, 21 per cent firm federalists, and 50 per cent ranging across the various shadings of support for sovereignty-association.[11] Second, opinion on this issue is volatile. The clearest examples occurred when the Supreme Court ruled on Bill 101, the Quebec language law, and when the Meech Lake Accord failed to pass. Support for sovereignty rose dramatically, to peak at 58 per cent, with only 30 per cent opposed.[12] It has since declined. This shows not only volatility but also its major cause – perceived threats to the security of the French language in Quebec. As Stéphane Dion concluded, "A linguistic crisis has been at the root of each new outburst of nationalism in Quebec since the 1960s."[13] This volatility at the time of the rejection of the Meech Lake Accord also shows that opinion in Quebec is highly sensitive to perceived opinion in ROC, and especially to events that can be interpreted symbolically as rejection, contempt, or humiliation.[14]

There are other important features of polling data about support for separation. Many studies have shown that reported opinion is very sensitive to the question posed. For instance, there are substantial differences between support for "sovereignty," "independence," and "separation," and there is good evidence that these concepts have different connotations in Quebec: in a straight question about them, 69 per cent of Quebecers agreed that "sovereignty" and "independence" meant different things.[15] This shows that the substance of a referendum question is very important at the margin, for when further information about the implications of sovereignty is provided to respondents, opinion shifts significantly. During the 1992 referendum campaign, for instance, respondents were randomly asked either for their opinion on Quebec sovereignty per se or on Quebec sovereignty, "that is, Quebec is no longer a part of Canada." The proportion that was very favourable was 47 per cent on the first question and only 39 per cent on the second.[16] This reveals the scope for political argument about the implications of sovereignty to move the Quebec electorate through the course of a referendum campaign. The perceived effects of sovereignty, including the substance of arrangements to be concluded between Quebec and Canada, would be a major determinant of how the moderate nationalists vote. Blais and Nadeau, for example, found that economic expectations strongly affected the propensity to opt for sovereignty: "Everything else being equal, support for sovereignty is 19 points lower among those who expect their standard of living to go down."[17] Similarly, Pinard concluded that support for independence drops 6 to 7 per cent when questions specify that this means the absence of political and economic ties with the rest of Canada.[18] Finally, polls consistently overestimate support for sovereignty and for the PQ – or, rather, they have done so in the past.[19] This, along with other sources of error and the close balance between sovereigntists and federalists, means that the outcome of a referendum campaign on sovereignty would very likely be in doubt until the votes were finally counted.

Comparative experience shows that partisan considerations are vital in cases of secession, because political parties and their leaders are the vehicles for formulating, presenting, and defending the various constitutional options. While the partisan and personal character of constitutional negotiations is often overshadowed by a focus on the substantive issues and the "interests" of various states, Cairns's comments about earlier negotiations would remain true both before and after a Quebec referendum on sovereignty: "Thus the constitutional struggle of recent years in Canada cannot be understood without reference to the clashing wills, ambitions, and visions of that small group of political leaders who happened to be on the stage when the time came for Canadians to have that constitutional rendezvous with destiny which they had so long avoided."[20] Of course, leaders are constrained by opinion within their parties and the general public, and constitutional debates also involve the media and organized interests; but in a system of representative parliamentary democracy, it is the elected members, organized into hierarchical parties, who make collectively binding decisions. Since leaders must make momentous and rapid decisions in cases of secession, and since the high degree of uncertainty that prevails in such unprecedented circumstances allows them considerable autonomy in their choices, it is important to analyse the partisan forces in the Canada-Quebec case.

The firm position of the federal Liberal Party is that there should be no reopening of constitutional issues. The leader, Jean Chrétien, has a mandate to provide good government and economic growth. This is a recent and strong mandate: the Liberals have 176 seats in the House of Commons, enough to govern with a comfortable majority even if they lose the support of all their members from Quebec. The party does not, however, control the Senate. In any referendum campaign about Quebec sovereignty, the Liberals would be the main federal defenders of the constitutional status quo. And as the governing party, they would be most unlikely to split and lose control of the House of Commons, whatever the outcome of a referendum in Quebec.

The Progressive Conservative party is rebuilding after its massive defeat in the 1993 election. Its precise constitutional policy is unclear, but the interim leader, Jean Charest, is a credible defender of federalism and has a substantial incentive to improve his fortunes and those of his party by doing so. Initial indications are that Mr Charest will distinguish his party within the federalist camp by advocating some form of "third way" between the constitutional status quo and sovereignty, perhaps by proposing that new power-sharing agreements be entrenched in the constitution.[21]

The federal New Democratic Party is also rebuilding. Its current constitutional position has not been enunciated, and it will have difficulty formulating one because of internal divisions between the Ontario and western memberships, between trade unionists and members of social movements, and between centralists and provincialists. It has never had electoral success in Quebec.

On constitutional matters, the Reform Party occupies a strategic position. This is a classic populist party with a weak organizational structure and a dominant leader. Its platform generally favours less interventionist government, and on specific issues – bilingualism, social welfare, minority and group rights – its position is antithetical to traditional Liberal policies.[22] Constitutionally, Reform makes common cause with Quebec nationalists by supporting decentralization, but it threatens Quebecers with other policies, such as equality of the provinces, an equal and elected Senate, and weak commitment to bilingualism, group rights, and redistribution.[23]

Reform is a "movement-party" based on discontent and active participation at the grassroots level, so it must keep its momentum going and its members mobilized. The party has three options. First, it could continue to spread into Ontario, the Atlantic provinces, and Quebec, aiming at the next election, though this could not occupy the members for four years, and the party's prospects in Quebec are dismal. Second, Reform could abandon its exclusively national focus and enter the provincial realm, especially in Ontario, aiming to occupy potential Progressive Conservative bases and to supplant the PC conclusively as the right-of-centre party in both orders of government. But this would create competing centres of power within the party, and in fact the option was defeated at the October 1994 Reform Party convention. Third, Reform could focus on the constitution, aiming to draw support by using the sovereigntists as a foil in a strategy of polarization. Quebec could be the keystone of other elements of the Reform philosophy too, because "it is seen as both the strategic key to demands made of the federal system by special interests, and as a continuing guarantee that attempts to downsize the welfare state will be maximally difficult."[24] So at the same time as he could criticize the governing Liberals for their inadequate defence of federalism, Preston Manning could seek support through counterattacking the sovereigntists' provocations. The Reform Party could thus gain support from both those favouring a functional federation in which Quebec was treated like any other province and those concerned, in the event of sovereignty, with retribution or with safeguarding their interests by taking a hard line in dealings with Quebec.[25] Mr Manning, in short, could presume to act as the tribune of ROC.

On the Quebec side, three political formations are important. First is the provincial Liberal Party. While it lost power in September 1994, its strong showing confirmed Daniel Johnson's leadership position. As the leading force in the No umbrella organization (assuming that Quebec referendum legislation is not amended), the party could find opportunities for reorganization and mobilization in the struggle to defend federalism. On the other hand, its constitutional position is ambiguous. Mr Johnson appears prepared to defend the existing federal constitution as supple enough to accommodate Quebec's evolution; however, the party's association with firm demands for constitutional change, through Meech, the Allaire Report, and Charlottetown, would make its position difficult and could possibly weaken its unity if no offers of renewed federalism were forthcoming before or during a referendum campaign.[26]

The Parti québécois would of course be in power at the time of a referendum. This is a strongly institutionalized party, with a large membership base and established links with powerful organizations of workers, teachers, the cultural milieu, and small business. Its commitment to sovereignty has evolved from one contingent on continued association with Canada to an absolute drive towards independence, softened by the prediction that ROC, in its own rational self-interest, would cooperate economically with a sovereign Quebec. So the economic costs to the citizens of each country would be minimized. The party is more popular than its leader, Jacques Parizeau, who is regarded by many as somewhat antiquated and erratic. But barring a major gaffe or illness, Premier Parizeau and the highly centralized inner cabinet will lead a united party in a referendum campaign. Mr Parizeau's entire political career has been devoted to the cause of sovereignty, and there is no evidence that he would stray from this course even if it were to impose large costs on the citizens of the province.

The final Quebec party is the Bloc québécois, the federal counterpart of the PQ. Although the Bloc rests to some extent on the PQ organizational base, it possesses some autonomy because of its status as official opposition in the House of Commons, because of its elected members, and above all because of its leader, Lucien Bouchard, the most popular politician in Quebec. After the failure of the Meech Lake Accord, Mr Bouchard resigned from the federal cabinet and created the Bloc as the federal vehicle to facilitate Quebec's evolution towards sovereignty. He is a charismatic leader with great rhetorical ability to blend logic and emotion. Compared with other provincial and federal politicians, he is seen by Quebecers as both strong and trustworthy; even among non-sovereigntist francophones, his overall approval rating has been as high as Mr Chrétien's.[27] Mr. Bouchard is acutely sensitive and, according to insiders, is sincere in all the positions he adopts. On the other hand, he is relatively new to the sovereigntist movement and may not share the core PQ leadership's entire commitment to independence: there is some evidence of suspicion within that party about his dedication to it.[28] It is conceivable that the Bloc would stop short of sovereignty if the costs to Quebecers mounted or if a third option opened between outright independence and the constitutional status quo.

Other partisan forces are found at the provincial level; the other premiers and opposition leaders would not be able to escape involvement in constitutional debates, however much the lead roles were played by Quebec and federal politicians. Particularly important would be Clyde Wells of Newfoundland and Frank McKenna of New Brunswick – both Liberals experienced in these matters – and Roy Romanow of Saskatchewan. Ralph Klein of Alberta might enunciate a Reform-like position, while also attempting to solidify a western Canadian option in the event of a Quebec vote for sovereignty. The premier with the most to gain from the constitutional issue is Bob Rae of Ontario. Leading an unpopular government, but personally credible, Mr Rae could run in the upcoming Ontario election as the only leader experienced and capable enough to deal with the sovereigntist threat and with constitutional issues. Downplaying the social and economic issues that have divided the electorate and diminished NDP support, he could position himself as the guardian of Ontario's collective interest.

QUEBEC DECLARES ITS INTENT TO SECEDE

It must be assumed that Quebec's claim to sovereignty can only be based on a positive referendum result after a campaign in which the major protagonists would be those described above. The sovereigntists are absolutely committed to a referendum, although the PQ government could do much to promote sovereignty before it is held. Two further issues concern the legitimacy of the result. The first is whether Quebecers have the right to decide to secede. Public opinion in Quebec, backed by many pronouncements of the National Assembly (some made under Liberal governments), strongly supports the existence of this right, and while Canadian public opinion on this issue is not undivided, the preponderant view is that Quebecers do have this right. More important, by participating in the campaign, the protagonists implicitly accept the stakes. This seems unavoidable. Even the leader of the Reform Party is committed to fight in a Quebec referendum.[29] On the other hand, there certainly is no agreement in ROC about what the terms and mechanics of a separation will be if the Yes side carries the referendum.

The second issue is the question to be posed. For the referendum to be perceived as legitimate, the question must be clear and fair. This is an important matter, and one that is in the hands of the PQ government. It is likely that the question will be "Are you in favour of Quebec becoming a sovereign country?" The use of the term "sovereign" has been attacked as vague and deceptive by federalists who favour "separation" or "independence," but in fact "sovereignty" has a precise meaning in international law, whereas the other terms do not. The referendum campaign itself will focus on defining exactly what are the implications of this sovereignty. It is possible that the question could provide some information about these implications – for example, that the Quebec government would administer all taxes, have the right to sign international treaties, and pass all laws applicable to Quebecers. While these amplifications are true, they could justly be decried as selective, and the federalist forces will certainly make this argument. But, once more, participation in the campaign will tend to lock them in to accepting the outcome. On the other hand, if the question is heavily biased – by suggesting that tax savings or economic growth would result from sovereignty – some ROC formations, notably Reform, might reserve judgment on the appropriate response to a Yes vote. Because of such considerations, and also because many party militants want a clear outcome, the PQ will pose a clear question, with little amplification.[30]

The referendum campaign will be bitter. It will have three central elements. The first is constitutional. The sovereigntists' claim will be that constitutional amendment to meet Quebec's aspirations has proved impossible. Since the existing arrangements are cumbersome and inefficient and provide neither special recognition of Quebec nor adequate protection of its distinctiveness against the weight of the majority, sovereignty is the only solution. The Quebec Liberals, associated with demands for change in the past, have a strategic disadvantage on this front. For instance, their long-serving premier, Robert Bourassa, is on record as stating that "two avenues of action must be considered simultaneously: an in-depth reorganization of the existing federal system, or sovereignty for Québec. No other solution could meet the needs and aspirations of Québec society."[31] Moreover, unless the federal government's policy against formal constitutional reform changes dramatically, there will be nothing on offer except a defence of the existing constitution, along with such proof of its flexibility and capacity to accommodate Quebec's interests as can be mustered. Since the PQ, having been in office for several months, will have stymied constructive initiatives in the allocation of functions and joint programming, and since fiscal constraints will not allow many attractive new federal program initiatives, this proof will be difficult to demonstrate.

In a sense, the constitutional dimension of the referendum debate is part of the larger constitutional game that has gone on since the 1980 Quebec referendum and has progressively entrenched the notion that Quebec and ROC are entities seeking some compromise, without success. In 1980, the question asked for a mandate to negotiate sovereignty-association with Canada. The federalist side argued that a No vote would produce constitutional change; but although it did so, the 1982 amendments were rejected by the Quebec government and by the National Assembly (by a vote of 70 to 38).[32] Five years later, the Meech Lake Accord recognized the province's distinctiveness and collective rights, but it failed, partly because of strong opposition in ROC to the distinct society clause.[33] Quebec's strategic reaction was to threaten a referendum on sovereignty in order to win the gains of Meech, and much argument was devoted to showing that sovereignty was a credible threat.[34] But Canadian negotiators in the Charlottetown process insisted on enlarging the scope of the proposed amendments, introducing elements threatening to Quebecers and watering down recognition of its distinctiveness. In Whitaker's view, the threat of sovereignty was not taken seriously enough in the rest of Canada to produce proposals for asymmetrical federalism – for equality among the provinces in ROC and special status and powers for Quebec.[35] And the Charlottetown Accord was defeated both in Quebec and in much of the rest of Canada. By holding a referendum after all these interactions, the PQ government will force Quebecers to choose between the constitutional status quo and sovereignty, pure and simple.

The second element of the campaign will be emotional, involving notions of patriotism and national identity. Federalist forces will try to tap Quebecers' sense of affection for and identification with Canada – and there is considerable attachment. An extensive poll of Quebecers by CROP in 1992 found that 71 per cent affirmed that "being Canadian" was part of their identity, while 93 per cent identified with the beauty of the country; more important, 54 per cent wanted Quebec to remain a province of Canada.[36] According to Blais and Nadeau, the differential sense of attachment to Canada or Quebec is the strongest single predictor of support for sovereignty.[37] For their part, the sovereigntists will appeal to Quebecers' desire for autonomy, for constituting themselves finally as an independent nation. The electorate will be told that their language and culture are under constant threat in the federation and in North America, and that the only way to ensure their survival is to create a state with the sovereign power to do so. Sovereigntists also will argue that the referendum represents the last chance for Quebecers to assert their independence.[38] If they do not act positively now, Quebec will be weakened for years and will eventually be submerged in the federal system. As Mr Bouchard showed in the 1993 election, he can be especially effective in striking emotional chords, and he will be ready to state that here is Quebec's final chance to "get off its knees" at last. The importance of this emotional dimension will depend on how much polarization has taken place between the election of the PQ and the referendum.

The critical battlefront is likely to be the economic one.[39] Here the debate will centre around the costs of sovereignty. As has been shown, these are highly contestable, depending on assumptions about Quebec's long-term growth potential and, more centrally, about transition costs. The latter are largely a function of the politics of the separation and the negotiations about sovereignty. The federalist strategy will be to accentuate the costs, and high estimates of those costs will be defended as valid. This position will be buttressed if real uncertainty causes interest rates to rise, the dollar to fall, and firms to leave the province. Meanwhile, the sovereigntists will provide counter-estimates, and will argue that a Yes victory has already been discounted by the markets.

Basically, though, the federalists will continue their current policy of refusing to speculate about a Yes victory and the arrangements that would follow it. At the federal level, one reason is that the government cannot prepare for sovereignty: "In Canada-without-Quebec, the federal government loses territory, citizens, a historic identity, some of its bureaucracy, and many of the political responsibilities that flowed from its former management of a linguistically dual people. Little preparation by the federal government for such an unsought goal is likely."[40] More deeply, refusal to discuss the aftermath of a Yes vote will be part of a strategy to increase uncertainty. It is unlikely that the federal government would even state authoritatively what margin of victory, if any, it would accept. The constant position of the federalists will be that separation is risky and unnecessary, and that the electorate will reject it. Economically, the federalists will refuse to admit that there would be any cooperation between a ROC and a sovereign Quebec. To do so would be to follow a two-track strategy, providing Quebecers with information about the secessionist future, reducing uncertainty, and – assuming an emotional preference for sovereignty among the electorate – making Yes votes more likely.

Both sides will agree that there are mutual gains through maintaining the common Canadian economic space. But federalists will deny that the mutual gains would necessarily continue in the event of Quebec independence. Some will go further, employing a strategy of threats. They will predict that the variable costs of transition, which are partly under the control of ROC, will be high – that negotiations will be long, hard, and bitter, that fundamental issues such as borders and minority rights will be on the table, and that there will likely be temporary economic disruption and the erection of permanent barriers to trade. In the spring of 1994, for example, several premiers warned about the consequences of sovereignty. Mr Klein pointed out that the Seaway belongs to Canada, Mr Romanow explained that there was no provision in the constitution for secession, and Mr Harcourt spoke of the "terrible consequences for everybody .... They think it's going to be logical and civilized. Forget it, it won't be. There will be great bitterness and a nasty split. And they'll suffer, not just economically but they'll suffer every which way, the people of Quebec."[41] While there will be a range of threats emanating from ROC (and some offers of cooperation as well), the major federalist actors will be united in predicting big economic costs of sovereignty and in making no commitments about the consequences of a Yes vote.

The sovereigntists will counter these predictions and threats by pointing to past cases when threats of economic damage proved unfounded, such as the 1976 election campaign and the 1980 and 1992 referendums. More important, they will aim to expose the language of threat as part of a transparent strategy that is not credible. Of course, they will argue, the federalists want to avoid the costs of independence. So, *before* Quebecers have made their choice, it makes sense for the federalists to emphasize these costs, and it is rational to inflate them by making threats about noncooperation; but Quebecers could still choose independence, and at the precise moment when they do so, the federalist strategy will have failed. According to this line of reasoning, *after* it is clear that the federal strategy has failed,

ROC will immediately have to change its course in order to minimize its own economic losses. ROC is rational (and the argument is
often presented in such anthropomorphic terms), so it must opt for
cooperation, for the tranquil management of the transition, for joint
assurances to diminish uncertainty, and for an economic association
that would avoid the costs to its citizens of fragmenting the common
economic space. As the PQ has stated the argument, "Par stratégie,
les politiciens fédéraux peuvent être tentés de déclarer maintenant
qu'ils ne négocieront pas, pour dissuader les Québécois et les
Québécoises d'appuyer la souveraineté. Une fois devant le fait
accompli, cependant, par réalisme économique et politique, ils
changeront d'attitude."[42]

Several conclusions emerge from this analysis. First, having adopted
the position that the economic costs of separation would be high and
that the negotiation of post-secession arrangements in advance is inconceivable, the federalists will have to maintain their stance until
voting day. Since the referendum result will probably be close, the
uncertainty and the prospect of economic loss must be kept constantly
before the moderate nationalists in order to induce them to vote No.

Second, the economic debate will be infused with emotion. One
reason is that the federalist strategy will be depicted as cynical and
manipulative, and contemptuous of Quebecers. If Quebecers do discount the threats and opt for secession, the strategy will have raised
the cost of their decision, in reality. This is because all the uncertainty
about the constitutional and economic future that pre-negotiation
would have reduced will hit Quebec and ROC as a sharp shock on
the day after the referendum. So transition costs will be very much
increased by the federalists; indeed, the sovereigntists will argue that
it is hard to think of a more effective way of maximizing these costs
than by refusing to cope with sovereignty until it occurs. Less subtly,
threats of noncooperation may anger Quebecers when they are made
by federalist leaders who point to ROC extremists and declare themselves bound to take such views into account. As well, some difficult
transition issues about which threats of noncooperation will be made
involve minorities, Native peoples, and the provincial borders. To
all of these, Quebec public opinion is extraordinarily sensitive.[43]

Finally, there is much truth in the sovereigntist analysis of threats of
noncooperation. If, after a Yes result, the secession is to be peaceful,
negotiations on outstanding issues will be conducted, and at this point
ROC will have an interest in minimizing uncertainty and in negotiating
certain cooperative arrangements. But this is a superficial truth. It is
based on depicting the federal strategy as one of "permanent
retaliation," meaning that noncooperation by Quebec in the form of a

Yes vote would be followed by permanent noncooperation on the part of ROC. This is not credible. Negotiations would certainly occur. But these negotiations need not be easy, nor need they produce cooperative outcomes. Indeed, it would be entirely rational for ROC to be noncooperative if this stance could produce outcomes favourable to it in the long run – if it could force Quebec into compromises that are in ROC's interest. For instance, if ROC and a sovereign Quebec are to cooperate economically, decisions must be taken about the level of integration to be maintained and about what decision rules will settle future questions of economic management. ROC leaders might calculate that the losses consequent upon adopting a nonconciliatory stance in the short term would be more than recompensed in the long run if it could obtain its preferred outcomes or a favourable compromise on these issues. Immutable geography and economic forces make it clear, as the Quebec sovereigntists recognize, that negotiations between ROC and Quebec will continue indefinitely, whatever the constitutional framework. But from this observation, one cannot draw the conclusion that cooperation is inevitable.[44]

The federalists might well make this argument in the referendum campaign. As Julius Grey put it, "The theory espoused by the separatists that Quebec will get whatever it asks for must be laid to rest."[45] The federalists will also, somewhat contradictorily, appeal to Quebecers' sense of attachment to Canada and to the successful functioning of the Canadian constitution. Here, however, it is assumed that all the federalist arguments have failed and that there is going to be a Yes majority in the Quebec referendum.

CANADA WILL ACCEPT THE PRINCIPLE OF
SECESSION: NEGOTIATIONS WILL FOLLOW

The referendum campaign has been heated, and the result has been too close to call. Even if the Yes forces have had a substantial lead according to the polls, there has been no commitment by the federalists about the implications of a vote for sovereignty, the margin required to be decisive, or post-sovereignty arrangements. This, despite the fact that high levels of uncertainty are registering in all Canadian markets.

As the results come in, it is apparent that Quebecers have voted Yes. What is to be done? Who will speak for ROC? There is little doubt about the answer. The referendum result will be accepted, and it will be the Government of Canada that does so.

Accepting the result will be an agonizing decision, taken by politicians who are exhausted from the referendum campaign and who are meeting under intense time pressure in an atmosphere where news of the result will produce popular reactions ranging from jubilation to outrage. Yet the decision must be made. It will be taken by the federal cabinet after consultation with the opposition parties and the provincial premiers. The announcement will be made by the prime minister, accompanied by senior ministers and probably the leaders of the Reform Party, the Progressive Conservatives, and the NDP. The prime minister will state that Canadians accept the result and that Quebec will leave the federation. He will appeal for calm and will reassure both the citizenry and the international community that the process of separation will be peaceful, constitutional, and managed through negotiations. All international obligations will be met. There will be no change whatsoever in the constitution, existing law, government programs, or economic management until a settlement of outstanding issues has been reached with the Government of Quebec. Most of all, he will stress that Canada has not come to an end, that political leaders are unanimous in their determination to carry on, and that in this critical time all Canadians must be united as never before.

What are the alternatives to such a decision? First, the Canadian government could refuse to accept the popular verdict, particularly if the margin of the Yes victory was very thin. There are good arguments for requiring super-majorities to effect constitutional change, and recent secession referendums have carried by wide margins.[46] Yet the fundamental democratic principle is that the majority rules. Moreover, insofar as there are norms about referendum decisions in Canada, the operative decision rule is 50 per cent plus one of those voting. This was the rule understood to be operative in the referendum on the Charlottetown Accord. It is also the position of the Reform Party with respect to the referendums it favours on all constitutional amendments.[47] It is even the principle used by Scott Reid and others who have advocated local referendums in Quebec to allow secession from the province.[48] Apart from the principle, refusing the result would cause massive unrest in Quebec, as well as sympathetic and provocative demonstrations elsewhere in the country. It would implicitly support Aboriginal claims of the right of secession from Quebec, and it would create international concern about Canada's commitment to democracy, since Quebecers would have decided the issue in a campaign where the options were clearly sovereignty or the status quo. If the question was legitimate and the campaign fair, ROC could not refuse to accept the result.

A refusal, in any case, would have to be effected by force sooner or later. But the repression of Quebec might not be within Canada's power; nor would this option command support in ROC. A 1992 Decima poll found that only 7 per cent of respondents in ROC found the use of military force to prevent Quebec seceding to be somewhat or very acceptable.[49] Apart from any propensity to pacifism among Canadians, there is the question of the goal of repression, either economic or political: "What would the objectives of such a declaration of political war be? To restore federalism? To abolish the Québec National Assembly? To install a more 'sensible' provincial government? Would it indeed be in Canada's self-interest to exact as high a price as possible before acquiescing to Quebec's sovereignty? Would Canada benefit from a poor, unstable, and recriminatory neighbour?"[50]

Alternatively, the government could resign in favour of new leadership. But the confusion and delay that this would engender makes this option highly irresponsible. In any case, a new government would still have to depend on the support of the Liberal majority in the House of Commons. The prime minister could resign, and this would be a possibility after a losing campaign, but it, too, would increase uncertainty and would be a neglect of duty.[51] The opposition parties could not force a resignation, and it is more likely that leadership within the government would become focused in a small number of senior ministers.

The federal government could call an immediate election. Having lost the referendum battle, the Liberals might be disorganized and discredited. There certainly will be calls for a change of government in order to choose an administration with a mandate to deal with Quebec and to manage the reconstitution of Canada.[52] But this course of action would extend and deepen uncertainty, and it could promote profound divisions within ROC by making the response to Quebec a partisan rather than national matter. There is also the problem of what specific platforms the federal parties could present, especially on constitutional change in ROC. More seriously, no party would be likely to secure a working majority in the House of Commons, and the passions of an election campaign would make a collective ROC position very difficult to frame in these circumstances. There also remains the obvious problem that Quebecers could not be excluded from participating in the election, even though they had just voted to exit from the Canadian community. (Amending the Elections Act to permit an election in ROC alone probably would be unconstitutional.) In the view of some, after the implications of the Yes vote have been registered by Quebecers, an election would allow them a second chance to cast a vote for federalism. But such an election would be highly divisive in the province, where it might be boycotted or might simply result in the re-election of Bloc members. The

Quebec vote might well prevent the formation of a majority government based in ROC and capable of coherently expressing a Canadian position about dealing with Quebec or reconstituting Canada.

Another possibility is for Ottawa to organize its own referendum after the Yes vote in Quebec. There are several forms this could take. A referendum restricted to Quebec might pose a different question about sovereignty, perhaps specifying different implications of the choice. Or it could be the same question, but one that was presented after some implications of the first vote had sunk in. Once more, though, this would prolong the process. By negating the first result, the gesture itself would promote demonstrations, a boycott, and violence at the polls.

Alternatively, a referendum confined to the rest of Canada might ask whether the Quebec decision should be accepted. Again, this would delay matters for at least the thirty-six days of campaigning specified in the Referendum Act, and it might not be conclusive. What would be the effect on national unity and Canada's negotiating power if some provincial electorates agreed and others did not? If the popular decision went against accepting the Quebec result, the federal government's room to manoeuvre would be very restricted. It could not negotiate the terms of separation, and the PQ government could be forced into a unilateral declaration of independence (UDI). If Canadians accepted the Quebec Yes vote, then negotiations would begin, but only after a costly delay.

Then again, rather than hold a referendum about accepting or rejecting Quebec sovereignty, the federal government could pose other questions in a referendum. It could ask whether Canadians favoured sovereignty or the constitutional status quo or negotiations to renew the federal system. Or it could put before the electorate specific constitutional proposals, perhaps the essence of the Meech Lake Accord or a package of generally decentralizing amendments. Such a referendum could be held in ROC alone or throughout Canada.

Some Quebecers would favour this outcome, because in the larger constitutional game, a Yes vote can be seen as the final card that would force ROC to negotiate seriously. Two positions are blended here. In the first, a vote for sovereignty would arm Quebec with sufficient power to negotiate post-separation arrangements that approximate "special status," the province's traditional demand. Hence sovereigntists such as Mr Bouchard both advocate and predict that confederal structures join Quebec and Canada after sovereignty is achieved.[53] In the second and softer position, a Yes vote would force ROC to negotiate and to meet Quebec's demands, but within the constitutional framework, so sovereignty might not be achieved – or it might be. Such ambiguity is expressed by Mario Dumont's Parti action démocratique, and it resembles the Slovak proposals for a "state treaty" – a way to achieve, as Mr Dumont puts it, sovereignty but not separation.[54] This position accords with many moderate nationalists' desire to have sovereignty – or at least national autonomy – without breaking the attachment to Canada, and it corresponds with some popular expectations that "sovereignty" would permit this.[55] If Canada held a referendum, the result might show that ROC finally understood how serious Quebecers' disaffection was, while in Quebec the moderate nationalists might swing away from sovereignty. The economic impact of the Yes vote might help produce these results.

But it is unrealistic to think that Ottawa will seek a mandate to negotiate constitutional change after a Yes vote, or that it would receive one in a referendum. First, whether a referendum question presented broad constitutional options or a set of constitutional proposals, uncertainty and confusion would be prolonged, not only during the referendum campaign but also while negotiations proceeded (if they did). If the federal government received only a mandate to renew federalism, this crude result would not dictate to the negotiators – the governments in place, with all their historical animosities – what should be the parameters of a settlement.

In any case, public opinion in ROC probably would not endorse major constitutional changes in order to keep Quebec in the federation. A 1992 poll on this question found opinion evenly divided, and sentiment in favour of "closure" undoubtedly has hardened since then.[56] There could be some support in ROC for a constitutional package that would decentralize powers in order to keep Quebecers in the federation, but there would be almost none for any form of special status.[57]

Any referendum campaign would be enormously divisive in ROC. Whatever the question posed, it is likely that some provincial electorates would be favourable while others would not be. MPs from these provinces and the provincial governments would be in an impossible situation, both during any negotiations and when any proposed amendments resulting from them were submitted for ratification. Quite apart from the provincial dimension, any referendum would create sharp divisions of opinion in ROC. After all the delay and debate, Ottawa could emerge with only a slim mandate to take any course of action, and the degree of opposition to it would have been precisely measured in the voting booths. More practically, the campaign in ROC would be along party lines. If the federal government supported negotiations or a specific set of proposals but the electorate did not, its legitimacy would be impaired. In any referendum the government would run the risk of having to resign after the vote.

Moreover, whatever the outcome of a referendum held in ROC, there is no reason to expect that the Parti québécois government would negotiate anything other than sovereignty, however much the moderate nationalists might support talks about constitutional renewal. Under a PQ government, the National Assembly would pass no constitutional resolution to renew federalism. If a federal referendum was conducted in Quebec, it would certainly be boycotted, and opposed physically at every polling station. The Quebec government would refuse to be bound by the result, and the National Assembly could pass a UDI, had it not done so already. Then the Quebec government, ready to negotiate the terms of sovereignty, would confront a ROC badly divided by a referendum campaign and led by a much weakened federal government. Given all of this, the referendum alternative is not a viable one.

Finally, the federal government could do nothing. It could wait for the National Assembly to act, since referendum results have no legal, binding weight in a parliamentary system. But this would be a short delay only, for the PQ majority would ensure quick passage of a resolution accepting the results and demanding negotiations. Even then, Ottawa could continue to make no response, but this would be unsustainable in the atmosphere of uncertainty that would result. Foreign powers concerned about their military and diplomatic interests would soon press for some resolution of the issue. The deteriorating economic situation would be another spur, as it would be in every alternative where Ottawa failed to take fast, decisive action.

A Yes referendum result would shake foreign confidence in Canada, and a result that did not meet with a clear, fast response would produce even more downward pressure on the dollar and a sharper rise in short-term interest rates: "The inevitable question on the mind of the foreign investor would be: 'Do I really want to play in the traffic while Canadians sort out these matters? Would it not be better to park, temporarily at least, my investments elsewhere?'"[58]

The financial consequences of any delay would be severe for individuals, firms, and governments, especially the last. As of January 1994, the federal government had $165.9 billion in outstanding treasury bills at terms of less than one year. It had another $193.3 billion in loans in the form of bonds, with an average time to maturity of less than five years. An increase in interest rates would make refinancing this debt much more expensive. For example, a 2 per cent rise in rates would cost an extra $4.32 billion in interest payments over the course of a year.[59] The provincial governments would be similarly affected, except that because more of their borrowing is in foreign currencies, they would also bear the cost of a depreciating dollar.

An even stronger stimulus to determined action will be domestic uncertainty. In Canada, some have discounted the argument that Quebec secession will produce a crisis (and this propensity increases as one moves west across the land). But a Yes vote will cause profound uncertainty throughout the country. This is a term that is used so often that it can take on an air of meaninglessness or unreality, but uncertainty is all too tangible. It implies precisely the kind of changes in calculations and attitudes and lifestyle that individuals make when the company they work for is taken over and the probability of keeping their jobs is reduced. A Yes vote in a Quebec referendum will dramatically reduce the probability of many things remaining unchanged – not only items that are normally volatile, such as the interest rate, but also much of the unquestioned background of everyday life: the currency in use, the security of bank deposits and pension-fund assets, and one's citizenship. To start with, Quebec citizens and firms will not know where their taxes should be paid. People there will be unsure of their rights and of whether government services will continue. Anyone with links to the province will also face uncertainty. The whole legal structure of trade will be uncertain: firms will not know whether their customers and suppliers will be staying in the same country and whether they will be governed by existing law, and every contract with Quebec interests will become insecure. Uncertainty will affect behaviour in every sector of the economy. Firms in the direct-mail business will have to wonder about the future of the post office. Wheat farmers shipping by rail will not know whether the CNR will serve them next year; they will not know what port their produce will move through and whether federal subsidies and stabilization plans will remain in effect. In the financial-services sector, there will be uncertainty about clearing trades on the stock exchanges, cashing cheques, and the nationality of assets and liabilities. In oil, cars, and lumber, hundreds of thousands of people will not know whether the FTA and NAFTA will continue to govern international commerce. Meanwhile, the whole retail sector will be seized with the question of whether Canadians will continue to spend when interest rates are rising and the future is so murky.

This is uncertainty. People will pay a lot to avoid it. (Consider how much most people would pay in order to know that their jobs were secure for a decade.) Consequently, after a Yes vote, Canadians will demand decisive action to reduce uncertainty, even at a price. And this price includes not only economic losses but also political costs –

the distaste of having matters handled by a government that one did not support, the frustration of having decisions made without participating in them, and the irritation of one's leaders making deals with separatists.

The whole force of uncertainty will be against any indecision and delay. Nevertheless, Ottawa might still resist this pressure and try to wait Quebec out. Then what? One possibility is that the PQ might crumble, and there might not be a majority in the National Assembly to support the next step – a unilateral declaration of independence. This seems unlikely, however, given the PQ government's current composition and orientation, the widespread sentiment in Quebec that its citizens have a right to self-determination, and the basic principle of majority rule. If the National Assembly did pass a UDI, Canada would then have the choice of recognizing the new state or not. If it did not do so, the result eventually would have to be either negotiations or a contest for control of the territory. On the other hand, if Canada recognized a Quebec UDI, two results follow. First, Quebec would no longer be part of the country, so both *de facto* and *de jure* the constitution would no longer apply to it. This would be convenient, in a way, since Canada would not have to proceed with constitutional amendments in order to eliminate Quebec from the country. However, it would then fall to the courts to interpret how the constitution would work in practice without Quebec, and the courts' interpretation would be cautious. There would be no court-ordered changes to language rights, the Senate, or the amending formula, yet these are amendments that the citizens and governments of ROC might want to make in order to fit the country's basic law to its new circumstances. Hence, the constitutional outcome would be inferior to what would otherwise be possible. Second, after a recognized UDI, Canada and Quebec would have to start negotiations about various urgent issues. So there would be no advantage to Canada if it waited out the result and forced a UDI.

It is clear, then, that all the alternatives would be unsatisfactory. The Yes verdict will therefore be accepted. And on referendum night, the federal government will speak for Canada.

QUEBEC SECESSION WILL BE A MOMENTOUS AND GALVANIZING EVENT

Until the referendum result was in, Canadians and Quebecers did not know what their collective future would be. The Yes vote will produce a sudden, definitive answer: the future will be very different. This shock will create enormous anxiety (and some anger). There had, of course, been intense discussion, reflection, and contingency planning about various options prior to the vote, but it was all hypothetical. Now, no one is at all certain how events will actually unfold.

In this context, power, legitimacy, and initiative will flow to the federal order of government. Only it can take the lead in resolving the uncertainty; only it can embody the solidarity Canadians will seek to deploy against Quebec and to maintain against the possibility of fragmentation; and only it has the requisite powers to keep order.

A Yes vote will plunge Canada into a crisis. Uncertainty will be felt by every citizen. There will be some variance in this, of course. The anxiety level of most federal employees in Kingston or Halifax will be much higher than that of most Vancouver real estate agents. But the Yes vote will unsettle every Canadian. Quite apart from their material interests, they will be unsure about their citizenship, about what community they now belong to. They will need reassurances about these matters, and Ottawa will supply them. So will the provincial governments, and it would be most unlikely in the immediate crisis for these governments to send messages contradicting those that emanate from the centre.

There will be a tremendous drive towards solidarity in ROC, and its only possible focus is the central government. Since the Yes vote will represent a profound rejection by Quebecers of the national community as it exists, there will be doubt about whether Canada can continue. Ottawa's message will be that it can. As is well understood, ROC does not really exist, but the rejection of all other Canadians by Quebec will help create it. For one thing, Quebec will have to be dealt with on new terms, and it will be essential to have unity in order to conduct negotiations in ROC's interest. An external threat is always highly conducive to internal solidarity, and as in wartime, the central government will be the agency that deals with the threat.

Beyond this, there is every indication that the citizens of ROC will prefer to continue as a country.[60] One major alternative is integration with the United States, but while Canadians may have lost some affection for their country's traditional symbols, the elements that do command support are touchstones of difference from that country, such as Canada's lack of violence and its health-care system.[61] In 1992 one straightforward poll question asked whether respondents would take the opportunity for their province to join the United States as a normal state with full political representation, and 79 per cent said no.[62] These *ex ante* sentiments will be strengthened when the event occurs, because at a much deeper level internal solidarity is a predictable consequence of Canadians' various senses of national identification. There is one identifiable group, among them the *bon voyagistes*, for whom francophone and alien Quebec has always been an anomaly in their essentially geographic conception of Canada; although they will be discomfited by noncontiguity, they will favour unity in order to deal – preferably harshly – with the "other." A different sense of national identification stresses the regions and provinces of Canada, viewing the whole rather like a family; that family must unite in a crisis. Then there are those who understand Canada to be a constructed society, different from and superior to the United States; they too will support a central leadership that promises to reconstruct and maintain their county.[63]

These deep structures of national identification suggest that in accommodating the shock of Quebec secession, the citizens of ROC will tend to support national leadership rather than provincial alternatives. Further evidence is available from survey research. It is true that the Environics data cited in Chapter 7 above showed declining levels of identification with Canada, as opposed to the provinces, over the 1980–91 period. But any questions about people's underlying sense of identification are intrusive, and the results are sensitive to the question posed. Environics asked "Do you feel you are more a citizen of Canada or more a citizen of this province?" In 1991, the proportions answering "Canada" were still 49 per cent in the Atlantic region, 57 per cent in the West, and 69 per cent in Ontario.[64] Gallup asked a different question in 1991 – "Generally speaking, would you say your primary allegiance is to Canada, to this province, or to this particular local community?" Even with a third response option, those choosing "Canada" were 57 per cent in the Atlantic provinces, 74 per cent in Ontario, 64 per cent on the Prairies, and 69 per cent in British Columbia.[65] In late 1993, another Gallup poll asked, "Do you think of yourself *first* as a Canadian or as a Newfoundlander?" (or "Albertan," "Ontarian," and so on). Respondents answering "Canadian" were 72 per cent in Atlantic Canada, 94 per cent in Ontario, 80 per cent on the Prairies, and 60 per cent in British Columbia.[66] Another survey asked a similar question and found that only 22 per cent of Canadians – including Quebecers – thought of themselves first as residents of a particular region or province, and in ROC, apart from respondents in the Atlantic region, the lowest "Canadian" identification was in Alberta, at 74 per cent.[67]

One cannot know with certainty how this strong and widespread attachment to Canada as a whole would change under the impact of a Yes vote, though comparative analysis suggests that it would strengthen. Moreover, there are some data concerning Canadians' expectations about the outcome of a Quebec secession. If Quebec separates, most Canadians anticipate that the rest of Canada would emerge from the event as a "strong united country," rather than breaking up into smaller countries or having parts absorbed by the United States. The proportions of respondents expecting unity and continuity were 48 per cent in the Atlantic provinces, 66 per cent in Ontario, 62 per cent on the Prairies, and 61 per cent in British Columbia.[68] Of course, these responses are sensitive to the question asked, and they concern hypothetical events – but they strongly suggest that the citizens of ROC would be prepared to accept the federal government's lead during a secession crisis.

Finally, only Ottawa has the power to maintain order. When secession is accepted, the use of force to maintain the existing state will be renounced simultaneously, but the Yes vote will undoubtedly cause unrest and sporadic outbreaks of violence. These will be concentrated in Quebec and on its borders, especially in Montreal, in anglophone regions, and wherever Aboriginal people choose to manifest their refusal to accept the result without their consent, but unrest and civil disobedience will not be limited to Quebec. The federal government controls the armed forces and the RCMP, and these agencies may well have to be deployed. Moreover, the central government can equip itself with extraordinary powers under the Emergencies Act, which defines a "national emergency" as "an urgent and critical situation of a temporary nature" that "seriously threatens the ability of the Government of Canada to preserve the sovereignty, security and territorial integrity of Canada."[69] If the government considered that threats of violence were being used for political objectives, it could declare a "public order emergency" in all or parts of Canada, and could equip itself with powers to prohibit public assemblies and control the use of specified property – which would allow, notably, the freezing of bank accounts.[70] This would be an extreme measure, but if the crisis is serious it would be difficult for opposition parties or the provincial governments to oppose it. In Quebec, obviously, the Emergencies Act would not be invoked without the approval of the provincial government; indeed, the Act could not legally be invoked in Quebec alone without that approval,[71] but this would be forthcoming if Ottawa accepted the referendum result and the domestic situation was slipping into disorder.[72]

This account of Ottawa taking the lead of an anxious public galvanized into unity by the reality of secession is supported by comparative experience and evidence from Canada, but it is contestable in theory. It will not be contestable in reality. Although one could argue that the federal government would be delegitimized by its failure to defeat the separatists, it seems unlikely that this would be the case. Since most Canadians regard secession as irrational, the blame for the Yes vote will be laid on Quebecers rather than on those who defended Canada. Some Canadians, like some analysts, will see in the crisis an opportunity to create a Canada more to their liking than the country and system of government that now exist, and they will be suspicious of Ottawa because its initial actions will reduce the chance of later countering central power. But the issue of how ROC will reconstitute itself will not be at the top of the agenda yet. As Gibson shrewdly recognized, "the first matter is to secure and nail down the internal and external status quo, at least temporarily."[73] Only Ottawa can do this. In theory, the provincial governments could object to Ottawa's taking the lead, but they will be able to offer no credible alternative. There is no mechanism for them to assume the initiative in dealing with Quebec, and they are divided by interest and ideology. In any case, some provincial governments will be immediately supportive of Ottawa, because not to do so would open the route to national disintegration. As the York study group advised,

If Québec secedes, we recommend that Ontario take a leading role in resisting the pressures to decentralize by committing itself to the values of sharing and common citizenship which have characterized Ontario's role in the past. It is essential that Ontario take this leading role, because a failure to do so would effectively subvert any attempt to maintain a political union among the remaining nine provinces. We believe that the disintegration of the remaining provinces into discrete political units would be contrary to the interests of these provinces, including Ontario. It would further complicate and increase the burden associated with Québec secession from Canada.[74]

In the short term at least, this support would leave other provinces open to criticism if they undermined a national response to the crisis. The same holds true for the opposition parties in Parliament, and especially for Reform, the critical actor. However uncomfortable some members might feel, these parties will have nothing to gain by strenuously resisting the federal government's attempts to deal with the grave threat posed by the Yes vote. In fact, both the provinces and the opposition parties will be brought into the negotiating process.

THE GOVERNMENTS WILL BE BROADENED
AND STRENGTHENED: THERE WILL BE A PREMIUM
ON SOLIDARITY

The first step in the secession is to begin negotiating the separation of Quebec from Canada. This cannot be delayed. The politicians in place will have to take charge of the process immediately. They will then create structures to guide and shape the negotiations.

There will be differing views in Canada about the course of action to be followed in the aftermath of the Yes vote, and about ROC's negotiating positions and Canada's optimal long-term relationship with Quebec. These differences will be submerged, temporarily, for their expression will be muted by the crisis and by the need for solidarity to frame a collective response to Quebec right away. Second, all political factions will become involved in the negotiations. This will be an indirect involvement for the most part, but it will be enough to ensure that the participants are fully informed about the conduct of the negotiations and that they can debate the positions taken by the Canadian side. It will be difficult for any leader to refuse to become involved in this process; and in the short term, any minority making strong public criticism of it will risk being regarded as disloyal.

The negotiations will be led by the federal order of government, which will have taken the initiative immediately. It has the power to recognize other states, and it takes the lead in international diplomacy. Executing agreements with Quebec will mainly require changes in federal rather than provincial law, for most will involve matters falling within federal jurisdiction. But the government will be broadened and strengthened in order to represent Canada fully. This will be necessary to maintain Ottawa's stock of legitimacy and support. The structures set up will evolve under the pressure of events, public opinion, special demands, and partisan incentives, and they will have many levels.

The basic entity will be a large joint committee of the House of Commons and the Senate. It might be called the Joint Committee on Canada-Quebec Separation (JCC-QS). This will resemble the Bélanger-Campeau Commission that was set up to inquire into Quebec's constitutional future. There will be about fifty members, at least half coming from the House of Commons, and the parties will be represented proportionately. The party leaderships, including members of the cabinet and the prime minister, will be members. Power, information, and responsibility will be concentrated in this large committee.

The JCC-QS will be the parliamentary body to which negotiators report. Meetings initially will be for the negotiators to share information and receive direction. Later, draft agreements will flow into the JCC-QS, to be debated in detail. Still later, some will take the form of bills that will be referred to the committee or to normal standing committees, and these will proceed through the standard legislative process (with proclamation delayed appropriately).

If the Emergencies Act is invoked, the JCC-QS could also serve as the parliamentary review committee that would oversee orders and regulations under that Act. A difficulty here is that all parties with at least twelve MPs must be represented on the review committee, and this means that the Bloc québécois will be entitled to membership. However, the Bloc might well withdraw its members from Parliament as soon as the referendum result has been accepted; alternatively, House of Commons rules and the Emergencies Act itself could be quickly amended to exclude them: one way or another, the Bloc will play no part on the Canadian side. Its members certainly will not participate in the JCC-QS.

The same is not true of the provinces. The provincial governments will have three interests in how the crisis is managed. First, their citizens and their treasuries will be affected by the prevailing economic uncertainty. Second, they have a direct stake in some of the matters to be negotiated with Quebec. Third, the separation will require constitutional amendments to effect it and to reconstitute a new Canada without Quebec. These amendments will require provincial assent, so it will be prudent to involve the provincial governments in the separation negotiations, even though these negotiations are independent of the constitutional amendment process. There are three avenues for provincial involvement. First, representatives will sit on the JCC-QS.[75] This will be the main body to which information about the negotiations is channelled, and every provincial government will have full access to it. These governments will then be able to take some responsibility for the Canada-Quebec arrangements. Second, a separate joint committee will be established to consider how to redraft the Canadian constitution, and this will have provincial representation, even though amendments will also be discussed in First Ministers' Conferences. Finally, some premiers will take a direct part in the negotiations.

The negotiating group will report to the JCC-QS. It will also report to cabinet, and probably to a special cabinet committee of the strongest ministers and those whose departments are most directly affected by the substance of the talks. Maintaining cabinet (and caucus) solidarity will be imperative, for the government must continue to operate and to be seen to be in control. But as noted above, crises both elicit determined leadership and offer few incentives for publicly defying it.

Would the government itself be broadened by taking opposition leaders into the cabinet? Probably not. The offer of a coalition was not made even during World War II. Moreover, it is unlikely that the only relevant potential partner, the Reform Party, would accept such an arrangement. Its western base is sceptical of Ottawa's intentions and wary of the Liberals, and the party is ideologically more disposed to locate legitimacy in the legislature as a representative whole rather than in the executive. So although Reformers will sit on the JCC-QS and Mr Manning will be part of the negotiating group, the Liberal majority will take responsibility for governing Canada during the transition.

This raises the issue of Liberal MPs and ministers from Quebec. Their continuing participation in the government and even the House of Commons will be questioned in some quarters – there will be distrust of "Quebec negotiating with itself." These are real concerns. But they will be countered. In the first place, under the operative constitution, the Quebec members were legitimately elected. The Liberal MPs, along with Mr Charest, are federalists all, and other members will not reject them, thereby immediately denying representation to their constituents. In the aftermath of the Yes vote, the federal cabinet will be broadened, and Quebec ministers will be massively outnumbered by those from elsewhere in the country. Some will be shed. It will be essential, for example, to have a non-Quebecer as minister of finance. Further, the JCC-QS membership will be overwhelmingly, if not exclusively, from ROC. Most important, apart from the prime minister (at the outset), the Canadian negotiating team will include no Quebecers. So the presence of Quebec representatives on the government side will not impede a solidaristic and collective ROC response to the Yes vote. On the other hand, the anomaly of there being any Quebec MPs at all in the House of Commons after a Yes vote, and especially from the Bloc, is one reason why a federal election will have to be called after the immediate crisis has passed.

In Quebec a parallel process will occur. The PQ government formed after the 1994 election is organized around a tight cadre of senior ministers that will dominate a raucous National Assembly through firm party discipline. After the referendum result, however, this will change. The PQ will set up a broad legislative steering committee with Liberals included. As in Canada, the Quebec government will seek the legitimacy that comes from concentrating power in a broad and representative body. And when Canada has accepted the referendum verdict, at least some Liberal MNAs will be drawn into the separation process. How else could they protect the interests of their constituents? In fact, some Liberals probably will be included on the Quebec negotiating team.

THE NEGOTIATIONS WILL INVOLVE FEW PARTICIPANTS

Secessions are negotiated at the highest level, and consequently few actors are involved. Although increasing numbers of politicians and civil servants come to participate in the process as it unfolds, the difficult questions are always resolved by small groups of leaders from each side. Extensive powers are delegated to these few individuals. This is because the situation is unprecedented and the crisis has to be resolved in short order. But large amounts of information are conveyed back from the negotiators to the bodies to which they are responsible, and to the public; and as debate takes place, the parameters of settlements acceptable to the domestic constituencies become apparent. On the other hand, the negotiators have considerable autonomy, since only they deal directly with the other side. Because the matters discussed are complex and urgent, secessions offer much scope for leadership – for the shaping of legislative and public opinion through explanation of the issues, the stakes, and the positions of the other side.

The initial talks with Quebec will be by telephone on the day of the Yes referendum result. They will involve aides to the prime minister and Mr Parizeau, who will agree on statements about the immediate situation and will arrange for a meeting to be held within two or three days. The leaders will speak briefly to confirm these matters. Subsequent negotiations will be conducted by a small delegation from each side. The prime minister and the premier of Quebec will probably not meet directly before this group is assembled, though their aides will certainly be in continual contact about the modalities of the negotiations.

The Canadian side initially will be led by the prime minister, though he will delegate day-to-day responsibility for the negotiations to another cabinet minister. The Canadian delegation will also include the minister of finance and two or three senior ministers who have wide credibility and experience in federal-provincial matters. Some regional balance will be essential. A strong and respected senator could also be included. But this is not sufficient. Even though the provincial governments will participate through the JCC-QS, it will be desirable to involve some provincial premiers directly in the negotiations. Their numbers must be limited, though. Negotiating a secession is not like negotiating a new GATT agreement. There are tight deadlines, and the same actors must confront each other repeatedly on tough issues. Large delegations consume time and inhibit agreement.

It seems that three premiers at most could adequately represent the provinces: a set such as Mr Rae, Mr Klein, and Mr McKenna would suffice. This group has regional and partisan balance, and includes the two provinces with the most at stake economically in the secession. If the other premiers resisted such a selection, an alternative structure would resemble that used in negotiating trade agreements. The federal team would conduct the negotiations and report to the

JCC-QS, but there would be a parallel set of provincial representatives – premiers, leading cabinet ministers, and key officials – to which the primary negotiators, along with their supporting officials, would also report.[76] A single premier, the chair of the group, could attend the negotiating sessions as an observer. Through this mechanism, all the provinces would have more sustained input into the negotiations, but it would be more cumbersome. Moreover, provincial participation is not strictly necessary to consummate the agreements that will be negotiated with Quebec.

This point needs to be clarified. The provinces will certainly have to agree to the constitutional amendments that seal the secession, but this is a separate matter from negotiating the terms of Quebec's exit. Most arrangements made with Quebec will not impinge on areas of provincial jurisdiction, and even if they did, treaties could still be signed by Ottawa under the "national concern" branch of the Peace, Order and Good Government power.[77] The constitution and the agreements could be linked politically, of course, by provincial governments that either were opposed to some terms of the separation or were determined to achieve some particular constitutional provisions. But none could stymie the separation deal. (And none will later be in a position to hold up Canada's reconstitution in order to gain particular terms of separation.) As a matter of practicality, premiers will be included in the negotiations with Quebec because they have credibility and popular support. So, with Ottawa necessarily taking the lead, some premiers will be integrated directly into the Canadian negotiating team, and all provinces will be represented on the JCC-QS.

Then there is Mr Manning. His position will be difficult. He leads a dynamic and growing party with a populist membership that opposes much of what "Ottawa" has done. When Bloc members resign from the House of Commons, or are expelled or become ineligible to sit, if not before, Mr Manning will be leader of the opposition. Since his party will have a very good chance of taking power at the next election, there will be incentives for it to resist federal – and Liberal – dominance of a process that would seem to offer opportunities for the fundamental changes demanded by many of his supporters. These pressures could keep Reform out of a coalition government. But Mr Manning would find it difficult not to take a direct part in the negotiations. He will be ineluctably involved, first by agreeing to accept the Yes verdict and by standing with other leaders as the representatives of Canada. Then, as the leader of the Loyal Opposition (and as champion of those most hostile to Quebec), could he refuse a public call to help negotiate on behalf of Canada? No. Moreover, although Reform, like the premiers, may feel increasingly uncomfortable with the process and with some of its outcomes, and although the incentives for partisan opposition will re-emerge as the sense of crisis lessens, Mr Manning will find it awkward to break with the Canadian position, because he will share responsibility for what it has accomplished. The appropriate time for political contestation in ROC will be during an election campaign or a referendum. The price of Mr Manning's presence on the Canadian team may well be a commitment to hold such a popular consultation as soon as the immediate issues of the secession have been agreed. But this will be necessary in any case.

The core Canadian negotiating group, then, will consist of about eight people. It will be supported initially by a few senior officials from Justice, Finance, Foreign Affairs and International Trade, and from the Privy Council Office. There will be some pressure to expand this group, but the immediate resistance will have been co-opted in the service of the national interest, and other pressures will take time to build. As this happens, they will be accommodated. Aboriginal peoples, for example, will be represented on the JCC-QS, and they will be involved in detailed negotiations about Aboriginal issues, most of which will already have been settled in principle. The same is true of special interests, other provinces, and the rest of the cabinet. Thus, while the negotiations will spread quickly as the sides engage, the negotiating parameters will be set by a small group that has the power to take the crucial initial decisions and later to resolve the most difficult and contentious issues.

QUEBEC SEPARATION WILL BE
ACCOMPLISHED QUICKLY

There are three major tasks to be accomplished after a Yes vote in the referendum. First, Canada and Quebec have to negotiate the modalities of the secession, including some transitional and long-term arrangements. Second, each country must equip itself with a new constitution. Finally, in Canada at least, the new arrangements must be ratified by the public, through either an election or a referendum.

There are good domestic reasons for all this to be done quickly. In the immediate aftermath of the Quebec referendum, Canadians will experience enormous uncertainty. Emotions will be running high, and there will be movements of people, demonstrations, and sporadic violence. The economic costs will be mounting. So there will be both a need and a demand for firm leadership and a rapid resolution of some big issues, and negotiations will have to begin at once. Then, as decisions are taken and as the realization spreads that the secession is irreversible, the prevailing public sentiment will favour settling the separation as quickly as possible in order to minimize the costs of transition, to stabilize the country, and to leave the past behind. The issues to be settled will be unprecedented, and this, along with the sense of urgency and the solidarity among the negotiating leadership, will give politicians considerable latitude in their dealings with Quebec. But dissent and conflict along several dimensions will re-emerge, for it will be difficult to sustain unity as the crisis fades. The very success of the crisis management will permit partisan, ideological, and regional differences to become more sharply expressed. This is another argument for haste – to allow for a broadening public debate about what has been done, and then for the popular ratification that will legitimize it.

In the first phase after the Yes vote, simultaneous with its acceptance by Canadian leaders, immediate statements will be forthcoming from Ottawa, Quebec City, and other provincial capitals. The leaders will abjure the use of force and will pledge themselves to settle matters through constitutional means. They will promise to protect the security and rights of all citizens. And they will declare that all existing laws will remain in effect – in particular, that there will be no alteration in economic management and regulation. (This last commitment represents an "economic standstill.") Finally, they will state to the world that Canada and Quebec will fully honour all international treaties and all obligations to foreigners.

In the next stage, Canada and Quebec will reach agreements in principle on the most pressing issues of the separation. This must happen fast, and it will. Assuming that the Quebec referendum was held on 19 June 1995, the first formal meeting between leaders from the two sides could be held on 22 June. Subsequent top-level meetings could occur on 29 June, 6 July, and 20 July. These meetings should suffice to settle most principles of the secession and to set up working groups of officials and politicians to work within frameworks as soon as they are agreed. Further meetings will certainly be necessary, including one or two in the autumn to resolve hard issues arising from the working groups, but the most crucial work will have been completed in about a month or six weeks. This should come as no surprise in light of the comparative experience of secession and the costs of delay and uncertainty in Canada. Some analysts, for example, foresee very long and hard negotiations about the division of the debt, but this issue could be settled in principle in ten minutes.

One of the most important decisions will be to establish a schedule and a deadline for achieving the separation. Assuming a June 1995 referendum, the most likely date would be 1 January 1996. Although constitutional amendments and a Canadian referendum or election would have to happen in the interim, this is a feasible schedule. An alternative would be 1 April 1996, a date that has the advantage of coinciding with the end of the fiscal year, but not much else to recommend it. Or the deadline could be set for the summer of 1996. In this case, one simple but symbolically important problem would be whether the date would be 24 June or 1 July. Only one date is possible. Far more important, though, this schedule would prolong the process for an entire year. Such a long delay would be improbable, given comparative experience, and it is not necessary. The essential tasks could be accomplished by 1 January 1996, with arrangements being made to tidy up outstanding details after that date. Speed will be essential in order to resolve economic uncertainty, and since a considerable proportion of this uncertainty will concern not the shape of Canada-Quebec relations but the continuity and structure of Canada itself, the Canadian reconstitution must start soon after the Yes vote and be occurring simultaneously with the Quebec negotiations. The Canadian side will insist on a firm and early deadline to drive the talks forward.

The negotiations with Quebec, then, will be largely settled by the end of September 1995. Canadians will commence the process of constitutional amendment in July, and this should be completed by September, setting the stage for a referendum or an election in early November. This popular consultation would ratify both the provisional separation arrangements and the reconstitution of Canada – or it might fail to do so. Assuming that ratification is given, Quebec's accession to sovereignty will take place at 12:01 am on 1 January 1996 at the same instant as the new Canada emerges.

FOREIGN POWERS WILL PLAY AN IMPORTANT ROLE IN THE SECESSION

The international community will watch the Canada-Quebec separation closely. In this larger context, Canada's interest, shared in part with Quebec, is to achieve a quick transition and a stable outcome in order to avoid foreign interference and to secure international support where it is feasible.

This should be possible. It will also be a strong incentive to negotiate quickly and efficiently. The major international organizations along with the important foreign powers share a primary interest in stability. This should lead to supportive action in the short term, and as long as the transition is occurring smoothly there will be no cause for foreign actors to contemplate intervention. But if the processes of disengagement and the reconstitution of Canada are delayed or if they collapse, the level of international anxiety will rise, simply because other states will have to make policy choices about what side to support, where to stand on "domestic" Canadian issues, and, ultimately, what to do in a situation in which government has broken down.

The major actor, of course, will be the United States. With the end of the Cold War and the shift of the PQ from socialism to a pro-business platform, the United States' concern for stability will be less acute than it was.[78] Its "tilt" in favour of Canadian unity may also become less apparent. But even a Yes vote will not cause a fundamental reassessment of American policy. The United States will favour a peaceful, constitutional, and rapid transition to Quebec sovereignty, one in which the huge economic interests of American firms in Canada and Quebec are unimpaired and the transborder flows of trade and money are unimpeded. There are many American jobs that depend on this relationship. If uncertainty about ROC-Quebec relations persists, however, economic activity will be affected, and U.S. concern will deepen considerably if Canada itself appears unstable. A new, more active policy would then be required.

One possible long-term outcome for Canada is that it fragments, with portions opting to join the United States. The reappraisal caused by a Yes vote will produce some thought of annexation in the Atlantic provinces, and British Columbians have become more conscious of their Pacific Rim position and the interests shared with Alaska, Washington, and Oregon. No country could fail to be attracted by this rich and strategically located province.[79] However, in the rapid events following the referendum, pro-annexationist sentiment will not swell enough to make provincial politicians impede the separation process and the reconstitution of Canada, let alone champion the notion of union with the United States. More important, if the transition is managed peacefully and rapidly, the American administration will be most unlikely to change that country's basic policy of supporting a stable state – or two stable states – on its northern frontier.

More generally, there are four critical areas where foreign powers will play an important role. The first is economic, especially in the immediate aftermath of the Yes vote. Given the pledges by Canada and Quebec to maintain an economic standstill until negotiations are complete, the G-7 countries might stand ready to support the Canadian dollar, which will be under pressure. Along with the Bank of Canada, the central banks of these countries are powerful enough to protect the currency against massive devaluations. Their incentive to do so will be to avoid disruption in international financial markets, to maintain the value of their citizens' and firms' investments in Canada and Quebec, and to help avoid financial panic in Canada. But these motives will not persist long; nor will concerted action alter the expectations of investors about the long term. Only visible progress in accomplishing the separation and evident stability in Canada will be able to do that.

Canada's most pressing problem will be to prevent a sell-off of bonds and to secure the placement of new issues. Again, international actors will help. The International Monetary Fund will make credit available, and some of this will be passed through to the provinces and to Quebec. But this will help only in the very short term, and Canadian debt dwarfs the amount of assistance likely to be available. In theory, the G-7 governments could extend guarantees to their citizens about the payment of interest, at least, on Canadian debt. This would be unprecedented, but so would be the breakup of a G-7 country. Such a move seems improbable, however. The burden would be unequally distributed across countries, the support levels and duration of the intervention would be hard to decide, and governments would risk criticism for taking on contingent liabilities and subsidizing those investors who held their Canadian bonds. So concerted international action to alleviate the financial crisis in Canada and Quebec will be unlikely. The only possible solution to this crisis will be firm assurances from politicians about future stability, followed by rapid and demonstrable progress towards a managed disengagement, and clear evidence of normalization in Canada. In domestic politics both in Canada and Quebec, the precarious economic situation will be a powerful spur to the occurrence of these very same phenomena.

The second international issue concerns the recognition of Quebec. Other countries and international agencies will not proceed to a sudden recognition. They will await evidence that the soon-to-be sovereign state will behave normally with respect to international obligations and human rights. Foreign governments will wait for a Canadian signal. Time will need to pass before it is entirely evident that the secession will not be contested by force. The agreements-in-principle, at a minimum, must be completed before other countries will deal formally with Quebec. Transitional arrangements enacted in the autumn of 1995 would permit Quebec to reach international agreements before it finally achieved sovereignty, and these agreements would constitute conditional recognition of the new country. But full sovereignty and its international recognition would await the constitutional separation of the two states on 1 January 1996.

The third concern of foreign states will be Canada's various rights and obligations under international treaties. Here there arises the possibility that the general interest of the international community in stability would be outweighed by specific advantages to be won through renegotiating treaties with a weakened partner or a fledgling state. And some modifications to existing treaties will have to be made. Generally, though, Canada's position will be secure, so long as it does not fragment. There is no doubt that it would be the successor state to all relevant international agreements. So its position as a treaty signatory will be unchanged, except where separation could be interpreted as representing such a fundamental change in circumstances that treaties must be renegotiated.

Military obligations will depend on arrangements about the Canadian Armed Forces. Doubtless, Canada will maintain membership in NORAD and NATO, and Quebec will probably enter these treaties. Some other bilateral and multilateral defence agreements might be broadened to include Quebec. In the short term, these matters will not be pressing to Canada's allies.[80]

Regional and bilateral trade treaties with the United States raise the most delicate issues. These include the Auto Pact, the Defence Production/Defence Sharing agreements, the FTA, and NAFTA. The Americans might demand that these treaties be reopened as a consequence of the separation.[81] The likelihood of this depends on the secession process and the economic arrangements negotiated between Canada and Quebec. Whether Quebec accedes to the FTA and NAFTA is a vital matter. If it does, these agreements will constitute a floor beneath which the level of Canada-Quebec economic integration cannot fall. But Canada has the legal right to veto Quebec's entry to NAFTA, and Canadian leaders will not provide any assurances not to use this veto power until negotiations are well advanced. While this move will probably not be countered by overt American pressures or statements to the contrary, the Canadian side cannot use this leverage indefinitely without stimulating general international concern about the country's economic stability – and also arousing American displeasure about the potential ending of NAFTA guarantees of its trade and investment relations with Quebec.[82]

The final international concern will be minority and Aboriginal rights. This will be deflected by the rights regime adopted by Quebec and the arrangements negotiated about First Nations. Fundamentally, the enforcement of human rights covenants is a matter of exposure and suasion rather than sanctions. Quebec will adopt model legislation and will be prepared to sign treaties and covenants about minority rights, and if implementation later is flawed, the international community (and perhaps Canada) will have the usual recourse. For the First Nations, the situation is similar. From the perspective of sovereign states, relations with indigenous peoples are *de facto* considered to be domestic issues. It is true that many citizens of countries such as Germany and the United Kingdom have great sympathy for Canadian First Nations, and they are capable of raising funds and putting pressure on their own governments on behalf of Aboriginal peoples. But if Aboriginal issues are successfully negotiated between Canada and Quebec, no official international action will be forthcoming. Even in the most extreme case – that some Quebec First Nations declare their sovereignty and stand prepared to defend their claim by force – other states or international organizations will be unlikely to recognize the claim, and they certainly will not countenance violence to achieve it.

To summarize, foreign powers will have great interest in the secession, but their stance generally will be benign. Their real interests lie in stability and therefore in a speedy and managed resolution of the crisis. Active policies or interventionist pressures will not be exerted by governments unless the separation process threatens to break down. The sovereign Quebec that will emerge from secession will be admitted into the international community as a normal member.

Foreign investors and firms are another matter. There will be a crisis of confidence in the Canadian currency and Canadian securities, and this will affect all governments and citizens. There will be some international assistance, but the crisis can only be resolved when uncertainty about Canada is reduced by coherent leadership, clear and explicit goals, and rapid and successful negotiations. Foreign governmental and economic pressures may not be sufficient to produce such a separation, but they will form an environment highly conducive to it.

CHAPTER THIRTEEN

The Negotiations

THE CANADA-QUEBEC NEGOTIATIONS WILL INVOLVE A RELATIVELY SHORT LIST OF ISSUES

Quebec secession will be accomplished when the Canadian constitution is amended to eliminate Quebec and the new constitution of Quebec becomes effective. Then relations between the two states will be conducted as is normal between sovereign entities. In the period between the referendum and the separation, the two sides will negotiate the modalities of the secession, along with agreements – which will become international treaties – about some of their future relationships. These negotiations will happen quickly. In the course of a few weeks, the shape of the secession will clarify, and as negotiations begin to produce agreements, each side will become more sharply defined, both as it will become legally and as it exists in the view of the public.

Although the negotiations will be fast, they will not be easy. Both Canada and Quebec will have to make unwelcome concessions. They will do so in the first instance because reducing international and domestic uncertainty will be imperative. Since the occasion will be unprecedented and since interests and opinion will take time to mobilize, the negotiators will have considerable autonomy to shape the course of events, especially in the early stages. Later, they will become more constrained by domestic interests. The negotiations will be the focus of immense national attention, and each side will have to become increasingly sensitive to domestic opinion. Each will have a fragile legitimacy. In Quebec, the bitterness and divisions of the referendum battle will be fresh, and public anxiety and civil disorder will be greater. In Canada, the politicians in place will have to respond to the referendum result, and while national solidarity will support them through the negotiations about separation and the longer-term issues that have to be settled quickly, this support will not endure for very long, nor will it be open-ended. In particular, the negotiators will be conscious of having no mandate to create permanent political structures joining Canada and Quebec.

A danger during the negotiations is that public opinion could polarize. This would most probably happen if Quebecers interpreted the agreements struck as punitive, for many Yes voters will have expectations that there will be a high level of cooperation between the two countries after the separation.[1] But this will not be the case, despite the fact that ROC's positions will be based on self-interest rather than spite, just as the sovereigntists predict. In contrast to some optimistic views, rational self-interest is not identical with cooperation. Canada's primary objective after a Yes vote will be national survival. In order of priority, this will require re-establishing stability, reconstituting the country, and making agreements with Quebec about the separation. This ordering immediately implies that suboptimal agreements with Quebec could well be tolerated for political reasons, especially for considerations of national unity.

Beyond this, Canadian negotiators will be responsive only to domestic interests. After secession, Quebecers will no longer vote for Canadian politicians, and the current incumbents managing the negotiations will respond only to Canadian problems. They will face a different configuration of interests and political demands than exists in Canada now. During the negotiations and after the separation, Canadian decision makers certainly will have to take Quebec into account, but only insofar as the effects on that country of their decisions will have negative second-order consequences for their own domestic constituency, and even these will be weighed against the offsetting Canadian benefits that would accrue. What is good for Quebec, in short, will not necessarily be good for Canada. And vice versa. In international relations, of course, it is perfectly normal to find noncooperation through self-interest.[2]

As is also common in international negotiations or in any strategic bargaining, countries adopt noncooperative positions in order to achieve long-term goals, or larger benefits in other areas if issues can be linked. So it is possible to categorize issues according to the sort of position that the Canadian side will adopt; and the same can be done for Quebec. First are cases where Canada's interests are highly congruent with Quebec's. For example, in the financial-services sector, both sides will agree that stability absolutely must be assured. In other areas, some compromise will result easily because Canada's immediate interest is bound up with the effects of outcomes on Quebec. The incentives offered to public servants to work for the Quebec government will be a case in point. Then there are areas where Canada will largely ignore the implications for Quebec and will act within its powers to achieve its interests as defined domestically. On citizenship, for example, Canadian negotiators will have to balance the pressures against allowing Quebecers to retain the right to move into Canada with those against abandoning its loyal nationals in Quebec. Similarly, companies with federal charters must by law maintain their head offices in Canada. Why would Canada change this legislation? The only motives would be to avoid imposing sudden costs on the firms and to maintain aggregate demand in Montreal for Canadian exports. It would be foolish to make firms move precipitously, but if the costs of lost markets would be outweighed by the benefits of gradually acquiring head offices, then the law might be amended to allow for a two-year adjustment period. Fourth, there are issues where Canada will refuse to cooperate in order to secure concessions elsewhere or in the future. Delaying Quebec's accession to NAFTA is a case in point. Finally, there are dossiers where Canada's position would be dictated by retribution. In a democratic system, public sentiments cannot be ignored by politicians, and separation is a symbolic and emotionally charged event. But there should be few if any issues where revenge predominates. As Gibson recognized, the Canadian side must act *strictly on the basis of what is good for us, and most definitely not on the basis of what is bad for them.*[3] This will probably occur. The danger is that Quebecers will demand radical counter-moves or retaliation by their government, because they will misinterpret Canadian noncooperation as malevolent when in fact it will simply be the rational exercise of self-interest, which realists understand to motivate sovereign states. But the prospects for polarization during the negotiations appear limited, for between Canada and Quebec there is sufficient mutual interest to produce a number of agreements that will be tolerable if not entirely satisfactory to either side.

Despite the high level of political, economic, and social integration that exists between Canada and Quebec, negotiations will centre on a small number of critical issues. The final statutes implementing the separation arrangements will run into several volumes as treaties are passed and statutes are amended, but the core issues to be decided are few, and agreements-in-principle can be stated succinctly.

The timing of agreements and the order in which they are reached are important. The first post-referendum announcements will embody the initial agreements: Canada accepts the result; force will not be used; only constitutional means will be employed by both sides; citizens' rights and security will be assured; all laws and regulations will continue in effect throughout the country; and all international obligations will be met. Reaction to this initial announcement will shape the agenda for the first meeting between the two sides. Assuming that relative calm prevails, at that meeting the negotiators will inscribe these principles in a formal document. They will also briefly engage all the major issues, considering the options and assessing the other side's preferences. After the initial meeting, a communiqué will state that discussions took place about all these matters – and they will be listed – but that the talks were limited to an exchange of views. Thus would the agenda be set for the public and for subsequent negotiations. But the real substance of the first meeting will concern the most urgent matters, and it will be essential to reach agreement on them immediately.

The Armed Forces and the Public Service

In sovereign states, the armed forces are the ultimate guarantor of national security and internal order. After a Yes vote, the single most pressing issue will be the conduct and future of members of the Canadian Armed Forces. There will be unrest to cope with, and the army may need to be deployed immediately. If deployed in Quebec, even at the request of the provincial government (to which Ottawa must respond), the army could provoke resistance. Another risk, if there is much ill-will and sporadic violence between Canadians and Quebecers, is that members of the armed forces might disobey orders or comply only with reluctance.[4] In any event, their surnames and those of their commanders will suddenly become significant to the public in both Canada and Quebec.

The long-term equilibrium outcome in this dossier is that Quebec will have its own armed forces. Otherwise it would be quite anomalous among nation-states, with no independent means of ensuring its national security and internal order, and unable to play a constructive international role. The country will enter alliances for defence, but to leave a core state function to other nations is inconceivable. It is also evident that the Canadian Armed Forces will divide. Quebec will receive some share of military assets and, more important, it will attract some proportion of the serving personnel. As in all similar issues, the operative principle of division in the separation will be individual choice. Members of the military will be able to decide whether to serve Quebec or Canada.

These principles will have to be agreed at the initial meeting, if not before. All members of the armed forces will be informed of them. They will be given long-term assurances that their choice will be free and that pensions and other conditions of service will be fully respected by both states. Beyond this, it should be clearly understood that existing units, their current deployments, and the structure of command will be maintained until the situation has stabilized. The Quebec government will agree entirely with this position. The army must maintain its professional discipline. And here it is interesting to note the role of the crown. Under section 15 of the Constitution Act, 1867, the command of all armed forces in Canada, including the militia, is vested in "the Queen," and this is reiterated in the National Defence Act, where it is stated that the "Canadian Forces are the armed forces of Her Majesty." Commissions of officers are granted by the crown (at pleasure). More important, members of the Canadian Armed Forces swear an oath of loyalty, and that oath is made not to Canada but to the crown. Finally, persons enrolled in the military must continue to serve until they are "in accordance with regulations, lawfully released."[5] All this implies that in the consciences of members of the forces, as well as in law, they are not the creatures of the government of the day or even of Canada per se, and they must continue their service until they cease to be enrolled. Undoubtedly, military personnel will be reminded of this by both sides and by their commanders.

Still, the military is under Canadian command through the minister of national defence. Given the situation likely to prevail right after the referendum, division of the forces would not be able to take place immediately. So if the army is required to maintain order, Canadian command will raise two problems: it could make Quebecers wary and defensive, and it could lead to international apprehensions of bias or oppression during the transition, particularly if deployment involves the First Nations. At this time in the separation, Canada will not accept any formal arrangements for sharing command with Quebec authorities; nor will it place the forces under the command of a neutral power – unless civil order and military discipline break down entirely. But the two sides will quickly agree to invite foreign observers to any military operations. Rather than approaching the United Nations for this role, Canada and Quebec could turn to the Scandinavian countries to send officers, who would be attached to headquarters and all active units.

Following these basic decisions, one immediate task of the Quebec government will be to designate a minister responsible for defence and to begin to build a department. Once it has seized the military dossier, the Quebec government might also contemplate one advantage of retaining the monarchy.

Like military personnel, members of the Canadian public service will be assured that they can continue in their posts under prevailing rules about termination. For those working in Quebec, obviously, some relocation will be necessary. The Quebec government will desperately need to attract expert personnel who are experienced in the new functions it will take on, and it will offer attractive incentives. Ultimately, public servants will have to choose where their allegiance lies, at the same time as they make choices about citizenship. In the interim, faced with personnel surpluses, Ottawa will permit its public servants to work for Quebec under normal provisions about unpaid leave of absence.

At the higher levels of the federal administration, incumbents may be asked to declare their provisional citizenship preference. As well, adjustments of personnel will be made: Quebec francophones will not occupy many sensitive positions during the negotiations.

Borders

This issue must be laid to rest immediately. Canada will agree that Quebec will become sovereign with its existing borders intact. No other outcome is feasible if the secession is to be rapid and peaceful. It is this issue, which is strictly associated with the position of Quebec's Aboriginal peoples and anglophone minority, that leads normally calm commentators to suspect that the secession could be contested: "The confrontation would not be over the right of French-speaking Quebeckers to form their own sovereign nation, but about their right to force ethnic minorities in Quebec, especially Aboriginal peoples, to be part of a sovereign Quebec. Such circumstances would pose a tremendous challenge to Canada's civilized ways; violence could supplant tedium as the central feature of our constitutional politics."[6]

Some of these issues are taken up below, but if the border question remains unsettled, it will only encourage resistance to the Quebec government. Civil unrest would be fanned in the Outaouais, the Eastern Townships, and in the Aboriginal communities, and irredentist movements would become active in Canada. Having decided to accept the secession, destabilization of either government is not in Canada's interest. Moreover, refusal to accept the border would solidify Quebecers behind their government, for there is massive public opposition to any form of partition.[7] This is bipartisan, as shown by then-premier Daniel Johnson's reaction to the suggestion by the federal minister of Indian affairs that in the event of a secession, Quebec Aboriginals might choose to remain in Canada: "What I say to people like Mr. Irwin and those who think like him or comment on hypothetical situations is that we, here, have a responsibility to defend the territorial integrity of Quebec ... The position of all those elected to the Quebec legislature, the premier, the government and obviously the opposition is to defend everywhere and forever the territorial integrity of Quebec."[8]

Arguments have been advanced for border adjustments on both geopolitical and democratic grounds.[9] But nothing would solve the basic Canadian problem of noncontiguity except massive changes – such as retaining the south shore of the St Lawrence – which have no justification in law or history and which could be accomplished only by force. There will be areas in Quebec whose citizens have voted massively against Quebec sovereignty, but they have no legal right to secede from Quebec. Moreover, opening the border issue could require referendums in New Brunswick and Ontario, where francophones might demand to join Quebec. It would also raise enormous disputes about the criteria to be used for drawing boundaries according to people's "expressed will."[10]

Aboriginal peoples raise special problems about the border. In the North, if secession materially changes the agreements between Native peoples, Quebec, and Canada, their extinguishment of land claims could be voided. These Aboriginals could then join the general argument made by many First Nations that as peoples they have the right to reject Quebec sovereignty and that their right of self-determination extends to a right of secession which would allow them and their lands to remain in Canada. This argument is explosive in Quebec and could result in a damaging backlash against Aboriginal peoples. It also poses a threat to Canada's own territorial integrity. There are no benefits in this issue for Canada: it has a responsibility towards Aboriginal peoples in Quebec and an obligation to protect their rights, but it has little interest in maintaining jurisdiction over them or their lands.

On this issue, therefore, Canada and Quebec will agree that the Quebec border will remain intact (including the disputed Labrador boundary that was set in 1927 by the Privy Council). The two sides will announce that in their joint view, Aboriginal rights do not extend to secession. They will then offer to open tripartite consultations immediately. One set will be with all Quebec Aboriginal peoples, and another will involve the signatories to the northern agreements.

Finally, both governments will pledge to maintain intact all existing Aboriginal rights of self-government and self-determination.

One other issue that will have to be settled is Quebec's maritime boundary. Drawing it in the Gulf of St Lawrence and Hudson Bay will not be a simple matter. As well, there may be isolated instances, as when the existing land border crosses through a town, where some minor adjustment would be advisable. Having accepted the principle of Quebec's territorial integrity, the negotiators will agree to establish a joint commission, with third-party representation, to make recommendations about the maritime boundary and other border issues. This should report in the autumn of 1995.

Access

The Quebec negotiators must give unequivocal guarantees that transport between the Atlantic provinces and the rest of Canada will be unimpeded. Obviously, full resolution of this matter will depend on later decisions about trade and the economic union, but the principle of free access must be agreed now.

The transit agreement will cover overflights, transport by train and highway, and shipping. It will extend to military passage, and it will also cover the movement of people – Canadian citizens and landed immigrants – subject to possible identity verification. Quebec will further guarantee the right of Canadian firms to use the Port of Montreal (and perhaps others) along with associated train and truck facilities. Beyond this, Quebec will commit itself to maintaining unchanged the existing St Lawrence Seaway accords, with arrangements about ownership and management to be decided. (Talks with the Americans on this issue will begin soon.)

The Debt

The final issue to be settled at the first meeting is how to divide the national debt. Undoubtedly, Quebec would prefer to settle the division of assets simultaneously, but that question is far more complicated and less pressing. The domestic and international investment communities will require a quick resolution of the debt question.

The equilibrium position on the debt is that it will be divided on a per capita basis. Legally, Quebec might not have to assume any responsibility for the federal government's debt, but this would be totally unacceptable to Canada. If this were Quebec's position, the negotiations would end abruptly, but it will not be. It is not in Quebec's interest to become a pariah in international capital markets by renouncing its obligations. International investors would be dismayed by any complete renunciation.

For dividing the debt, several formulae have been proposed. These include the Bélanger-Campeau mechanism, which is based on asset values, and the historic-benefits approach, based on the location of past federal expenditures. Other alternatives are division by ability to pay, as measured by shares of GDP or federal tax revenues, and the population principle, which allocates on a per capita basis.[11] The differences in debt allocation that these formulae produce are huge. Quebec's share ranges from 18.50 per cent under the Bélanger-Campeau formula to 32.03 per cent under the historic-benefits approach, while division by GDP and population produce shares of 23.15 per cent and about 25 per cent, respectively.[12] The differences amount to billions of dollars.

All methods except the population principle have two defects: they are complex and contestable, and they have no obvious fairness. Using the Bélanger-Campeau approach, it would be necessary to evaluate all federal assets and allocate the portion of the debt incurred for each. The historic-benefits approach requires estimating net federal spending by province (and "spending" can include tax expenditures and price distortions caused by regulation). Even the GDP approach requires agreement on when and how to measure a province's share. By contrast, the population principle is simple and just, on communitarian principles. The national debt was accumulated by all Canadians, and funds were spent by a national government for purposes that benefited all members of the collectivity. So when a community is fractured, those who choose to separate take their fair share – an equal proportion per person. The per capita formula has the great advantage of being simple enough to be understood by the public, and it has international precedents, notably in the Czech-Slovak case. Most analysts use it as a baseline, and so does Mr Parizeau, who has said, "We will, I suppose, haggle for a few weeks before we come to something like a quarter."[13] This is what the negotiators will quickly decide.

One important question will be when to take the measure of the populations of Canada and Quebec. This is relevant not only for the debt division but for other matters as well. Some logic would dictate that the date should be 1 January 1996, when the separation is effected; but this would disadvantage Canada, because outmigration from Quebec in the interim will exceed immigration. More important, without this essential figure, arrangements could not be finalized. One solution would be to take the Statistics Canada estimate as of 1 July 1995; another would be simply to agree on a figure of 25 per cent for the Quebec population and to use the 3:1 ratio in all calculations.

A greater problem than division will be how to accomplish the payment. Quebec cannot issue new debt to recompense Ottawa for one-quarter of its outstanding liabilities: the market would not absorb it, especially given the uncertainties attendant on separation. Quebec could perhaps guarantee that it would pay its share of interest and also its share of capital on maturity (which would mean taxing the population and issuing Quebec bonds as the federal issues came due), but Canada would have no guarantee that Quebec would not renege on its obligations if its economic position deteriorated, and particularly if its government blamed Canada for this. One solution would be for Quebec to issue new securities for its full portion of the debt and transfer them to Canada.[14] These would match the term structure, currency, and interest rate of the federal debt but would be for one-quarter of the amount. (Other arrangements would have to be negotiated for particular liabilities, such as unfunded civil service and military pensions). In one scheme, Canada would exchange these Quebec bonds for cash as they matured; alternatively, they could be used as a guarantee of the cash flow and would be marketable if the obligations to Canada were not met, thus exposing Quebec to the market's disciplines for default.[15] But this would not provide perfect security, and neither would any guarantee that was offered by Quebec, and investors will realize this. Hence, after separation, Canada will inevitably pay a risk premium on its debt, because it will remain liable for 100 per cent of outstanding bonds but will be able to tax only 76.8 per cent of the former GDP to meet its obligations.[16] Canada might well demand that Quebec pay a share of this risk premium, the size of the share being determined by a panel of experts; alternatively, Quebec could forgo its share of seigniorage from using the Canadian dollar as compensation for the added costs of borrowing imposed on Canada.

Whatever the method of payment ultimately decided on, the negotiators will agree on the basic principles at the initial meeting: Quebec will assume its share of all existing federal debt and other liabilities; the basis of division will be population; and Canada will receive some form of guarantee that Quebec will meet its obligations. The two sides will also agree that subsidiary negotiations will be launched to investigate Canada's liabilities and to find solutions to particular problems within this framework of principles; these negotiations will involve private-sector participants on both sides and also perhaps as fact finders, and it may be decided to have them chaired by neutral parties. Canada and Quebec will later agree to establish a bipartite commission to deal with outstanding debt matters and unexpected developments, and the final arrangement will be embodied in a detailed formal treaty between the countries. But the core of the debt problem will be decided right away.

At the end of the first negotiating session, then, the most critical issues will have been decided. Physical security will be assured, and some certainty will have been provided about economic matters. Since the package is broadly symmetrical, it can be defended as just. The session will demonstrate that progress can be made, and this will be its most significant result, one that will reassure the populace(s) and foreign powers. More subtly, the conclusion of agreements will demonstrate that the separation is really going to happen: people will be able to plan around this assumption, so uncertainty will be reduced substantially. The process will also show that the negotiating table is where big decisions are being made, even if they have to be provisional until the whole process is complete. This will make the Canada-Quebec nexus absolutely central for a while, and the media barrage will reflect and reinforce this fact. At its core is the confrontation between the two entities, an inescapable symbolism that will strengthen the internal solidarity of each, for every citizen clearly now is on one side or the other. Finally, the first session will establish some fundamental principles: Quebec is a unit; populations are being divided and are the basis for division; people can choose which community they will join; and Quebec will extend special consideration to Canadians and Canadian commerce (or, more deeply, each side has some interest in the social and economic well-being of the other).

The final communiqué will list the remaining items on the negotiating agenda, and these will be dealt with over the next few weeks. There are basically two sets of issues: economic ones (assets, treaties, commercial and economic relations, currency, and mobility), and others (citizenship, immigration, social entitlements, Aboriginal rights, the environment, and minority rights). At the second and third meetings, all will be discussed intensively. The issues interlock, and the two sides will have different opinions about which need to be settled first, given their domestic situations and agendas and also the likely rhythm of concession, threat, and cooperation in the talks. They are taken up here in the order in which they could well be announced as two packages of agreements in principle.

Assets

The Canadian state possesses billions of dollars' worth of assets, and secession means that they must be divided between Canada and Quebec. Negotiations on this dossier will be difficult, not only because of the material stakes and the symbolism of some assets but also because of the diversity of federal holdings. Broadly speaking, they consist of financial assets (movables), fixed assets (immovables), and special cases.

In general, the negotiations will be characterized by speed and disengagement, and by the application of simple principles that can be readily understood, and that will be the case here: fixed assets will be allocated by location; financial assets, as with the debt, will be divided on a per capita basis. But the special cases will need to be handled differently, and there will be some exceptions. This is because the two sides share some common interests. They must be concerned with the other state's viability and with moderating, if not minimizing, economic disruption.

The financial assets include holdings of gold and foreign currencies, receivables (mostly taxes owed), and loans held by federal lending agencies. Taxes pose no problem, since they will be paid solely to Quebec or Canada after the separation date (with adjustments to be made when the fiscal year is complete). Liquid holdings will be split on a per capita basis. They may be retained by Canada and deducted from Quebec's share of the debt. Loans could continue to be administered jointly, but it is more likely that the location principle will intrude here, so that credit extended to Quebec firms and residents by agencies such as the Federal Business Development Bank and the Canada Mortgage and Housing Corporation will be administered by Quebec agencies, with the assets so transferred being part of Quebec's overall per capita share. A special problem concerns the cash flows to the federal government from the Bank of Canada, which consist mostly of seigniorage on the currency. Resolving this will await a decision about what currency Quebec will use.

The immovable assets are massive. In Quebec, they include national parks, bridges (both interprovincial and intraprovincial, including the Jacques Cartier and Champlain bridges), the major ports at Montreal and Quebec City, land holdings in the old areas around these ports, hundreds of small-craft harbours, over six thousand buildings, airports at Mirabel, Dorval, and Quebec City, and the major military bases at Bagotville, Montreal, St-Jean, and Valcartier.[17] All this will become the property of Quebec, and that country will have no claim on fixed assets in Canada. There is no practical alternative to the location principle. The only other procedure would be to evaluate all property, not just in Quebec but in the entire country, and to divide the total according to some formula. But what is the market value of the Quebec Citadel, the federal land in the High Arctic, or the New Westminster Railway Bridge?[18] This complex, contestable and time-consuming process would never substitute for the rough justice of location. A sovereign Quebec, therefore, will own all federal assets within its borders.

However, efficiency and other considerations will dictate some exceptions to these basic principles. Crown corporations are one problem, especially those such as Via Rail, Air Canada, and Canada Post that provide common infrastructural services. In the long term, joint participation in their management and ownership is unlikely because there would be disagreement over the location of investments and, more fundamentally, about whether control should be shared on the basis of equality, population, or the location of markets. In the short term, some will be fully privatized or will have their shares distributed between Canada and Quebec in the 3:1 ratio (Air Canada), and some will quickly be broken up (the CBC). Others, such as Canada Post, will be run for an interim period after separation by a joint board of directors (with one-third being neutral members chosen by the other appointees).

By treaty, Canada will have guaranteed access to the ports of Montreal and Quebec and to the St Lawrence Seaway. The Seaway Authority will be reconstituted after negotiations with the Americans to provide for joint Canada-Quebec management of Canada's current responsibilities. Here the United States will be a moderating influence. It will be necessary to divide the cost of icebreaking and other operations, and one solution would be to make the Seaway Authority operate on a full cost-recovery basis.

Since the National Capital Region will cease to exist in its current form, the federal government will lose possession of dozens of buildings in and around Hull. On the other hand, two major office buildings are occupied through lease-purchase arrangements, and these buildings could continue to be used by federal public servants, regardless of what general labour-mobility provisions are negotiated by the two sides.

Defence equipment is another special case. Here, the population principle will be applied, so Quebec will be entitled to one-quarter of all materiel, including planes and ships. Currently, on Quebec territory there are adequate army facilities, a surplus of aircraft (with no control system), and few naval vessels and facilities. In subsidiary negotiations, conducted under the aegis of NATO or the Permanent Joint Board on Defence, the two sides will have to negotiate a rational division of these assets, one that provides for effective units. Neither side has an interest in any other outcome, and the principle of division will be settled in these initial negotiations.

Many other assets will require special agreements. Difficult matters will include the holdings of museums in both Quebec and Canada, the National Archives, federal databases, and the files of the RCMP and CSIS. Some will be resolved through other treaties, such as one providing for cooperation between police and security forces. Others will be solved by guaranteeing access, perhaps with user fees. Still other assets, especially culturally significant ones, will need special arrangements, and the two sides will establish a bipartite commission, perhaps with a neutral chair, to reach proposals about them. This will be set up in the late summer of 1995, after negotiators have settled as many of the issues about assets as is possible.

Environmental Issues

Quebec and Canada will have many common environmental interests, including boundary rivers and waters, the St Lawrence Basin, and air quality. By their nature, many pollution issues transcend boundaries, and this area of policy will be a test of regulatory cooperation. Moreover, the environment is important to many Canadians and Quebecers, and for substantial numbers it is of primordial significance. So it would be appropriate to reach an accord on environmental matters early in the negotiations.

Quebec, of course, will set its own environmental policy, though if it accedes to NAFTA it will be bound by the side agreement on the environment. But after consultation with the United States, the parties will announce that Quebec will become a member of the International Joint Commission (IJC), to be involved in research and recommendations where its interests are affected. As well, the negotiators could agree to establish a Canada-Quebec environmental commission, along the lines of the IJC, to work on bilateral pollution issues – though this might be too ambitious for the Canadian negotiators. In any case, the two sides will agree to a general framework treaty on environmental cooperation, one that provides for sharing information, consulting on standards, and undertaking collaborative research. It will also commit the parties to common goals about the environment.

Citizenship

This is a very difficult issue. It lies at the cutting edge of sovereignty, because states alone can define the composition of their national communities. It also raises deep symbolic issues about community membership, and these are mixed with practical considerations because of the rights citizens enjoy and the benefits to which they are entitled (and the possibility that residence in a country will be necessary to secure these).

In law, a sovereign Quebec is capable of extending citizenship to all residents of its territory (and perhaps even to people outside Quebec). It will do this. But one major concern of the government will be to retain its population: an exodus of anglophones, allophones, staunch federalists, and people afraid to become non-Canadians would greatly damage the economy. So Quebec would prefer a system of dual citizenship.[19] It would be even better for Quebec if Canada decided to allow Canadian citizenship to be retained only by Canadians living in Quebec but not born there, and by people born in Quebec but now living in ROC. For Quebec, this would avoid the problem of having large numbers of residents who possessed another citizenship.[20]

The federal government of Canada has the power to determine who will be a Canadian. Here it should be remembered that under the Charter of Rights and Freedoms, citizens have the right to enter and remain in Canada, and also to move to any province and take up residence; as well, they have the right to vote and stand for office. Unless these provisions were changed, Canadians who acquired Quebec citizenship would continue to enjoy these rights. Second, the Canadian side will have no interest in the short term in promoting massive economic dislocation in Quebec, which it could do by requiring citizens to reside in Canada as a condition of keeping their status, for this would diminish foreign confidence in Canada itself and would disrupt its economy. Such a policy would be anomalous in any case, since Canadians have the right to leave the country and therefore to reside outside it. On the other hand, it is exceedingly improbable that public opinion in Canada will countenance any arrangement that would allow Quebecers *en masse* to maintain their Canadian citizenship and rights. It will be recognized that those who voted No should not be penalized by being stripped of their citizenship. But the Yes vote will represent a fracturing of the Canadian community, a rejection of it, and as Canadians come to accept this and begin to cohere around a new community, one defined in part through the absence of Quebec and through confrontation with that entity, there will be no support for the notion that Quebecers can stay Canadian while also being citizens of the new sovereign state.

The Canadian position, then, will be that Quebecers will have some period, perhaps two years, in which to make a choice about their citizenship. In order to retain their Canadian citizenship, they will have to make a formal renouncement of the Quebec citizenship extended by the new state. Dual citizenship will not be allowed in normal circumstances. As under current legislation, children of non-resident citizens will be entitled to choose to remain Canadian until they reach a certain age (though this right could later be restricted to the first post-separation generation).[21] Because landed immigrants and resident aliens currently living in Quebec already have been admitted to Canada under Canadian law, they will be able either to move out of Quebec or to remain there under Quebec's citizenship laws. Even though these arrangements open the possibility of a future outmigration or of having a large population of resident non-citizens, the Quebec side will have no choice but to accept the position at this time.

This solution settles the issue by following the principle of individual choice. It will also relieve uncertainty. Yet people will not need to make hurried decisions. They can continue their normal activities, secure in the knowledge that they will be able to make a fundamental choice later, in the light of future developments. Second, it allows for the reconstitution of Canada: constitutional amendment and elections must occur very soon, and it is essential that there be a clear understanding of the nature of the underlying community. (In connection with elections, it should be noted that most Quebec residents who retain Canadian citizenship will not be eligible to vote, because non-resident electors must have lived in, and must register in, a particular constituency in Canada – and Quebec will no longer be part of Canada.) Third, this solution is independent of any arrangements to be made about the economic union or mobility rights. These can be made in the context of the agreement on citizenship. Finally, the two-year period wins time for modifications later. These might be negotiated by a newly elected Canadian government with a fresh mandate, and it might also be possible for Quebec and Canada to moderate the citizenship regime at the regulatory level.

At this stage of the secession, however, it will be made quite clear that Quebecers will not automatically remain Canadians.

First Nations

The referendum result will bring Aboriginal issues to the forefront. Most Aboriginals on reserves will have boycotted the referendum, arguing that it is an external imposition on their powers of self-government;[22] and some First Nations will have held their own referendums to legitimize the position that they have the right not to remain in a sovereign Quebec. In Quebec, there will be unrest on

Aboriginal lands. First Nations will refuse to accept the result, and they will initiate moves to adhere to Canada or will take the opportunity to declare sovereignty. They will be supported by Aboriginal people throughout Canada and will also attract moral, financial, and physical support from Aboriginals throughout the hemisphere. As at Oka and Kahnawake, tactics of public disturbance, civil disobedience, and armed resistance may require a military response. Although foreign powers and international agencies will consider this matter largely to be an internal affair, appeals will be made to them by the First Nations, and they will watch the dossier closely. Meanwhile, the Native people will demand to be represented directly in the negotiations. All of these tactics are very rational manoeuvres to maximize their bargaining leverage. Their negotiating stance will be that they cannot be forced to stay in Quebec without their consent, and they will demand that their terms be met. But their position is precarious, as it has been ever since colonization, and they will have a considerable stake in the outcome of Quebec sovereignty.

There are four basic issues of concern to Aboriginals. First is the status and continuity of existing treaties. Second is the process and outcome of negotiating land claims. Third is the recognition of the right to self-government, with its constitutional and practical implications. Fourth are the flows of money and programs to Native people, both on and off the reserves. In every case, the fear is that Aboriginals in Quebec will receive worse treatment than they would in Canada: that treaty provisions will be ignored by the government or narrowly interpreted by Quebec courts; that land-claims negotiations will be more difficult and drawn out, and the results less generous; that the right to self-government will not be recognized either in the constitution or in its implications for language use, education, taxation, and policing; and that a sovereign Quebec government under fiscal pressure will reduce the funds and services received by Native people.

There is some justification for these apprehensions. The Parti québécois program envisages a new social contract with all Aboriginal nations, through which they and Quebec would become "partners" in developing the sovereign state. The new constitution would define the right of Aboriginals to give themselves responsible governments, and powers would be transferred to these by negotiation. While these Native governments would at first be financed by taxes, resource revenues, and subsidies, they would look forward to assuming their financial responsibilities fully. The self-government agreements would replace existing treaties, though they would not extinguish existing rights, which would be interpreted by Quebec courts according to the Quebec constitution. Under these agreements, there would be joint management of Aboriginals' traditional territories.[23]

This PQ program will be moderated, however, because this is a serious problem for Quebec sovereigntists. Civil unrest will mar the secession, and failure to settle Aboriginal issues could delay international recognition of the new state. The importance of the dossier is shown by Mr Parizeau's retention of this portfolio, and the Quebec government clearly is ready to bargain. The premier's parliamentary secretary and special negotiator has said that "we are just about open to anything" in the self-government agreements, and that there would be no "grey zone" in Quebec's full recognition and protection of native rights.[24] On the other hand, sweeping concessions to First Nations, such as recognizing an uncircumscribed inherent right of self-government, could reinforce their claims to sovereignty and threaten the territorial integrity of Quebec. This would not be acceptable.

On the Canadian side, there will be considerable public sympathy for Native people in Quebec.[25] As well, one current of opinion holds that Canadian support for extreme Aboriginal demands could be used to punish Quebec for the decision to separate, perhaps by diminishing its territory as First Nations secede. This will not attract the Canadian negotiators, who will have accepted Quebec's borders and will be anxious to proceed with more important issues, especially economic ones. Moreover, they will not support Aboriginal positions that could be turned against Canada by First Nations living on Canada's borders, for example, or those living in the West, where there are massive land claims pending.

Essentially, there are two possible solutions here. Canada could simply turn over all its existing treaty obligations and program responsibilities to Quebec; or the two sides could reach agreements that would provide permanently for a single, uniform regime for Aboriginals, whatever their country of residence. By fully harmonizing their policies and law on Aboriginal matters, Canada and Quebec would, in effect, render the border and the secession itself irrelevant for Native people.

Although the second option is attractive, it could not be realized. In the urgent post-referendum atmosphere, it would be impossible to settle the complexities of Aboriginal matters, including the status of treaties, the position of Métis, the land-claims policies, the meaning of an inherent right to self-government, and the full range of existing programs. Nor, politically, could such substantive matters be decided without full Aboriginal participation and consultation. More important, no mechanism could credibly commit the parties to harmonization after the separation. A bipartite or tripartite commission, for example, could hardly bind sovereign states even if its powers were inscribed in their constitutions (which are amendable). Moreover, were such a body established, Canada would not accept a decision rule based on equality, and Quebec would not place its whole Aboriginal policy under a Canadian majority. Similarly, neither side could commit to accept decisions of the other country's Supreme Court. Nor would either give up jurisdiction to international agencies or courts. There is no way, in short, to provide for permanent policy harmonization.

Hence, Canada will have to transfer to Quebec its authority over Aboriginals living there and its obligations to them. Some of the constitutional implications of this are considered below. Here it suffices to note that important treaty obligations already have passed from the British monarch to the crown in right of Canada, and further transfers are possible.[26] Tripartite negotiations about how this will occur will be opened immediately by Canada, Quebec, and the First Nations.

Quebec will provide strong guarantees to its Aboriginal population. This will be essential in order to obviate claims that the Native peoples' right to self-determination has been violated. Some protections will be written into Quebec's constitution. One provision could recognize the First Nations' right of self-government. Another could embed existing treaties and self-government agreements in the constitution. There will also be a provision that any amendment affecting Aboriginals will require their consent. Further protection could involve language rights, as well as a provision that all past decisions of the Supreme Court of Canada concerning Aboriginals and treaties will continue to apply in Quebec.[27]

Beyond this, Canada and Quebec will agree to guarantee the full and unimpeded mobility rights of Aboriginals, through a bilateral treaty. Further protection will be afforded by the citizenship arrangements. Native people, like others in Quebec, will be able to choose to remain Canadian citizens. Since this could lead to political as well as legal difficulties, the two sides might agree from the outset to allow all Aboriginal people in Quebec to maintain dual citizenship. Finally, Canada and Quebec will agree to establish a tripartite First Nations Commission, with a mandate to conduct research, provide advice to governments, and encourage harmony in law and policy in the two countries.

All of this will not satisfy Quebec First Nations, however. They will pursue their interests in the courts, before international agencies, and by appealing to public opinion, and they may resort to civil disobedience and violence. But in law there is nothing to stop this outcome, and since there is so much else at stake in the separation, *realpolitik* dictates that Aboriginal people living in Quebec will pursue their struggles for justice and autonomy within the context of that sovereign state. This will prove to be a heavy responsibility for Quebec.

At this stage of the separation, many of the most important issues will have been settled. The second package of agreements-in-principle (covering assets, the environment, citizenship, and First Nations), is roughly symmetrical. It will demonstrate progress and will show that the secession is being managed. Most important, by dealing with citizenship and assets, it will provide further evidence that the secession is inevitable. This will be reinforced, giving extra momentum to the whole process, by a joint announcement of the target date for the new constitutions to come into effect and the separation to occur.

At this time, working groups of officials, led by ministers, will be fleshing out the substance of the agreements so that they can take the form of treaties and bills. These groups will be reporting to cabinets and to the legislative committees. Meanwhile, other groups will be preparing options and positions about the issues that remain to be settled. And Canadians and Quebecers will be reacting to the accords that have been reached. There will be great speculation and debate about how the matters still outstanding will and should be resolved, and governments and parties will be floating trial balloons to test opinion. Uncertainty will be eased to some extent because the process is under control, yet some critical issues still remain to be settled.

These issues have been left unresolved not because they are the most difficult or important but because, before settling them, the negotiators need to gauge public reaction to the process, to consult foreign powers, and to assess the economic situation. As well, these issues require some articulation with the constitutional drafting processes that are underway. But now they must be settled.

Minority Rights

The Canadian constitution contains sections protecting minorities and conferring particular rights on them. These apply principally to linguistic minorities. Hence, under the Constitution Act, 1867, there are guarantees for denominational schools (s. 93) and the right to use English and French in Parliament and the courts, both in Quebec and federally (s. 133). Under the Constitution Act, 1982, the latter right is reaffirmed and is extended to New Brunswick (ss. 17–19). As well, English and French are recognized as official languages, and the right to communicate with government in either language is affirmed (s. 16, s. 20). Finally, there are provisions for minority-language educational rights, notably the right of citizens to move within Canada and to have their children educated in the official language of their own primary school instruction (s. 23).

Minority rights will be an issue in both Canada and Quebec. It will be of most concern to the Government of Quebec, which will be anxious to show that the new state will adhere to international human rights norms, in order to attract immigrants and to reassure its anxious anglophone and allophone populations that secession will not threaten them. On the Canadian side, there will be public concern about the future of the Anglo-Quebec minority, and also debate about whether to maintain special language rights in Canada.

It is possible that these conditions could lead to a formal agreement between the sides that would establish a homogeneous rights regime across the two countries.[28] This, notably, would encourage labour mobility and therefore economic efficiency, and it would also assuage people's concern about their relatives and compatriots living in the other state. But such a treaty is unlikely. The situations are not symmetrical. Although the numbers of the respective minority-language communities are roughly equal, their proportions are not: the anglophones are 10 per cent of Quebecers, while the francophones will be 3–4 per cent of Canadians after separation. Moreover, Quebec will be anxious to provide reassurances about strengthening minority rights, whereas the pressure of opinion in Canada will be towards reducing them.[29] Finally, rights beyond those in the Canadian constitution could not be negotiated by Ottawa, since even a treaty would involve matters that fall mainly within provincial jurisdiction. So no formal treaty can be envisaged.

As well as signing international accords, Quebec undoubtedly will embed in its constitution the rights now inscribed in its Charter of Human Rights and Freedoms. With sovereignty providing the means to ensure the collective linguistic future, Quebec will add rights for using English in official dealings, rather like those in sections 133 and 20 of the Constitution Acts, 1867 and 1982, respectively. It will also provide minority-language education guarantees for the existing population and for some immigrants. Stronger rights for other cultural minorities will be included in the Charter.

Canadian constitutional redrafting is discussed below. The principles that will guide it are continuity and minimal change. These imply the continuation of existing minority-language rights, though there will be powerful political pressures to the contrary. If the citizenship arrangements are as envisaged, many francophone Quebecers might choose to remain Canadian and to migrate to Canada. Maintaining the existing structure of minority-language rights would encourage this.

But there will be no formal, detailed treaty about minority rights. Each side will deal with the matter according to domestic pressures and external considerations. The two sides will, however, frame a general treaty about the treatment of citizens when they are resident in the other state. This will specify, for example, that such citizens will be accorded all the rights and privileges enjoyed by resident aliens under the respective Charters of Rights, as well as under the normal statutes governing immigration and citizenship. While this is but a vague goodwill gesture, agreements beyond this are improbable.

Quebec's Succession to Treaties

Canada has signed a great number of bilateral and multilateral treaties. There is no doubt that it will be the successor state after separation, retaining its rights and obligations under these agreements (as long as it does not fragment, and unless Quebec's separation causes a fundamental change in the matters covered by a treaty). In many cases, Quebec will have a choice about succeeding to treaties, as will its potential partners. Quebec will apply for NATO membership, for example, and it will be free to negotiate a whole range of agreements about taxation, extradition, aviation, and so forth. On local border treaties, it will have no choice but to assume Canada's existing rights and responsibilities. About these two classes of treaty, then, there is nothing for Canada and Quebec to negotiate.

Some other treaties will involve very little negotiation. Canada's dues and rights in organizations such as the United Nations, the World Bank, and the International Monetary Fund will be split with Quebec according to formulae agreed with these agencies. Population, GDP, and export share are the obvious bases of division. The extent of change will depend on the degree of economic integration that obtains between Canada and Quebec. If a customs union is maintained, for example, arrangements under various commodities regimes, and Canada's European Community quotas, will not need to be renegotiated with third parties.

Other treaties raise the possibility – or necessity – of joint action. This is especially true of economic agreements. Each party's stance towards these agreements, and the nature of the joint action, will be determined largely by the level of economic integration to be maintained between Canada and Quebec. This is discussed in the following section. In essence, though, Canada and Quebec will maintain the FTA/NAFTA floor, will operate a temporary customs union, and will preserve some elements of the economic union by special agreement and voluntary harmonization.

Under these arrangements, Canada will support Quebec's entry into GATT. This will be straightforward if Quebec agrees to maintain the existing tariff schedule, along with other border measures negotiated in the Uruguay Round. Any other arrangement is difficult to envisage, simply because Quebec would have to undertake long multilateral negotiations in order to accede to GATT with a different array of tariffs. This means that Canada and Quebec will maintain a *de facto* customs union, although Quebec will henceforth act independently in multilateral talks.

The other agreements involve the United States. On the military side, Quebec will be admitted as a member of the Permanent Joint Board on Defence.[30] Since the Canadian defence industry is highly integrated and the Defence Production/Defence Sharing agreements are flexible and relatively informal, it will be possible to incorporate Quebec as a participant. Until its defence purchases rise, however, Quebec producers will be vulnerable to truncated markets. The Auto Pact will also be extended to Quebec. Canada has a large stake in this agreement and an interest in maintaining stability. If the Auto Pact did not apply to a sovereign Quebec, American manufacturers potentially would face restricted access to an important market, and the United States might seek to renegotiate the agreement. This might occur in the medium term in any event, because Canadian production now far exceeds the safeguard levels of the Auto Pact. But there is little current pressure from the industry to reopen the agreement. More important, the Pact can be abrogated on twelve months' notice, and since renegotiation can be forced at any time, the United States is unlikely to seize the occasion of secession to do so.

In general, the United States will be prepared to admit Quebec to the FTA and NAFTA. As long as the secession is being competently managed, there should be no fundamental reassessment of American policy towards Canada and Quebec. The primary U.S. concerns will be to protect American investment and to minimize the dislocation to trade flows (and their effects on American jobs and the profitability of subsidiaries in Canada and Quebec). This means that the United States will support extending the agreements to Quebec with as little modification as is necessary to incorporate another member. Canada, too, has an interest in Quebec's accession, because if this did not occur, the FTA/NAFTA regime might cease to apply to Canada itself. Some analysts have suggested that this might be acceptable to Canada, because ROC opinion is less supportive of continental free trade than is true of Canada-with-Quebec.[31] But this is most improbable. Not only has the Canadian economy already adjusted to the FTA, but in the midst of the secession Canadian governments are unlikely to add yet another element of uncertainty. Instead, Canada will argue quite the opposite – that it is bound to the treaties by its status as the successor state. And it will support Quebec's entry to the treaties, unless the negotiations come to an impasse on other issues. In this, Quebec will have little choice. The FTA/NAFTA regime will be the main vehicle for securing its access to markets in both Canada and the United States. By being exposed in the treaties as a sovereign entity rather than a subnational unit, Quebec's policy autonomy will be constrained in new ways, but it will nevertheless be anxious to be admitted to the agreements.

Commercial and Economic Relations

A crucial issue for the negotiators to decide will be the extent of economic integration to be maintained after the separation. Until the separation occurs, all existing laws and regulations will continue to apply in Canada and Quebec. There will be an economic standstill (one that will become increasingly awkward as time passes and decisions are made in the shadow of the separation), and yet the two sides will have to agree on a framework for the longer term, because economic actors need a predictable environment. The negotiators will confront a menu of possibilities ranging from the GATT floor to the existing economic union. Their positions and choices will be shaped by domestic politics (as these evolve through the intense process of separation), by outside pressures and opportunities, and by awareness of the economic losses that will be incurred if the economic union disintegrates.

The core problem here is that the two sides will be unable to establish a supranational locus of authority. A full economic union requires a legislature with the capacity for redistribution; positive integration requires institutions capable of promulgating some regulations across state borders and providing efficient common services and facilities; and negative integration is more certain with an authoritative adjudication mechanism to settle disputes. But Canada and Quebec will not be able to agree on a set of common institutions for economic management. In the first place, there is no obvious decision rule. The choice will be between making decisions on the basis of equality, which will be unacceptable to Canada, or making them on proportionality, which will be unacceptable to Quebec. Since the negotiators will be under considerable time pressure, it will be difficult to design new institutions.[32] Moreover, the Canadian side will be politically incapable of committing to new structures for economic management that are elaborate or powerful. The material interest in the Quebec economy is very weak in western Canada, where there will be little support for institutions that would preserve the economic union at the cost of allowing Quebec a voice in managing the western economy.[33] Maintaining national unity will be the primary concern on the Canadian side. As well, the federal government alone is not constitutionally capable of implementing an agreement that would impinge on areas of provincial jurisdiction. In any event, the Canadian negotiators' legitimacy will be weakening as partisan and regional forces gain prominence now that the immediate crisis has passed. Finally, the process of redrafting the Canadian constitution will be well underway, and there will be no question of providing for supranational authorities in this. Among the sovereigntists, Mr Parizeau at least is quite aware of this. In late 1993, when addressing proposals for complex supranational political institutions, he said sarcastically: "Il ne faut pas rêver et demander la lune ... Et, déja pas très contents que le Québec devienne souverain, ces Canadien-anglais, pour nos beaux yeux, pour nous faire plaisir, pour imiter vaguement ce que certains croient qu'il se passe, en Europe de l'Ouest, accepteraient ainsi de chambarder leur vie politique, eux, qui ont toujours refusé d'accorder le moindre pouvoir additionnel au Québec et pour qui l'égalité des provinces est un principe sacré."[34]

Still, both Canada and Quebec have an interest in providing a stable and predictable environment right away. They also have a mutual interest in preserving the advantages of a common economic space, with the efficiency gains this allows, as well as some interest in the viability of each other's economy, simply because it is an important market. On the other hand, these interests are not symmetrical. Canada is the larger economy, and the extra efficiency gains accruing from access to Quebec are not as great as those realized in Quebec from access to Canada. And at the grossest level, Canada exports under 5 per cent of total GDP to Quebec, while Quebec exports 15.2 per cent of GDP to Canada; in manufactured and primary products, the respective proportions are 6.3 and 24.0 per cent. There are regions and sectors of much higher dependence and interdependence, of course, but the gross figures, along with the political considerations noted above, dictate which side will make the policy adjustments.

Apart from the standstill announced by the two governments, which will be maintained until the date of separation, the economic and commercial arrangements will consist of five elements. Not all of these will take the form of treaties.

First, Quebec will adopt the existing Canadian tariff structure. The two countries will agree not to impose tariffs on each other's products (and this will require GATT approval). This outcome will preserve the customs union, minimizing disruption and easing Quebec's entry into GATT and other agreements. On the Canadian side, there will be less interest in maintaining the current levels of protection, especially in the West. But no precipitous action is likely, since the question will be put off until after the separation. Then, after full consultation with affected interests, Canada might choose to make such unilateral tariff reductions as appear beneficial. Quebec would have the choice of dropping its own tariffs or setting up border posts. Of course, if Quebec made unilateral reductions, Canada could also establish border controls.

Second, Quebec will be admitted into the FTA and NAFTA. These agreements will set the basic level of Canada-Quebec economic integration. This is the equilibrium position on this issue, at least for this phase of the relationship; Canada and Quebec will not be able to negotiate formal arrangements to preserve higher levels of integration, yet neither party will have any interest in the short term in not maintaining FTA/NAFTA coverage of the common economy. The FTA/NAFTA solution is, in fact, very convenient. The rules of trade are known to many businesses; consultative and dispute-settlement mechanisms are provided for, with no extra requirements for institutional design; the federal-provincial implications have already been worked out; and the solution should be acceptable to the public. Quebecers, on average, might favour a higher level of integration, to be secured through a separate bilateral treaty, but the FTA/NAFTA agreements do provide some security. And although some Canadians will resist economic integration with Quebec, the arrangement can be presented as one that is necessary for Canada as well as offering continuity with what already exists.

The third component of the economic arrangements will be voluntary harmonization of laws and regulations, and of tax structures and levels. At the time of the separation, economic integration between Canada and Quebec will be at 100 per cent of the current levels. There will have been a substantial economic evolution after the referendum, including outmigration, shifts in product sourcing and marketing, altered investment decisions, and changes in the pattern of government spending. After the separation, the economic union will be considerably weakened, despite the FTA/NAFTA floor. The interprovincial trade agreement signed in July 1994, for example, will no longer extend to Quebec, nor will other reciprocal agreements between provinces. Labour mobility will be constrained by the citizenship provisions. There will be no common competition policy, and, generally, the federal government as a force for positive economic integration will no longer reach into Quebec. The two states will be able to apply anti-dumping, countervailing-duty, and safeguards measures against each other's products. Nevertheless, it will be possible to maintain integration above the FTA/NAFTA floor and to preserve important elements of the common market, simply by not changing much of the legal framework of commerce. The regulatory environment can be harmonized if the states adopt identical legislation or, more realistically, if Quebec enacts legislation that duplicates what now exists in Canada. If Canada makes changes to the legal and regulatory framework of commerce to suit its own purposes, Quebec can choose whether to modify its own laws accordingly. If it does not do so, interstate commerce will face new barriers and this will impose costs, but Quebec governments will take these decisions at a rhythm dictated by the country's own economic evolution and political dynamics.

The fourth element is consultation. There are provisions for regular ministerial-level meetings in the continental trade agreements, but the two sides will agree to a very general treaty about the desirability of regular consultation about economic, fiscal, and commercial matters. Specific commitments about timing, or engagements to consult in advance of introducing new measures, will not be contained in this.

Lastly, the economic and commercial package will involve at least two specific agreements. One will cover the financial sector, where both sides will have a strong incentive to provide maximum stability.[35] Unless there is cooperation about deposit-taking institutions and insurance companies, several major institutions will be in violation of national ownership laws. At the FTA/NAFTA floor, this problem is avoided, but only because, under its national-treatment principle, firms have to incorporate subsidiaries to manage their operations in the other country. This could prove difficult and costly in the short term, and so would the adjustment of portfolio balances in a time of high uncertainty. The negotiators thus have an incentive to agree to supersede national treatment by extending mutual recognition of each other's firms. This would reduce transition costs and impede operations far less. On the other hand, it would require regulatory coordination; otherwise, one country would be insuring depositors and policy holders for assets under the prudential regulation of the other.[36] Provision for this coordination will be made in a separate treaty, which will involve the Bank of Canada and the new state Bank of Quebec as joint overseers of national regulatory authorities. In the longer term it might be possible to establish a joint regulatory agency. Also in this sector, the parties will agree to maintain full access to the Canadian payments system. But both elements of this agreement are likely to be temporary. Quebec's regulatory regime is diverging from Canada's, and payments-system arrangements in the longer term will depend on how currency issues are resolved. Hence, the agreement will have a two-year expiry period.

The other area where some arrangement must be made is agriculture. This is a highly sensitive sector, because of the political power of farmers, the interregional differences in both farm specializations and ideological support for supply management, and uncertainties arising from the FTA/NAFTA and the Uruguay Round settlements. The immediate issue will be the allocation of production quotas in the supply-managed commodities of milk, eggs, and poultry. Industrial milk is the critical commodity because of the size of the market and the fact that Quebec farmers have over 47 per cent of Canada's total market share quota. This has been estimated to provide a direct surplus on processed dairy products of $1 billion.[37] There will be no support in Canada for the current allocation of quota in this sector. As long as supply management and quotas or very high tariffs persist in agriculture, the implicit standard is national self-sufficiency, and this will be applied in the Quebec-Canada separation. The long-term result in Canada may be that producers in other provinces lobby successfully to take up Quebec's lost quota; or it may be that processors will be able to win access to cheaper foreign supplies. In any case, the problem will be to achieve adjustment without any massive disruption to the farming and food-processing industries and without having to establish border controls. The two sides will agree to adjust domestic production levels to match final domestic consumption plus exports to third parties, perhaps over a three-year period. (It should be noted that the FTA contains provisions outlawing export subsidies and permitting the application of anti-dumping laws in this sector.) This will be embodied in a treaty (to apply also to eggs and poultry),[38] which will be accompanied by whatever support programs each country is prepared to introduce to ease the transition. Inevitably, agricultural trade problems will add to the other factors tending in the long run towards the establishment of border controls.

The net economic result of this entire package will be that much of the economic union will be retained, though some will be lost. The FTA/NAFTA floor provides important guarantees about national treatment, capital mobility, access to procurement, and many other features of the Canadian economic union. On the other hand, labour mobility will be restricted under this regime; there will be much scope for establishing new barriers to trade; and commercial relations fundamentally will take on a state-to-state form, because disputes will be managed on this basis and current universal access to the Canadian courts will end. The internal regulatory environment will remain largely harmonized, by voluntary action, into the medium term. The commercial arrangements alone do not require that border controls be established. On the other hand, the legal weakening of the union between the Canadian and Quebec economies, and the increase in obstacles to trade, will undoubtedly lead to some trade diversion in the future, and there will be further losses as positive economic integration between Canada and Quebec is much lessened.

Politically, the package makes sense. It will help resolve the immediate uncertainty of economic actors. It will maintain the commercial and financial systems while postponing larger decisions about the latter, and it will retain the FTA/NAFTA status quo. As well, it embodies no new long-term commitments of the kind that would prove divisive and beyond the legitimacy of the Canadian negotiators to make; instead, it allows for flexibility and adjustment by firms and governments. Most important, it creates very few supranational political or regulatory institutions with binding authority. When separation takes place, economic integration will be at 100 per cent of current levels, but political integration will be almost at zero.

The Currency and Monetary Policy

This is an absolutely crucial issue. The stakes involved are very high. It may need to be settled before this point in the separation process if there is a crisis of confidence in the Canadian dollar. This is because, in normal circumstances, governments have little control over individual depositors or the activities of firms and investors, especially foreign ones. The Yes vote could produce a liquidity crisis as depositors withdraw funds, and also a currency crisis as investors shift to assets not denominated in Canadian dollars. In the most recent peaceful secession, the Czech-Slovak case, these possibilities were limited, because the currency was not readily convertible and because foreign debt was both relatively small and mainly held by international organizations and governments. This is not true of Canada, where the economy is open, the dollar floats freely, foreign debt is very large, trading in Canadian securities is international, and individuals can choose the currency in which many assets – certainly, their savings accounts – are denominated. A currency crisis would affect every Canadian, through its implications for the value of pensions, savings, and wages, as well as interest rates and the cost of servicing government debt. If there is a crisis of confidence, the Canadian government could introduce foreign-exchange controls, and, possibly under the Emergencies Act, it could freeze deposits. But such disruptive measures could not be maintained for very long; moreover, their imposition would simply reduce confidence in the currency and the country's capability of servicing its debt. Whatever arrangements were announced before the controls were lifted would have to be extremely credible to withstand the renewed speculative pressure caused by their very imposition. All this could force a quick and stable resolution of the currency question at the first meeting of the negotiators.

Alternatively, the issue could remain open. Because of the announced economic standstill, the decisive and peaceful handling of the separation process, the debt agreement, and the firm action by the Bank of Canada with international support, a crisis of confidence in the currency might have been avoided. The negotiators will have discussed the several options open to them in this dossier. Central to these talks will not be the relatively minor issues of seigniorage and transaction costs, but how to produce an arrangement that will meet the core needs of each side while avoiding uncertainty and speculative attacks on the currency. Long-term seigniorage and transaction costs pale into irrelevance when set against the potential effects on government finances and the underlying economy of a sharp increase in the prime rate, a plunging Canadian dollar, or a liquidity crisis in the financial system – or all three simultaneously. Temporary controls and international coordination could only postpone such effects if the currency settlement was not certain, stable, and credible.

Of the options available, there are only three that meet these criteria. One is that Quebec declares that it will introduce a separate, floating currency. Another is that Quebec decides to use the U.S. dollar. The third is that the Canadian monetary union will be maintained, with full Quebec participation in setting policy. Quebec could introduce a separate currency pegged either to the American or the Canadian dollar, but there would be huge costs in establishing its credibility, as well as inevitable speculation against the level of the peg, and at the same time none of the benefits of the other options would be realized. The two sides will agree on the third option. This will not be the result of unacrimonious negotiation, because both sides have a lot at stake and each option imposes asymmetrical costs and benefits. But in this crucial dossier the advantage lies with Quebec.

If Quebec were to establish its own floating currency, the issue would be credibly settled. There would be costs for Canada in terms of speculative pressures, transaction costs, and lost seigniorage, but these would not be crippling. Quebec would incur the very large costs of establishing confidence in its currency, and these would be taken up front. Afterwards, the situation would normalize, and the country would have the benefits of policy autonomy and a separate currency as a mechanism of adjustment. But while this is a credible outcome, the huge short-term costs of this option render it very unattractive.

Canada's preferred option will be to maintain the currency union, but without Quebec participation in setting policy. It would be difficult politically to extend formal decision-making power to the seceding country, let alone to make payments to it for seigniorage. But to be a pure taker of Canadian policy will be unacceptable to Quebec. If this is the only option, Quebec might choose to adopt the American dollar; it might be better off as a taker of Washington's monetary policy. Although this choice could not be definitely made at the outset of the separation negotiations, before there were American assurances of admission to the FTA/NAFTA and before the Canada-Quebec economic and commercial framework had been agreed, it could be deployed early on as a threat, and it is a credible one. The option would cause great damage to Canada at little economic and political cost to Quebec, relative to that country's other alternatives.

Hence, Canada will concede to joint management of the currency union. This is a stable outcome and is more credible than maintaining the union without participation (because observers would expect Quebec to become dissatisfied with such an arrangement). Quebec will establish a central bank, and representatives of this institution will sit on the board of the Bank of Canada, with full voting power. Quebec will also gain the power to appoint a member of the management committee of the bank or a senior vice-president. The two sides will conclude a treaty to this effect, which will also provide for seigniorage to be paid to Quebec according to its 25 per cent of the Bank of Canada's equity, and for there to be a full exchange of information between the two institutions. As well, the agreement will provide for regular meetings of the two countries' ministers of finance about fiscal and monetary issues. Finally, it will embody a joint commitment to price stability as a leading, though not exclusive, goal of the monetary union: this will both set a common purpose and reassure investors.

This will be a very difficult concession for the Canadian side to make. It will create great suspicion in the Canadian West and will enrage all those who favour cutting relations with Quebec or punishing the "treasonous province." But there is little choice. Quebec cannot be forced to establish an independent currency. Nor is it evident that Canada could prevent it from adopting the U.S. dollar without using measures that would be costly to itself. If Quebec chose the U.S. dollar, Canada might well be forced to peg to the U.S. dollar or to adopt it as well. If this alternative is even less politically palatable than shared monetary management at a time when the unity and continuity of Canada itself are questionable, then the joint arrangement must be the outcome.

This agreement will be supported by most of the Canadian business community and by all financial institutions. It could be made more acceptable by some elaborations. For instance, the Bank of Canada Act could be amended to provide for more effective regional representation on the board and even for provincial or regional appointments. Alternatively, the bank's structure could be regionalized through the creation of regional central banks to carry out some functions that are now centralized in Ottawa.[39] The presidents of these banks – among them, the Central Bank of Quebec – would sit on the Bank of Canada's board, along with federal (and Quebec) appointees. Through such devices, Quebec's participation in managing the monetary union could be rendered less extraordinary, while the suspicions of the West and Atlantic Canada could be allayed somewhat.

Despite this, the agreement will erode support for the federal negotiators. But their role will be coming to an end. In any case, there is no more agreeable choice open to them. Indeed, Quebec's position on this issue seems strong enough that it could win concessions in other areas as well. The only comparable Canadian bargaining cards are citizenship and the veto over Quebec's admission to NAFTA.

Mobility and Immigration

The mobility of people within the Canada-Quebec economic space and the admission of people to it will be matters of concern in the negotiations. Under the FTA and NAFTA, individuals who are in certain occupational classes or performing certain functions have a limited right to enter the other countries for work. In the period before Quebecers have to choose a citizenship, they will of course be able to work in Canada, and those who decide to remain Canadians rather than becoming citizens of Quebec will have the right to enter the country and seek work anywhere. Other Quebecers seeking to work in Canada will need employment authorization. Whether Quebec decides to allow Canadians resident in Quebec to work there, and whether it will admit Canadians to work under easier terms than the FTA/NAFTA provisions will be an autonomous policy choice. It does not appear to be in Quebec's interest to encourage residents to leave, though Canadian citizens will probably require work permits.

As for non-work travel, there would seem to be no interest on either side in imposing visa requirements on people who aim to spend money in the country. Hence, there will be no need for border controls. Of course, the lack of controls opens up the possibility of smuggling, should tax regimes come to vary widely. More seriously, people crossing the border could work "underground" in the other country. If these became widespread problems, controls would have to be established.

Immigration is a different matter. If admission policies vary substantially and there are no border checkpoints, then each country will be surrendering some control of its population base to the other. Since this issue, in the medium term, is the only possible cause of establishing highly inefficient border controls, there is a strong incentive to reach a treaty on immigration. Quebec certainly has a major interest in immigration, and not only to maintain population levels while integrating newcomers into the French language and Quebec culture. One significant advantage of sovereignty is that the province will be better able to retain immigrants: it will no longer be competing with the attractions of the rest of Canada, but only with the immigrant's home country or alternative destinations. An agreement on immigration would not impair this advantage much, because new Quebec citizens or permanent residents could not emigrate to Canada to work without securing employment authorization, resident status, or landed-immigrant status from the Canadian authorities. Canada has a less substantial material interest in immigration, but it is a highly sensitive symbolic issue, and there will be no support for a regime that would admit "undesirables" into Canada through Quebec. On the other hand, Canada has no interest in letting this issue be the sole cause of border posts coming into immediate operation.

The solution will be a treaty similar to the agreements on immigration that Canada and Quebec have reached in the past. Under the 1978 Cullen-Couture agreement, Canada and Quebec each established a set of criteria for admission, and either could veto an immigrant who failed to reach 30 per cent of the possible points on their scale. Admission to Quebec was, however, subject to the statutory requirements for admission to Canada.[40] Under the 1991 agreement, Canada sets national standards and defines the classes of immigrants, as well as those who are inadmissable. Within these constraints, Quebec has the power to select Quebec-bound immigrants and to veto unacceptable ones (except in the Family and Assisted Relative classes). There is provision for consultation over every refusal.[41]

A treaty could provide that the two countries each establish whatever standards, classes, and objectives seem appropriate to it, along with admission procedures, with each having a veto over every case according to its own standards. This might work well in practice, and it might be the long-run equilibrium position, but it will not be politically acceptable in the wake of the referendum, especially in Canada, where opinion will not countenance the reach of Quebec policy over domestic Canadian matters. Alternatively, the two sides could agree on common standards, with separate application. Despite the current harmonious working relationship, this would require a level of trust not likely to be present after secession; moreover, it will take Quebec some time to build up the organization necessary to administer a fully independent system. The solution therefore will be that the current agreement will be extended, with slight modifications. Quebec will set its own immigration targets, it will have a veto over all Quebec-bound immigrants and visitors, and Canada will be able to define the "inadmissable" class, thus retaining the right to veto undesirable Quebec-bound immigrants. Those admitted to Quebec would have no right of later entry to Canada, and vice versa. Given the citizenship choices to be made in two years, the term of the treaty will also be two years.

Social Entitlements

This is an area where scope exists for fruitful cooperation. In particular, maintaining a common "entitlement space" would promote labour mobility. It would also avoid the transaction costs of splitting the administrative systems that provide benefits, and it would reduce the number of people who will resettle in order to retain benefits. But the negotiators will not agree to cooperation at this level. Social programs channelled through the federal government involve regional redistribution, and after Quebecers have voted to rupture the political community, there will be no support for any such redistribution towards Quebec. In Quebec, the provincial government will require the autonomy to design an integrated and efficient social-welfare system. And given the fiscal situations of the two countries, neither side will be interested in committing to fixed regimes of benefits.

There is one basic principle that can be agreed, however. This is that eligibility for social benefits will depend on residency rather than citizenship. This principle is analogous to the "national treatment" of firms. If this were not agreed, rather severe complications would result. One is deciding what government would be responsible for benefits in the period before the definitive citizenship choice. Beyond this, tying benefits to citizenship could provide powerful incentives for people to migrate to the other country for non-economic reasons and for reasons possibly rooted in false expectations about the home country's viability. Moreover, the citizenship criterion would restrict labour mobility long after the secession, when there would already be the barrier that acquiring resident status would require the approval of immigration authorities. So Quebec, raising all taxes from residents, will be responsible for their social entitlements. And in Canada, the federal government will extend social programs to all residents, without discrimination.

This will apply to social assistance (where the provinces also control access), to old age security and guaranteed income supplement payments (or their Quebec equivalents), and to unemployment insurance. In health care, provincial residency will be required, and the provinces will continue to establish rules about out-of-Canada coverage, which will apply to Quebec as well as other countries. The Canada and Quebec pension plans, by treaty, will be coordinated as they are now. Private pensions pose more difficult problems. It is likely that the pension funds of out-of-country employees of firms will have to become registered in the country or province where they work. This will apply also to Quebec-based employees of industries currently regulated by the federal government.

As for individual pensions, in the form of registered retirement savings plans (RRSPs), there is potential for acrimony. Through allowing deductions for contributions to these plans, Ottawa has, in effect, deferred taxes on the income that will flow from them. There is a case to be made that Canada should impose a tax on the Quebec-based assets in these funds and that Quebec should do the same.[42] On the other hand, these deferred taxes are not carried as assets on the government's books, and sophisticated financial management generally ensures that most taxes deferred from RRSPs are never collected anyway. So there will be no point in fighting this issue out in the autumn of 1995.

A more serious problem concerns the ceilings on non-national holdings in private and individual pension funds. If the Canadian laws are applied immediately, fast and costly liquidations of Quebec assets would be required. Canada could introduce legislation providing for a transition period, perhaps of five years, for pension funds to adjust their Quebec holdings to comply with the ceiling. Quebec might prefer not to retain the existing requirement, or it might adopt mirror legislation.

Finally, there are the pension entitlements of public servants, MPs and senators, an issue that overlaps to some extent with the settlement of the national debt. Canada will agree to pay normal pensions to all retirees in the period before citizenship choice, and to all who retain Canadian citizenship afterwards: Quebec will take responsibility for the others. As for incumbent public servants, Canada will maintain its normal commitments even if these individuals are seconded to the Quebec government; after the citizenship choice, those who opt not to remain Canadian will have transferred to the Quebec authorities their full pension entitlements until the date of departure from the public service. This will be costly, but there will be a strong incentive for Canada to do this, given its interest in reducing the size and changing the composition of the public service.

Overall, these arrangements will involve substantial transition costs. There is much potential for acrimony here, but also much to be done to avoid instilling fear in the population and panic in some quarters. Although the principle of supplying benefits only to residents will inhibit labour mobility and weaken the economic union, there is no realistic alternative. As in the case of firms, "national treatment" will prevail in most social programs – after people have met the immigration and residence requirements established by the two countries.

Other Matters

There will be many other issues about which the two sides will make agreements. These include cooperation at the border, cooperation in defence manoeuvres, cooperation between police forces, extradition, disaster planning, public health, higher education, fisheries, and taxation. Some of these matters will be highly complex, and they are all important. But they are not unprecedented, and they need not be settled immediately by the primary negotiating teams. For the most part, they will be resolved according to standard international practice. Canada has many such treaties with other countries. So these matters can be safely delegated to working groups of officials, with draft treaties to be signed later (but before the separation). Officials in both countries will also be working furiously to change normal statutes and regulations so as to accommodate the separation, but the redrafting will follow the main principles to which the two sides have agreed.

At this point, the negotiating teams have completed the essential work that must be done for the secession to take place. They have reached agreement on these central issues under severe time constraints, and in a terribly difficult political and economic context. In so doing, they have established the shape of the new bilateral relationship, crystallizing it in a form that will endure for years. The transition has produced a new institutional order.

CHAPTER FOURTEEN

The Rest of the Separation

SECESSION WILL OCCUR CONSTITUTIONALLY

At the same time as the negotiations with Quebec are being undertaken, Canada will also be creating new domestic institutions; it will be reconstituting itself. Even though this will be a separate process from dealing with Quebec, some of the leading actors will take part in both. Because of this and because of the sense of urgency that will infuse both processes, the negotiations and the constitutional debates will each shape the other. On the one hand, the solidarity necessary for effectively dealing with Quebec will help prevent dissension on constitutional issues, since profound constitutional disagreements obviously would impair the capacity of Canadian politicians to accomplish the separation. Conversely, because the constitutional debates will be the more critical for ROC, they will constrain the agreements that can be made with Quebec.

Quebec will also be finalizing a new constitution, and the substance of these reconstitutions will be discussed in the next section. Much redrafting will be necessary on the Canadian side – to excise Quebec, to ensure legal continuity, and to make the adjustments needed to have the fundamental law reflect the new shape of the federation. The guiding principles will be to write Quebec out of the basic law, to make minimal changes to the status quo, and to opt for flexibility where changes must be made.

The issue here is how to accomplish the secession. It is clear that for separation to take place legally, the Constitution Acts must be amended. Until this happens, Quebec will remain a part and a province of Canada. Most notably, this means that no federal election could be held without Quebecers participating. And yet this election must occur to legitimize the principle of the separation, the agreements reached with Quebec, and the constitutional amendments themselves. It will also be necessary to choose a fresh government with a mandate to chart Canada's future course.

The Constitution Acts must of course be amended constitutionally. If this did not occur, there would be a fundamental discontinuity in the basic law, precisely analogous to a UDI by Quebec. At its core, Canada would be an illegal state, assuming that it continued to exist (and the illegality of its reconstitution would justify internal claims, and perhaps some external ones, that the authority of the state need not be respected). In order to accomplish the secession, many changes to the constitution will be required. The question is how these amendments must be made. In particular, will it be necessary to have the unanimous agreement of the provinces?

In the Canadian constitution there are several amending formulae.[1] The most general procedure is for a proclamation to be issued by the governor general after resolutions assenting to the amendment have passed the Senate, the House of Commons, and the legislatures of at least two-thirds of the provinces that have at least 50 per cent of the population. This procedure – the general amending formula – is contained in sections 38 and 39 of the Constitution Act, 1982 (CA1982). According to section 42 of CA1982, the general formula must be used to effect amendments about certain matters, including the Supreme Court, the powers of the Senate, and the enlargement or establishment of provinces. Some other amendments require the unanimous consent of the provinces and the federal government. Under section 41 of CA1982, unanimity is required to make amendments to the constitution "in relation to the following matters": (1) "the office of the Queen, the Governor General and the Lieutenant Governor of a province";(2) the right of a province to have as many MPs as senators; (3) the use of the English or the French language; (4) the "composition" of the Supreme Court; and (5) the amending formulae themselves. Subject to these provisions, each province can amend its own constitution, and the federal Parliament can amend the constitution regarding the executive government of Canada, the Senate, and the House of Commons. As well, in matters that concern at least one province but not all of them, and involve interprovincial boundaries or the use of English or French within a province, amendments can be made under section 43, through proclamations authorized by Parliament and the legislatures of the provinces concerned.

Now, if Canadians proposed constitutional changes that required unanimity, Quebec would have to agree to the amendment. Since Quebec will retain its present status until the constitution is changed, a resolution would have to be approved by the National Assembly along with all the other provincial legislatures. This is an interesting problem overhanging Canada's reconstitution. As for the specific issue of an election, it might seem possible to use the general formula to amend the constitution, and then amend the Elections Act, so as to exclude Quebecers from participating, but this would be questionable, since it arguably would derogate from the powers of the province (under section 38), and it could affect the right of the province to have at least as many MPs as senators (section 41). Hence, either Quebec's assent or provincial unanimity would be required to hold an election before the whole constitution is amended.

Another relevant aspect of the amending procedure is that according to section 39, no amendment under the general formula can be made within one year of the resolution being initiated, unless every province's legislature has either consented or dissented. Hence, if unanimity is not required, Quebec or any other province could stall the process for a year, simply by not acting at all. If, on the other hand, reconstituting Canada requires some amendments that clearly fall under the unanimity provisions of section 41, there are no such time constraints: provinces could pass resolutions overnight, or never. Whether unanimity will be required to effect a constitutional separation, therefore, is an arcane but important point. It involves the bargaining relationship with Quebec and – more important – it will affect the political dynamic within Canada itself.

Despite some arguments to the contrary, it seems that the amendments required to achieve the secession will indeed need unanimous provincial consent.[2] First, some amendments will affect "the office" of a lieutenant-governor "of a province," namely Quebec. Where references to the powers and office of lieutenant-governors are written in general language, it might be possible to maintain the fiction that since other amendments render Quebec a non-province, the offices of the lieutenant-governors in "Canada" will not have been affected, so the general amending formula will suffice. But other sections are more specific. Section 71 of the Constitution Act, 1867 (CA1867), for example, provides explicitly for a lieutenant-governor to be part of the Quebec legislature, and it is hard to see how excising this section would not affect the office.[3]

Second, amendments must be made to provisions about the Supreme Court. The Supreme Court Act currently states that "at least three of the judges" shall be appointed from among those on the Court of Appeal or the Superior Court of Quebec, or from advocates at the Quebec bar. Some commentators have held that the federal Parliament can change the Supreme Court's composition by ordinary statute, under its power to constitute, maintain, and organize a general appeals court (CA1867, s. 101).[4] This argument hinges mainly on the proposition that the Supreme Court Act is not part of the constitution, and although this is debatable, there are strong indications that the constitution does indeed include this Act.[5] Moreover, there are the explicit references to the Supreme Court in sections 41 and 42 of CA1982. Given the short list in the former section of matters requiring unanimity, and given the gravity of placing anything in this category, changing the composition of the Supreme Court will require the unanimous agreement of the federal Parliament and all provincial legislatures. Of course, if the reconstitution of Canada involves amendments to the amending formulae or to language rights, then unanimity certainly will be required.

To reconstitute Canada without Quebec, then, will require that resolutions to amend the Constitution Acts be introduced in the House of Commons, the Senate, and the legislature of every province, and that they all be passed. Quebec will not impede this process. If the province is to become sovereign, the only way to do so constitutionally is by making these amendments. But the negotiations will be continuing until (and after) the separation, and the Quebec government might be tempted to obstruct Canada's reconstitution in order to win concessions on other issues, delaying the separation until it gains better terms. Or it might seek modifications in the amendment package, aiming perhaps to constitutionalize some treaties or joint decision-making structures. However, because the process will have proceeded so far, the threat of obstruction would be an empty one. The entire momentum on the Canadian side will be towards accepting secession, negotiating arrangements in the national interest, and collectively setting up the framework of a country. Since there will be much resentment towards Quebec for having forced these events, there would be very little support for a Canadian government that did not meet the threat of obstruction with firm determination. So Canada would counter with threats of its own – to effect a nonconstitutional separation or one based on the general amending formula. If this were subsequently found to be illegal (by Canadian courts), it would be too late for Quebec. In any case, since the constitutional amendment package was being designed for the continuity of Canada, there would be no international sympathy for a Quebec government that delayed this to win substantive concessions. Moreover, after a UDI, even a forced one, Quebec's status as a successor state to treaties would be doubtful.

Of course, there will be a bitter fight in Quebec and in the National Assembly as federalists engage in the final battle to stop the separation. But if the secession process has unfolded as described here, and if the economic situation is relatively stable, fighting the constitutional amendment will be to resist a *fait accompli*.

The question of the other provinces is much more pressing and delicate. Constitutional amendments will be debated in a joint Senate and House of Commons committee of Parliament and also in every provincial legislature. As has been the case in the past, albeit with much protest and little success, they will also be discussed in First Ministers' Conferences. There will certainly be disagreement about what Canada's new constitution should contain, and the negotiations with Quebec could spill over into the constitutional arena, with some provincial governments aiming to hold up constitutional change in order to force the Canadian negotiators into certain positions *vis-à-vis* Quebec. If unanimity is the requirement for reconstitution, any provincial government would appear to have tremendous leverage. Paradoxically, however, the unanimity requirement will make rapid passage of the constitutional changes more probable than would be the case if the consent of only seven provinces were required. If only seven were needed, any provincial government could refuse the amendment without bringing the whole reconstitution process to an end. But unanimity raises the stakes enormously, and so it makes consent more likely. Once the secession is taking place, it will acquire a momentum of its own. The whole chain of decisions, agreements, and commitments that makes up the separation process involves not only Canada-Quebec relations but also the future shape of Canada. Yet the internal debate about this will not be intense when the first principles of separation are being negotiated, for strong dissent would weaken the Canadian bargaining hand. Later, a fundamental challenge to the emerging constitution would destroy what the negotiators had accomplished, and the country would be plunged again into uncertainty. As the separation gathers momentum, the main order of business for Canadians will be to eliminate Quebec so that they can regain stability, make collective choices, and secure a national future. If most provincial governments are prepared to do this, others will not stand in the way by obstructing constitutional amendments. Consequently, the necessary amendments will be through all the provincial legislatures by October 1995 at the latest.

How could this be? Some provinces have laws requiring extensive consultation or referendums about constitutional amendments. These are normal statutes, though; they cannot bind future legislatures (all of which will be in session during the crisis). Provincial legislators can amend laws about constitutional amendments, and participatory exercises can be accelerated. But why should this be done? Inevitably, as the crisis fades and as the results of the negotiations are discussed, there will be growing dissatisfaction in Canada, and the legitimacy of those managing the process will decline. Disagreement about the future configuration of Canada will become more manifest. So why would the provincial governments in Alberta, British Columbia, Ontario, and Newfoundland – to name only those least likely to be in accord with the process – agree to rapid constitutional amendments?

There are three reasons. First, the amendments will be minimal. Their whole thrust will be to accept and constitutionalize the fact that Quebec is no longer part of the Canadian community. Apart from this, the status quo will obtain. If there are any further amendments, they will only be such as to make the status quo easier to change; hence, the constitutional proposals will embody continuity and flexibility. Second, it will be clear that a referendum, or more probably an election, will follow passage of the amendments. Canadians will then have an opportunity, free of Quebecers' participation, to define their collective future; more concretely, the election campaign will allow parties to take competing positions about the agreements with Quebec and about how Canada should be reconstituted. For any province to resist the amendments at this point would be to deny the opportunity for the first Canadian elections without Quebec. Third, there will be an enormous sense of urgency and a perception that the stakes are very high: both elements are conducive to successful constitutional change.[6] Non-passage of the amendments in any province would represent a fundamental break with the rest of Canada. It would probably force a UDI by either Quebec or Canada. The government of the recalcitrant province would have to be prepared to risk the whole federation – or to take its citizens out of Canada, to inflict further economic loss on them, to risk that treaties would no longer apply on its territory, and, following the Quebec precedent, to assume a share of the national debt proportional to its population. This is improbable. Canadian solidarity will have been heightened in the first phases of the secession process, and in no province will there have been time to establish a consensus in favour of an independent, non-Canadian alternative, either provincial or regional. The amendments will therefore pass through the provincial legislatures.

Apart from the provinces, there are two other groups that will make claims about the constitutionality of the secession. These are the federalists in Quebec, particularly the anglophone minority, and the Aboriginal peoples. The Protestant minority in Quebec, as dissentient school supporters, possesses educational rights under section 93 of CA1867 (as do Roman Catholics in Ontario), along with the right to appeal provincial legislation affecting them to the federal government and to have remedial federal legislation if necessary. The existing Canadian constitution also guarantees the right to use English in the Quebec legislature and courts, and to be served by the federal government in English. Native peoples have rights under treaties with the crown in right of Canada, and they may have a claim to retain federal authority over themselves because they now fall under federal jurisdiction. Under recent court decisions, Ottawa also has a general fiduciary responsibility for Aboriginal peoples.

These matters involve the morality of the separation; more precisely, the morality of Canada surrendering authority over citizens who wish to continue to be members of the polity.[7] As well, there is the issue of whether these people have a right to participate in an amendment process that will result in Canada abandoning its authority over them and obligations to them. Morality will be a concern in the separation process. After a Yes vote, however, if secession is to occur peacefully, the moral question will be not whether Canada can abandon these people, but whether Quebec is providing an adequate framework of rights for them; and if secession is to occur constitutionally, the legal question will be whether any claims on Canada can be constitutionally extinguished so that Canada will have no specific obligations to people living within Quebec's territory.

There are no legal grounds to prevent the constitutional secession of Quebec.[8] The Constitution Acts contain no provision that the federation is immutable, indestructible, or indissoluble; hence, there is nothing to prohibit a constitutional amendment that arranges for the secession of part of the country.[9] As well, there is no right for citizens to insist, under the Charter, that some order of government must protect their rights.[10] The dissentient schools arrangement, for example, was part of the historic compromise made in 1867, and when that compromise ends there will be no grounds to appeal to Ottawa, even assuming that Quebec would not be prepared to continue a system at least as generous. More generally, there is no existing constitutional provision that limits what amendments can be made: in law, any duty or obligation of the federal government can be revoked.[11]

This still leaves the issue of procedure, which involves the Aboriginal peoples' participation in the amendment process. The First Nations in Quebec have no general legal entitlement to retain federal jurisdiction over themselves. But, in fact, do First Nations have a special right to participate in making constitutional amendments that affect them, and do they have a right of veto over such amendments?

Section 35.1 of CA1982 commits the federal and provincial governments to the principle that the prime minister will convene a constitutional conference with the provincial premiers and that representatives of the Aboriginal peoples "will" be invited to participate in discussions when amendments are contemplated to section 91(24) of CA1867 or sections 25 and 35 of CA1982. The first of these makes "Indians, and Lands reserved for the Indians" a matter of federal jurisdiction; the second protects Aboriginal rights from abrogation or derogation by the Charter; and the last recognizes and affirms "the existing aboriginal and treaty rights" of Native peoples. This would seem to imply that Aboriginal peoples must play a special role in the amendment process. But the reconstitution of Canada need not involve any change whatsoever to the specified sections, which will continue to define the division of powers in Canada as it will come to exist, and thus there may be no constitutional obligation to consult with Aboriginal representatives. Moreover, the phrasing commits the Canadian government only to the "principle" of the conference and to Aboriginal participation, and this may not be legally enforceable. Even were a conference held, as it will be, there is no implication that Native peoples' views about the amendment must prevail.

Beyond these legalities is the general fiduciary responsibility of the crown to Native peoples. The government's actions towards them are reviewable by the courts, and in the Sparrow case the Supreme Court set out conditions to be satisfied when the crown acts as "trustee" for Native peoples, including the requirement to consult the Aboriginal groups affected by the crown's actions.[12] But the fiduciary relationship, by its nature, does not oblige the crown to act in accord with Aboriginal peoples' views. It does appear, though, that there is an obligation to ascertain these views, and this will require consultation.[13]

Finally, there may exist a constitutional convention that Native peoples participate in constitutional discussions affecting them and that they have a veto over relevant amendments. This may have been established by the four conferences in the 1980s devoted to Aboriginal rights and by the participation of Aboriginal leaders in the 1992 constitutional negotiations. Moreover, the Charlottetown Accord provided that amendments affecting one or more of Canada's Aboriginal peoples would be made only if these amendments had received their "substantial consent," and this would buttress the convention. On the other hand, since the Accord did not pass, the strict constitutional requirement for consent is not in place. Beyond this, discerning consent in such disparate groups is not simple, and governments may not believe themselves bound by the conventional "rule" in any case. Constitutional conventions are enforceable not by the courts but, ultimately, by public opinion and the political process. There will be considerable sympathy in Canada for Quebec's Aboriginals, but not enough to derail the entire secession.[14]

The result is that there will be consultation with Aboriginals. They will be incorporated into the Joint Committee on Canada-Quebec Separation, and their leaders will be invited to a formal First Ministers' Conference. But the necessary amendments to the constitution can be made without the consent of Aboriginal peoples. As discussed earlier, however, the separation process would be considerably eased if the Quebec constitution contained clauses identical to sections 25 and 35 of CA1982, along with provisions about consultation and consent in future constitutional changes; in fact, Quebec will do far more than this to extend constitutional guarantees of self-government to its Aboriginal peoples.

If the constitutional proposals are passed by late September or early October, a Canadian election can be held in November. Or a referendum could be held. In the view of many observers, constitutional change can no longer be accomplished in Canada without this device, "at least for any significant package of constitutional proposals."[15] A referendum on the constitutional amendments, or on them and the principle of separation and the agreements with Quebec, would very likely carry right across the country. It would seal the process with popular approval. Thus, depending on the public's mood, the federal government might opt to hold one. On the other hand, referendum campaigns are unpredictable, and some question might fail to carry in some province, despite the enormous stakes involved. Given these high stakes, both federal and provincial politicians might well argue that an election is necessary in any event, that it will allow fuller debate, that the separation is inevitable, and that the constitutional changes are minimal departures. Thus, the referendum might be avoided.

An election raises one more constitutional difficulty. If the entire package of amendments is passed, the separation will take effect when the governor general issues the proclamation. This would be premature, since the new Canadian constitution is to come into effect, along with Quebec's sovereign constitution, at midnight of 31 December 1995. Moreover, if the constitutional changes were made irrevocably, the election debates would be artificial. On the other hand, if the amendments had not actually been made, the Canadian election could not be held constitutionally in ROC alone. There are two ways around this difficulty. One is to insert a new section in the constitution stating that it will become effective only on 1 January 1996, except for those amendments necessary to hold an election in Canada as it will then be constituted (and the relevent sections could be specified or not). Another method, less constraining of the election debate, would be for the House of Commons to pass the entire package except for one section that does not affect the election. This could be an important section, perhaps the amending formula itself if it had become the focus of discord, or perhaps section 4 of CA1867: "Unless it is otherwise expressed or implied, the Name Canada shall be taken to mean Canada as constituted under this Act." Then, in order to accomplish the secession and reconstitute Canada, the newly elected House of Commons would have to pass this final section. Assuming that this occurs, the governor general will proclaim the new Canadian constitution effective 1 January 1996. Quebec will follow the same process. And the separation will have been done constitutionally.

THERE WILL BE NO OTHER SUBSTANTIAL CONSTITUTIONAL CHANGES IN EITHER STATE

After the Quebec referendum, Canadians will experience a high degree of uncertainty, and they will begin a painful process of adjustment. Rather than relations with Quebec, what will soon preoccupy them most will be the make-up of Canada itself. Between the election of the PQ government and the referendum, the options open to Canada will have been canvassed and debated at great length by think-tanks, academics in conferences, and the media. Depending on the strategies that political parties and governments adopt, and the degree of polarization that obtains, the debate will have extended into political parties and perhaps, in some provinces, into official bodies such as task forces and legislative committees. Despite the array of alternatives that will have been assessed, after the event Canada will have a constitution that resembles the current one very closely. This conclusion is supported by comparative experience, though it flies in the face of some Canadian commentary. Focusing on Ontario's predominance in federal institutions, for example, Roger Gibbins has claimed that "it would be naïve to assume that Quebec could be plucked out of the existing system and that the federal arrangements now in place would remain more or less intact."[16] He suggests a number of potential reforms, including strict representation by population in the House of Commons, a reformed Senate to express regional interests (as well as gender and ethnic differences), and an elected prime minister or president to "knit together" a disparate country: "If one thing is certain, it is that the institutional and constitutional status quo could not hold."[17]

But it will hold, for the most part. There are several reasons why. Post-separation constitutional arrangements will depend critically on how the transition actually takes place. In the immediate aftermath of the Yes vote, Canadians' uncertainty will produce support for stabilizing measures, not only in relation to Quebec and the economy but also with respect to the make-up of Canada. Just as Quebec will have an incentive to adopt a constitution with few alterations from the status quo, in order to reassure citizens and gain international credibility, so in Canada will there be pressure to make the immediate adjustments required to cope with the secession and then quickly to find a new equilibrium. While there will be strong advocates of more profound constitutional changes, such as rearranging borders, abolishing the Senate, altering the distribution of powers, or inscribing new rights in the Charter, there will be no consensus on these proposals and little time to forge one. More important, no such change will be necessary, in the sense that excising Quebec from Canada will be regarded as absolutely essential: upon this, consensus will be reached easily. Nor is there any urgency to make some of the amendments that are likely to be proposed. They can be debated and adopted later, by the new Canadian community. After Quebec has separated, the source of much constitutional stalemate will be eliminated, and appropriate amendments can be made when this has happened and the situation has become stable. It will not yet have been demonstrated that the current constitution cannot work for ROC; and as the proposed alterations would be untried, their effects could not be predicted, and there would be little support for introducing yet more uncertainty into an unstable economic and political environment. Citizens, firms, and governments will face enough transition costs without having to discover and accommodate themselves to a new constitutional order. As well, the argument will be made that Canadian governments would remain free to make policy changes without formal constitutional amendments.

Given these reasons, and the transition process as described above, the main principles guiding the reconstitution of Canada will be simple. First, it will be an autonomous process in which Quebec representatives will not participate, except to pass the amendments through the National Assembly. Second, the basic goal will be to eliminate Quebec entirely from the constitutional order. Canada will have its own constitution in which there will be no reference to Quebec. Third, the minimal amendments necessary to accomplish this will be passed; there will be no sweeping institutional redesign. Finally, insofar as amendments will be made that do not involve Quebec, or when Quebec's excision dictates that some choice will be made, the thrust of the changes will be towards maintaining flexibility. Canadian governments and citizens will prefer to keep open their constitutional options once the immediate task is completed.

Constitutional amendment will therefore be a process that starts from the status quo rather than *de novo*. This, despite the fact that analysts and advocates from both the left and right wings of the political spectrum have argued for a constitutional or constituent assembly that would throw open the whole constitution and allow for radical change to Canada's institutions.[18] There will not be a constituent assembly. There is no procedure to set one up. And not only will the politicians and governments in power manage the process, but they will have popular support in doing so, given the anxieties of the time and the urgent need to accomplish the separation. So the existing Constitution Acts will form the baseline for change.

Many provisions of the Constitution Acts lend themselves to a simple deletion of Quebec. This will be necessary to remove Canada's power over Quebec – in the area of taxation, for example – and to remove claims of Quebecers upon Canada. When Quebec is no longer a "province," for instance, it will lose the right, under section 121 of CA1867, to have its products "admitted free into each of the other provinces." Deleting Quebec involves rewriting history. Section 5 of CA1867, for example, defines the core entity that other provinces later joined; it will simply be rewritten to state that "Canada shall be divided into Three Provinces, named Ontario, Nova Scotia, and New Brunswick." Other parts of the constitution refer only to Quebec, such as sections 71–80 of CA1867, which provide the legal underpinnings of the Quebec legislature; they can be eliminated. Simple deletions of references to Quebec and of provisions exclusively about Quebec can easily be made in twenty-five sections of CA1867 and one section of CA1982. In fact, it is surprising how little excision is required to eliminate Quebec from the constitution.

In other areas, it will be necessary to preserve continuity. The original British North America Act which brought Canada into being divided "Canada" as it then existed into Ontario and Quebec. Many of the provisions of CA1867 were thus concerned with effecting the transformation of "Canada" into the two new provinces. Some of these provisions are spent and can be repealed, and others can be safely deleted; but before references to Lower Canada and Quebec are eliminated from a few other sections, they will require either a new interpretive clause or some phrasing that allows for judicial discretion, in order to preserve continuity and prevent a vacuum of law.

Another issue to be resolved concerns assets. Section 113 of CA1867 conferred the assets of the former Canada upon the new provinces of Ontario and Quebec conjointly. Most of these assets have probably been divided, so the section can be eliminated. But section 108 transfers certain public works and property "of each Province" to the federal government. If a suitable agreement on the division of assets has been reached with Quebec, this section can stand unchanged, since other amendments will redefine "Province" so as not to include Quebec.

A more difficult issue concerns the language rights enshrined in the existing constitution. There is a case to be made for maintaining these unchanged, because Quebec francophones will be able to remain Canadian citizens for two years – and longer, if they so choose – and because of the substantial francophone populations in New Brunswick and Ontario. But these rights are unsustainable. Minority-language education rights have provoked much resentment among anglophone taxpayers and recent immigrants in Ontario and throughout the West. More important, the Yes vote will have destroyed two symbolic conceptions of Canada, views that have been in competition but that have both sustained these rights. First, secession will end any remaining conception of Canada as essentially dualistic, as a partnership of two founding communities. Second, it will terminate the liberal conception that language rights inhere in individuals, who should be able to exercise them anywhere in the country, for there will not be enough francophone individuals in Canada to justify special treatment.[19] People who speak "non-official" languages at home greatly outnumber French-speaking Canadians in every province except Prince Edward Island, Nova Scotia, and New Brunswick, and the disproportion is much larger where "mother tongue" is concerned.

As a consequence, section 133 of CA1867 will be deleted, and so will sections 93(3), 93(4), and the parts of 93(2) that refer to Quebec. Alternatively, the whole of section 93 could be deleted, along with references to separate schools in the Acts and Orders-in-Council admitting the various other provinces to the federation; then amendments to maintain francophone schools – in Prince Edward Island and Ontario, for example – could be made under section 43. In CA1982, sections 16–23 will be eliminated, except for those subsections concerning the use and status of English and French in New Brunswick. New Brunswick's francophone majority is so large that the province would be ungovernable without linguistic guarantees. It is also possible that the Government of Ontario would entrench similar rights for the province's francophone minority, but since this could be done at any time under section 43, it need not take place during this amendment process. The result of these changes is that Canada will have no official language. Customary use will prevail.

258 The Dynamics of Quebec Secession

Other changes will be even more contentious. One concerns representation. The provision in the Supreme Court Act guaranteeing three Quebec judges will be eliminated, and it is unlikely that any other regional qualifications will be inserted. More important is the Senate. The minimalist approach is simply to shrink it. Hence, section 22 of CA1867 will be amended so that it simply specifies that there will be three divisions of the Senate and there is no mention of Quebec and its twenty-four senators. Section 21 will state that the Senate will consist of eighty members.[20] Table 5 lays out the new distribution of Senate seats by province, along with the existing distribution.

It is worth noting, first, that the underlying disproportion between seats and populations will remain unchanged. Nova Scotia now has 1.12 Senate seats per 100,000 citizens while Ontario has 0.25, and this will continue. Second, all provinces will increase their relative weight in the Senate by the same proportion – about 30 per cent. What will change are the relative weights of provinces and regions. The Atlantic provinces will move from 28.8 per cent of the votes to 37.5 per cent, and the West (including the territories), will move from 25 per cent to 32.5 per cent. Ontario's relative weight will also increase, to 30 per cent.

This result will not prove popular in the West, where there is much support for an equal, elected, and effective Senate. However, one criticism of the current distribution is that the Senate does not adequately represent the regions outside central Canada, and this will be rectified to some extent; with Quebec eliminated, central Canadian seats will fall from 46.2 to 30 per cent. Second, there is nothing in the constitution to prevent Senators from being elected; the governor general has the power to summon any "fit and qualified" person to the chamber, and one such summons has already been extended to the winner of an election (though this was in anticipation of the Meech Lake Accord being passed). As well, the existing legislative powers of the Senate are fully equivalent to those of the House of Commons, except that money bills must be introduced in the House. Finally, there is no evidence that Senators actually vote *en bloc* according to their province of origin. There has been no systematic analysis of Senate voting patterns, but in the crucial vote over the second set of constitutional proposals in December 1981, for example, the 23 Nays included members from every province except Manitoba and the territories, and the major cleavage was along party lines. One keen observer has argued that a triple-E Senate would be likely to vote on party lines; as such, it would be an "institution of little value."[21] Another, from the West, rejects a triple-E Senate as "inherently centralizing" and prefers an expansion of provincial jurisdiction instead.[22]

Table 5
Distribution of Senate Seats: Current and Excluding Quebec

	Current		Excluding Quebec	
	Seats	Percentage	Seats	Percentage
Newfoundland	6	5.8	6	7.5
Prince Edward Island	4	3.8	4	5.0
Nova Scotia	10	9.6	10	12.5
New Brunswick	10	9.6	10	12.5
Quebec	24	23.1	–	–
Ontario	24	23.1	24	30.0
Manitoba	6	5.8	6	7.5
Saskatchewan	6	5.8	6	7.5
Alberta	6	5.8	6	7.5
British Columbia	6	5.8	6	7.5
Yukon/Northwest Territories	2	1.9	2	2.5
Totals	104	100.1	80	100.0

Note: The figures do not change significantly when provision is made for the extraordinary allocation of eight extra senators (currently) or six extra (in the new configuration)

These arguments and others will be heard in the reconstitution debate. But if there is a consensus to eliminate Quebec but no consensus on Senate reform, the minimally changed status quo will prevail.[23]

Representation in the House of Commons raises similar issues in more acute form. Following the principle of minimal modification, the constitution will be amended to eliminate Quebec's 75 members, and section 37 of CA1867 will specify that the House consist of 220 members. The formula for allocating seats among the provinces is contained in section 51, which was last amended by the Representation Act, 1985; there is no need to alter this, since the formula is no longer based on the Quebec seats.

Once more, it is instructive to examine the new distribution of seats by province.[24] As table 6 shows, all provinces will increase their strength in the House of Commons by roughly the same amount (32–38 per cent), but the relative power of provincial and regional blocs will change substantially. Ontario will come close to commanding a clear majority in the House, with 45.0 percent of the members; the weight of the Atlantic provinces will increase from 10.8 to 14.5 per cent; and the West, including the territories, will come to hold 40.5 per cent rather than 30.2 per cent. Again, under the assumption that central Canada is a now dominant bloc, its weight without Quebec will fall from 59 to 45 per cent.

Still, for the West, the make-up of the House of Commons will be seen as cause for apprehension, with respect to both policy and future constitutional change. On normal legislation, Ontario members will almost have the capacity to secure changes they desire and to block those they oppose. On the other hand, representation by population is a basic principle in democratic communities and is defensible as such. Moreover, Ontario's dominance will be offset by the composition of the Senate. More practically, divisions in the House are along party lines rather than provincial ones. And pragmatically, the Reform Party, which is most inclined to champion western interests, might sense itself poised for a breakthrough in Ontario in the first election to be held without Quebec, so it might not oppose the new House of Commons. Nevertheless, it is the provincial governments that will have to agree to these constitutional amendments, and the threat of Ontario dominance in the Commons might be severe enough to force amendments to the Senate's composition so that provincial equality would prevail there.

A closely related issue concerns the amending formulae. The general formula need not be redrafted, but Quebec's absence will have consequences. Currently, the general formula requires that Ottawa and seven provinces with 50 per cent of the population must approve an amendment for it to pass; without Quebec, amendments would require the assent of Ottawa and six of the nine provinces having 50 per cent of the population. So the "blocking coalitions" would change. This is a term used by political scientists who have devised intricate measures of the power of provinces and their citizens in constitutional amendment processes.[25] What often counts here are the coalitions capable of blocking amendments. Under the current general formula, the blocking coalitions are:

1 the federal Parliament,
2 any four provinces,
3 Ontario and Quebec,
4 Ontario and British Columbia and any province other than Prince Edward Island, and
5 Ontario and Alberta and Manitoba.[26]

With Quebec out of the constitution, the blocking coalitions under the general formula would be:

1 the federal Parliament,
2 any four provinces, and
3 Ontario and any province other than Prince Edward Island.

Table 6
Distribution of House of Commons Seats: Current and Excluding Quebec

	Current		Excluding Quebec	
	Seats	Percentage	Seats	Percentage
Newfoundland	7	2.4	7	3.2
Prince Edward Island	4	1.4	4	1.8
Nova Scotia	11	3.7	11	5.0
New Brunswick	10	3.4	10	4.5
Quebec	75	25.4	–	–
Ontario	99	33.6	99	45.0
Manitoba	14	4.7	14	6.4
Saskatchewan	14	4.7	14	6.4
Alberta	26	8.8	26	11.8
British Columbia	32	10.8	32	14.5
Yukon/Northwest Territories	3	1.0	3	1.4
Totals	295	99.9	220	100.0

Ontario's capacity to block amendments, both as a province and through its members in the House of Commons, would increase substantially. (The Senate is less relevant because the seat distribution by province is more equal and the upper chamber can block amendments for only 180 days.) Because of the 50 per cent population requirement, the governments of Ontario and any other province except Prince Edward Island could defeat any amendment under the general formula, such as proposals to establish an elected Senate, to include property rights in the Charter, or to decentralize powers. Similarly, on the dubious assumption that members of Parliament vote as a bloc on constitutional amendments, Ontario MPs would need to find only ten other members in order to prevent passage of an amendment. For amendments that it proposed, the Ontario government would need to recruit among the provinces only five of eight potential allies (62.5 per cent) rather than six of nine (66.7 per cent), and its MPs alone would almost suffice to pass them through the House of Commons. In theory, based on 1992 population figures, amendments could be passed against the wishes of provincial governments representing 34.0 per cent of the population (British Columbia, Alberta, and Manitoba). But this is the case now! In fact, the blocking power of the peripheral provinces would be much increased in the new House of Commons. On proposed amendments favourable to "central Canada," they would have 70 per cent of the Senate and 55 per cent of the House, rather than the 54 per cent and 41 per cent that they now control. Indeed, Ontario could be stymied in the new system, and it could easily be overwhelmed if the other provinces combined against it.

Still, given its position in the House of Commons, Ontario's power would be regarded as threatening. There are two solutions. One is to increase the veto capacity of provinces other than Ontario. This could be accomplished by eliminating section 47 of CA1982, thereby allowing the Senate to block amendments permanently, or by amending it to provide that Senate vetoes could be overridden only by a two-thirds House majority, rather than a simple majority. The second solution is to change the formula by raising the population level required under section 38 of CA1982 from 50 per cent to, say, two-thirds. This would enable Alberta and British Columbia, along with either Manitoba or Saskatchewan, to block amendments. But both of these devices would reduce constitutional flexibility at a time when Canada's rapid evolution will require the capacity to adjust.

The more probable solution will be to make amendments easier to accomplish. One device would be to include in the constitution provisions allowing for the interdelegation of powers and for cooperative federal-provincial contracts, as envisaged by the Beaudoin-Dobbie Committee, and also to expand the areas of concurrent jurisdiction, where both Ottawa and the provinces can legislate.[27] Another would be to reduce the population requirement in the general amending formula so as to remove Ontario's near-veto. Amendments might require the assent of two-thirds of the provinces with 40 per cent of the population. In this case, to block an amendment, the Ontario government would have to ally with Alberta, with British Columbia, or with Manitoba and Saskatchewan. Of course, Ontario would still have the power (if its MPs voted as a bloc) to stop amendments in the House of Commons by finding only a few allies. But Ontario could not impose its will without recruiting five other provincial governments.

The amending formula issue is a critical and complex one. Its outcome will depend on the provincial premiers and their reading of public sentiment, especially in the West. If normal provincial procedures for ratifying proposed amendments are to be compressed or ignored in order to reconstitute the country quickly, then there certainly will be some extra resistance to a status quo constitution; and if suspicion of Ontario begins to match pro-Canadian solidarity as the immediate crisis fades, then the minimally changed status quo will not prevail. But it can be presumed that the Ontario government will be accommodating, as in the past. The result will be that the amending formula will be changed to provide greater flexibility; as well, there may be a consensus that the provinces should have equal representation in the Senate. Of course, changing the amending formula will definitely require unanimity among the provincial governments.

At the same time as Canada is reconstituting itself, Quebec will be finalizing its constitution. There need be no coordination of these processes, nor will the substance of the constitutions be interrelated. The only requirements are that both become effective at the same time and that Quebec's National Assembly pass the Canadian amendment package.

The Quebec drafters will face a more difficult task than their Canadian counterparts, for they will have to design a whole new constitution, rather than simply making minimal changes like the Canadians. There will be many tough issues for Quebecers to face, including whether to establish an upper chamber, how much to decentralize, how to make constitutional amendments, and what rights to inscribe in the document. Based on comparative experience, Quebecers will make as few changes as possible to the existing order. This raises again one issue of mutual interest – the Quebec head of state. It is widely presumed that Quebec will become a republic by stipulating in the constitution a method of selecting a president or other head of state. But there are good reasons for not doing so. A new system would be untried and unpredictable in its effects, while retaining the monarchy would be a statement of continuity. As noted above, members of the military have sworn an oath to the crown. Equally significant is the fact that early treaties made by Native peoples were agreements with the crown. As the courts have firmly decided, these rights and obligations have passed to the crown in right of Canada, and it would be much more difficult for the Aboriginals in Quebec to contest in the courts the transfer to Quebec of historic treaty rights and Canadian fiduciary responsibilities if these too pass to the crown in right of Quebec. As a consequence, it is quite possible that Quebec will continue as a constitutional monarchy, at least for some time.

POLICIES IN THE TWO STATES WILL SOON BEGIN TO DIVERGE

As in any secession, policy divergence will result from the different social and economic forces bearing on politics in the two states, as well as the impact of the transition to sovereignty. The foreign policies of Quebec and Canada should not diverge much. For both, the principal preoccupation will be the United States and the hemisphere as a whole. Quebec's military role will be muted for some time, but the government will have to engage in a substantial diplomatic effort to forge treaties akin to the Canadian ones that no longer apply to the new country. Undoubtedly, Quebec will tilt towards France and *La francophonie*, while Canada's orientation towards the Pacific Rim will become more developed. All of this need produce no discord between the two states.

Domestically, there will be divergence in the treatment of minorities. Francophone privileges outside Quebec will be curtailed, except in New Brunswick. Within Quebec, the treatment of the anglophone minority will very likely improve as Quebecers finally feel secure about their linguistic future and as the government seeks to retain skilled labour and capital. On the other hand, relations between Quebec and its Aboriginal population will be tense. Although programs and funding will be plentiful, negotiating self-government agreements will be very difficult: any sovereign Quebec government would be loath to reach the type of generous land-claims agreement that will continue to be made in Canada, or to accept an unconstrained Aboriginal right to self-government.

There will be some continuing disagreements between Canada and Quebec. These can be anticipated about the division of certain assets, the location of the maritime boundaries, environmental spillovers, the fisheries, labour mobility, access from the Atlantic provinces through Quebec, and many other matters. Even so, there is no reason to expect such disputes to be so acrimonious that the governments will abrogate treaties.

Some of the treaties will lapse, however. The immigration agreement will not long endure the different external and economic orientations of the two states. This alone would necessitate border controls, but they will go up in any case. While both countries will continue to adhere to NAFTA and the FTA, the customs union will not survive beyond the next round of multilateral trade negotiations, in which Quebec will be a free agent. This means that commerce between the two countries will be encumbered by rules-of-origin requirements and other border measures.

It is in economic policy that the policies of the two countries will diverge most, because their overall stances towards the role of the state will inevitably differ. At the very least, there will be noncoincidental oscillations between *dirigisme* and *laissez-faire* in Canada and Quebec. This will pit state spending, economic regulation, and comprehensive social policies against restraint, deregulation, and targeted welfare programs. Initially, Canada will probably move towards the right, while the Quebec government will have a more interventionist philosophy. Voluntary harmonization will erode over time, therefore, and there will be less cooperation in measures of positive economic integration.

Beyond this predictable outcome will be the ideological difficulties of Quebec governments. Currently, the PQ melds a confident, business-oriented wing (which is interested in trade liberalization, competition, and supportive state policies) with a more traditional wing, based in the trade unions and social movements (which favours national solidarity and redistributive policies). To some extent this cleavage coincides with the regional division between Montreal and the periphery. With the national question finally settled, these divisions will continue to be submerged in the short term, as sovereigntist Quebecers, at least, make sacrifices to achieve the collective benefits of independence. Before long, however, differences will emerge about how best to generate in the long term the economic growth that benefits all. There is no evidence to show that easy solutions exist to this basic problem. Politically, the PQ will be unable to abandon the right wing to the opposition – assuming that the provincial Liberals have regrouped around the pro-business end of this dimension – which means that after the rigours of the transition, if not during them, Quebec's economic landscape will be punctuated with labour and social unrest. Even if the political system finds equilibrium in a stable two-party arrangement, as will probably be the case in Canada, the governmental cycles in the two countries will be unlikely to coincide. At the very least, the two governments will have different responses to external economic shocks. Since economic interdependence will decline after the separation, the effects of this divergence in economic policy will become less serious over time; they will, however, contribute independently to declining interdependence. It is also possible that conflicting orientations will fracture the currency agreement. In this case, Quebec could adopt the U.S. dollar; alternatively, having passed through the major adjustments of the transition, it could more safely introduce an independent, floating currency. As for Canada, the threat posed by either of these alternatives will have been much reduced by a successful transition and new economic stability. Ending joint management of monetary policy would not threaten the viability of an independent, floating Canadian currency.

In sum, the two states will tend to drift apart on various policy fronts. This tendency will be moderated by their continuing integration into the North American, hemispheric, and world trading and security systems, and by a few enduring agreements between them. But in the absence of common political institutions, and within the range permitted by outside forces, policy in the two states will evolve independently.

QUEBEC SECESSION WILL BE IRREVOCABLE

After the tension of the immediate post-referendum period, the re-drafting of the Canadian constitution, the writing of Quebec's, the difficult negotiations, the signing of international treaties, the creation of barriers to mobility, the formal dissolution of the existing community and the end of redistribution, the transformation of the party systems, and the gradual development of different policy environments, it is inconceivable that Quebec and Canada would reunite. The process of peaceful secession has a momentum that has never been reversed and that will not be reversed in this case.

CHAPTER FIFTEEN

Reprise: Secession with Polarization

The depiction of Quebec secession presented above rests on a large number of assumptions. These are too numerous to list, but some of the most critical ones are the following:

- Before the referendum, there is no official, public contingency planning by Canada and no negotiations with the sovereigntists.
- The referendum result is close and unpredictable.
- There is a very high level of uncertainty after the Yes result is known; this is economically damaging but not disastrous.
- There is a widespread sense of crisis in Canada, and Ottawa takes the lead in handling the situation. As it does so, allegiance, legitimacy, and power flow to the central government.
- The Liberal Party is able to continue to govern more or less intact; it neither resigns nor fragments.
- National solidarity is maintained in the transition process. In particular, no provincial government is prepared to impede Canada's reconstitution.
- The stance of the United States and other foreign powers is to favour competent, rapid management of the crisis and the re-establishment of stability.

All these assumptions are contestable, of course. Whether they will hold cannot be known unless secession actually takes place. The purpose here is not to justify each of them any further or to relax individual assumptions in order to make variations on the basic scenario.

The assumptions form a package, based on analysis of Canada, comparative experience, and an historical sense of how the complex dynamics of the separation would play out.

Nevertheless, the basic account of the transition to Quebec sovereignty may also rest on a more general assumption about the level of polarization that exists between Quebec and the rest of Canada (ROC). By polarization is meant simply the degree of mutual hostility between the communities, and the uniformity and intensity of desires within each community for political separation. Generally, it has been assumed that opinion within each community is divided, with a substantial majority in ROC favouring the existing order and with a majority in Quebec (probably a narrow one) eventually opting for sovereignty. After the referendum, of course, polarization would increase as a consequence of the crisis and the collective solidarity that the bilateral negotiations would engender.

But what if there is much polarization before the referendum takes place? This phenomenon was evident in the Czech-Slovak case. There were political incentives for Meciar and Klaus to foster polarization, because this increased their support, and after the 1992 elections they were able to use state resources to move public opinion further in favour of separation. On both sides, the leaders induced people to re-evaluate and reinterpret the risks and benefits of profound political change, and opinion in each state consolidated around the view that separation was desirable and inevitable. In Canada, there is considerable potential for polarization. Our purpose here is to explore how this might occur and to assess whether a high degree of polarization could invalidate the assumptions underlying the separation scenario, thereby producing a substantially different outcome.

UNDERLYING FACTORS

There are some basic elements of the Canadian landscape that allow for polarization. The first is the economic situation. Continuing high levels of unemployment in Quebec provide openings for sovereigntist politicians to claim that only radical constitutional change can bring improvement. In ROC, it is widely believed that constitutional uncertainty has decreased foreign investors' confidence in the Canadian economy, causing the value of the Canadian dollar to decline and interest rates to rise. This slows the economic recovery and imposes costs on all debtors, including governments, and the blame for this is laid on the sovereigntist aspirations of Quebecers. The federal and provincial governments' deficits are another cause of high interest rates, and efforts to correct them have led the governments to run surpluses on operating accounts. One result is that Canadians now are paying more in taxes than they are receiving in services, and this undoubtedly has contributed to both a general disaffection with government and critical scrutiny of redistributive spending.

Another consequence has been continuing federal-provincial and interregional conflicts. All provincial governments have condemned Ottawa's off-loading of responsibilities. Ontario, British Columbia, and Alberta have been penalized financially by the federal cap on Canada Assistance Plan payments at the same time as these provinces are the paymasters of the equalization system. These tensions and others make for visible conflict in federal-provincial relations, heightening the public's perception that the system is fragile and unfair. In this context, too, sharp and suspicious attention is paid to the regional or provincial impact of federal expenditures and even regulatory measures such as pharmaceutical patent protection. It is common to hear in Ontario, for example, that Ottawa funds 50 per cent of welfare costs in Quebec but only 30 per cent in Ontario.

Regional economic differences coincide to some extent with an ideological cleavage about the role of the central government and governments in general. In some quarters, the view persists that Ottawa is a creative force, capable of improving the economy, promoting necessary change, maintaining the social safety net for all Canadians while providing special programs for those who need them, and acting as trustee of the sharing community within which redistribution occurs. This confronts a view that big government is itself a major problem, that federal programs are often wasteful and dysfunctional, that individuals, groups, and provinces are fundamentally equal and should receive no special treatment, and that redistribution is excessive, at least until fiscal balance is restored. These ideological currents were evident during the public debates about the Meech Lake and Charlottetown accords, and some of their conflicting elements provide scope for polarization.[1]

Finally, there is constitutional fatigue. In Quebec, most citizens may be fundamentally ambiguous about their political identity and national allegiance, but the sovereigntists are not, and they want the past three decades of constitutional discussion to culminate, at long last, in an independent Quebec. Since no offers for constitutional change will be forthcoming from the federal Liberal government, the Parti québécois administration will settle the issue by forcing Quebecers to choose between the status quo and sovereignty. And a strong current of opinion in ROC wants just that. There is much support for "closure"– for settling the interminable, frustrating, and costly constitutional wrangling "once and for all." As Jeffrey Simpson put it,

"The rest of the country, having rebuffed Meech Lake and Charlottetown, is insisting that Quebec take the current constitutional arrangements and put them to the test in the confrontation with secession."[2]

All of these conditions provide some opportunity for polarization. They establish incentives for political actors, and some will respond.

THE ACTORS AND THE STRATEGIES

The Parti québécois has the strongest incentive to deepen divisions between Quebecers and other Canadians, and as the governing party it will have abundant resources to do so. For many in the organization, this term of government is the last chance to realize the goal that has animated their political lives. There can be little doubt that the party leadership will be determined enough to use the state instruments at its disposal in order to increase support for sovereignty. It will aim to polarize. In fact, it must do so: poll results consistently show that a majority of Quebecers would not choose sovereignty in a referendum. In a 1980-style referendum, in which people in the rest of Canada would be little involved except as concerned spectators and in which the debate, while heated, would be among Quebecers, it is most unlikely that the PQ's option would carry. The 1994 vote for the PQ was not high enough to create a sense of momentum towards an inevitable sovereignty, and polarization is therefore the sovereigntists' main hope. What is needed are measures that do not seem unreasonable to a majority of Quebecers but are highly provocative to other Canadians. The hostile reactions that such measures elicit will make Quebecers feel insulted, frustrated, anxious, and insecure in the federation, and they will be more likely to vote for secession. Hence, the PQ will act as a *gouvernement provocateur*.

This strategy requires great delicacy. It could backfire if Quebecers see particular initiatives as unjustified or unfair and if they lose trust in the PQ government. But there are many tactics available for antagonizing Canada while consolidating domestic opinion behind the sovereignty option. Some are primarily symbolic, others are economically disruptive or threatening to Canada, and a third group involves putting in place what Vaclav Havel called "structures" – measures that actually lay the groundwork for sovereignty, while making it seem more reasonable and probable. It is no surprise that Mr Parizeau has formed his government around a small, coherent, and dedicated inner cabinet, capable of strategic planning, while abolishing all other cabinet committees and harnessing a number of backbenchers by making them regional delegates.[3] An extensive set of special National

Assembly committees will probably keep many other backbenchers active and involved as the core group assumes "la responsabilité d'enclencher le processus devant mener à la souveraineté."[4]

A first symbolic initiative of the PQ government could be to introduce in the National Assembly a resolution affirming Quebec's right to self-determination. In itself, this language would not be unprecedented, for the assembly used such terminology in the preambles to various Acts under the former PQ government, and so did the Liberals in Bill 150. But a new resolution could go much further and be more explicit. It could specify that a simple majority vote in a referendum would be taken as a definitive expression of Quebecers' choice to secede, that Quebec's borders are inviolable and will remain intact if the province secedes, and that sovereignty will be attained peacefully and constitutionally. Such a motion would place the provincial Liberals in an awkward position. They could abstain from voting on a resolution which presumed that sovereignty would occur; on the other hand, they might have to support it, simply because of their historical position about self-determination and because of the consensus in the electorate about Quebecers' right to secede with their territory. Such a motion in itself would be highly provocative in ROC, because it would be seen as an attempt to pre-empt the ground rules of separation. If the provincial Liberals also supported it, the perception in ROC of the other community as homogeneous would be reinforced, and Quebecers would be regarded as presumptuous – or, in common parlance, "uppity."

Another symbolic move would be to pass a declaration of Quebec's intent to achieve sovereignty. This would not be legally binding, but it would be very provocative because of doubts that the government had an electoral mandate to proceed with it. Beyond this lies a whole range of actions. The PQ could establish a committee of the National Assembly to study federal operations and expenditures in Quebec. It could establish a committee to study the conditions of francophones outside Quebec and to plan for future relations with them; it also could start to fund these communities. It could make an offer to employ federal public servants and start attracting them from their current posts. It could decrease funding to voluntary associations with pan-Canadian operations and offer incentives to establish Quebec associations. It could restrict minority rights by reversing the recent liberalization of rules about signage in business premises or by tightening controls on access to English schools in the province. The PQ also could open the Aboriginal dossier, either by extending rights and programs superior to those available elsewhere or by constricting Native autonomy in areas such as policing and taxation. Conflicts with Ottawa over land claims and native rights would be highly provocative. Beyond this are economic initiatives. The PQ could encourage the Caisse de dépôt to reduce investments in non-Quebec firms. Even more sensational would be a government-backed bid to take control of a flagship company such as Canadian Pacific or Bell Canada.

Then there is the type of action that would be costly or threatening to Canadians. For instance, the PQ government could seek to impair the functioning of the federation. It has already refused to cooperate in major reforms to the social-policy framework, demanding full control over these areas of jurisdiction and denouncing federal interference.[5] It could also obstruct joint action in education, fishing, tax reform, the environment, and fiscal arrangements. It could challenge the Canada Health Act. It could systematically employ welfare recipients in order to make them eligible for unemployment insurance. Beyond this, it could break interprovincial agreements, especially about procurement and the construction industry. All of this would be done with the purpose of demonstrating to the domestic constituency that federalism cannot work in Quebec's interests, while at the same time increasing frustration in the rest of Canada. As Mr Parizeau has said, "After all, we are not there to make the system operate as smoothly as possible. We are there to get out of the system."[6]

Another sensitive dossier is international. The PQ could establish a National Assembly committee on the foreign relations of a sovereign Quebec. It could invite foreign officials from abroad to address this topic, and it could certainly hear from foreign experts about Quebec's probable relations with the United States and the European Union, as well as about its accession to GATT, NAFTA, and the FTA. A very active foreign policy, with official visits and new "embassies," would provoke Ottawa and irritate English Canadians while advancing the cause of secession.

Another set of initiatives would lay the foundations of sovereignty. One obvious move is the creation of a National Assembly committee to prepare the constitution of a sovereign Quebec. At first, this committee might only explore options, but its debates and hearings could be well publicized, with wide consultations, plenty of expert witnesses, and appearances by English Canadians and foreigners. The drafting of a constitution could deepen the sense that secession is inevitable. More concretely, the government could prepare a complete and formal set of negotiating positions for post-secession relations with Canada. These could be made to appear quite reasonable to Quebecers, and the government could demand that negotiations start before the referendum. It would point out that pre-referendum talks would serve to clarify the choice for Quebecers, reduce uncertainty, and avoid the costs to both Canada and Quebec of leaving matters unsettled until after the referendum. The National Assembly could vote on these proposals, and it could resolve that negotiations begin immediately.

Finally, the PQ could directly challenge Ottawa's constitutional authority. The ferry that Mr Parizeau has proposed to operate between the Magdalen Islands and the Gaspé is only one example.[7] There are other initiatives that would be both popular in Quebec and obviously unconstitutional. The government could encroach on Ottawa's authority over telecommunications, especially with respect to regulating data transmission and licensing radio and television operations. It could build lighthouses. It could even move to establish a militia.

All such initiatives would have the same purpose. They would irritate Canadians outside Quebec, provoking hostile reactions from individuals, associations, the media, and perhaps governments. Quebecers would be exposed to this antagonistic reaction and would be pressed either to condemn their own government or to support it in opposition to the rest of Canada. These measures would place the provincial Liberal Party in the same awkward position. If moderate nationalist support was flowing towards the PQ, the Liberals would be divided and would be less capable of fighting the referendum campaign. Moreover, some of the provocative measures would be constructive, in the sense of providing plans and structures that would prepare for the secession.

At the same time, the PQ would be trying to force responses from the federal government. Ottawa would prefer to ignore some measures, waiting for the referendum, but others, especially the obstruction of its own initiatives, would require action. The PQ measures would also be aimed at the parliamentary opposition in Ottawa, especially the Reform Party, and would be designed to provoke its criticism, both directly and because of the Liberals' inaction. The manifest groundwork for sovereignty being laid by the PQ would show strikingly that ROC had no such plans and preparations, so the pressure to contemplate its collective future would increase substantially. The PQ measures would also diminish ROC's solidarity if they provoked regional or federal-provincial differences about how to respond to them.

In the polarization scenario, the Bloc québécois will face difficult choices. Its members are in Ottawa and in the House of Commons, where there are some incentives to act in a moderate and collegial fashion. As well, there is a weakness in the logic of polarization. At the same time as it promotes antagonism in ROC and more cohesiveness and solidarity among Quebecers, it undercuts the long-standing argument that English Canadians, after secession, would be cooperative and rational, and that the economic costs of separation would therefore be modest.

So Mr Bouchard would focus his party's attention at the federal level, rather than attempting to defend the Quebec government's actions. His would be the high road. One thrust would be to emphasize the coherence of ROC, stressing its distinctiveness, common interest, and national character. Mr Bouchard would urge Canadians outside of Quebec to contemplate their collective future, and he would travel extensively for this purpose. Another line of attack would be to press the argument that the federation no longer works either for Quebecers or for other Canadians – that the system is conflict-ridden and inefficient, and the debt cripples the future of all, and that both Canadians and Quebecers have an interest in disentanglement and reform. Hence, the oft-repeated line, "At the core of the economic crisis is a political crisis ... The political problem with Canada is Quebec, and the problem of Quebec is Canada."[8] At the same time, by defending all social programs and protesting any spending cuts in Quebec while condemning as discriminatory any major federal expenditures elsewhere in the country, Mr Bouchard would convince more people in ROC that "Quebec" is indeed the problem.[9] The BQ could also resolutely demand that the federal government prepare itself for the secession and that it begin negotiations with Quebec before the referendum takes place. The party would continually ask about the federal position on the debt, citizenship, and all the other issues raised by the separation. In the House of Commons it would keep the pressure directly on the federal Liberals in a way that the Government of Quebec cannot do.

A more critical actor at the federal level would be the Reform Party. This party needs to regain and maintain momentum.[10] If the sovereigntist polarization strategy appeared to be successful in Quebec and ROC, then Reform's temptation would be to focus fully on the Quebec issue, with Preston Manning playing Klaus to Parizeau's Meciar. In the view of one shrewd observer, Reform has already benefited from polarization, in the 1993 election: "Although neither the Bloc nor Reform ran candidates in each other's territory, and thus did not confront each other directly, they fed on each other's growing strength in the polls throughout the campaign. All reports of growing Bloc strength were ammunition for the Reform thesis of the need for a strong uncompromising counter-presence of a take-it-or-leave-it voice from ROC in the House of Commons."[11]

To polarize, Reform would draw attention to the Quebec government's provocations, making them much more visible, and the party's interpretation would make them appear more irritating and even dangerous. As well, the party would argue that the federal government's preoccupation with Quebec and its constitutional challenges was deflecting attention and energy from Canada's urgent problems, especially the deficit. Here, Reform could make common cause with the Bloc, driving home the message that coherent and determined federal action is not possible in the system as it is constituted. In opposition to Mr Bouchard, however, Reform would criticize federal spending in Quebec on regional development, crown corporations, and infrastructure, as well as any other measure especially beneficial for the province. Beyond this, Mr Manning could urge the federal Liberals to prepare for separation. He would want to know the government's position on all the critical issues. Indeed, he has already asked, formally and publicly, for the government's response to twenty detailed questions about how Ottawa would react to a secession.[12] He would demand responses to the PQ's negotiating positions. He might advocate that English Canada's post-separation policies be formulated through a grassroots consultative process or that they be the subject of a referendum. Finally, the Reform Party itself could advance a set of proposals for negotiating the separation, as well as a redesigned constitution for ROC.

In doing this, Reform would articulate the views of its core supporters, who disproportionately tend to resent Quebec's distinctiveness and the policies, such as bilingualism, that it has engendered. More important, the party could aim to accumulate the support of those ROC citizens who have been made angry, anxious, and impatient by Quebec's initiatives. It could focus on these initiatives and seek to frame ROC's response. Carried to its limit, the polarization strategy implicitly would represent an abandonment of Quebec and of Canada as it now exists. But as Roger Gibbins has noted, "the Reform Party is appealing to a kind of nationalism that makes sense if Quebec leaves – and makes no sense if Quebec stays."[13] The Reform Party would never make a statement in favour of separation; instead the general position would be that Quebecers need to make a clear and final choice about their adherence to Canada, under the constitutional status quo, and that the citizens of ROC must start preparing to cope with the separation because Quebecers might vote Yes. As Mr Manning said in 1989, after listing Reform's constitutional principles, "If these principles of Confederation are rejected by Quebec, if the house cannot be united on such a basis, then Quebec and the rest of Canada should openly examine the feasibility of establishing a better but more separate relationship between them, on equitable and mutually acceptable terms."[14] Reform would insist that it did not favour Quebec secession – it favoured a united Canada – but its underlying message would be that Quebecers must choose, that the issue must be settled once and for all, and that the choices were separation or the constitutional status quo – a country that was one nation, where all provinces were equal, where citizens had equal rights, the Charter was supreme, and majorities ruled; a nation where official bilingualism should be abolished and where Reform could well form the next federal government. All this would be provocative to Quebecers; it would provide fertile ground for the message that their future was threatened under the constitutional status quo and could be secured only through sovereignty. In the rest of Canada, this strategy would draw people's attention to Quebec's provocations, muster anti-Quebec sentiment, focus the growing anxieties and frustrations of English Canadians, and strengthen the coherence and self-consciousness of ROC. This is all part of polarization.

The provincial governments form another set of important actors. They have many options and would be unlikely to adopt a coherent and unified position. At times, some governments would echo the PQ's opposition to particular federal initiatives, but there would also be much criticism of an obstructionist and uncooperative Quebec government. While overt criticism of Ottawa's position on the constitution and the Quebec referendum would be unlikely, some provincial governments might establish task forces or legislative committees to formulate new constitutional proposals or, more likely, to explore post-secession options and arrangements. Once more, these would reinforce the view that separation was imminent. Their deliberations and conclusions would be transmitted to Quebecers, with the same effect. Such exercises could lead some provincial governments to adopt particular stances on issues such as citizenship, currency, and trade with Quebec, or to favour certain constitutional provisions for ROC and the processes to secure them. These might be hard to abandon later. On the other hand, the period before the Quebec referendum will not be long enough for most provincial governments to reach firm conclusions to which they are publicly committed. More important, there is little incentive for most provincial politicians to contribute to polarization, and they will be reluctant to challenge overtly the view that the federal arena is the appropriate one for grappling with the Quebec government's challenges.

The last set of actors are nongovernmental. Individuals, firms, and associations could all contribute to increasing the degree of polarization between ROC and Quebec. It must be stressed that these actors are entirely beyond governments' control. There is a wide range of opinion about Quebec sovereignty, and there would be some extreme reactions to both provocative acts by the PQ and the responses emanating from ROC. There would be demonstrations against the PQ's provocations, and although these might be organized and spearheaded by tiny groups, anti-Quebec symbolism has proven in the past its potency to attract media attention and to arouse Quebecers' anger; flag burnings, effigies, and ugly slogans would certainly be offensive and threatening. Demonstrations against Quebec positions by Aboriginal organizations, either inside the province or without, would also be highly inflammatory. Of course, there would also be demonstrations in favour of federalism and in favour of Quebec remaining in Canada, but these could be outnumbered by the negative ones and might well be less remarkable than them. Polarization would increase when extreme or threatening reactions were portrayed and interpreted as typical, as expressing the sentiments and inclinations of a whole mass of people. In polarization, members of each community come to see the stakes as high, the positions as irreconcilable, and the members of the other community as homogeneous, different, and hostile.

There might also be boycotts of Quebec products. This would be very offensive to Quebecers and could cause counter-boycotts. But the normal activities of firms might be more provocative. Given rising uncertainty in Quebec, it would be rational for companies to diversify their sources of supply, so Quebec firms might lose Canadian markets. Head offices and other facilities could be moved from the province. And it is probable that private investment in Quebec would decline somewhat. All of these behaviours could be portrayed as conscious attempts to threaten Quebecers and impose costs upon them. In such circumstances, a public reaction in Quebec of greater support for sovereignty might seem irrational, insofar as these individual and corporate actions would be harbingers of the reaction to separation itself, but it is not unlikely. Moreover, the public might more staunchly support its provincial government's efforts to compensate for the loss of markets and jobs. As well, the PQ might retaliate against offending firms by denying them government business.

Finally, associations, labour unions, academics, think-tanks, and the media will all engage in debates about separation. Activity will be feverish. Although extreme views and provocative positions will be advanced by both Quebecers and English Canadians, it is not likely that these debates will contribute directly to polarization between the two communities. What they will do is make the probability of separation seem greater. The debates will also make more obvious and problematic the lack of preparation in ROC and the absence of a sound constitutional framework for it. So they will increase the pressure on the federal government to take positions on the issues surrounding secession and on the constitutional make-up of ROC. These discussions might also produce powerful demands for a constitutional convention or an estates-general of ROC to be held.

All of this suggests that there is a significant potential for polarization between ROC and Quebec, analogous to what took place between Slovakia and the Czech Republic. A PQ government in Quebec would have the resources of the state and a National Assembly majority at its command, and these could be used to provoke English Canadians, who would not only object to particular initiatives but would also deny the legitimacy of any movement at all towards separation without a prior referendum mandate. These reactions in turn could cause resentment in Quebec, the rallying of opinion in support of the provincial government, and increased support for sovereignty. At the federal level, both the Bloc and Reform could gain from polarization. As the process continued, Quebecers and citizens of ROC would increasingly come to see members of the other community as unreasonable, homogeneous, and distinct. They would perceive, correctly (as the polls would show), that the probability of separation was growing. This would only increase anxiety and the sense of threat in each community and the level of mutual hostility between them.

CHECKS ON POLARIZATION IN CANADA

However realistic this polarization scenario may appear, it is essential to recall some basic differences between the Czech-Slovak and Canadian cases. In Canada, there has been no fundamental change in regime, with its attendant uncertainties in the social, economic, legal, and political spheres. Second, the economic situation is relatively stable: it will be improving, not deteriorating, and the hardships that do exist – and that provided a fertile ground for nationalist unrest in Slovakia – cannot be unambiguously attributed to the federal government's policies. Third, the system of proportional representation in Czechoslovakia and its republics, and also the rules of the legislatures, meant that power was shared within shifting coalitions. In Canada, the counterparts of Mr Klaus are relegated to the opposition.

There are also four major factors that limit the potential for polarization in Canada. First, there would be several constraints on the polarization tactics available to the PQ government. One is provided by financial markets. The cost to the province of government borrowing – more precisely, the risk of credit downgrades – could limit the funds available for economic intervention, competition with Ottawa, and social-welfare spending to bolster popularity. As well, the sensitivity of private direct investment to the political climate could restrain PQ brinkmanship. Over the short term, a truly determined government might be able to ignore these counterbalances, perhaps even trying to blame them on federalist fear-mongering, but this tactic would be limited by another basic check on the ability of the government to shift opinion – the fact that Quebec is a mature democracy.

The PQ confronts a viable opposition party that is capable of exposing and reinterpreting its tactics. The provincial Liberals, most notably, could refuse to cooperate or participate in National Assembly committees charged with preparing the ground for sovereignty. Rebuilding after a defeat, they would mobilize around the referendum to come. As well, the Quebec media are alert and are prone to criticize governments. Most important, the electorate is experienced and relatively sophisticated. Voters would not be unresponsive to the view that job losses were caused in part by the policies of the Quebec government and that federal-provincial initiatives were failing because of PQ obstruction. The electorate's concern about the provincial deficit would help constrain provocative expenditures, such as hiring federal public servants or encroaching on federal jurisdiction. As well, most Quebecers have a sense of democratic fairness and pragmatism. Many would resent the government's pre-referendum moves towards sovereignty on the grounds that no clear mandate had been given to so proceed.[15]

The third major check on polarization is the federal government itself. The Liberals possess a majority strong enough to command the House of Commons, the party has broad regional representation, and the government has considerable depth and experience. The prime minister is credible in both ROC and Quebec. Structurally, there is no competitive centre of power that could respond authoritatively to Quebec in the same way as the Czech Republic became the Slovak interlocutor. Indeed, if the Reform Party attempted to enunciate a ROC counter-position, the federal Parliament would become even more central to the debate in ROC.

Despite provocation and polarization, the essence of the federal government's strategy will remain unchanged. It will attempt to produce attractive programs and constructive reforms, both to improve the economy and to show that the federal system works. The government will count on continued economic growth that will improve the conditions of Canadians along with its own finances. And it will maintain its posture on the issue of separation. Difficulties with the

Quebec government, especially over noncooperation in reasonable reforms, will be blamed on sovereigntist obstruction. The polarizing thrusts of the opposition parties will be condemned as partisan manoeuvres that are insulting and harmful to Canadians. Government leaders will appeal to Quebecers' affinity for Canada at the same time as they stress the illogic of secession and the costs and dangers it would involve. Ottawa will also counter erroneous information emitted by the PQ. Most emphatically, the government will insist that Quebecers do not want separation and that the option will definitely be rejected in any referendum. The federal Liberals have no mandate to reopen the constitutional dossier and, they will say, they have no intention of doing so. They will refuse all opposition demands for contingency planning or pre-negotiation with Quebec as hypothetical responses to an event that will not take place. No matter what pressures are mounted from Quebec and ROC, it is most improbable that Mr Chrétien's Liberals would budge from this position. As the prime minister has said, "I am not spending one minute on this impossible scenario."[16] So although the federal government will help fight sovereignty in the referendum campaign, it will not contemplate it publicly in advance. This will diminish the impression that sovereignty is inevitable.

The final check on polarization will be the referendum itself. In contrast to the Czech-Slovak case, the separatist party is irrevocably committed to holding one; so the polarization that took place there as governments proceeded to negotiate, and the concomitant sense of the secession's inevitability, are far less likely to occur in Canada. The negotiations were enormously important in Czechoslovakia, and they monopolized the public's attention, as will the events unfolding after a Yes vote in Quebec. But in Quebec there has to be a referendum, and until that event, citizens in the province can suspend judgment. They can safely abstain from involvement in all these disputes, watching the politicians' machinations with their usual degree of attentiveness. Meanwhile, they need not commit to either side of the struggle or even follow it very closely. The same is true in ROC, although the electorates' positions are not symmetrical because English Canadians, to the frustration of many, will not be able to pronounce on the issue through a referendum. They must wait, and the sense of powerlessness and impatience this causes will feed support for polarizing responses to sovereigntist thrusts. But in ROC, too, there are moderating forces – the sense that separation is irrational, the somewhat contradictory view that the choice lies with Quebecers, and hesitation to follow the Reform Party on the constitution when its other policy positions are farther to the right than most

Canadians can accept. In any case, there will be some polarizing responses, and these will cause reactions in Quebec. But the citizens there will know that they have time to make up their minds, and a ballot to cast on referendum day.

REPRISE

In the period between the election of a PQ government and the referendum, there is potential for polarization between ROC and Quebec. But the checks in the system should hold it to moderate levels. Under conditions of moderate polarization, would the assumptions underlying the secession scenario be altered? Would the flow of events change, and would the arrangements negotiated with Quebec be different?

Few assumptions would be violated. The PQ government would call the referendum at the most opportune time; that is, when Quebec public opinion was most favourable to sovereignty, perhaps in reaction to threats and insults emanating from ROC. But the result of the referendum would still be unpredictable. In the last instance of polarization, after the Meech Lake Accord failed to pass, support levels in Quebec for "sovereignty" and "independence" rose to a range of 60–65 per cent. Under similar conditions, the No forces would face a difficult campaign, but the outcome would remain in doubt until the ballots were counted, and so there would be no pre-negotiation with Quebec. In ROC, many more ideas would be circulating about post-secession strategies and arrangements with Quebec, but the federal government would not need to commit itself to a set of positions about borders, the debt, and other issues. After a Yes vote, as a consequence of polarization, there would be a higher level of unrest and a worse economic situation. There would be more emigration, boycotts, demonstrations, Aboriginal unrest, and so on, and domestic and foreign economic actors would expect difficult negotiations and continued uncertainty. But Ottawa would still take the lead in managing the situation. There would be sharper resistance to this in some quarters because provincialist and decentralist opinion would have been primed in the period before the referendum. On the other hand, the major tribune of ROC's opinion and interests, Mr Manning, operates in the federal arena.

It is not clear whether the Liberal government could continue in office if it maintained its phlegmatic stance and then lost the referendum. The prime minister would probably have to resign in a polarized environment. This could lead to a government of national unity, a Reform-Liberal coalition. Alternatively, Mr Manning could be called on to form a government if he could count on substantial Liberal support. Neither situation would be very stable, given the animosity that would have developed between the parties in the pre-referendum period. Reform would blame the Liberals for ROC's lack of preparation and for losing the referendum about which they had been so overtly confident of victory, while the Liberals would hold Mr Manning responsible for Quebecers' alienation from Canada and their choice to secede. This means that it will remain very critical that an election be held in Canada, though it is conceivable that a union government could hold together until the separation was accomplished.

National solidarity in ROC would be maintained. In fact, while polarization will have sharpened divisions within the country about its future constitutional make-up and about how to deal with Quebec, the same process, paradoxically, would have rendered more acute the public's sense of ROC's distinctness and collective interest. This would be reinforced through the confrontation to come with Quebec in post-referendum negotiations. So it is not likely that provincial governments would impede federal management of the crisis or block the process of reconstituting Canada. Finally, with few signs of ROC fragmentation but with more uncertainty because of polarization, foreign powers would be important moderators, seeking and supporting competent, fast management of the crisis.

Overall, then, there is no major change in the basic scenario. The big imperative would still be to resolve uncertainty. It would be necessary to settle matters with Quebec as quickly as possible and to reconstitute Canada quickly too, and then to secure public ratification of what was done. Mr Manning's greater influence could lead, however, to some modifications. The constitutional amendments would very likely have to include Senate reforms congruent with Reform's long-standing position on the issue. The amending formula itself might be changed to require ratification of amendments by referendum. The Reform Party and the much larger body of supporters it would have after polarization might require that the constitutional amendments that were made, and even the arrangements that were negotiated with Quebec, should be ratified by referendum. This would prolong uncertainty. On the other hand, polarization itself would make ratification very likely, and if the government was stable enough to see the separation through, a referendum could obviate the need for an election.

Polarization would produce some change in the set of agreements negotiated with Quebec. There would be a somewhat different mix of political forces in ROC, and Mr Manning would play a more prominent role in the negotiations. Presumably, his party would be identified with, if not entirely committed to, a set of negotiating positions, and presumably these would be hard-line.[17] On the other hand, Reform would be constrained by the great bulk of Liberals from Ontario in the House of Commons. Nevertheless, polarization would reinforce the internal solidarity of the communities and raise the level of resentment directed towards the "other," and both effects would increase people's willingness to bear economic loss. As a consequence, the package of agreements would be a minimalist one. On symbolic issues there would be much less cooperation. There would be no environmental treaty, none about immigration, and much less flexibility about citizenship (with the period of choice being reduced). Border posts would be erected, and although the NAFTA/FTA floor of economic integration would be retained, special agreements on financial institutions and agriculture would be more difficult to reach. Quebec would want to use the American dollar as its currency, but a threatened veto of NAFTA membership or a tougher stance on citizenship would make it a taker of Canadian monetary policy for a while. The basic parameters of debt and asset division would remain, though there would be fewer joint management bodies and much more acrimony about lumpy assets that cannot be privatized. A taxation treaty would be signed, but cooperation in other matters, such as emergency planning, would be unlikely.

In short, moderate levels of polarization would make the transition more acrimonious and would increase the cost for each side, and the animosity accompanying the separation would not quickly fade. More important, the structures put in place between Canada and Quebec would be less conducive to economic and political integration over the long term. On the other hand, the core scenario requires little modification. It holds. Hence, having described the transition to sovereignty, it is now possible to reach some conclusions about the longer-term future of Canada and Quebec. Before doing this, however, it is appropriate to review the course of this study, by briefly revisiting all the terrain that we have traversed to this point.

PART FOUR

Conclusion

CHAPTER SIXTEEN

Summary

This study had several purposes. On the assumption that Quebec secedes, it proposed to describe Canada as it would then exist, to survey the institutional arrangements that the country might adopt, to lay out the possible economic and political institutions that might link Canada and a sovereign Quebec, and to reach conclusions about both the long-term structure of Canada and the relationships between Canada and Quebec.

Much of the basic work was presented in the first part of the book. Initially, we examined some core characteristics of the rest of Canada (ROC), discussed them briefly, and found that by most standard indicators, Canada without Quebec would be a viable state, perhaps even more so than Canada as presently constituted. Next, we considered the range of possible constitutional outcomes for Canada. For those familiar with the issues, this was a rather straightforward exercise; nevertheless, each of the alternatives has its advocates, and each has been selected by some observers as the most probable outcome, so it is useful to have them all laid out and analysed. The foundations of the analysis were standard – whether governments could deliver services efficiently, whether decision making would be effective, and whether citizens' loyalties would support particular degrees of centralization and decentralization. In this, there was much attention paid to the West and to the overlapping economic and ideological cleavages that seem to divide it from the rest of the country. The Atlantic region was presumed to be a hostage to the continuation of transfers and to be supportive of a central government powerful enough to redistribute income to the region. Much less attention was devoted to Ontario, despite its serious deficit problem, its position as paymaster of the federation, its lessened trade dependence on the Canadian market, and its strong links with Quebec. In reacting to Quebec secession and in reconstituting Canada, Ontario's position will be pivotal, but our analysis presumed, not without justification, that the Ontario government would support efforts to hold Canada together and that it would not attempt to usurp federal leadership unless managing the secession proved beyond the capacity of the central government.

The next section reviewed the types of economic relations that might be maintained between the two independent countries of Canada and Quebec. It made the usual assumption that an economic union is the relationship most conducive to growth and overall efficiency, and that lower levels of integration impose losses on firms, individuals, and governments. The basic trade-off underlying this treatment was that between efficiency and autonomy. In Quebec, the sovereigntist hope is that a more autonomous economic policy can produce a more competitive and dynamic economy, through coordinated state intervention and more appropriate and flexible policy, as well as through more efficient administration. In the standard analysis, however, access to larger markets through free trade agreements restricts the range of state action, while higher levels of integration, as in a customs union or economic union, impose even greater constraints.

A separate section explored the alternative arrangements that might be made about currency and monetary policy. In the event of Quebec secession, this would be a critical issue, with short-term ramifications for the domestic financial system and international confidence in the two states, and with longer-term implications for efficiency in economic transactions. We raised the possibility of joint management of monetary policy, and also the relatively unexplored alternative that Quebec might simply adopt the U.S. dollar, a course of action that could be very damaging to Canada.

Next came the political relationships between the two countries. There exists a very large array of possible institutional arrangements here. Most analyses concentrate on legislative bodies, quasi-judicial mechanisms to resolve disputes, and normal state-to-state negotiations, but there can be interesting variations on each of these, and other devices such as special-purpose agencies, consultative bodies, and voluntary harmonization also could be put into place.

Among analysts from English Canada there is a wide consensus that economic and political integration are interdependent, so this was the focus of the next section. This is a very abstract question, revolving around several subquestions: how barriers to commerce can most surely be reduced, how joint international negotiations can work, how and whether positive integration can be achieved without a central authority, and, finally, what political mechanisms sustain common entitlements to mobility and redistribution. The conclusion was that the relationship between economic and political integration is not a close one. In theory, states can maintain economic integration at a high level through voluntary harmonization and the use of quasi-judicial bodies and special-purpose agencies, while a common legislature and a responsible executive seem necessary only for measures that touch the core of citizenship – movement and sharing within the community. For economic integration between two sovereign states, what counts, bluntly, is whether governments have the capacity to implement policies that substantial numbers of their citizens disagree with, and in the short term at least this is a function of national solidarity. As well, it is unclear how much economic loss would result from forgoing some of the central-government measures that are positively integrating, especially redistribution, which might not be very efficient at high levels. Similarly, labour mobility might not be very important economically when other adjustment mechanisms are available.

The last section of the descriptive survey examined the underlying societal factors conducive to centralization and decentralization within and between states, focusing on the initial creation of political institutions, both within a new Canada and between Canada and Quebec. For Canada, the analysis was inconclusive, because there was no overwhelming tendency towards a more decentralized or centralized constitution; instead, the factors conflicted. Between Canada and Quebec, the underlying conditions pointed towards much less integration than currently exists. In both cases, the conjunctural factors are the ones that would predominate, especially the stance of foreign actors, the sense of emergency or threat, and political leadership. Given the public anxiety accompanying fundamental political change and the scope for interpreting the relevance and force of underlying factors, leadership would be particularly important in shaping the course of events. As Vaclav Havel wrote of such times, "It is largely up to the politicians which social forces they choose to liberate and which to suppress, whether they rely on the good in each citizen or on the bad."[1]

These findings strengthened the conclusion that the whole process of secession – the transition to sovereignty – has to be thoroughly understood in order to predict the long-term structure of Canada and Canada-Quebec relations. We began to examine this in the next part, first arguing that the transition is crucial because secessions are indeterminate: many alternatives are open, public attitudes are volatile, leaders have much autonomy, and decisions are taken under tight time pressure. Big choices with enduring effects are made during secessions. As well, institutions are set up then, and these have a tendency to persist and to structure economic and political activities far into the future. In sum, the outcomes of a secession depend on how it actually takes place.

Consequently, we moved on to survey the extant studies of how the transition to Quebec sovereignty might occur. This analysis reinforced the view that the process itself is crucial and that the politics of the event have primacy. The various economic studies show that transition costs could be very large indeed or rather limited; more important, most of the potential costs described by economists are variable, and their magnitude would be a function of the degree of political cooperation that existed at the time. The legal studies reinforce this conclusion. While they are useful in isolating some legal issues that will have to be resolved during the secession (about matters such as treaties, assets, debts, and Aboriginal rights), the major legal question is whether Quebecers have the right to choose to become a sovereign state. Despite the tortured arguments of jurists, this boils down to whether the Quebec government can exercise effective control of its territory and whether other states will recognize it. Both matters are political, and in both the position of Canada would determine the medium-term outcome.

This brought the study to political scenarios, some of which envisage great conflict, including armed conflict, between Canada and a Quebec that has unilaterally declared its independence. Our study assumed at the outset that Quebecers would clearly decide to secede, that Canada would accept this decision, and that the secession would be peaceful (even though this is a rarity: most secessionist movements are violent, and most secessions are contested). The study of more extreme scenarios showed what has to happen for the assumption of a peaceful secession to hold. There must be a clear referendum question, a fair campaign, a Quebec commitment to economic and social policies that are not highly offensive or costly to Canadians, and a sense among people in ROC that the separation would not very much threaten their collective future. Similarly, Quebecers must not feel deeply threatened or oppressed – the political scenarios suggest that contesting Quebec's borders could quickly lead to organized violence.

Finally, there was a brief survey of more detailed studies of the mechanics of the transition. Some of these usefully discuss matters that will have to be settled during the separation, but they differ wildly in their predictions about how the secession will take place and what the outcomes will be. While each has its logic, and each has its adherents, there is no detailed and reliable guide to how the process of Quebec's separation would unfold.

In order to help provide one, we turned to other cases of peaceful secession. There are only a few such cases, but they proved very instructive, because the comparative analysis revealed a pattern in the politics of peaceful secession. This consisted of a set of inductively derived empirical generalizations about such secessions; that is, features of the process that occur with regularity. Of course, these generalizations do not form a theory of peaceful secession. Nor was it suggested than any of them are of particular importance, though clearly the decision by the predecessor state to accept the principle that separation will take place is critical in distinguishing peaceful from contested secessions. As well, the generalizations were derived from historical and comparative study, which can only produce conclusions that hold true until they are broken in some instance. Every secession is unique, and the separation of Quebec from Canada could be qualitatively different from those found elsewhere and in the past. On the other hand, the pattern composed by the generalizations is a robust one – most of them characterize every case – and since there is clearly a logic underlying the pattern of political disengagement, this basic framework was used to approach the Canada-Quebec case in the next part of the study.

First, however, it seemed important to investigate the most recent peaceful secession, the breakup of the Czech and Slovak Federal Republic. Here again the pattern held, though there were a few exceptions: the Czechs accepted only gradually the notion that the separation would occur, and the government of each state formed a narrow coalition rather than the broad, representative coalitions found in most cases. Essentially, these deviations occurred because the Slovaks never made any clear, unequivocal statement of their intent to secede, through either their government or a referendum. Instead, the separation was marked by polarization, a process that took place as party leaders in each state found it profitable to confront each other, to gain domestic support by doing so, and to drive the other state's citizens towards supporting the extreme position advocated by the opponent. This dynamic may have been peculiar to the Czechoslovak case, where there was a massive social transformation after the fall of the Communist regime, a high level of economic uncertainty, and a turbulent young democracy; but polarization also marked other peaceful secessions, especially after the negotiations had begun and national solidarity was essential – or was said to be – in order to confront the other country and deal with the crisis. It might be that closer study of the political dynamics that precede secessions, including contested ones, would reveal the same phenomenon. In any event, how polarization took place in Czechoslovakia is a reminder that political competition is not restricted by the rules of the game: politicians will try to shift public opinion and even to reshape society for their own advantage. Beyond this, with the few exceptions noted, the Czech-Slovak separation conformed closely to the generalizations about peaceful secession. That these held true even in this modern, industrial, democratic, and East European country increased our confidence in their universality and generalizability, and helped justify applying them to a Quebec secession from Canada.

This was the next major subject. How would the transition take place in the Canada-Quebec case? The approach here was to rely on the material from other studies, the lessons of comparative analysis, and a wide political and economic literature in order to depict in detail how the separation would occur. First the background was set, and within the context of the economy, fiscal problems, the recent constitutional history, and existing public opinion, most emphasis was placed on the incumbent leaders and political formations. Some other studies have presumed that in the secession crisis, political initiative will somehow be wrested from the established leaders; but elected politicians have constitutional authority and state resources at their disposal, and they have a responsibility to exercise them. This is a representative democracy, and unless the political order breaks down entirely, it will be the incumbent politicians who will deal with the secession.

There followed a brief account of the issues in the campaign leading to the referendum on sovereignty. This will be a tough campaign, forced on a populace that includes many citizens who are reluctant to end their ambiguity and choose between sovereignty and the constitutional status quo. There will be no advance negotiation about the terms and conditions of post-secession relations between Canada and Quebec, for most strategists on the federalist side presume that the francophone Quebecers' emotional preference for autonomy is restrained by their fears about the costs of sovereignty; thus, a federal commitment to any proposals that could reduce uncertainty about these costs would tend to increase the Yes vote. On the sovereigntist side, this approach will be decried as blackmail and an empty threat. More emotionally, the argument will be that Quebecers have only this final chance to choose independence, because a No vote would weaken the nation and leave it, along with the survival of the French language, permanently subject to the preferences of the anglophone majority. Offensive and threatening signals coming from ROC during the campaign would reinforce this sense of insecurity.

This analysis presumed that there will be a Yes vote for sovereignty. Another assumption was that this verdict will be accepted, and this turned out to be a defensible assumption, for all other courses of action appear to produce inferior results (if the question and campaign are fair). Some of them would lead to the use of force, others would produce very heavy economic costs because they would prolong the crisis and increase uncertainty, and others would divide and weaken ROC.

In Canada at the present time, some people discount the argument that Quebec secession would produce a crisis, a propensity that increases as one moves from east to west across the country. But throughout Canada a Yes vote in the Quebec referendum is bound to cause profound uncertainty. While it is an abstract and overused term, uncertainty is all too tangible in fact. A Yes vote will dramatically change people's expectations that many things will remain unchanged, and this includes not only normally volatile items such as interest rates but also much of the unquestioned background of everyday life – the currency Canadians use, the security of bank deposits and the value of pension funds, the language of their children's education, and even their citizenship. Economic uncertainty will affect every sector and region of the country. Consequently, after a Yes vote, Canadians will support decisive action to reduce the uncertainty, even at a price. This price will include not only the costs of making some compromises with Quebec but also the political price of settling for deals one may not like, having matters handled by a government one did not elect, and seeing decisions made without participating in them. But the secession crisis will not merely engender grudging tolerance of government action; it will also produce strong positive support for the Canadian politicians who are prepared to manage the crisis and see the country through it.

Quebec's secession will be a momentous event. As the Yes vote is accepted, there will be a clear sense that the community has changed. Suddenly, Quebec will have left and will be foreign. But Canadians will want to carry on, and as leadership is assumed by Ottawa, power and legitimacy will flow to the federal government. There is a lot of opinion-poll data to show that Canadians will support a national response to the secession crisis, and in the first instance, the provincial governments will have neither the capacity nor the will to resist this. Later they will become participants in defining Canada's future as the separation gathers momentum.

Thus we come to the negotiations, which were covered in some detail in our study. These will be accomplished quickly, but they will not be easy. In the post-referendum environment, leaders from Canada and Quebec will have a common interest in reducing uncertainty by managing the crisis, and they will also have a joint concern that the economy should not be disrupted too much. But this does not mean that the negotiations will produce cooperative outcomes. As our analysis showed, a common misconception among sovereigntists is that after a Yes vote all the earlier ROC threats of noncooperation will prove to be unfounded. But when two sides in negotiations have separate interests, when they have a large agenda to deal with, and when they expect to have other negotiations and relationships in the future, noncooperation can be entirely rational if it is a by-product of achieving one's priority objectives, or if it establishes the credibility of future threats or secures one's ends in the future or in some other dossier. Throughout the Canada-Quebec negotiations, relative power will count. This includes the power to cause damage, though each side has only a few credible threats. (For instance, threats to close the Seaway or seal the borders or renege on debts are not credible, because they inflict too much damage on the threatener or on third parties.) Nevertheless, Quebec can threaten to use the U.S. dollar, and Canada can threaten to veto Quebec membership in NAFTA (for a while) and, more credibly, to cause disruption through its laws about citizenship.

These strategic considerations make it possible that the Canada-Quebec negotiations would break down, but stronger forces point towards a fast settlement of the major issues. These forces include the anxiety of both citizenries, the need to reassure investors, and the mutual desire to show foreign governments that the crisis is being managed. As in other secessions, the pattern will be that the core negotiators establish framework agreements that are later fleshed out by large teams of officials and politicians. Although the negotiators will have assumed a massive authority, this will be compensated for by their reporting to large representative committees in each state.

Our analysis holds that there will be three essential tasks for Canada. The first is to reach agreements with Quebec to accomplish the political disengagement while avoiding economic dislocation. The next is to amend the constitution so as to excise Quebec and provide a stable framework for the new Canada. The third is to legitimize both the agreements and the constitution through a popular consultation, probably in the form of an election.

The details of the agreements were discussed in chapter 13, though only the most critical and unprecedented ones were covered, because many other matters can be handled through standard off-the-shelf treaties. Some Canada-Quebec agreements will clearly be temporary. They will envisage gradual disengagement and will simply provide time for adjustment. For example, although the basic level of economic integration will be set by the FTA/NAFTA floor, other arrangements will preserve the customs union, stabilize the financial system, maintain regulatory uniformity, and keep some transnational facilities running. Similarly, citizenship arrangements will provide time for adjustment. Other agreements will dispense rough justice; this will be the case in the Aboriginal dossier, where the two governments will effectively collude to hand over responsibility for Native peoples living in Quebec. In some areas, agreements will not be reached – for instance, about mobility, language rights, the environment, and social entitlements – and this will make life very difficult for some people.

On the Canadian side, Ottawa will take the lead in negotiations, with some form of provincial participation. The provinces will be much more involved in the task of constitutional amendment, however, since reconstituting Canada will require unanimous provincial consent. This will be achieved under the pressure of necessity and because amendments to the constitution will be minimal and will provide for future flexibility. Items about which there is no consensus will be put off until after the separation. Refusing to pass the amendments would bring the whole process to a halt and would amount to a declaration of independence, and no provincial government will be in a position to take this step.

Finally, but before the separation is accomplished, there will be an election in ROC. The legitimacy of the government will have worn thin throughout the negotiations, and the reconstitution will have bypassed normal consultative processes. An election will produce some instability, of course, because some parties will campaign against elements of the agreements with Quebec or for further constitutional amendments, but it will be essential to have popular consent for what has been accomplished, and to equip the country with a government that has a mandate to achieve the rest of the separation and to steer the course of the new Canada.

The core scenario laid out in our study depicts gradual disengagement between Canada and Quebec as the policies in the two states diverge. Quebec will establish a full governmental apparatus, with an army, a diplomatic corps, and a complete range of programs. As economic and political conditions evolve, each state will implement different policies, and the level of economic integration will erode. People will make citizenship choices, and agreements will terminate in immigration, agricultural marketing, and perhaps financial services; crown corporations will be sold off or broken up; border posts will come into operation; and there will be less voluntary harmonization of economic regulation. Within the framework of multilateral and continental treaties, relations between the states will take on the normal international form.

At this point in our study, having covered the whole transition to separation, we moved to take it up again, this time on the assumption that polarization existed. This modification was suggested by the Czech-Slovak case, which showed how public opinion can be moved before the separation occurs. Clearly, the Government of Quebec might act as a *gouvernement provocateur*, aided by the Bloc québécois. In the months leading up to the referendum, it could purposely act in a way that would irritate and frustrate English Canadians and provoke offensive and threatening responses that would make Quebecers more likely to vote for sovereignty. A critical force here would be the Reform Party, whose leader might try to capture more support by acting as the tribune of ROC, focusing Canadians' frustrations on Quebec. Polarization could help produce a Yes vote in the referendum on sovereignty; indeed, given the historical support levels for sovereignty, polarization might be the only way for the PQ to achieve a Yes majority.

There are, however, counterweights to polarization in Canada and Quebec. There is a strong majority government in Ottawa, one unlikely to budge from its core position of refusing to contemplate secession, let alone negotiating it in advance, while trying to offer attractive programs to all Canadians. The Quebec government will be constrained not only by financial markets, the media, and an informed public, but also by its promise of a referendum, which allows voters to ignore the issue for the duration. So polarization should not rise above moderate levels, and if Quebecers were then to vote for separation, there would be no fundamental change in the basic scenario. Mr Manning would play a more prominent role in the negotiations, perhaps even as prime minister, and the reconstitution of Canada would include a triple-E Senate. The agreements reached with Quebec would form a minimal package, but the core described earlier in this study would still emerge.

CHAPTER SEVENTEEN

The Long-term Outcomes

CANADA

If the separation of Quebec unfolds as depicted here, Canada will undergo a transition period lasting three to five years as the immediate shocks of the secession continue to have repercussions throughout the country. In the period between the referendum and the separation, the country will reconstitute itself and arrange for some continuity in its relations with Quebec, and the public will pronounce on the politicians' handling of the secession by choosing a new federal government. In this period, citizens will be anxious, governments will be in a state of frenetic activity, and firms will be reassessing their plans and reorienting themselves to the new realities. After the separation, adjustment will continue, though the size of the changes necessary will vary by region, economic sector, and the personal circumstances of individuals.

Adjustment costs will continue to be registered for some time. In the economy, all Canadians will bear the effects of higher interest rates and a depreciated Canadian dollar. These will not abate fully until well after the separation. More substantial will be the effects of a sharp decline in investment, particularly in central Canada, where the disruption of commerce will be seen as more probable. Provincial and federal government finances will be strained by these developments, and services will be further reduced. In some sectors, adjustment will be especially hard. These include the sectors directly affected by the separation agreements – for example, financial services, agriculture, transportation, and all public enterprises – as well as those with the strongest linkages into Quebec, such as textiles, paper, chemicals, and oil and gas.

There will also be a hard psychological adjustment to make. The first sense of deep shock in ROC will be followed by the gradual realization that the nature of the country has changed profoundly. In geographical conceptions, the "hole" in Canada where Quebec "was" will continue to be troubling; in terms of a community or family, the whole will have lost an important if demanding member; and the more cosmopolitan view of Canada as a society consciously constructed around certain fundamental features, including francophone Quebecers, will have been shaken to its foundations. Of course, a few Canadians will remain quite oblivious to all of this – life will go on – but for most the secession will represent a profound loss. At the same time, there will be no choice except to see it also as an opportunity, a chance to discover what a new Canada can be and what can be achieved by its people.

Canada will emerge from the transition with a constitution that closely resembles the existing one, though some of the minor changes will be potentially decentralizing. These include provisions for the delegation of powers between the two orders of government and provisions for more concurrent powers; but such devices may also allow for centralization, in practice, or for a variety of arrangements in different provinces: they are flexible. Some changes will definitely create a more centralized system. The elimination of minority-language rights will mean the end of dualism, enshrining a pan-Canadian homogeneity of individual rights, and the absence of Quebec will tend to delegitimize collective rights generally, so there will be fewer grounds for the devolution of resources and power to other minorities, including the Aboriginal peoples. If a triple-E Senate is introduced, it might effectively reinforce the federal order of government. This will depend on how the party system evolves, but a new Senate might well provide more scope for the expression of regional interests and their incorporation into central-government policy. On the other hand, if the Senate is elected and if national parties are strong, divisions within it would be likely to occur around partisan cleavages as much as regional ones, and provincial governments would be less able than now to claim that they best represent the interests and preferences of their citizens. Beyond this, the strong centralizing elements of the current constitution will remain intact. If no areas of jurisdiction are transferred to the provincial order, Ottawa will retain its important responsibilities, along with its spending power.

The institutional structure, therefore, will be at least as conducive to central power as it is at present.

Over the long term, many factors will affect how the new Canadian federation evolves. Other scholars have listed and analysed the factors conducive to stability and instability in federal systems, just as they have assessed those that determine the degree of centralization written into constitutions when federations are first forming.[1] The factors on which there is some agreement can thus readily be explored in the Canadian case.

First is the continued sense of emergency and the struggle for independence. The sense of national emergency in ROC will support determined and rapid management of the immediate crisis, and a united focus on the need to deal with Quebec will help get Canada's new constitution into operation. The uncertainty of the external environment, especially the country's relations with the United States, will have a similar effect. But then the immediate perception of crisis will fade, and partisan, ideological, and regional cleavages will resurface. The sense of emergency will not be long sustained after the separation, particularly if an election produces a majority government. But although the crisis will have produced no massive centralization in Canada's institutional framework, it will have renewed the perception that Ottawa is the active centre of the Canadian polity, and this will take much longer to erode. Moreover, since the new system will be untried and potentially fragile, there will be some pressure to allow it to work, to see what results it produces, and to avoid the uncertainty that fundamental challenges to it would create. All these tendencies will promote stability.

A second factor is the economic performance of the federation, and this should be positive. During the transition, of course, there will be losses, big ones, as investment drops and interest rates rise. The GDP of ROC could easily drop by more than it does in a normal recession. Firms and individuals will have to adjust to the end of the economic union, and they will make further adjustments through anticipation that Canada-Quebec links will become even weaker. Government finance will be more precarious since spending will undoubtedly increase during the crisis at the same time as the cost of borrowing rises. (Government borrowing will probably become concentrated in very short-term maturities during the transition, in anticipation that rates will later fall; Ottawa might also take advantage of increased patriotism by issuing special Canada Savings Bonds on the domestic market.) While not all of these costs will show up as measurable declines in GDP, there certainly will be a sharp recession.

In Canada, however, the recession will be relatively short. First, the separation will take place at a time of general economic growth, especially in the United States, and expanding foreign markets will help growth resume. Second, separation will resolve the constitutional uncertainty that has lowered investors' confidence in Canada for several years. Once it is clear that the country is politically stable, investment should resume and interest rates will be able to drop. Finally, although times of uncertainty and dramatic change in basic economic and institutional arrangements are costly, they shake up the policy environment and create new opportunities and alliances; in the view of some analysts, transformative change increases growth.[2] So Canada's economic performance should not create much disaffection – greater wealth is highly conducive to stability.[3]

After the transition, though, there could be sharply uneven growth rates within the federation, and deepening regional inequalities are widely held to be destabilizing. For long-term stability, it seems essential that the central government should have the capacity to offset short-term regional economic declines and to compensate for enduring disparities in tax revenues.[4] But Ottawa would still be able, constitutionally, to redistribute to those provinces that are currently receiving equalization; in fact, both the ability and the willingness to do so would be greater in the absence of Quebec. The only serious obstacle would be Ontario, if the disruption of its economic links with Quebec makes the transitional recession deeper and longer there. Generally, though, economic conditions will not tend to cause serious centrifugal forces in the new Canadian federation, at least in the medium term.

A third factor conducive to stability is constitutional flexibility. After the secession, this will be increased in Canada in two ways. First, the constitution will become easier to amend formally as the population requirement under the general formula is reduced and provisions are made for interdelegation. Second, amendments will become more feasible politically. Since Quebec's particular requirements will no longer dominate the agenda, centralizing changes will be made more easily, and decentralizing amendments will no longer raise the objection that they are easing the way to Quebec secession. As well, the peculiar position of the Atlantic provinces could induce still more constitutional flexibility by requiring asymmetrical arrangements to meet its unique circumstances.

Long-term stability also depends on the balance of power within the federation. Persistent demands for regional autonomy are destabilizing, and they arise most strongly when central-government policies are not responsive to regional preferences and interests. In turn, comparative experience shows that this is accentuated when the number of units is small and especially when one unit is preponderant in the federation. The latter factors are associated with both political instability and the potential for secession.[5] Once again, this suggests that the preponderant position of Ontario could make for interregional conflict, disaffection, and long-term instability in the federation.

There are some important countervailing factors, however. First, Canadians will resist the uncertainty of further structural changes and will allow the new system time to work. Having experienced the event of secession once – in fact, they will still be witnessing its effects on Quebec – they will not be interested in repeating the experience. The core of the constitution will remain a relatively centralized one, and this will be buttressed by the new attention and even loyalty focused on Ottawa.[6] Canadians' community of outlook will be greater than in the existing federation. If a more equal and elected Senate is part of the new constitution, the West will have won a major concession, and one that might well reduce direct federal-provincial confrontation in the long run. Of at least equal importance is the system of political parties; competitive national parties are more influential than any other factor in reducing the potential for secession, because they help prevent an unequivocal expression of provincial preferences, while ensuring the representation at the centre of regional interests.[7] In post-secession Canada, a two-party system will probably emerge, with more political debate taking place along ideological lines than on regional ones. This might cause economic policy to be less consistent, but it would be a strong force for the stability of the federation.

So, after a Quebec secession, into the medium term at least, it is predictable that Canada will cohere and that the constitutional structure will much resemble that of the present federation. The initial tendency will be towards rather more centralization than currently exists, even though federal governments might be much less activist than they have been since World War II. Over the longer term – that is, beyond two decades – prediction fails. Canada would remain a somewhat artificial country, with a small market and a fragile culture, subject as ever to changing external forces and the continual integrating pressures of the continental and global systems. The country might fragment. It might dramatically change its constitution. Or, if the economy works well and there is sufficient public commitment to a distinct mix of national policies, then Canada might continue to persist in much the same form as it assumed after Quebec's separation.

QUEBEC

The shape of relations between Canada and Quebec in the long term will, of course, depend on the decisions made and the structures established during the transition to sovereignty, but they will also be affected by the repercussions of secession in Quebec, both economic and political.

Economically, Quebec's situation will be difficult for some time. There will be substantial costs to bear in setting up a full government. After the referendum, although ROC will not have a constitution, the federal government will still be equipped with a complete administrative machine, but Quebec will have to create one. Even if some savings from eliminating duplication do accrue to the government, the fiscal position of the newly sovereign Quebec will worsen as it assumes responsibility for programs and for its share of the national debt. Moreover, the costs of uncertainty will be much higher in Quebec than in Canada, and they will be longer lasting, in part because of economic fundamentals such as greater adjustment costs but also because the policy environment will be less predictable. Investment will stay depressed until the province's prospects have clarified, and this will take some time.

Quebec's big economic advantages, fundamentally, stem from its cultural homogeneity, its social solidarity, the fast transmission of information within the society and its businesses, the supportive stance of government towards business, and the linkages between financial firms and other companies in manufacturing and commerce. In a world in which treaties provide secure market access and business is global, these features might allow Quebec to attain more rapid economic growth as a sovereign state than as part of the Canadian federation. Despite the direct losses that the separation causes, it could reinforce some of these long-term advantages. In particular, the urgency of the crisis, and the focus of the whole collectivity on the negotiations with Canada, could strengthen the sense of national solidarity. So could the prospect of embarking on a new national project. Indeed, separation will bring a sense not only of autonomy but also of isolation, and there will be no choice for many Quebecers except to make their country work (or to leave). Further, as in Canada, structural transformation in the policy-making and economic arenas could create new opportunities and stimulate growth.

But some factors will operate so as to weaken this solidarity and its concomitant advantages. There will be continued difficulties with ethnic minorities. Emigration will be an economic depressant. More important, during and after the transition, a substantial and bitter federalist rump will hold the government responsible for the economic hardship brought on the province (an effect that will be absent in Canada, where the entire blame will be laid on Quebec). After the transition, the Government of Quebec will also be more obviously accountable for economic conditions. In federations, responsibility is blurred, and disaffection can be directed towards the other order of government, an outlet that will no longer be available after Quebec achieves sovereignty; so domestic politics will acquire a greater salience there. This raises a most difficult problem – the alignment and realignment of political forces in the sovereign Quebec.

Since 1970, politics in the province have come to be oriented around the national question. In particular, the quest for sovereignty has been the glue holding the Parti québécois together. Presumably, the PQ government could continue in office for at least two years after the separation, but there would be much uncertainty about its economic-policy orientation, especially given the difficult conditions of the time. Its programmatic inclination would be towards a corporatist model of economic planning, involving the state, the private sector, public enterprises, unions, cooperatives, and social movements.[8] The party's left wing would expect the state to combine a neo-Keynesian full-employment policy with indicative industrial and regional planning, and with some protection for strategic firms. This would be accompanied by expanded social-welfare programs. But in the post-secession period, in view of the heavy losses of the transition and the fiscal position of the state, this role could not be fulfilled. As Mr Parizeau remarked during the 1994 provincial election campaign, when it was noted that the party was not emphasizing its commitments about more aid for the poor, more generous health programs, and universal day care, "We haven't got the money for that sort of thing at the present time. That's why it's not in the platform but it is in the program. And once the finances of Quebec will be in better shape, sure we'll do that sort of thing."[9] But the Quebec government will face decreasing revenues and rising social needs as a consequence of the separation, at the same time as investors will be more wary of the province because of the PQ's social-democratic orientation. And although a move towards corporatism and planning might create growth, this would be constrained by the country's new exposure to FTA, NAFTA, and GATT disciplines on subsidies, foreign investment controls, public enterprises, and discriminatory procurement. As a consequence, it will be difficult for the government to form a coherent economic policy that builds on Quebec's strengths. National solidarity might compensate for economic decline and the economically depressing effects of policy incoherence, and might carry the party through another election; or the government might call and win an election soon after the separation. In either case, though, there would be deep uncertainty about the framework of economic policy, dissension within the governing party, and, probably, unrest among its working-class and rural supporters.

On the other hand, if the Liberal Party were to be elected after sovereignty was attained, some of these effects would be lessened. The Liberal Party is more firmly oriented towards fiscal restraint, liberalized trade, deregulation, and competition, though it is still committed to a catalytic role for government and its state enterprises. A Liberal regime would give the PQ time in opposition to reorient itself; but if the PQ regrouped on the left, the ideological distance between the two major parties would be greater than before, and there would be sharp conflict over economic policy. Whatever the medium-term political outcome, Quebecers will face a harder transition, more costly adjustments, and a slower re-emergence from the recession caused by the separation.

CANADA-QUEBEC RELATIONS

Long-term relations between Canada and Quebec will be shaped by the agreements made at the time of the separation as well as by the political and economic developments that take place later within the two states. In a nonpolarized environment, the principal loci of political integration after the secession will be in the management of monetary policy and the financial sector, a few special-purpose agencies and joint systems, and consultation and cooperation about Aboriginal peoples, the environment, defence, policing, and other matters. Economic integration at the level of a customs union will be maintained, but through no formal mechanism. If the political environment is polarized before the secession, political integration will be even less.

Many of the agreements will lapse, however. Even if neither state reduces external tariffs unilaterally, the customs union will not survive the next round of multilateral trade talks. The immigration agreement will not be renewed, voluntary regulatory harmonization will be reduced because of different domestic political pressures, and the currency agreement might break down after a relatively short time if the two governments have very different attitudes towards inflation or the exchange rate. Economic integration will erode as Quebec becomes a more autonomous state. There will be much less labour mobility, in part because of the decline of French-language education in Canada. Large Canadian firms based in Quebec will shift their head offices over time, and this, along with the diminution of Quebec's anglophone community, the reduced number and scope of public enterprises operating transnationally, and some inevitable weakening of capital-market integration, will tend to divert trade away from crossing the Quebec-Canada border. At the margin, the flow of business will shift to the two internal markets and, more substantially, to the United States and other foreign markets.

All this will entail economic losses for both countries. To the immediate and considerable costs of the transition will be added the burden of adjustment to a gradual decrease in positive integration between them. These costs will accrue slowly, but compared with the alternative of a full economic and political union, they will mount noticeably. The costs of the transition and of later adjustment will be greater for Quebec than for Canada. There will be more uncertainty about the new country, especially on the political front; as the smaller economy it will have to adjust more, proportionately; and there will be the added costs caused by the end of redistribution, the mutual-insurance support provided by the federation, and the restriction of an important adjustment mechanism – labour mobility. The main question is whether Quebec's particular social advantages could be brought into play to compensate for all this. The answer will depend on the degree of national solidarity and patriotism occasioned by sovereignty and how it was accomplished, the creativity of the government and business, and the success of partisan realignment.

Over the longer term, more cooperation between the two countries will be possible. Inevitably, they will share common interests and problems, and costly irritants will provide incentives to reach new agreements. The countries' joint position in the global and continental systems will encourage this. But even over the long term, cooperation is far less likely to occur if the secession is accomplished through polarization. Moreover, governments will always face political incentives to perpetuate conflictual relations with other states, because problems and failures can then be attributed to the "other." But this is only to encounter once again a dynamic that had helped produce the separation in the first place; it could persist.

In the end, then, the original questions animating the study are answered. If the transition occurred as depicted here, Canada and Quebec would undergo a wrenching adjustment to the new political and economic order. Substantial costs would be incurred over the transition period, particularly in Quebec. Many lives would be greatly disrupted, and every person who is now a Canadian would have to make adjustments. But, for most, the change would not be catastrophic.

Canada would emerge as a stable country, rather like what it is now but with a higher degree of centralization, at least temporarily. There would be few special political links with Quebec, and economic relations would erode as their policy framework gradually settled to the level of integration prevailing among the countries of North America. Within this framework, Quebecers would have their chance to fashion a more autonomous future, having taken the risk that the costs of the transition and the residue it left could be compensated either by their society's special capacity to achieve economic growth or by the security of sovereignty.

Selected Characteristics of Canada, Quebec, and ROC

Table A1
Selected Characteristics of Canada, Quebec, and ROC

	Canada	Quebec	ROC	ROC as % of Canada
1 Area (km²)	9,970,610	1,540,680	8,429,930	84.5
2 Population (000s) 1992	27,409	6,925	20,484	74.7
3 GDP				
(a) at market prices ($ millions) 1991	671,668	155,864	515,804	76.8
(b) per capita ($ 1991)	24,505	22,507	25,180	
4 Manufacturing shipments ($ millions) 1992	283,559	68,678	214,881	75.8
5 Manufacturing value-added				
($ millions) 1989	127,407	34,160	93,247	73.2
6 Domestic exports ($ millions) 1992:				
primary	34,025	3,132	30,893	90.1
secondary	119,730	22,423	97,307	81.3
total	153,755	25,555	128,200	83.4
7 Exports to the US ($ millions) 1992	118,677	19,328	99,349	83.7
8 Federal government revenues ($ millions):				
PIT 1990	59,562	12,717	46,845	78.6
CIT 1987	45,655	10,703	34,952	76.6
9 Assets & liabilities of chartered banks				
($ millions) 3rd quarter, 1992: assets	675,649	80,006	595,643	88.2
liabilities	675,649	70,734	604,915	89.5
10 Investment ($ millions)				
(a) total public & private:				
preliminary actual 1992	158,537	34,791	123,746	78.0
intentions 1993	163,181	34,578	128,603	78.8
(b) public: preliminary actual 1992	41,685	11,399	30,286	72.6
11 Immigrants from outside Canada (1988–91)	593,480	93,610	499,870	84.2
12 Mother tongue (single responses, %):				
English	62.1	9.0	80.2	
French	24.5	83.3	4.6	
non-official	13.4	7.7	15.2	
13 Home language (single responses, %):				
English	68.7	10.7	88.3	
French	23.5	83.9	3.1	
non-official	7.8	5.4	8.6	
14 Seats in House of Commons: 1984	282	75	207	73.4
1988	295	75	220	74.6
(proposed) 1996	301	75	226	75.1
15 Popular vote – federal election				
(a) PC % 1984	50.3	50.2	49.7	
1988	43.0	52.7	39.5	
1993	16.0	13.6	17.0	
(b) NDP % 1984	18.8	8.8	22.5	
1988	20.4	14.0	22.7	
1993	6.9	1.5	8.9	
(c) Reform % 1993	18.7	0.0	25.8	

Table A2   Selected Characteristics of ROC

	Nfld Actual	% ROC	PEI Actual	% ROC	NS Actual	% ROC	NB Actual	% ROC
1 Area (km²)	405,720	4.8	5,660	0.1	55,490	0.7	73,440	0.9
2 Population (000s) 1992	575	2.8	130	0.6	907	4.4	728	3.5
3 GDP (a) at market prices ($ millions) 1991	9,312	1.8	2,078	0.4	17,605	3.4	13,689	2.6
(b) per capita ($ 1991)	16,195		15,985		19,410		18,803	
4 Manufacturing shipments ($ millions) 1992	1,366	0.6	407	0.2	4,989	2.3	5,590	2.6
5 Manufacturing value-added ($ millions) 1989	810	0.8	156	0.2	1,935	2.1	2,145	2.3
6 Domestic exports ($ millions), 1992: primary	450	1.5	159	0.5	1,065	3.4	705	2.3
secondary	771	0.8	16	0.01	1,259	1.3	2,308	2.4
total	1,221	0.9	175	0.1	2,324	1.8	3,013	2.3
7 Exports to the U.S. ($ millions) 1992: total	616	0.6	102	0.1	1,577	1.6	1,935	1.9
8 Federal government revenues ($ millions): 1990 PIT	715	1.5	175	0.4	1,512	3.2	1,094	2.3
1987 CIT	404	1.2	115	0.3	839	2.4	711	2.0
9 Assets & liabilities of chartered banks ($ millions) 3rd quarter, 1992: assets	4,962	0.8	1,214	0.2	10,720	1.8	7,714	1.3
liabilities	4,154	0.7	1,159	0.2	8,714	1.4	6,670	1.1
10 Investment ($ millions) (a) total public & private: preliminary actual 1992	2,743	2.2	519	0.4	3,864	3.1	3,357	2.7
intentions 1993	3,123	2.4	503	0.4	3,837	3.0	3,156	2.4
(b) public: preliminary actual 1992	783	2.6	171	0.6	1,207	4.0	1,445	4.8
11 Immigrants from outside Canada (1988–91)	925	0.2	430	0.08	3,640	0.7	1,915	0.4
12 Mother tongue (single responses, %) 1991: English	98.7		94.6		94.0		65.4	
French	0.4		4.2		3.8		33.4	
non-official	0.8		1.1		2.2		1.2	
13 Home language (single responses, %) 1991: English	99.3		97.4		96.5		68.3	
French	0.2		2.3		2.4		31.0	
non-official	0.5		0.3		1.1		0.6	
14 Seats in House of Commons: 1984	7	3.4	4	1.9	11	5.3	10	4.8
1988	7	3.2	4	1.8	11	5.0	10	4.5
(proposed) 1996	7	3.1	4	1.8	11	4.9	10	4.4
15 Popular vote – federal election: (a) PC % 1984	58		52		51		54	
1988	42		41		41		40	
1993	27		32		24		28	
(b) NDP % 1984	6		6		15		14	
1988	12		7		11		9	
1993	4		5		7		5	
(c) Reform % 1993	1		1		13		9	
16 Popular vote – last two provincial elections (%)	Apr 20/89		May 29/89		Sept 6/88		Oct 13/87	
	NDP 4		NDP 4		NDP 16		NDP 10	
	PC 48		PC 36		PC 43		PC 28	
	Lib 47		Lib 60		Lib 40		Lib 61	
	May 3/93		Mar 29/93		May 25/93		Sept 23/91	
	NDP 7		NDP 5		NDP 18		NDP 11	
	PC 42		PC 40		PC 31		PC 21	
	Lib 49		Lib 55		Lib 51		Lib 47	

Ont Actual	% ROC	Man Actual	% ROC	Sask Actual	% ROC	Alta Actual	% ROC	BC Actual	% ROC	Yukon/NWT Actual	% ROC	ROC
1,068,580	12.7	649,950	7.7	652,330	7.7	661,190	7.8	947,800	11.2	3,909,770	46.4	8,429,930
10,098	49.3	1,096	5.4	994	4.9	2,565	12.5	3,305	16.1	84	0.4	20,484
270,463	52.4	23,340	4.5	19,985	3.9	72,168	14.0	84,088	16.3	3,076	0.5	515,804
26,784		21,296		20,106		28,136		25,443		36,619		25,180
149,114	69.4	6,153	2.9	3,530	1.6	19,410	9.0	24,322	16.0	N/A	N/A	214,881
65,328	70.0	3,060	3.3	1,388	1.5	6,707	7.2	11,682	12.5	35	0.03	93,247
4,628	15.0	1,718	5.6	4,460	14.4	13,488	43.6	3,844	12.4	376	1.2	30,893
72,783	74.8	1,800	1.8	1,734	1.8	4,202	4.3	12,435	12.8	1	0.0	97,307
77,411	60.4	3,518	2.7	6,194	4.8	17,690	13.8	16,279	12.7	377	0.2	128,200
68,424	68.9	2,102	2.1	2,757	2.8	13,838	13.9	7,993	8.0	4	0.0	99,349
26,251	56.0	1,847	3.9	1,531	3.3	5,728	12.2	7,605	16.2	191	0.4	46,845
19,491	55.8	1,148	3.3	924	2.6	6,544	18.7	4,136	11.8	167	0.5	34,952
223,951	37.6	12,284	2.0	9,621	1.6	43,461	7.3	61,018	10.2	931	0.1	595,643
204,051	33.7	13,649	2.6	11,895	2.0	39,183	6.5	57,022	9.4	809	0.1	604,915
59,432	48.0	4,957	4.0	5,710	4.6	19,845	16.0	22,318	18.0	1,004	0.8	123,746
62,502	48.6	5,071	3.9	5,200	4.0	20,375	23.6	23,871	18.6	965	0.7	128,603
14,237	47.0	1,931	6.4	1,622	5.3	3,465	11.4	4,885	16.1	539	1.7	30,286
328,105	65.6	16,110	3.2	4,255	0.8	48,940	9.8	95,025	19.0	200	0.04	499,870
77.5		76.1		85.2		83.5		81.4		66.5		80.2
4.7		4.5		2.0		2.0		1.4		2.6		4.6
17.7		19.4		12.8		14.5		17.2		30.9		15.2
86.0		88.6		94.9		92.2		90.3		77.3		88.3
3.1		2.2		0.7		0.7		0.4		1.2		3.1
10.9		9.1		4.4		7.1		9.3		21.5		8.6
95	45.9	14	6.8	14	6.8	21	10.1	28	13.5	3	1.4	207
99	45.0	14	6.4	14	6.4	26	11.8	32	14.5	3	1.4	220
103	45.6	14	6.2	14	6.2	26	11.5	34	15.0	3	1.3	226
48		44		42		69		47		47		50
38		37		36		52		35		30		40
18		12		11		15		13		6		17
21		28		38		14		35		24		23
21		21		44		17		37		37		23
6		17		27		4		16		21		9
20		22		27		52		36		10		26

Ont	Man	Sask	Alta	BC
May 2/85	Mar 18/86	Oct 20/86	Mar 20/89	Oct 22/86
NDP 24	NDP 41	NDP 39	NDP 26	NDP 42
PC 37	PC 41	PC 59	PC 45	SC 50
Lib 38	Lib 14	Lib 2	Lib 29	Lib 7
Sept 6/90	Sept 11/90	Oct 21/91	June 15/93	Oct 17/91
NDP 38	NDP 29	NDP 51	NDP 11	NDP 41
PC 24	PC 42	PC 25	PC 45	SC 24
Lib 32	Lib 28	Lib 23	Lib 40	Lib 33

Sources, tables A1 and A2: (1) Statistics Canada, *Canada Yearbook 1990,* table 1.1; (2) Statistics Canada, *Postcensual Annual Estimates of Population,* table 2; (3) Statistics Canada, *Provincial Economic Accounts: Annual Estimates, 1981–1991,* table 1 (Per capita figures are derived from the data in rows 2 and 3a); (4) Statistics Canada, *Monthly Survey of Manufacturing,* table 10; (5) Statistics Canada, *Manufacturing Industries of Canada,* tables 5–27; (6) Statistics Canada, *Summary of Canadian International Trade,* table x-4 (Primary exports comprise the categories of live animals, inedible crude materials, and food, feed, beverages, and tobacco. Secondary exports comprise inedible fabricated materials, inedible end products, and special transactions); (7) Statistics Canada, *Exports: Merchandise Trade,* table 3; (8) Revenue Canada, *Taxation Statistics, 1992,* table 11, and Statistics Canada, *Corporation Taxation Statistics, 1987,* table 11; (9) Bank of Canada, *Bank of Canada Review, Spring 1993,* tables C5 and C6 (Percentages do not add to 100% because the remaining assets and liabilities are international or are attributed to head office); (10) Statistics Canada, *Private and Public Investment in Canada: Intentions,* tables 7 and 7D; (11) Statistics Canada, *Immigration and Citizenship,* table 6 (These statistics refer to 20% sample data from 1988–1991. Immigrants from outside Canada refers to persons who resided outside Canada after 1988 but in Canada on 1 June 1991); (12) Statistics Canada, *Mother Tongue,* table 1 (Mother tongue refers to the first language used at home in childhood and still understood by the individual. Single responses were 97.3% of all responses in Canada: multiple responses were highest in Manitoba at 3.8%); (13) Statistics Canada, *Home Language and Mother Tongue,* table 1 (Home language is the language spoken most often at home by the individual. Single responses were 98.2% of all responses in Canada: multiple responses were highest in the Yukon and NWT at 3.0%); (14) Statistics Canada, *Canada Yearbook 1990,* table 19.3, and Elections Canada, *Redistribution,* n.p., n.d., "Representation Formula: Detailed Calculation"; (15) Canada, Chief Electoral Officer, *Report of the Chief Electoral Officer, 1984,* table 6, *1988,* table 6, and Elections Canada, "Percentage of Popular Vote by Province," unofficial results reported by Media Election Consortium, 28 October 1993; (16) (Newfoundland) *Evening Telegram,* St John's, 21 April 1989 and 4 May 1993; (Prince Edward Island) *Evening Telegram,* 22 April 1986 and 30 May 1989; (Nova Scotia), *Halifax Chronicle Herald,* 7 November 1984 and 7 September 1988; (New Brunswick), *Halifax Chronicle Herald,* 14 October 1987 and *Globe and Mail,* 24 September 1991; (Ontario), *Globe and Mail,* 3 May 1985 and 7 September 1990; (Manitoba), *Winnipeg Free Press,* 19 March 1986 and 12 September 1990; (Saskatchewan), *Winnipeg Free Press,* 21 October 1986 and 23 October 1991; (Alberta), *Calgary Herald,* 21 March 1989 and 16 June 1993; (British Columbia), *Vancouver Sun,* 23 October 1986 and 19 October 1991.

Notes

CHAPTER ONE

1 In fact, Canada would not be entirely discontiguous if Quebec were to separate with its borders intact. On Killinek Island, off the northern tip of Labrador, between Hudson Strait to the west and the Labrador Sea and Davis Strait to the east, the Province of Newfoundland and Labrador meets the Northwest Territories. These two components of Canada share a border on the island that is approximately 8 kilometres long.

2 See the figures in Reid and Snoddon, "Redistribution under Alternative Constitutional Arrangements," 77–80. Major federal-provincial transfers in 1988 would have cost 5.7% less than they did.

3 Some weakness in these data should be noted. Dating from 1989, they do not reflect rising exports to the United States since the Canada–U.S. Free Trade Agreement came into effect. As well, some Quebec "exports" to Ontario may be transshipments of goods actually destined for other markets.

CHAPTER TWO

1 Some of this ground is covered by the contributions in Simeon and Janigan, *Toolkits*, 142–81. See also Covell, *Thinking about the Rest of Canada*.

2 Archer, "The Prairie Perspective," 249.

3 Usher, "The Design of a Government."

4　Boothe, "Constitutional Change," 40–5.

5　Young, "What Is Good about Provincial Governments?"

6　Covell, *Thinking about the Rest of Canada*, 13.

7　Kwavnick, "Québécois Nationalism," 54.

8　Resnick, *Toward a Canada-Quebec Union*, 53; Resnick, *Thinking English Canada*, 85: "What is crucial, however, in thinking English Canada (as opposed to Canada as a whole) is to free ourselves from the bane that Quebec, ever since the Quiet Revolution, has introduced into our political life, namely, the incessant demand for increased provincial power."

9　See Canada, *Shaping Canada's Future Together*, 33–9; Allaire Report, *A Québec Free to Choose*.

10　Boothe, "Constitutional Change," 26–7, 42.

11　Harris and Purvis, "Some Economic Aspects of Political Restructuring," 210.

12　Covell, *Thinking about the Rest of Canada*, 12.

13　Chambers and Percy, "Natural Resources and the Western Canadian Economy," 85.

14　From survey results about attitudes towards the various elements of the Charlottetown Accord, Johnston et al. conclude that "the various regions outside Quebec were *not* at odds with each other" ("The People and the Charlottetown Accord," 24; emphasis in the original). Another survey probed attitudes towards four central aspects of the Accord: the elected Senate, Native self-government, guaranteed seats for Quebec, and the transfer of power to the provinces. Taking the four regions of ROC – the Atlantic provinces, Ontario, the Prairies, and British Columbia – the maximum interregional difference in support for these elements was 13%, 14%, 10%, and 9%, respectively. The differences between support in ROC as a whole and in Quebec were 32%, 17%, 41%, and 32% respectively (Gallup, *Gallup Report*, 24 September 1994). On national identification, see the data reported in chapter 12, below.

15　Gibson, *Plan B*, 145–56.

16　There would also be the problem of internal regional governance. Chambers and Percy argue that only a unitary regional government would make sense in the West: it "would be unrealistic to presume that the residents of the West would want to replicate a central government with many of the functions held by the current federal government yet on a smaller economic base" ("Structural Characteristics," 199).

17　Covell, *Thinking about the Rest of Canada*, 24.

18　For an analysis of various fragmentation possibilities, see Gibson, *Plan B*, 99–104, 145–56.

19　Whitaker, "Life after Separation," 74.

20 Lederman, "The British Parliamentary System," 37–8.
21 Covell, *Thinking about the Rest of Canada*, 22.
22 Economic Council, *A Joint Venture*, table 3-4, and material supplied by the council. In 1987 Ontario-controlled firms received $20.6 billion in revenues from Quebec and $39.5 billion in revenues from the rest of ROC, while Quebec-controlled firms received $30.3 billion in revenues from Ontario.
23 Leslie, "Options for the Future," 137–8.
24 On other potential demands, see, for example, Day, "Speaking for Ourselves."
25 See Young, Faucher, and Blais, "The Concept of Province-building."

CHAPTER THREE

1 For a critique, on the grounds that this integration limits the scope of government intervention, see Miriam Smith, "Québec-Canada Association."
2 Jockel, *If Canada Breaks Up*, 22.
3 Québec, Commission sur l'avenir, Secrétariat, "L'accès du Québec aux marchés extérieurs"; Hartt et al., *Tangled Web*; and Ritchie et al., *Broken Links*.
4 Maxwell and Pestieau, *Economic Realities*, 14.
5 For a good survey of these benefits and of the losses through decentralization and disintegration, see Royal Bank, *Unity or Disunity*, 9–13.
6 Hartt, "Sovereignty and the Economic Union," 14–23.
7 Economic Council, *A Joint Venture*, fig. 3-2; de Mestral "Economic Integration," 52–3.
8 Québec, Commission sur l'avenir, Secrétariat, "L'accès du Québec aux marchés extérieurs," 48–50.
9 Economic Council, *A Joint Venture*, 84-5.
10 Lipsey, Schwanen, and Wonnacott, *The NAFTA*.
11 Jockel, *If Canada Breaks Up*, 26–7.
12 Courchene, *In Praise of Renewed Federalism*, 30–4.
13 Lipsey, "Comments," 59.
14 The Bélanger-Campeau Commission put much stock in this possibility. See Québec, Commission sur l'avenir, *Report*, 56-8.

CHAPTER FOUR

1 See Leroy, "Les options monétaires."
2 On "hysteresis," see Pierre Fortin, "La question de l'emploi," 216–20, and Scarth, "A Note," 70–2.

3 See Boothe, "Constitutional Change," 41: "If economic conditions differ across regions, small regions such as western Canada generally get the 'wrong' macro policy."

4 On the importance to sovereigntists of monetary policy as an adjustment mechanism and policy tool, see Leslie, "Equal to Equal," 17–23.

5 In the Canadian case, see the data in Royal Bank, *Unity or Disunity*, 42–3.

6 The basic source is Bernard Fortin, "Les options monétaires."

7 Ibid., 288; Laidler and Robson, *Two Nations, One Money?* 40–1.

8 Laidler and Robson, *Two Nations, One Money?* 41–5.

9 Rousseau, "L'intégration politique," 139–41.

10 Courchene, *In Praise of Renewed Federalism*, 64–5.

11 Ibid., 61, 65; Lucas, "Comment," 437.

12 Arguably, the countries' representation on the bank's board of directors would make little practical difference. In all likelihood, the governor of the bank would make the important decisions, and there is no reason in principle why this individual could not serve two governments, unless their policy preferences about inflation were widely divergent. Still, the appointment process would raise symbolic problems, as would the perceptions of the publics of Canada and Quebec about the distribution of power over monetary policy.

13 Royal Bank, *Unity or Disunity*, 14–16.

14 Laidler and Robson, *Two Nations, One Money?* 34–7.

15 In "The Case for a Single Currency," for example, Donner and Lazar do not give it any consideration.

16 Québec, Assemblée nationale, Commission d'étude, *Les options monétaires d'un Québec souverain*, 6. ("Still, the use of the American currency by a sovereign Quebec could be contemplated, given the rising commercial and financial exchanges between Quebec and the United States. Moreover, using the American dollar would avoid conflicts with Canada.") All translations by the author.

17 If the value of the Canadian dollar dropped sharply because of Quebec's announcement, then Quebecers as well as all Canadians would see their assets shrink, because their Canadian-dollar holdings would take time to convert. Moreover, Canadians' assets would recover in value if their currency was sustainable. Quebecers would incur a permanent loss.

18 Lucas and Reid, "The Choice of Efficient Monetary Arrangements."

CHAPTER FIVE

1 Resnick, *Toward a Canada-Quebec Union*, 77–89.

2 See Bergeron, "Projet d'un nouveau Commonwealth," and Turp, "Réponses," especially 1083–1115. The latter envisages a joint

parliamentary conference (with parity in representation), a council of ministers, a secretariat, and a court, as well as a joint central bank. Turp also includes a draft treaty creating the Canada-Quebec economic union.

3 Resnick, *Toward a Canada-Quebec Union*, 100.
4 See the account of negotiations between the Czechs and Slovaks about the "state treaty" in chapter 11.
5 Smiley, "The Association Dimension."
6 Johnston et al., "The People and the Charlottetown Accord," 24; Gallup, *Gallup Report*, 24 September 1992. The first places opposition to the guarantee in ROC at 78%, the second at 72%.
7 Franck, "East African Federation," 18–19.
8 May, *The Hapsburg Monarchy*, 38–41.
9 Dauphin and Slosar, "Étude des modalités," 161–72.
10 Monahan and Covello, *An Agenda for Constitutional Reform*, 108: "Democratic principles suggest than any common political legislative authority must derive its authority directly from a common electorate. In effect, the only common political legislative authority that is consistent with basic democratic norms is a legislative body which is elected directly by the residents of Québec and the rest of Canada."
11 Soberman, "European Integration," 202–3.
12 Courchene, *In Praise of Renewed Federalism*, 53.
13 Spiro, "The Federation of Rhodesia and Nyasaland," 78.
14 Smiley, "As Options Narrow," 6.
15 Pentland, "Association after Sovereignty?" 240.

CHAPTER SIX

1 Monahan and Covello, *An Agenda for Constitutional Reform*, 110.
2 Boadway, Purvis, and Wen, "Economic Dimensions," 18.
3 Murray Smith, "The Quebec Sovereignty Scenario," 481.
4 Maxwell and Pestieau, *Economic Realities*, 26.
5 Leslie, "Options for the Future," 137.
6 Canada, Federal-Provincial Relations Office, *Sovereignty-Association*, 1.
7 Grady, *The Economic Consequences*, 144.
8 Courchene, *In Praise of Renewed Federalism*, 40, 35. This relationship is sometimes seen as so close that the two separate dimensions of economic and political integration are conflated. So Watts, for example, despite his sophisticated treatments of the whole set of issues, wrote that when federations break down, an "alternative consequence of federal disintegration is the attempt to establish, as a substitute for the federation, an economic union or confederacy" ("The Survival or Disintegration of Federations," 70).

9   *Parti québécois, La souveraineté: Pourquoi? Comment?* 36. ("In becoming sovereign, of course, Quebec will cut the political link with the federal regime, but in the interest of Quebec and of Canada, many economic links will be maintained.")

10 Canada, External Affairs, *The Canada–U.S. Free Trade Agreement*, art. 605.

11 Courchene, *In Praise of Renewed Federalism*, 35.

12 Putnam, "Diplomacy and Domestic Politics."

13 Loungnarath, "A Comment," 65.

14 Grieco, "Anarchy and the Limits of Cooperation." See the application of these theories to post-secession Canada-Quebec relations in Pierre Martin,"Association after Sovereignty," 16–23.

15 Harris and Purvis, "Some Economic Aspects," 205–7. Politicians also have short-time horizons, and if the costs are immediate and the benefits are long term, they have little incentive to agree on a more efficient common policy.

16 Breton, "Supplementary Statement," 495–8.

17 Whalley, "The Impact of Federal Policies." As Peter Leslie dryly remarked, political union is justified on economic grounds partly on the supposition "that an interventionist state, governed by people no wiser than those we have the habit of electing, is capable of achieving welfare gains beyond those attainable through market integration alone" (*Federal State, National Economy*, 144).

18 Monahan, *Political and Economic Integration*, 39–43.

19 Dehem, *On the Meaning of "Economic Association,"* 2.

20 Courchene, "Toward the Reintegration of Social and Economic Policy."

21 Norrie, Boadway, and Osberg, "The Constitution and the Social Contract," 247–8.

22 Institute of Intergovernmental Relations, *Approaches to National Standards*; Monahan, *Political and Economic Integration*, 19–29.

23 Courchene, "Canada 1992," 60–2.

24 Such an asymmetry informs Rousseau's whole treatment of monetary and currency unions. See "L'intégration politique."

CHAPTER SEVEN

1   For federations, the classic source of this approach is Livingston, "A Note on the Nature of Federalism." See also Stein, "Federal Political Systems and Federal Societies."

2   Courchene and McDougall, "The Context for Future Constitutional Options"; Courchene, "Staatsnation vs Kulturnation," 2–7.

3   Whitaker, "Life after Separation." See also Ian Stewart's remarks in Simeon and Janigan, *Toolkits*, 160–2: the former clerk of the privy

council outlined a "prescriptive mythology" that would define factors supportive of a more centralized federation than many others envisage.

4 For an effort along these lines, see Gibbins, "Speculations on a Canada without Quebec." In Courchene's words, these are efforts to discern "the impact of the hole on the parts" ("Staatsnation vs Kulturnation," 2).

5 Lemco, *Political Stability*, 17.

6 Watts, *New Federations* and "The Survival or Disintegration of Federations"; Hicks, *Federalism*; Lemco, *Political Stability*.

7 Watts, *New Federations*, 41–92, and "The Survival or Disintegration of Federations."

8 Leslie, "The Fiscal Crisis," table 7.

9 Chambers and Percy, *Western Canada*, 21–44, 69–72.

10 Taylor, "Shared and Divergent Values," 54–8. See also McRoberts, *English Canada and Quebec*, 53.

11 May and Rowlands, "Atlantic Canada," 16–34, 43–6. These authors present scenarios for Newfoundland of net transfers being eliminated; real GDP would drop 40% by the year 2000, and either unemployment or outmigration would be massive.

12 Bickerton, "Alternative Futures," 16–21.

13 See McRoberts's ingenious analysis of the 7 July 1992 constitutional agreement reached before the Quebec government entered the negotiations ("Disagreeing on Fundamentals," 250–2).

14 Courchene, "What Does Ontario Want?"

15 Hicks, *Federalism*, 14; Franck, "Why Federations Fail," 173–4.

16 Dasko, "The Ties That Bound," 8. Direct questions about national and provincial identification are intrusive, and the responses vary with the form of the question posed. See the data reported in chapter 12.

17 Vernon, "The Federal Citizen."

18 Gibbins, "Speculations on a Canada without Quebec," 270.

19 Gibson, *Plan B*, 177–8. See also 204: "A central Parliament with real initiative is an appropriate instrument for a people who wish to do things together – a people who have an agenda, visions, and mutual goals that require proactive efforts by a centre that is larger than the constituent states. On the other hand, if our agendas, visions, and mutual goals as Canadians can be largely achieved in our own provinces, with the help of a central service organization, then a completely different structure is required."

20 Léon Dion, "Pour sortir de l'impasse constitutionnelle," 277.

21 Coleman, *Business and Politics*, 240–8.

22 Berger, "Quebec's Rendezvous with Independence," 318.

23 Wood, "Secession," 132.

CHAPTER EIGHT

1 Compare Stéphane Dion, "Why is Secession Rare?" 10–11, with Léon Dion, *Nationalismes et politique au Québec*.
2 Covell, *Thinking about the Rest of Canada*, 8.
3 Nordlinger, *On the Autonomy of the Democratic State*, especially 74–97.
4 Stéphane Dion, "Why Is Secession Rare?"
5 Wood, "Secession," 109.
6 Bookman, *The Economics of Secession*, 37–41.
7 Michael Atkinson, "Public Policy and the New Institutionalism."
8 For an application to federalism in Canada, see Cairns, "The Governments and Societies of Canadian Federalism"; more generally, see Young, "Tectonic Policies and Political Competition."

CHAPTER NINE

1 Buchanan, *Secession*; Buchheit, *Secession*.
2 McNaught, "A Ghost at the Banquet: Could Quebec Secede Peacefully?"; Morton, "The Canadian Security Dimension," 69–75; Bercuson and Cooper, *Deconfederation*, esp. 148–56; Reid, *Canada Remapped*.
3 Latouche, "Le Québec est bien petit et le monde, bien grand"; Parti québécois, *Le Québec dans un monde nouveau*; Pierre Fortin, "How Economics Is Shaping the Constitutional Debate"; Proulx, "L'évolution de l'espace économique"; Young, "Does Globalization Make an Independent Quebec More Viable?"
4 Economic Council, *A Joint Venture*, 115–18.
5 Ibid., 90.
6 Ibid., 90–1.
7 Grady, *The Economic Consequences*, table 37, 160.
8 Pierre Fortin, "Le passage à la souveraineté," 452–3.
9 Québec, Commission sur l'avenir, Secrétariat, "Analyse pro forma des finances publiques," 393–566.
10 Economic Council, *A Joint Venture*, 84–5.
11 McCallum, *Canada's Choice*, app., 39–42.
12 Such a program might consist of a 15% increase in all taxes, a 10% cut in all transfer payments, a 15% reduction in public- and para-public-sector salaries, and a 5% cut in government employment (McCallum and Green, *Parting as Friends*, 45–9).
13 Côté, "Souveraineté," 28–33, 35.
14 Pierre Fortin, "Le passage à la souveraineté." And the consequence is that "bref, le 'party de l'indépendance' devrait être limité à une seule nuit et il faudrait avoir, au préalable, envoyé en détention préventive les politiciens patriotards portés sur la dépense somptuaire" (458).

(In short, the independence celebration had better be limited to one night, and beforehand it would be best to send to preventative detention any super-patriotic politicians inclined to extravagant spending.)

15 Economic Council, *A Joint Venture*, 85–6.
16 Royal Bank, *Unity or Disunity*, 23. This study includes a useful chart of the factors taken into account in other analyses (table 8).
17 Raynauld, "Les enjeux économiques de la souveraineté," 44–7.
18 McCallum and Green, *Parting as Friends*, app. A, 69.
19 Ibid., table A-2, 70.
20 The author's calculations using Economic Council estimates from *A Joint Venture*, 85.
21 Royal Bank, *Unity or Disunity*, 23.
22 Ibid., table 6.
23 Ibid., 28.
24 Grady, *The Economic Consequences*, table 37, 160.
25 Pierre Fortin, "A Comment," 87. Grady presents an "apocalypse scenario."
26 Côté, "Souveraineté."
27 McCallum and Green, *Parting as Friends*, 50–55 and app.B.
28 See the comments by Polèse, Fortin, Vaillancourt, and Proulx in ibid.
29 Courchene, *In Praise of Renewed Federalism*, 58; Bouchard, *Un nouveau parti*, 77–83.
30 Mansell and Schlenker, "Regional Analysis of Fiscal Balances," 249.
31 Royal Bank, *Unity or Disunity*, 28.
32 See Association des économistes québécois, "Mémoire à la Commission sur l'avenir politique et constitutionnel du Québec," 17–20.
33 Whitaker, "Quebec's Right to National Self-Determination," paper for the Community Membership Seminar, 12 September 1991, 10–13, as summarized in Monahan and Covello, *An Agenda for Constitutional Reform*, 90–1.
34 Turp argues, to the contrary, that a referendum could "in itself constitute a mechanism for amending the constitution" ("Quebec's Democratic Right," 107). Presumably, this would involve a popular consultation on a direct question such as "Are you in favour of Quebec becoming a sovereign state on 24 June 1996?" But whatever the question, to recognize the result as self-executing would require a decision by the Supreme Court that the constitution can be amended by unconstitutional means, which seems unlikely.
35 A brief synopsis of these options is found in Québec, Assemblée nationale, Commission d'étude, "La déclaration de souveraineté."
36 Finkelstein and Vegh, *The Separation of Quebec*, 36.
37 Leslie, "Options for the Future of Canada," 132. Leslie argues that probably the federal authorities would lose the capacity to govern,

the constitution would sooner or later become inoperative, and the various "Humpty-Dumpty" options (of sovereignty-association, a confederacy, or reconfederation) would quickly prove to be impossible. However, this analysis drastically telescopes the process of the transition and conflates a UDI with any declaration of intent to secede: these are very different.

38 The basic sources are Brossard, *L'accession à la souveraineté*; Finkelstein and Vegh, *The Separation of Quebec*, 33–66; Williams, *International Legal Effects of Secession*; Beaudoin and Vallée, "La reconnaissance internationale"; Turp, "Le droit à la sécession", Woehrling, "Les aspects juridiques"; and Bernier, "Le maintien de l'accès aux marchés."

39 Scott, "Secession or Reform?" 156.

40 Brossard, *L'accession à la souveraineté*, 182–3.

41 Hence, Brossard contends that only Quebec francophones, bearers of the rights of the "people," could participate in a decision to accede to sovereignty. He then suggests that Quebec francophones might expressly consent to non-members of the people participating in the collective decision (*L'accession à la souveraineté*, 182–5, 305). A further problem is that secession is difficult to justify when the criteria defining the people are only linguistic and cultural (see Buchanan, *Secession*, 52–64, esp. 61).

42 Turp, "Le droit à la sécession," 55. ("The will to live together contributes even more to affirming the status of a people.")

43 Turp, "Quebec's Democratic Right," 108–9.

44 Quebec, National Assembly, *Bill 150*, 3.

45 Progressive Conservative Party, *Resolution Guide*, 59, resolution 244. Note that this resolution referred to the right to self-determination of Quebec men and women, not of "Quebec."

46 Williams, *International Legal Effects of Secession*, 20.

47 International Covenant on Economic, Social and Cultural Rights and International Covenant on Civil and Political Rights, cited in Turp, "Quebec's Democratic Right," 109. Note how Bill 150 echoed this phrasing.

48 Williams, *International Legal Effects of Secession*, 16–17. See also Turp, "Quebec's Democratic Right," 112–13.

49 Brossard, *L'accession à la souveraineté*, 225–6.

50 Turp, "Le droit à la sécession," 58. ("What is more, a refusal to act according to the constitutional convention authorizing Quebec to accede to sovereignty would be a grave violation of democratic principles, and would permit the conclusion that the Canadian state was violating the right to self-determination of Quebec; as a result of this the Quebec people possess a right to self-determination in the international sphere, including the right to secession, and this would conform with the United Nations Charter as amplified by the

Declaration concerning Friendly Relations.") See also Turp, "Quebec's Democratic Right," 114.

51 Williams, *International Legal Effects of Secession*, 9.
52 Monahan and Costello, *An Agenda for Constitutional Reform*, 98.
53 Williams, *International Legal Effects of Secession*, 5–6; Finkelstein and Vegh, *The Separation of Quebec*, 43–5. Note, though, that while recognition of other states is strictly an executive prerogative of the federal government, the implementation of treaties or agreements with any state requires provincial legislation when they require action in areas of provincial jurisdiction. As well, recognition of Quebec by Ottawa arguably would violate the common-law rule that government cannot override the constitution. Recognition could alter Quebec's status as a province under the Constitution Acts. The federal government could, however, grant conditional recognition.
54 Islam, "Secessionist Self-Determination."
55 Buchheit, *Secession*, 216–45 and app. 2.
56 Morton, "Reflections on the Breakup", 97.
57 Beaudoin and Vallée, "La reconnaissance internationale," 198. ("More than any other state, France, the historic leader of the francophone world and permanent member of the Security Council, would have the legitimacy and weight to begin, when the time comes, the process of international recognition of Quebec, and to help the process gain irreversible momentum.")
58 Toy, "Vive le Canada uni."
59 Lemco, "American interests," 13–15.
60 Jockel, "The USA Reaction," 144.
61 Williams, *International Legal Effects of Secession*, 45–6.
62 Beaudoin and Vallée, "La reconnaissance internationale," 181.
63 Finkelstein and Vegh, *The Separation of Quebec*, 43.
64 The normative component of his argument – that Quebec's "revolution" should be suppressed – is a separate matter.
65 Turp, "Le droit à la sécession," 59. ("Faced with the desire of peoples for freedom, the law has never been a decisive obstacle.")
66 Quebec, Commission sur l'avenir, *Report*, 52–3.
67 McNaught, "A Ghost at the Banquet."
68 See, for instance, Coon-Come, "The Crees," 11–12; *Globe and Mail*, 31 July 1991; and *Globe and Mail*, 12 February 1992, reporting the appearance of Ovide Mercredi, grand chief of the Assembly of First Nations, before the Quebec National Assembly Committee on accession to sovereignty. In a Washington speech Chief Coon-Come stated, "We Cree do intend to make our own choice, to assert a right of self-determination at least equal to that claimed by Quebec. The establishment of an independent Quebec through the process they describe will entail violations of our basic human rights and

fundamental freedoms. Among these violations are denial of our nationality, denial of our right of self-determination as people, unilateral abrogation of our treaty rights, and the imposition of a new international border between us and our brethren in the rest of Canada" (*London Free Press*, 1 October 1994).

69 *Globe and Mail*, 15 October 1994.
70 Coon-Come, "The Crees," 11.
71 Morse, "Comparative Assessments of Indigenous Peoples."
72 Finkelstein and Vegh, *The Separation of Quebec*, 60–4.
73 Buchanan, "Quebec Secession and Native Territorial Rights," 2–4. See also Turpel, "Does the Road to Quebec Sovereignty Run through Aboriginal Territory?" 99.
74 Bercuson and Cooper, *Deconfederation*, 147–56.
75 Franck et al., "L'intégrité territoriale," 444–5.
76 Monahan, *Cooler Heads Shall Prevail*, 28–33.
77 McNeil, "Aboriginal Nations," esp. 109, 115, 260–1n35, and 266–7n70.
78 Turp, "Quebec's Democratic Right," 116–21, esp. 120.
79 Reid, *Canada Remapped*.
80 Woehrling, "La protection des droits," 144. But they might not (see Parti québécois, *Programme*, 163–6).
81 Emanueli, "L'accession du Québec," 110–13.
82 Williams, *International Legal Effects of Secession*, 26–9. It should be noted that under the existing section 6 of the Canadian Charter of Rights and Freedoms, non-resident citizens, like others, have the right to enter, remain in, and leave Canada, and also to take up residence and pursue a livelihood in any province.
83 Ibid., 42–3.
84 Ibid., 44–8. See also Finkelstein and Vegh, *The Separation of Quebec*, 64–6.
85 Ibid., 33.
86 Bernier, "Le maintien de l'accès aux marchés," 2–3.
87 Ibid., 4; Williams, *International Legal Effects of Secession*, 41–2.
88 Canada, *North American Free Trade Agreement: An Overview*, vi.
89 Ibid., 19.
90 Canada, *North American Free Trade Agreement*; art.2204(1), art.2001(4).
91 Scenario painting may also carry the implicit message that the truth can lie only between the two extremes (see Pierre Fortin, "The Threat of Quebec Sovereignty," 388–9).
92 Simeon, "Scenarios for Separation."
93 Ibid., 192.
94 Ibid., 189.
95 Turp, "Quebec's Democratic Right," 114–15, 120–1.
96 See Watts, "Survival or Disintegration," 55: "In practice it has proved difficult to work out a peaceful and rationally negotiated secession or

325 Notes to pages 113–20

disengagement of a unit from a federation. A federation which has been in existence for any length of time builds up many internal links and with them vested interests which have a large and emotional stake in their continuation. In addition, the confrontations and controversies which lead to the contemplation of secession inevitably generate a mounting frenzy of emotional responses with a momentum of their own, stirring up resentments and hatreds which make a coolly negotiated separation very difficult."

97 Young, "National Identification in English Canada," 83.
98 Bell, "Getting to the Table," 52–5.
99 Simeon, "Scenarios for Separation," 197.
100 Boothe and Harris, "Alternative Divisions of Federal Assets," 453–73; Jordan, "Sharing the Seaway System."
101 Banting, "If Quebec Separates," 167.
102 Ibid., 168.
103 Ibid., 169.
104 Bercuson and Cooper, Deconfederation, 141, 161–2.
105 Ibid., 147. The Quebec MPs would "immediately be eligible to receive their generous parliamentary pensions" (147).
106 Ibid., 147–56, 161–70.
107 Lemco, Turmoil in the Peaceable Kingdom, 55.
108 Ibid., 126, 131, 137, 168–9.
109 Parti québécois, Programme, 18. ("The act of birth of the sovereign Quebec.")
110 Parti québécois, La Souveraineté: Pourquoi? Comment?, 16, 19–33.
111 Ibid., 34.
112 Parti québécois, Le Québec dans un monde nouveau, 64–5, 79–84, 80: "En ces matières, l'intérêt du Québec et du Canada coïncide tout à fait." (In these matters, the interests of Quebec and Canada coincide perfectly.)
113 Quebec, Commission sur l'avenir, Report, 54.
114 This is not true of the whole exercise. Some members of the commission refused to sign the report, or did so only with addenda attached (see especially those of Charles-Albert Poissant and André Ouellet). Neither is it true of all the experts consulted by the commission (see the presentations of Bernard, Courchene, Dion, Fortin, Latouche, Lemieux, Polèse, Robertson, Taylor, and Watts, in Québec, Commission sur l'avenir, Les avis des spécialistes).
115 Quebec, National Assembly, Commission d'étude, Draft Report, 104–5. See also 7–8, 137.
116 Ibid., 63.
117 Ibid., 64.
118 Lamont, Breakup, 172.
119 Ibid., 149–225.
120 Granatstein, "Canada, Quebec and the World," 103–6.

121 Lamont, *Breakup*, 26.

122 Ibid., 244. It is worth noting that the initial hard-cover print run of this book was 14,000 copies.

123 Monahan, *Cooler Heads Shall Prevail*, 3.

124 Ibid., 39.

125 Ibid., 64.

126 Gibson, *Plan B*. In line with this effort, the author's populist convictions are evident throughout the work. He claims, for example, that "the gatekeepers to reform are those in charge of our governments, and they are mostly against change," and that "'Ottawa' is a set of specific interests that are paid for by all Canadians, but really work for themselves" (ibid., 6, 22).

127 Ibid., 114–19.

128 Ibid., 181.

129 Ibid., 133. In this fundamental rethinking, citizens will appreciate that "Canada" is not "Ottawa" (191). For Gibson, the foe is precisely Ottawa, "the whole system of power and control and networks that has not only run this country but believes it is uniquely qualified to do so" (144n6)

130 Ibid., 167–70.

131 Ibid., 186.

132 Ibid., 196–204.

133 Covell, *Thinking about the Rest of Canada*, 10.

134 Ibid., 11.

135 Monahan and Covello, *An Agenda for Constitutional Reform*, 99.

136 Ibid., 100.

137 Ibid.

138 Ibid., 100–4.

139 Thorburn, "Disengagement."

140 Ibid., 208.

141 Ibid., 204.

CHAPTER TEN

1 This chapter draws heavily on Young, "How Do Peaceful Secessions Happen?"

2 Schroeder, "On the Economic Viability of New Nation-States"; Etzioni, "The Evils of Self-Determination."

3 Buchanan, *Secession*; Heraclides, "Secession, Self-Determination and Nonintervention."

4 Wittman, "Nations and States"; Simard, "Compétition électorale"; Young, "The Political Economy of Secession."

5 Buchanan and Faith, "Secession and the Limits of Taxation"; Stéphane Dion, "Why Is Secession Rare?"; Hechter, "The Dynamics of Secession."

6 These cases are discussed in Franck, *Why Federations Fail*. The "neoclassical" appellation is from his concluding essay, "Why Federations Fail," 195. The other cases include the breakup of the West Indian Federation, the non-formation of the East African Federation, and the disintegration of Rhodesia and Nyasaland (the Central African Federation). As well, the secession of Iceland from Denmark (1944) is of some interest. See also Watts, *New Federations*, and Hicks, *Federalism*.

7 Watts, "Survival or Disintegration." See also, for example, Nafziger and Richter, "Biafra and Bangladesh," and Bookman, *The Economics of Secession*.

8 Bookman, *The Economics of Secession*, table 1.2, 31–4. She counts Malaysia-Singapore as a non-peaceful case, presumably because of the race riots that occurred around the secession; obviously, though, this one is at the margin of violence.

9 Here we leave aside a third class – the few instances, like Western Australia in 1933–35 and Nova Scotia in 1868 – where secessionist movements captured the support of a majority of the population or of elected representatives but were simply ignored or "waited out." The focus here is on cases where secession did occur.

10 Tihany, "The Austro-Hungarian Compromise," 115–16.

11 May, *The Hapsburg Monarchy*, 495–6n22; Huertas, *Economic Growth and Economic Policy*, table 8, 37–8.

12 May, *The Hapsburg Monarchy*, 34–6.

13 Wendt, *Cooperation in the Nordic Countries*, 21.

14 Lindgren, *Norway-Sweden*, 49–51.

15 Ibid., 62–5.

16 Ibid., 95–111.

17 Drake, "Singapore and Malaysia: The Monetary Consequences," 28.

18 Chan, *Singapore: The Politics of Survival*, 36–7.

19 Fletcher, *The Separation of Singapore*, 12–16.

20 See Watts, *New Federations*, 177, 257.

21 Fletcher, *The Separation of Singapore*, 16–23; Vreeland et al., *Area Handbook for Malaysia*, 74; Ongkili, *Nation-building in Malaysia*, 181; Lee, "Emergency Powers in Malaysia," 134–56.

22 Ongkili, *Nation-building in Malaysia*, 184–5.

23 Fletcher, *The Separation of Singapore*, 50–1, 56–66.

24 Lyon considers the possibility that the secession was a "contrived withdrawal" by Lee Kuan Yew; on balance, though, he agrees with most analysts that the event was an eviction (Lyon, "Separatism and Secession in the Malaysian Realm," 74–6).

25 May, *The Hapsburg Monarchy*, 34.

26 Lindgren, *Norway-Sweden*, 130–1.

27 See Watts, *New Federations*, 311–12.

28 Ongkili, *Nation-building in Malaysia*, 186.
29 Lindgren, *Norway-Sweden*, 133–4.
30 May, *The Hapsburg Monarchy*, 50–1; Tapié, *The Rise and Fall of the Hapsburg Monarchy*, 304–5.
31 Lindgren, *Norway-Sweden*, 189–90.
32 Ongkili, *Nation-building in Malaysia*, 187–90.
33 Lindgren, *Norway-Sweden*, 128. The committee refused to abide by the views of the ministry just before the decisive vote, but there was no ministerial crisis: "The times demanded that there be no constitutional or parliamentary conflicts."
34 Ibid., 149–51.
35 Ibid., 167; Andrén, *Government and Politics in the Nordic Countries*, 121.
36 Vreeland et al., *Area Handbook for Malaysia*, 75; Fletcher, *The Separation of Singapore*, 3.
37 Lindgren, *Norway-Sweden*, 155–66.
38 Means, *Malaysian Politics*, 294–5. The agreement is in Chan, *Singapore: The Politics of Survival*, 58–9.
39 Boyce, *Malaysia and Singapore in International Diplomacy*, 24–5, 88–92.
40 Vreeland et al., *Area Handbook for Malaysia*, 358–9; Chan, *Singapore: The Politics of Survival*, 41–7; Jenkins, "New Life in an Old Pact," 26–8.
41 Mason, *The Dissolution of the Austro-Hungarian Empire*.
42 Hence Deák's remark that "for us Austria's existence is just as necessary as our existence is for Austria" (Tihany, "The Austro-Hungarian Compromise," 118).
43 Lindgren, *Norway-Sweden*, 112–14, 127–31.
44 Ibid., 182–6.
45 Lindgren, *Norway-Sweden*, 145–51.
46 In fact, it was passed unanimously, the PAP members having absented themselves by prior arrangement.
47 Franck, "Why Federations Fail," 170.
48 Andrén, *Government and Politics in the Nordic Countries*, 97–8.
49 May, *The Hapsburg Monarchy*, 37–8.
50 Mason, *The Dissolution of the Austro-Hungarian Empire*, 16–18; May, *The Hapsburg Monarchy*, 46–69.
51 Ongkili, *Nation-building in Malaysia*, 194–5; Vreeland et al., *Area Handbook for Malaysia*, 94; Watts, *New Federations*, 234.
52 Chan, *Singapore: The Politics of Survival*, 48–51, 22–5; Bedlington, *Malaysia and Singapore*, 210–43.
53 Lindgren, *Norway-Sweden*, 235, 245–6.
54 Leistikow, "Co-operation between the Scandinavian Countries," 311–18.
55 Lindgren, *Norway-Sweden*, 7.
56 Wendt, *Cooperation in the Nordic Countries*; Solen, *The Nordic Council and Scandinavian Integration*, esp. ch. 3.

329   Notes to pages 143–52

57 Spiro, "The Federation of Rhodesia and Nyasaland," 80.
58 Franck, "East African Federation," 6–11, 17–18.
59 Chan, *Singapore: The Politics of Survival*, 29–32.
60 Pang and Lim, "Foreign Labour and Economic Development in Singapore."
61 Chan, *Singapore: The Politics of Survival*, 39.
62 Bedlington, *Malaysia and Singapore*, 247–8.
63 Chan, *Singapore: The Politics of Survival*, 33 n. 48; Vreeland et al., *Area Handbook for Malaysia*, 338.
64 Watts, "Survival or Disintegration," 69.

CHAPTER ELEVEN

1 This case is treated in much more detail in Young, *The Breakup of Czechoslovakia*.
2 Saladin, "Self-Determination, Minority Rights," 195–201.
3 Barbieri, "Czechoslovakia's Movement toward a New Constitution."
4 Pehe, "Czechoslovakia: An Abrupt Transition"; Draper, "New History of the Velvet Revolution."
5 Obrman, "Civic Forum Surges."
6 Musil, "Czechoslovakia in the Middle of Transition."
7 See Adam, "Transformation to a Market Economy."
8 Svec, "Czechoslovakia's Velvet Divorce"; Pehe, "Growing Slovak Demands."
9 Richard Rose, "Czechs and Slovaks Compared," Studies in Public Policy no. 198, Glasgow, University of Strathclyde, Centre for the Study of Public Policy, cited in Olson, "Dissolution of the State," table 1, 306.
10 Kusin, "Czechs and Slovaks," 6.
11 Pehe, "Referendum Controversy," 37. See also United States, Foreign Broadcast Information Service (hereafter cited as FBIS), 24 July 1992, 6.
12 Draper, "End of Czechoslovakia," 25.
13 Obrman, "Language Law Stirs Controversy."
14 Pehe, "Growing Slovak Demands," 5–6.
15 United States, FBIS, 14 March 1991, 17.
16 Ibid., 6 March 1991, 29–33.
17 Pehe, "Growing Slovak Demands," 7–8.
18 Obrman, "Further Discussions on the Future," 8.
19 Pehe, "Czechoslovak Federal Assembly Adopts Electoral Law," 6.
20 Pehe, "The State Treaty," 14.
21 Pehe, "Czechoslovakia's Changing Political Spectrum," 6.
22 United States, FBIS, 18 February 1992, 11.
23 Ibid., 19 February 1992, 4.

24 Wightman, "The Czechoslovak Parliamentary Elections."
25 *Keesing's Record of World Events*, June 1992, 38944-5.
26 *Facts on File*, 11 June 1992, 421.
27 Obrman, "Czechoslovakia: Stage Set for Disintegration," 26-7.
28 *New York Times*, 17 June 1992.
29 United States, FBIS, 22 June 1992, 12.
30 Ibid., 22 June 1992, 20.
31 Obrman, "Czechoslovakia's New Governments," 3.
32 Pehe, "Scenarios for Disintegration," 30.
33 Obrman, "Slovakia Declares Sovereignty," 25.
34 United States, FBIS, 16 June 1992, 8.
35 Obrman, "Slovakia Declares Sovereignty," 28.
36 United States, FBIS, 23 July 1992, 9.
37 Pehe, "Czechs and Slovaks Prepare to Part," 14.
38 Ibid., 15.
39 Barbieri, "Czechoslovakia's Movement toward a New Constitution,"
    117–18.
40 Pehe, "Bid for Slovak Sovereignty," 13.
41 Pehe, "Growing Slovak Demands," 6–7.
42 Ibid., 8.
43 This report, as well as two others, is discussed in Martin, "Slovakia:
    Calculating the Cost."
44 Pehe, "Bid for Slovak Sovereignty," 13.
45 Obrman, "Czechoslovakia's New Governments," 5.
46 *New York Times*, 7 June 1992.
47 United States, FBIS, 22 June 1992, 12.
48 *Financial Times* (London), 22 June 1992.
49 United States, FBIS, 18 June 1992, 3.
50 Obrman, "Czechoslovakia's New Governments," 5.
51 *Facts on File*, 23 July 1992, 553. The foreign debt was $9.3 billion,
    mostly owed to international agencies and foreign governments.
52 Obrman, "Czechoslovakia: A Messy Divorce," 3.
53 Pehe, "The New Slovak Government."
54 Obrman, "Czechoslovakia's New Governments," 5–6.
55 United States, FBIS, 1 September 1992, 10.
56 Obrman, "Czechoslovakia: A Messy Divorce," 3.
57 Pehe, "Czechoslovak Parliament Votes to Dissolve Federation," 4.
58 Young, *The Breakup of Czechoslovakia*, 40–63.

CHAPTER TWELVE

1 The best general account is Russell, *Constitutional Odyssey*.
2 Monahan, *Meech Lake*.
3 McRoberts and Monahan, *The Charlottetown Accord*.

4 Cairns, "The Charter, Interest Groups, Executive Federalism," 20.

5 In the wake of the PQ victory, a Southam–Angus Reid poll found 33% choosing national unity as the country's most pressing problem, almost matching the proportion choosing "jobs" (*London Free Press*, 5 October 1994).

6 Adams and Lennon, "The Public's View of the Canadian Federation," fig. 5.3.

7 Stéphane Dion, "The Importance of the Language Issue."

8 Quebec, Ministère des finances, *1993–94 Budget*, tables B.a.3, c.13, and c.14.

9 Cloutier, Guay, and Latouche, *Le Virage*, 31–73.

10 Johnston, et al., "The People and the Charlottetown Accord," 35.

11 Cloutier, Guay, and Latouche, *Le Virage*, 169.

12 Pinard, "The Secessionist Option," 2. Between 1980 and 1989, support for sovereignty-association ranged between 36% and 42%, but it rose to 60% in 1990 (Pinard, "The Dramatic Reemergence," table 2).

13 Stéphane Dion, "Why Is Secession Rare?" 12.

14 Pinard, "The Dramatic Reemergence," 487–8; Nemni, *Canada in Crisis*, 15–18.

15 Pinard, "The Secessionist Option," 2, reporting results from a CROP survey. See also Cloutier, Guay, and Latouche, *Le virage*, 45, and Pinard, "The Dramatic Reemergence," 481–2.

16 Johnston et al., "The People and the Charlottetown Accord," 42–3 n20.

17 Blais and Nadeau, "To Be or Not to Be Sovereignist," 96.

18 Pinard, "The Secessionist Option," 4.

19 Blais, Crête, and Lachapelle, "L'élection québécois de 1985," table 3. Again, the form of the poll question can be important. Even thinking more concretely about casting a ballot can diminish support. Questions asking how people would vote in a referendum show about 5% less support for sovereignty than questions asking about general attitudes towards this constitutional option (Blais, "Will Quebec Secede?").

20 Cairns, "The Politics of Constitutional Renewal in Canada," 135.

21 *Globe and Mail*, 5 October 1994.

22 Reform Party of Canada, *Blue Sheet*.

23 Archer and Ellis, "Opinion Structure of Party Activists," 297.

24 Laycock, "Reforming Canadian Democracy," 226.

25 Mr Manning's initial speech in the House of Commons failed to mention the constitution at all (Canada, House of Commons, *Debates*, 19 January 1994, 45–7). In contrast, his speech to the Reform convention in October 1994 was built around the theme of a New Canada that would provide a "third option" between separatism and

status quo federalism (Manning, "A New and Better Home for Canadians," 4–11). See also Simpson *Faultlines*, 123–6.

26 *Globe and Mail*, 19 October 1994.
27 Blais, "Quebec: Raising the Stakes," 10–12.
28 Fournier, *Autopsie du lac Meech*, 201–2; Bourgault, *Now or Never!* 58, 93–99.
29 Manning, "A New and Better Home for Canadians," 9–10.
30 Bourgault, *Now or Never!* 127–32.
31 Quebec, Commission sur l'avenir, *Report*, 86.
32 Mr Bouchard has called this a "quasi-unanimous repudiation by the Quebec National Assembly" (Canada, House of Commons, *Debates*, 19 January 1994, 35).
33 Blais and Crête, "Pourquoi l'opinion publique au Canada."
34 Fortin, "The Threat of Quebec Sovereignty"; Imbeau, "Le compromis."
35 Whitaker, "The Dog That Never Barked," 109.
36 "Le Canada dans le peau," 21–8.
37 Blais and Nadeau, "To Be or Not to Be Sovereignist," 95–6.
38 See Simpson, *Faultlines*, 303–4.
39 The strategies and outcomes here have been explored more comprehensively in Young, "The Political Economy of Secession."
40 Cairns, "Constitutional Change and the Three Equalities," 95.
41 *Globe and Mail*, 26 and 27 May 1994, 17 May 1994.
42 Parti québécois, *La Souveraineté: Pourquoi? Comment?* 35. ("As a strategy, federal politicians might be tempted to say now that they will not negotiate, in order to dissuade Quebecers from supporting sovereignty. But when the event occurs they will change their attitude, because of political and economic realities.") See also Tremblay, "Constitutional Political Economy," 77–8: "Here again, it is necessary to distinguish statements and actions before and after secession. It could indeed be good tactics for some politicians and opinion leaders in English Canada to engage in some posturing to influence the issue for an eventual sovereignty referendum in Quebec ... Threatened political empires always resort to intimidation to preserve their hegemony ... Yet since Toronto – and Ontario in general – is the hub of interregional corporate, commercial, financial, and banking activities, east and west of the Ottawa River, such a dismantling of the common market and monetary union would clearly be a case of shooting oneself in the foot!"
43 André Blais has argued that any entry of Aboriginal issues into the referendum debate would increase support for sovereignty ("Will Quebec Secede?"). For an analysis of why Quebecers are so sensitive to this issue, see Young, "Aboriginal Inherent Rights," 37–41.
44 Young, "Le Canada hors Québec: Voudrait-il cooperer?" More generally, see Axelrod, *The Evolution of Cooperation*.

45 Julius Grey, "Winning Quebec for Canada," 21.

46 Referendums in Slovenia, Croatia, Lithuania, Estonia and Latvia found over 70% of voters favouring sovereignty. See Lukic, "Twilight of the Federations," 581–2.

47 Reform Party of Canada, *Blue Sheet*, 3.

48 Reid, *Canada Remapped*, 67–100.

49 Maclean's/Decima Poll, "Cross-Canada Opinions," 66. When the question asked, however, was whether force by Canada was acceptable "to protect its interests in Quebec," the figure rose to 35%.

50 Latouche, "Canada: The New Country," 332.

51 Preston Manning has stated that Mr Chrétien would have to resign after a Yes vote, because of his failure to defend the status quo successfully, and because he would be in a conflict of interest (*Le Devoir*, 26 May 1994).

52 Robertson, "The Atlantic Provinces," 116–17; Gibson, *Plan B*, 117–19.

53 Bouchard, *Un nouveau parti*, 92–5, 117–20.

54 *Globe and Mail*, 16 September 1994.

55 A recent poll found that "if Quebec became a sovereign state" 27% of Quebecers thought it would not issue passports, 20% thought they would still elect MPs, 31% thought Quebec would still be part of Canada, and 40% thought they would keep their Canadian citizenship (*Globe and Mail*, 3 June 1994).

56 The poll asked, "If Quebec decided to separate, do you think the rest of Canada should do everything it can to convince them to stay, or just let them go?" In ROC, 49% chose the first option, while 50% favoured letting "them" go (Maclean's/Decima Poll, "Cross-Canada Opinions," 65).

57 In 1994, 64% were in favour of transferring powers to all provinces in order to keep Quebec in the federation, but only 17% would extend special status to Quebec for the same end (Maclean's/Decima Poll, "In Search of Unity," 19). See also the *Globe and Mail*, 22 April 1991: 76% of respondents in ROC opposed special powers for Quebec, even "if that's what it takes to keep Quebec within Canada." As for the decentralization of powers, it should be noted that while 55% of people in ROC favoured the Charlottetown Accord proposal to transfer powers to the provinces, this was in the context of a much larger package, and 27% still opposed this very modest transfer of jurisdiction (Gallup Canada, *Gallup Report*, 24 September 1992).

58 Lloyd Atkinson, "A Comment," 53.

59 Bank of Canada, *Bank of Canada Review, Winter 1993–1994*, tables F1, F7, and G6. This assumes gross new bond issues of $50.04 billion, as they were in 1993.

60 Whitaker, "Life after Separation."

61 Well over 90% of Canadians consider the U.S. health care system to be inferior: Gallup Canada, *Gallup Report*, 13 September 1993.

62 Maclean's/CTV Poll, "Voices of Canada," 44. See also Maclean's/CTV Poll, "How We Differ," 11: in late 1993 a survey question asked whether respondents agreed with the statement that "Canada would not be any worse off it became part of the United States." In no province in ROC did more than 29% agree with the statement. The percentage agreeing was particularly low in the western provinces, where it ranged from 11% to 20%

63 Young, "National Identification in English Canada."

64 Dasko, "The Ties That Bound," 8.

65 Gallup Canada, *Gallup Report*, 13 August 1991.

66 Ibid., 2 December 1993.

67 Maclean's/CTV poll, "How We Differ," 11.

68 Maclean's/Decima Poll, "In Search of Unity," 18.

69 Canada, *Statutes*, 1988, ch. 29, s. 3.

70 Ibid., part 2.

71 Ibid., s. 25 (3).

72 As a province of Canada still, Quebec could also avail itself of the "Aid of the Civil Power" provisions in the National Defence Act. When riot or disturbance occurs or is thought likely, this permits the attorney general of a province to "require" that the Canadian forces be called out on service. The Act leaves some discretion to the chief of the defence staff about the nature of the response, but stipulates that he "shall" call out the forces he thinks necessary to suppress or prevent riots or disturbances (Canada, *Revised Statutes*, ch. N–5, ss. 274–85).

73 Gibson, *Plan B*, 37.

74 Monahan and Covello, *An Agenda for Constitutional Reform*, 118. The group took this position despite their erroneous view that Ontario's economic links with Quebec outweigh those with the other eight provinces (116).

75 Non-MPs have served on parliamentary committees in the past as non-voting members but with full rights to speak and to question witnesses. Ministers have also sat on them, as voting members (See Fraser, Dawson, and Holtby, *Beauchesne's Rules*, 224).

76 Brown, "The Evolving Role of the Provinces."

77 Richards, "The Canadian Constitution and International Economic Relations."

78 As Fry puts it, the "strategic-military implications of an independent Quebec for the United States are presently quite minor, and the North American relationship would continue to be relatively secure with or without a new nation along the 49th parallel" (*Canada's Unity Crisis*, 3).

79 Lamont, *Breakup*, 230–7. The author portrays American policy makers as torn by a request from some province to join the union. On the one

hand, they would not want to fragment the rest of Canada, absorb people difficult to assimilate, upset the domestic political balance, or take on a financial burden; on the other hand, there are the defence benefits and the resources, especially water: they opt for admission.

80 Jockel notes that "the ability of the United States to substitute its forces for Canada's, if need be, is very great"; that is, the United States could insist on access to Canada and Quebec if the Canadian Armed Forces could not fulfil their defence obligations ("The USA Reaction," 146).

81 Wonnacott, "Reconstructing North American Free Trade," especially 31–8 on the Auto Pact.

82 Jockel claims it would be "astonishing" if the USA did not favour extending the trade agreement to a sovereign Quebec (*If Canada Breaks Up*, 24).

CHAPTER THIRTEEN

1 As the Parti québécois will repeat during the referendum campaign, "En ces matières, l'intérêt du Québec et du Canada coïncide tout à fait" (In these matters, the interests of Quebec and Canada coincide perfectly). See Parti québécois, *Le Québec dans un monde nouveau*, 80.

2 Sometimes this fact is ignored in English Canada too. Daniel Drache, for example, strictly identifies noncooperation between Canada and Quebec with revenge ("Negotiating with Québec," 20).

3 Gibson, *Plan B*, 111 (Emphasis in original).

4 Haydon, "General Security Analysis of the Scenarios," 29.

5 Canada, *Revised Statutes*, ch. N-5, ss. 14, 20, 23; Canada, Department of National Defence, *The Queen's Regulations and Orders*, art. 6.04.

6 Russell, "The End of Mega Constitutional Politics," 218.

7 Reid, *Canada Remapped*, 3, citing a June 1991 Angus Reid poll that found 82% of Quebecers opposed to territorial partition.

8 Montreal *Gazette*, 19 May 1994. For Mr. Irwin's comments, see the Globe and Mail, 18 May 1994.

9 Bercuson and Cooper, *Deconfederation*, 148–53; Reid, *Canada Remapped*, 37–66.

10 McRoberts, "Protecting the Rights," 184–5.

11 Boothe, Johnston, and Powys-Lybbe, "Dismantling Confederation," 30–6.

12 Ibid., tables 3, 5, 6.

13 Parizeau, "What Does Sovereignty Association Mean?" Notes for a speech to a joint meeting of the Empire Club of Canada and the Canadian Club, Toronto, 11 December 1990, 10, cited in Grady, *The National Debt*, 8.

14 Boothe and Harris, "Alternative Divisions," 462–6.
15 Chant, "Dividing the Debt," 90.
16 Monahan, *Cooler Heads Shall Prevail*, 49–50.
17 Canada, Treasury Board, *Directory of Federal Real Property*; Canada, Task Force on Program Review, *Real Property*.
18 Some of the difficulties in this approach are described in Ip and Robson, "Liquidating the Federal Balance Sheet."
19 Parti québécois, *Le Québec dans un monde nouveau*, 69–70, 83.
20 Quebec, Commission d'étude, *Draft Report*, 12.
21 Canada, *Citizenship Act*, ss. 3, 8. Note that under this legislation, people born outside Canada to Canadian citizens can opt to remain Canadian, before reaching the age of 28, only upon making an application to do so and either residing in Canada for a year before applying or establishing "a substantial connection with Canada."
22 Turpel, "The Charlottetown Discord," 142.
23 Parti québécois, *Programme*, 29–33.
24 *Globe and Mail*, 19 October 1994.
25 A COMPAS poll found 81% of ROC respondents agreeing that Quebec Aboriginals should have the right to determine their future by referendum (*Financial Post*, 26 June 1994). Generally, though, support for Aboriginal rights may be broad but shallow in English Canada. In ROC, the percentage endorsing the Charlottetown Accord provisions about Native self-government was lower, at 55%, than the proportions supporting an elected Senate (82%) and stronger economic ties within Canada (82%). See Gallup Canada, *Gallup Report*, 24 September 1992.
26 See Hogg, *Constitutional Law of Canada*, 216–17, on the divisibility of the crown and the Alberta Indians case.
27 Parti québécois, *Le Québec dans un monde nouveau*, 67.
28 McRoberts, "Protecting the Rights," 186–8.
29 In ROC there is much stronger mass support for anglophone rights in Quebec than for francophone rights elsewhere. See Sniderman et al., "Political Culture and the Problem of Double Standards," 263–9.
30 Bland, "Defence North of the 49th Parallel," 211.
31 Lemco, *Turmoil in the Peaceable Kingdom*, 159.
32 Dauphin and Slosar note these problems and conclude that a customs union is the most that could be negotiated during the transition ("Étude des modalités," 172–6).
33 This sentiment is not found only in the West. Pierre Martin has analysed polls that investigated attitudes towards post-secession economic association. The responses vary according to the precise question posed and the range of possible response options; generally, though, a consistent 21–24% in ROC opposed any association. About 50–60% favoured a close or loose association. An Angus Reid poll in

June 1994, however, found 52% opposed to a formal economic union. These opinions are therefore volatile, and they are also strongly related to the view that Quebec would lose economically from sovereignty and that it would lose more than Canada. See Martin, "Association after Sovereignty?" tables 1, 2.

34 *La Presse*, 3 December 1993. ("One mustn't dream and ask for the moon ... So, already not very happy that Quebec is becoming sovereign, these English Canadians, because of our pretty face, in order to make us happy, or to vaguely imitate what some people think is happening in Western Europe, would agree to turn their political system upside down – they, who have always refused to give Quebec the tiniest extra power, and who believe that the equality of the provinces is a sacred principle.") See also the *Globe and Mail*, 20 May 1994.

35 Informetrica, *Financial Sector: Deposit-Taking Institutions.*

36 For a comprehensive treatment of legal problems in this sector and of the advantages of mutual recognition, see Coulombe, "La souveraineté du Québec et les institutions financières."

37 Informetrica, *Supply Management: Dairy*, 15.

38 Quebec is a net exporter of poultry and an importer of eggs (Informetrica, *Supply Management: Poultry and Eggs*).

39 Howitt, "Constitutional Reform and the Bank of Canada," 403–7.

40 Canada, Federal-Provincial Committee, *Agreement between the Government of Canada and the Gouvernement du Québec.*

41 Canada, Employment and Immigration Canada, *Canada-Québec Accord.*

42 Informetrica, *Registered Pension Plans*, 11.

CHAPTER FOURTEEN

1 See Hogg, *Constitutional Law*, 51–77.

2 For an argument to the contrary, see Hogg, *Constitutional Law*, 102–3 and note 109.

3 Finkelstein and Vegh, *The Separation of Quebec*, 6.

4 Hogg, *Constitutional Law* 66, 186. See also note 56 and references cited therein.

5 The argument turns on what is "an amendment to the Constitution of Canada," the wording that introduces both sections 38 and 41 of CA1982. The constitution is defined in section 52(2) of CA1982 to include the Constitution Acts, the Acts and orders listed in the schedule to CA1982, and amendments to the above. Hogg considers this list to be exhaustive, despite the schedule not including many Acts and orders commonly thought to be part of the constitution, because there must be some defined limit on what is the supreme law

of the land, entrenched in the constitution and alterable only through the amendment process. The Supreme Court Act is not listed in the schedule, so Hogg concludes that it is amendable by the federal Parliament alone. But this seems wrong. As Hogg recognizes, the definition of the constitution in section 52(2) uses the term "includes," which implies non-exhaustiveness. As well, section 55, which provides for the translation of the instruments in the schedule, states that a "French version of the *portions* of the Constitution referred to in the schedule shall be prepared" (emphasis added).

6 Banting and Simeon, "Introduction," 20.

7 These will be inflammatory matters. See Hodgins, "The Northern Boundary of Quebec," 148: Quebec could not assume full jurisdiction over its northern lands and Aboriginal peoples without Canada's "cowardly connivance."

8 Finkelstein and Vegh, *The Separation of Quebec,* 8–32.

9 But see Hogg, *Constitutional Law* 102: there is no statement in the constitution that the union cannot be dissolved, "but the absence of any provisions in the Constitution authorizing secession makes clear that no unilateral secession is possible."

10 Finkelstein and Vegh, *The Separation of Quebec,* 11.

11 Ibid., 13.

12 Reesor, *The Canadian Constitution,* 382–5.

13 Finkelstein and Vegh, *The Separation of Quebec,* 26. If the amendments were so sweeping as effectively to terminate the fiduciary relationship between the crown and some Aboriginal peoples, the courts might rule that this could not be accomplished without both consultation and consent.

14 Legal arguments on these matters have continued. The main case concerns the Native Women's Association of Canada (NWAC), which went to court during the consultations leading to the Charlottetown Accord, seeking an order to bar further federal-government disbursements to the four national Native organizations until NWAC received equal funding, and also to require that NWAC be admitted to the constitutional review process. The main grounds were freedom of speech and gender equality, under sections 2(b) and 28 of CA1982. The arguments were that the four major Aboriginal organizations discriminated against women and were advocating that the Charter not apply to Native governments, which argument, if successful, would allow for further discrimination against women by those governments. Without funding and participation in the consultative process, NWAC could not argue effectively that the Charter should apply to Native governments. In March 1992, this order was refused by the Federal Court (*Canadian Native Law Reporter* 4 [1992]: 59–70.) In August 1992, however, the Federal Court of Appeal upheld NWAC's

appeal: the government had "accorded the advocates of male dominated Aboriginal self-governments a preferred position in the exercise of an expressive activity which had the effect of restricting the freedom of expression of Aboriginal women in a manner that was offensive to ss.2(b) and 28 of the Charter" (*Canadian Native Law Reporter* 4 [1992]:72). With respect to participation in conferences, however, the court held that no individual had the right to funding or to be present at constitutional conferences. More important, it reaffirmed earlier judgments about the courts' lack of power to intervene in legislative processes. The Charter provides grounds for court intervention in consultation or policy development, but not in the process of amending the constitution. This process, "as a legislative process, begins not later than when First Ministers are convened to agree upon a constitutional resolution they will put to their legislatures." In the words of Justice Mahoney, "I frankly cannot conceive of even Charter based circumstances in which a court could properly interfere, however indirectly, with the convening of a First Ministers' Conference or any other purely intergovernmental meeting and dictate to them whom they ought to invite to their table" (*Canadian Native Law Reporter* 4[1992]:87–8). In late October 1994, the Supreme Court unanimously overturned the main decision of the Federal Court of Appeal in favour of NWAC. On Native peoples' participation generally, see Turpel, "The Charlottetown Discord," 132–5.

15 Monahan, "The Sounds of Silence," 243.
16 Gibbins, "Speculations on a Canada without Quebec," 266.
17 Ibid., 267.
18 Gibson, *Plan B*; Cameron, "A Constitution for English Canada." See also Russell, "Towards a New Constitutional Process." On the alternative forms of such assemblies and the advantages and pitfalls of setting them up, see Fafard and Reid, *Constituent Assemblies*, esp. 44–7.
19 Gibbins, "Speculations on a Canada without Quebec," 271: the official-languages sections of the Charter "would be repealed at the first opportunity."
20 As for sitting senators from Quebec, under CA1867, section 31(5), they will "cease to be qualified" in respect of residence. Their places will become vacant: while the governor general "shall" summon some person to fill a vacancy, all questions concerning vacancies are settled by the Senate itself (according to section 33), and this should end the issue. Another matter is section 26, which deals with extraordinary additions to the Senate: it will be amended to provide for additions of three or six senators, representing equally the three divisions (with section 27 amended accordingly), and section 28 will read that the number of senators will never exceed 86.

21 Hogg, *Is the Constitution of Canada Ready*, 20. On the prospects for provincial bloc voting in the Senate, see also Richard Janda, *Re-balancing the Federation*.
22 Gibson, *Plan B*, 59.
23 On the intricacies of Senate reform, and, by extension, on the difficulty of reaching consensus on any specific amendments, see David Elton, "The Charlottetown Accord Senate."
24 Unless the Electoral Boundaries Readjustment Act is amended so as to accelerate the one-year adjustment period to the new constituencies proposed in mid-1994 by provincial commissions under Canada's chief electoral officer, a federal election in 1995 would be fought on the basis of the existing ridings, with the current distribution of seats. Were the Act to be changed or the election delayed, the new House of Commons would have 226 seats without Quebec; nevertheless, no percentage reported in table 6 would be altered by more than 0.6%. For an account of the 1985 changes to the Representation Act, see Sancton, "Eroding Representation by Population."
25 See, for example, Kilgour and Levesque, "The Canadian Constitutional Amending Formula."
26 This last combination is just at the cusp of having 50% of the population.
27 Canada, Senate and House of Commons, *A Renewed Canada*, 67–9.

CHAPTER FIFTEEN

1 See Watts, "Canada in Question, Again."
2 Simpson, "The Referendum and Its Aftermath," 199.
3 *Globe and Mail*, 27 and 28 September 1994. This structure puts the core group of six at the centre of fourteen other cabinet ministers and the fourteen regional delegates.
4 Parti québécois, *La Souveraineté: Pourquoi? Comment?* 3 ("the responsibility of throwing into operation the process that must lead to sovereignty").
5 *Globe and Mail*, 6 October 1994.
6 *Globe and Mail*, 29 September 1994.
7 *Toronto Star*, 19 June 1994.
8 Canada, House of Commons, *Debates*, 19 January 1994, 34.
9 Mr Bouchard often provokes an almost visceral negative reaction among English Canadians. The more calm and reasonable he attempts to be – as when he insists that the election of the Bloc and the prospect of sovereignty offer Canada and Quebec "a unique opportunity to seal a new relationship based on truth and respect" – the more irritation he seems to create (*La Presse*, 26 October 1994). A majority in ROC agrees that "there is no role for a separatist like

Lucien Bouchard in the federal Parliament," and only 22% thought that the Bloc should form the official opposition (*Globe and Mail*, 18 October 1993; Gallup Canada, *Gallup Report*, 18 November 1993). But antipathy in ROC towards the Bloc leader seems more widespread and intense than can be accounted for by disagreement with his goal of sovereignty or by rejection of the "two-nations" view of Canada that he powerfully articulates.

10 By mid-1994, Reform support had weakened considerably since the 1993 federal election. The party was less popular in British Columbia than the Liberals and was only marginally ahead of them in Alberta. By September 1994, its support had dropped to 10% nationally, as opposed to 19% in the election (*Globe and Mail*, 29 September 1994; *London Free Press*, 16 September 1994).

11 Cairns, "An Election to be Remembered," 227.

12 *Globe and Mail*, 9 June 1994.

13 In Simeon and Janigan, *Toolkits*, 114.

14 Manning, "Leadership for Changing Times," 80.

15 Before the 1994 election, 50% of Quebecers thought the PQ would "have the right to begin the process of sovereignty" if it won, but 37% disagreed (*Globe and Mail*, 15 July 1994).

16 *London Free Press*, 13 October 1994.

17 As Mr Manning has said about sovereignty-association, "There is no market for that outside Quebec. There is a greater market for straight independence" (Simpson, *Faultlines*, 140).

CHAPTER SIXTEEN

1 Havel, *Summer Meditations*, 4.

CHAPTER SEVENTEEN

1 Watts, *New Federations*, 103–10, and "Survival or Disintegration"; Hicks, *Federalism*, 171–96; Lemco, *Political Stability*, 16–18.

2 Mancur Olson, *The Rise and Decline of Nations*.

3 Lemco, *Political Stability*, 50.

4 Hicks, *Federalism*, 181–5; Watts, "Survival or Disintegration."

5 Watts, *New Federations*, 106; Hicks, *Federalism*, 179; Lemco, *Political Stability*, 49, 53.

6 In the only quantitative analysis of federal stability, the relationship between secession potential and the number and size of units disappears when the degree of constitutional centralization is introduced into the equation (Lemco, *Political Stability*, 78–9).

7 Ibid., 150–1; Watts, "Survival or Disintegration."

8 Parti québécois, *Programme*, 67–86.

9 *Globe and Mail*, 4 August 1994.

Selected Bibliography

Adam, Jan. "Transformation to a Market Economy in the Former Czechoslovakia." *Europe-Asia Studies* 45, no. 4 (1993): 627–45.

Adams, Michael, and Mary Jane Lennon. "The Public's View of the Canadian Federation." In Ronald L. Watts and Douglas M. Brown, eds., *Canada: The State of the Federation 1990*, 97–108. Kingston: Institute of Intergovernmental Relations 1990.

Allaire Report (Report of the Constitutional Committee of the Quebec Liberal Party). *A Québec Free to Choose*. For submission to the 25th Convention, 28 January 1991.

Andrén, Nils. *Government and Politics in the Nordic Countries*. Stockholm: Almqvist & Wiksell 1964.

Archer, J.A. "The Prairie Perspective." In R.M. Burns, ed., *One Country or Two?* 231–51. Montreal: McGill-Queen's University Press 1971.

Archer, Keith, and Faron Ellis. "Opinion Structure of Party Activists: The Reform Party of Canada." *Canadian Journal of Political Science* 27, no. 2 (1994): 277–308.

Association des économistes québécois. "Mémoire à la Commission sur l'avenir politique et constitutionnel du Québec," November 1991.

Atkinson, Lloyd C. "A Comment." In David E.W. Laidler and William B.P. Robson, eds., *Two Nations, One Money?* Canada Round Series no. 3, 53–5. Toronto: C.D. Howe Institute 1991.

Atkinson, Michael. "Public Policy and the New Institutionalism." In Atkinson, ed., *Governing Canada: Institutions and Public Policy*, 17–45. Toronto: Harcourt Brace Jovanovich 1993.

Axelrod, Robert. *The Evolution of Cooperation*. New York: Basic Books 1984.

Bank of Canada. *Bank of Canada Review, Spring 1993*. Ottawa: Bank of Canada 1993.

– *Bank of Canada Review, Winter 1993–1994*. Ottawa: Bank of Canada 1994.

Banting, Keith G. "Introduction: The Politics of Constitutional Change." In Banting and Richard Simeon, eds., *Redesigning the State: The Politics of Constitutional Change*, 1–29. Toronto: University of Toronto Press 1985.

– "If Quebec Separates: Restructuring Northern North America." In R. Kent Weaver, ed., *The Collapse of Canada?* 159–78. Washington: The Brookings Institution 1992.

Barbieri, Roberta. "Czechoslovakia's Movement toward a New Constitution: The Challenge of Establishing a Democratic, Multinational State." *New York Law School Journal of International and Comparative Law* 13, no. 1 (1992): 94–124.

Beaudoin, Louise, and Jacques Vallée. "La reconnaissance internationale d'un Québec souverain." In Alain-G. Gagnon and François Rocher, eds., *Répliques aux détracteurs de la souveraineté du Québec*, 181–205. Montreal: VLB éditeur 1992.

Bedlington, Stanley S. *Malaysia and Singapore: The Building of New States*. Ithaca, N.Y.: Cornell University Press 1978.

Bell, David. "Getting to the Table: The Prenegotiation of Deconfederation." In Daniel Drache and Roberto Perin, eds., *Negotiating with a Sovereign Québec*, 47–57. Toronto: James Lorimer 1992.

Bellemare, Diane. "Réponses aux questions posées par la Commission sur l'avenir politique et constitutionnel du Quebec." In Quebec, Commission sur l'avenir, *Les avis des spécialistes*, Working Paper no. 4, 21–44. Quebec 1991.

Bercuson, David Jay, and Barry Cooper. *Deconfederation: Canada without Quebec*. Toronto: Key Porter 1991.

Berger, Thomas R. "Quebec's Rendezvous with Independence." In J.L. Granatstein and Kenneth McNaught, eds., *"English Canada" Speaks Out*, 309–21. Toronto: Doubleday 1991.

Bergeron, Gérard. "Projet d'un nouveau Commonwealth canadien." *Journal of Canadian Studies* 12, no. 3 (July 1977): 8–17.

Bernier, Ivan. "Le maintien de l'accès aux marchés extérieurs: Certaines questions juridiques soulevées dans l'hypothèse de la souveraineté du Québec." In Quebec, Commission sur l'avenir, *Éléments d'analyse économique*, Working Paper no. 1, 1–17. Quebec 1991.

Bickerton, James. "Alternative Futures: Atlantic Canada and the Constitutional Crisis." Paper presented at the annual meeting of the

Atlantic Provinces Political Studies Association, Saint John, 25–7
October 1991.

Blais, André. "The Quebec Referendum: Quebeckers Say No." In Kenneth
McRoberts and Patrick J. Monahan, eds., *The Charlottetown Accord, the
Referendum and the Future of Canada*, 200–7. Toronto: University of
Toronto Press 1993.

– "Quebec: Raising the Stakes." Paper presented at the annual meeting of
the Canadian Political Science Association, Calgary, 12 June 1994.

– Will Quebec Secede?" Panel discussion, McMaster University, 19
September 1994.

Blais, André, and Jean Crête. "Pourquoi l'opinion publique au Canada
anglais a-t-elle rejeté l'Accord du lac Meech." In Raymond Hudon and
Réjean Pelletier, eds., *L'engagement intellectuel: Mélanges en l'honneur de
Léon Dion*, 385–400. Ste-Foy: Presses de l'Université Laval 1991.

Blais, André, and Richard Nadeau. "To Be or Not to Be Sovereignist:
Quebeckers' Perennial Dilemma." *Canadian Public Policy* 18, no. 1
(1992): 89–103.

Blais, André, Jean Crête, and Guy Lachapelle. "L'élection québécoise de
1985: Un bilan des sondages." *Canadian Journal of Political Science* 19,
no. 2 (1986): 323–36.

Bland, Douglas. "Defence North of the 49th Parallel: What Happens to
the Military?" In Daniel Drache and Roberto Perin, eds., *Negotiating
with a Sovereign Québec*, 204–12. Toronto: James Lorimer 1992.

Boadway, Robin W., Thomas J. Courchene, and Douglas D. Purvis, eds.
Economic Dimensions of Constitutional Change. 2 vols. Kingston: John
Deutsch Institute 1991.

Boadway, Robin W., Douglas D. Purvis, and Jean-François Wen.
"Economic Dimensions of Constitutional Change: A Survey of the
Issues." In Boadway, Thomas J. Courchene and Purvis, eds., *Economic
Dimensions of Constitutional Change*, 1:12–44. Kingston: John Deutsch
Institute 1991.

Bookman, Milica Zarkovic. *The Economics of Secession*. New York: St
Martin's Press 1993.

Boothe, Paul, ed. *Alberta and the Economics of Constitutional Change*.
Western Studies in Economic Policy no. 3. Edmonton: Western Centre
for Economic Research 1992.

– "Constitutional Change and the Provision of Government Goods and
Services." In Boothe, ed., *Alberta and the Economics of Constitutional
Change*, Western Studies in Economic Policy no. 3, 19–48. Edmonton:
Western Centre for Economic Research 1992.

Boothe, Paul, and Richard Harris. "Alternative Divisions of Federal
Assets and Liabilities." In Robin W. Boadway, Thomas J. Courchene,

and Douglas D. Purvis, eds., *Economic Dimensions of Constitutional Change*, 2:453–73. Kingston: John Deutsch Institute 1991.

Boothe, Paul, Barbara Johnston, and Karrin Powys-Lybbe. "Dismantling Confederation: The Divisive Question of the National Debt." In Boothe et al., *Closing the Books*, Canada Round Series no. 8, 26–55. Toronto: C.D. Howe Institute 1991.

Boothe, Paul, et al. *Closing the Books: Dividing Federal Assets and Debt if Canada Breaks Up*. Canada Round Series no.8. Toronto: C.D. Howe Institute 1991.

Bouchard, Lucien. *Un nouveau parti pour l'étape décisive*. Montreal: Fides 1993.

Bourgault, Pierre. *Now or Never! Manifesto for an Independent Quebec*. Toronto: Key Porter Books 1991.

Boyce, Peter. "Singapore as a Sovereign State." *Australian Outlook* 19, no. 3 (1965): 259–71.

– *Malaysia and Singapore in International Diplomacy: Documents and Commentaries*. Sydney: Sydney University Press 1968.

Breton, Albert. "Supplementary Statement." In Canada, Royal Commission on the Economic Union and Development Prospects for Canada, *Report*, 3:486–526. Ottawa: Minister of Supply and Services 1985.

Brossard, Jacques. *L'accession à la souveraineté et le cas du Québec: Conditions et modalités politico-juridiques*. Montreal: Presses de l'Université de Montréal 1976.

Brown, Douglas M. "The Evolving Role of the Provinces in Canada–U.S. Trade Relations." In Brown and Earl H. Fry, eds., *States and Provinces in the International Economy*, 93–144. Berkeley: Institute of Governmental Studies Press 1993.

Buchanan, Allen. *Secession: The Morality of Political Divorce from Fort Sumter to Lithuania and Quebec*. Boulder: Westview Press 1991.

– "Quebec Secession and Native Territorial Rights." *Network* 2, no. 3 (March 1992): 2–4.

Buchanan, James M., and Roger L. Faith. "Secession and the Limits of Taxation: Toward a Theory of Internal Exit." *American Economic Review* 77, no. 5 (1987): 1023–31.

Buchheit, Lee C. *Secession: The Legitimacy of Self-Determination*. New Haven: Yale University Press 1978.

Burns, R.M., ed. *One Country or Two?* Montreal: McGill-Queen's University Press 1971.

Cairns, Alan C. "The Governments and Societies of Canadian Federalism." *Canadian Journal of Political Science* 10, no. 4 (1977): 695–725.

– "The Politics of Constitutional Renewal in Canada." In Keith G. Banting and Richard Simeon, eds., *Redesigning the State: The Politics of Constitutional Change*, 95–145. Toronto: University of Toronto Press 1985.

- "The Charter, Interest Groups, Executive Federalism, and Constitutional Reform." In David E. Smith, Peter MacKinnon, and John C. Courtney, eds., *After Meech Lake: Lessons for the Future*, 13–31. Saskatoon: Fifth House 1991.
- "Constitutional Change and the Three Equalities." In Ronald L. Watts and Douglas M. Brown, eds., *Options for a New Canada*, 77–100. Toronto: University of Toronto Press 1991.
- "An Election to be Remembered: Canada 1993." *Canadian Public Policy* 20, no. 3 (1994): 219–34.
Cameron, Barbara. "A Constitution for English Canada." In Daniel Drache and Roberto Perin, eds., *Negotiating with a Sovereign Québec*, 230–43. Toronto: James Lorimer 1992.
Canada. *Citizenship Act: Office Consolidation*. Ottawa: Minister of Supply and Services 1990.
- *Revised Statutes of Canada, 1985*.
- *Shaping Canada's Future Together: Proposals*. Ottawa: Minister of Supply and Services 1991.
- *Statutes of Canada*. Ottawa: Queen's Printer 1984–93.
- *North American Free Trade Agreement*. Ottawa: Minister of Supply and Services 1992.
- *North American Free Trade Agreement: An Overview and Description*. Ottawa: n.p., August 1992.
- Chief Electoral Officer. *Report of the Chief Electoral Officer*. Ottawa: Minister of Supply and Services 1984, 1988.
- Department of Justice. *A Consolidation of the Constitution Acts 1987–1982*. Ottawa: Minister of Supply and Services 1983.
- Department of National Defence. *The Queen's Regulations and Orders for the Canadian Forces*. Vol. 1. Ottawa: Queen's Printer 1968 (updated).
- Employment and Immigration Canada. *Canada-Québec Accord relating to Immigration and Temporary Admission of Aliens*. Ottawa: Minister of Supply and Services Canada 1991.
- External Affairs Canada, *The Canada–U.S. Free Trade Agreement*. Ottawa: Department of External Affairs n.d.
- Federal-Provincial Committee, *Agreement between the Government of Canada and the Gouvernement du Québec*. Ottawa: Queen's Printer 1978.
- Federal-Provincial Relations Office, Canadian Unity Information Office. *Sovereignty-Association: The Contradictions*. Ottawa: Minister of Supply and Services 1978.
- House of Commons. *Debates*. 1993.
- Revenue Canada. *Taxation Statistics 1992*. Ottawa: Minister of Supply and Services 1993.
- Senate and House of Commons. *A Renewed Canada*, report of the Special Joint Committee of the Senate and the House of Commons, 28 February 1992.

- Task Force on Program Review. *Real Property*. Ottawa: Minister of Supply and Services 1986.
- Treasury Board Secretariat. *Directory of Federal Real Property*. Ottawa: Minister of Supply and Services 1992.

Canadian Parliamentary Guide. Ottawa 1980–92.

Capek, Ales, and Gerald W. Sazama. "Czech and Slovak Economic Relations." *Europe-Asia Studies* 45, no. 2 (1993): 211–35.

Chambers, Edward J., and Michael B. Percy. "Natural Resources and the Western Canadian Economy: Implications for Constitutional Change." In Norman Cameron et al. eds., *From East and West*. Canada Round Series no. 6, 59–85. Toronto: C.D. Howe Institute 1991.
- "Structural Characteristics of the Alberta Economy: Implications for Constitutional Scenarios." In Paul Boothe, ed., *Alberta and the Economics of Constitutional Change*, Western Studies in Economic Policy no. 3, 163–204. Edmonton: Western Centre for Economic Research 1992.
- *Western Canada in the International Economy*, Western Studies in Economic Policy, no. 2. Edmonton: University of Alberta Press 1992.

Chan, Heng Chee. *Singapore: The Politics of Survival 1965–1967*. Singapore: Oxford University Press 1971.

Chant, John. "Dividing the Debt: Avoiding the Burden." In Boothe et al., *Closing the Books*, Canada Round Series no. 8, 84–91. Toronto: C.D. Howe Institute 1991.
- "Financial Regulation under Alternative Constitutional Arrangements." In Robin W. Boadway, Thomas J. Courchene, and Douglas D. Purvis, eds., *Economic Dimensions of Constitutional Change*, 2:409–24. Kingston: John Deutsch Institute 1991.

Cloutier, Édouard, Jean H. Guay, and Daniel Latouche. *Le virage: L'évolution de l'opinion publique au Québec depuis 1960*. Montreal: Québec/Amérique 1992.

Coleman, William D. *Business and Politics: A Study of Collective Action*. Montreal: McGill-Queen's University Press 1988.
- "Standing Ready: Quebec's Quasi-State and Interest Associations." Paper presented to Conference on Nationalism, McMaster University, 2–4 May 1994.

Coon-Come, Matthew. "The Crees, Self-Determination, Secession and the Territorial Integrity of Quebec." *Network* 2, no. 5 (May 1992): 11–12.

Côté, Marcel. "Souveraineté: Les coûts de transition." Paper presented to conference Projet "90," Module Administration, Université du Québec à Montréal, 24 March 1992.

Coulombe, Gérard (Desjardins Ducharme). "La souveraineté du Québec et les institutions financières." In Quebec, Assemblée nationale, Commission d'étude, *Les implications de la mise en oeuvre de la souveraineté (deuxième partie)*. Exposés et études, 4:371–559. Quebec 1992.

Courchene, Thomas J. "Canada 1992: Political Denouement or Economic Renaissance." In Robin W. Boadway, Courchene, and Douglas D. Purvis, eds., *Economic Dimensions of Constitutional Change*, 1:45–76. Kingston: John Deutsch Institute 1991.

– *In Praise of Renewed Federalism*. Canada Round Series no. 2. Toronto: C.D. Howe Institute 1991.

– "Toward the Reintegration of Social and Economic Policy." In G. Bruce Doern and Bryne Purchase, eds., *Canada at Risk? Canadian Public Policy in the 1990s*, 125–48. Toronto: C.D. Howe Institute 1991.

– "The Community of the Canadas." In Courchene, *Rearrangements: The Courchene Papers*, 72–103. Toronto: Mosaic Press 1992.

– "What Does Ontario Want?" In Courchene, *Rearrangements*, 1–42. Toronto: Mosaic Press 1992.

– "Staatsnation vs Kulturnation: The Future of ROC." In Kenneth McRoberts, ed., *Beyond Quebec: The Canada that Remains*. Montreal: McGill-Queen's University Press. Forthcoming.

Courchene, Thomas J., and John McDougall. "The Context for Future Constitutional Options." In Ronald L. Watts and Douglas M. Brown, eds., *Options for a New Canada*, 33–51. Toronto: University of Toronto Press 1991.

Covell, Maureen. *Thinking about the Rest of Canada: Options for Canada without Quebec*. Study no. 6, Background Studies of the York University Constitutional Reform Project. North York: York University Centre for Public Law and Public Policy 1992.

Dasko, Donna. "The Ties That Bound: Canadians' Changing Perceptions of the Federal System." *Network* 2, nos. 6–7 (1992): 5–11.

Dauphin, Roma, and Stanislas Slosar. "Étude des modalités de maintien de l'espace économique canadien actuel après l'accession du Québec à la souveraineté." In Quebec, Assemblée nationale, Commission d'étude, *Les implications de la mise en oeuvre de la souveraineté (première partie)*, Exposés et études, 3:139–84. Quebec 1992.

Day, Shelagh. "Speaking for Ourselves." In Kenneth McRoberts and Patrick J. Monahan, eds., *The Charlottetown Accord, the Referendum, and the Future of Canada*, 58–72. Toronto: University of Toronto Press 1993.

Dehem, Roger. *On the Meaning of "Economic Association."* Montreal: C.D. Howe Research Institute 1978.

de Mestral, A.L.C. "Economic Integration under the GATT, the FTA, the Treaty of Rome, and the Canadian Constitution." In Stanley H. Hartt et al., *Tangled Web*, Canada Round Series no. 15, 31–53. Toronto: C.D. Howe Institute 1992.

Dion, Léon. *Nationalismes et politique au Québec*. Montreal: Hurtubise 1975.

– "Pour sortir de l'impasse constitutionelle." In Quebec, Commission sur l'avenir, *Les avis des spécialistes*, Working Paper no. 4, 269–80. Quebec 1991.

Dion, Stéphane. "Explaining Quebec Nationalism." In R. Kent Weaver, ed., *The Collapse of Canada?* 77–121. Washington: Brookings Institution 1992.

– "The Importance of the Language Issue in the Constitutional Crisis." In Douglas Brown and Robert Young, eds., *Canada: The State of the Federation 1992,* 77–88. Kingston: Institute of Intergovernmental Relations 1992.

– "Why is Secession Rare? Lessons from Quebec." Unpublished manuscript (December 1993).

– "Quebec Secession: What Are the Odds?" Paper presented at the Colloquium on Canadian Government and Politics, Bowling Green State University, 22 January 1994.

Donner, Arthur, and Fred Lazar. "The Case for a Single Currency and a Reformed Central Bank." In Daniel Drache and Roberto Perin, eds., *Negotiating with a Sovereign Québec,* 127–38. Toronto: James Lorimer 1992.

Drache, Daniel. "Negotiating with Québec: A New Division of Powers or Secession?" In Drache and Roberto Perin, eds., *Negotiating with a Sovereign Québec,* 13–29. Toronto: James Lorimer 1992.

Drache, Daniel, and Roberto Perin, eds. *Negotiating with a Sovereign Québec.* Toronto: James Lorimer 1992.

Drake, P.J. "Singapore and Malaysia: The Monetary Consequences." *Australian Outlook* 20, no. 1 (1966): 28–35.

Draper, Theodore. "A New History of the Velvet Revolution." *New York Review of Books,* 14 January 1993, 14–20.

– "The End of Czechoslovakia." *New York Review of Books,* 28 January 1993, 20–6.

Economic Council of Canada. *A Joint Venture: The Economics of Constitutional Options,* Twenty-Eighth Annual Review. Ottawa: Minister of Supply and Services 1991.

Elections Canada. *Percentage of Popular Vote by Province.* Unofficial results reported by Media Election Consortium, 28 October 1993.

– *Redistribution.* n.p. n.d.

Elton, David, "The Charlottetown Accord Senate: Effective or Emasculated?" In Kenneth McRoberts and Patrick J. Monahan, *The Charlottetown Accord, the Referendum, and the Future of Canada,* 37–55. Toronto: University of Toronto Press 1993.

Emanueli, Claude C. "L'accession du Québec à la souveraineté et la nationalité." In Quebec, Assemblée Nationale, Commission d'étude, *Les attributs d'un Québec souverain,* Exposés et études, 1:61–113. Quebec 1992.

Etzioni, Amatai. "The Evils of Self-Determination." *Foreign Policy* 89 (1992-93): 21–35.

Facts on File: Weekly World News Digest with Cumulative Index. New York: Facts on File, Inc. 1992.

Fafard, Patrick, and Darrel R. Reid. *Constituent Assemblies: A Comparative Survey.* Research Paper no. 30. Kingston: Institute of Intergovernmental Relations 1991.

Finkelstein, Neil, and George Vegh. *The Separation of Quebec and the Constitution of Canada.* Study no. 2, Background Studies of the York University Constitutional Reform Project. North York: York University Centre for Public Law and Public Policy 1992.

Flanz, Gilbert H. "West Indian Federation." In Thomas Franck, ed., *Why Federations Fail,* 91–123. New York: New York University Press 1968.

Fletcher, Nancy McHenry. *The Separation of Singapore from Malaysia.* Data Paper no. 73. Ithaca, N.Y.: Cornell University Southeast Asia Program 1969.

Fortin, Bernard. "Les options monétaires d'un Québec souverain." In Québec, Commission sur l'avenir, *Éléments d'analyse économique,* Working Paper no. 1, 283–302. Quebec 1991.

Fortin, Pierre. "How Economics Is Shaping the Constitutional Debate in Quebec." In Robert Young, ed., *Confederation in Crisis,* 35–44. Toronto: James Lorimer 1991.

– "La question de l'emploi au Québec: La photo et le film." In Québec, Commission sur l'avenir, *Éléments d'analyse économique,* Working Paper no. 1, 167–241. Quebec 1991.

– "The Threat of Quebec Sovereignty: Meaning, Likelihood and Economic Consequences." In Robin W. Boadway, Thomas J. Courchene, and Douglas D. Purvis, eds., *Economic Dimensions of Constitutional Change,* 2:335–44. Kingston: John Deutsch Institute 1991.

– "A Comment." In John McCallum and Chris Green, *Parting as Friends,* Canada Round Series no. 5, 87–90. Toronto: C.D. Howe Institute 1991.

– "Le passage à la souveraineté et le déficit budgétaire du Québec." In Alain-G. Gagnon and François Rocher, eds., *Répliques au détracteurs de la souveraineté du Québec,* 440–459. Montreal: VLB éditeur 1992.

Fournier, Pierre. *Autopsie du lac Meech: La souveraineté est-elle inévitable?* Montreal: VLB éditeur 1990.

Franck, Thomas M. "East African Federation." In Franck, ed., *Why Federations Fail: An Inquiry into the Requisites for Successful Federalism,* 3–36. New York: New York University Press 1968.

– "Why Federations Fail." in Franck, ed., *Why Federations Fail,* 167–99. New York: New York University Press 1968.

Franck, Thomas M., et al. "L'intégrité territoriale du Québec dans l'hypothèse de l'accession à la souveraineté." In Québec, Assemblée nationale, Commission d'étude, *Les attributs d'un Québec souverain,* Exposés et études, 1:377–445. Quebec 1992.

Fraser, Alistair, W.F. Dawson, and John A. Holtby. *Beauchesne's Rules and Forms of the House of Commons of Canada.* 6th ed. Toronto: Carswell 1989.

Fry, Earl H. *Canada's Unity Crisis: Implications for U.S.–Canadian Economic Relations.* New York: Twentieth Century Fund 1992.

Gagnon, Alain-G., and François Rocher, eds. *Répliques aux détracteurs de la souveraineté du Québec.* VLB éditeur 1992.

Gallup Canada, Inc. *Gallup Report*, 1989–93.

Gibbins, Roger. "Speculations on a Canada without Quebec." In Kenneth McRoberts and Patrick J. Monahan, eds., *The Charlottetown Accord, the Referendum, and the Future of Canada*, 264–73. Toronto: University of Toronto Press 1993.

Gibson, Gordon. "What If the Wheels Fall Off the Constitutional Bus?" Canada West Foundation. *Alternatives '92*, May 1992.

– *Plan B: The Future of the Rest of Canada.* Vancouver: Fraser Institute 1994.

Goldberg, Michael A., and Maurice D. Levi. "Growing Together or Apart: The Risks and Returns of Alternative Constitutions of Canada." Manuscript (September 1993). Forthcoming in *Canadian Public Policy.*

Gordon, Harold J., Jr., and Nancy M. Gordon *The Austrian Empire: Abortive Federation?* Lexington, Mass.: D.C. Heath 1974.

Grady, Patrick. *Economic Consequences of Quebec Sovereignty.* Vancouver: The Fraser Institute 1991.

– *The National Debt and New Constitutional Arrangements.* Economic Council of Canada Working Paper no. 26. Ottawa: Economic Council 1992.

Granatstein, J.L. "Canada, Quebec and the World." In Granatstein and Kenneth McNaught, eds., *"English Canada" Speaks Out*, 94–106. Toronto: Doubleday 1991.

Granatstein, J.L., and Kenneth McNaught, eds. *"English Canada" Speaks Out.* Toronto: Doubleday 1991.

Grant, John. "A Comment." In Daniel E.W. Laidler and William B.P. Robson, eds., *Two Nations, One Money?* 57–63. Toronto: C.D. Howe Institute 1991.

Grey, Julius H. "Winning Quebec for Canada." *Policy Options* 13, no.4 (May 1992): 20-1.

Grieco, Joseph M. "Anarchy and the Limits of Cooperation: A Realist Critique of the Newest Liberal Institutionalism." *International Organization* 42, no. 3 (1988): 485–507.

Harris, Richard G., and Douglas D. Purvis. "Some Economic Aspects of Political Restructuring." In Robin W. Boadway, Thomas J. Courchene, and Douglas D. Purvis, eds., *Economic Dimensions of Constitutional Change*, 1:189–211. Kingston: John Deutsch Institute 1991.

Hartt, Stanley H. "Sovereignty and the Economic Union." In Hartt et al., *Tangled Web*, Canada Round Series no. 15, 3–30. Toronto: C.D. Howe Institute 1992.

Hartt, Stanley H., et al. *Tangled Web: Legal Aspects of Deconfederation.* Canada Round Series no. 15. Toronto: C.D. Howe Institute 1992.

Havel, Vaclav. *Summer Meditations,* trans. Paul Wilson. Toronto: Vintage Books Canada 1993.

Haydon, Peter. "General Security Analysis of the Scenarios." In Alex Morrison, ed., *Divided We Fall,* 27–37. Toronto: Canadian Institute of Strategic Studies 1991.

Hechter, Michael. "The Dynamics of Secession." *Acta Sociologica* 35, no. 4 (1992): 267–83.

Heraclides, Alexis. "Secession, Self-Determination and Nonintervention: In Quest of a Normative Synthesis." *Journal of International Affairs* 45, no. 2 (1992): 399–420.

Hicks, Ursula K. *Federalism: Failure and Success.* London: Macmillan 1978.

Hodgins, Bruce W. "The Northern Boundary of Quebec: The James Bay Crees as Self-Governing Canadians." In J.L. Granatstein and Kenneth McNaught, eds., *"English Canada" Speaks Out,* 141–9. Toronto: Doubleday 1991.

Hogg, Peter W. *Constitutional Law of Canada,* 2nd ed. Toronto: Carswell 1985.

– *Is the Constitution of Canada Ready for the 21st Century?* Study no. 1, Background Studies of the York University Constitutional Reform Project. North York: York University Centre for Public Law and Public Policy 1992.

Howitt, Peter. "Constitutional Reform and the Bank of Canada." In Robin W. Boadway, Thomas J. Courchene, and Douglas D. Purvis, eds., *Economic Dimensions of Constitutional Change,* 2:383–408. Kingston: John Deutsch Institute 1991.

Huertas, Thomas F. *Economic Growth and Economic Policy in a Multinational Setting: The Habsburg Monarchy, 1841–1865.* New York: Arno Press 1977.

Imbeau, Louis-M. "Le compromis est-il encore possible? La négotiation constitutionnelle de l'après-Meech à la lumière de la théorie des jeux." In Louis Balthazar, Guy Laforest and Vincent Lemieux, eds., *Le Québec et la restructuration de Canada 1980-1992,* 283–309. Sillery: Éditions du Septentrion 1991. (English translation in University of Western Ontario, Political Economy Research Group, *Papers in Political Economy,* no. 23, May 1992.)

Informetrica Ltd. *Financial Sector: Deposit-Taking Institutions.* Economics of Confederation Study no. 6.0, Ottawa: Informetrica Limited 1991.

– *Financial Sector: Life and Health Insurance.* Economics of Confederation Study no. 9.0, Ottawa: Informetrica Limited 1991.

– *Registered Pension Plans.* Economics of Confederation Study no. 2.0, Ottawa: Informetrica Limited 1991.

– *Supply Management: Dairy.* Economics of Confederation Study no. 7.1, Ottawa: Informetrica Limited 1991.

- *Supply Management: Poultry and Eggs.* Economics of Confederation Study no. 8.0, Ottawa: Informetrica Limited 1991.

Institute of Intergovernmental Relations, Queen's University. *Approaches to National Standards in Federal Systems.* Research report for the Government of Ontario, September 1991.

Ip, Irene K., and William B.P. Robson. "Liquidating the Federal Balance Sheet: Some Additional Modest Proposals." In Paul Boothe et al., *Closing the Books,* Canada Round Series no. 8, 69–83.Toronto: C.D. Howe Institute 1991.

Islam, M. Rafiqul. "Secessionist Self-Determination: Some Lessons from Katanga, Biafra and Bangladesh." *Journal of Peace Research* 22, no. 3 (1985): 211–21.

Janda, Richard. *Re-balancing the Federation through Senate Reform: Another Look at the Bundesrat.* Study no. 11, Background Studies of the York University Constitutional Reform Project. North York: York University Centre for Public Law and Public Policy 1992.

Jenkins, David. "New Life in an Old Pact." *Far Eastern Economic Review,* 7–13 November, 1980, 26–8.

Jockel, Joseph. *If Canada Breaks Up: Implications for U.S. Policy.* Occasional Paper no. 7, Canadian-American Public Policy. Orono, Maine: University of Maine, Canadian-American Centre 1991.

- "The USA Reaction." In Alex Morrison, ed., *Divided We Fall,* 141–7. Toronto: Canadian Institute of Strategic Studies 1991.

Johnston, Richard, et al. "The People and the Charlottetown Accord." In Ronald L. Watts and Douglas M. Brown, eds., *Canada: The State of the Federation 1993,* 19–43. Kingston: Institute of Intergovernmental Relations 1993.

Jordan, F.J.E. "Sharing the Seaway System." In R.M. Burns, ed., *One Country or Two?,* 95–120. McGill-Queen's University Press 1971.

Keesing's Record of World Events, ed. Roger East. London: Longman 1992.

Kilgour, D. Marc and Terrence J. Levesque. "The Canadian Constitutional Amending Formula: Bargaining in the Past and the Future." *Public Choice* 44 (1984): 457–80.

Komlos, John. *The Habsburg Monarchy as a Customs Union: Economic Development in Austria-Hungary in the Nineteenth Century.* Princeton: Princeton University Press 1983.

Kusin, Vladimir V. "Czechs and Slovaks: The Road to the Current Debate." *Report on Eastern Europe* (Munich), 5 October 1990, 4–13.

Kwavnick, David. "Québécois Nationalism and Canada's National Interest." *Journal of Canadian Studies* 12, no. 3 (July 1977): 53–68.

Laidler, David E.W. and William B.P. Robson. "Two Nations, One Money? Canada's Monetary System following a Quebec Secession." In Laidler and Robson, eds., *Two Nations, One Money?* Canada Round Series no. 3, 1–51. Toronto: C.D. Howe Institute 1991.

Lamont, Lansing. *Breakup: The Coming End of Canada and the Stakes for America*. New York: W.W. Norton 1994.

Latouche, Daniel. "Canada: The New Country from Within the Old Dominion." *Queen's Quarterly* 98, no. 2 (1991): 319–37.

– "Le Québec est bien petit et le monde, bien grand." In Alain-G. Gagnon and François Rocher, eds., *Répliques aux détracteurs de la souveraineté du Québec*, 345–72. Montreal: VLB éditeur 1992.

Laycock, David. "Reforming Canadian Democracy? Institutions and Ideology in the Reform Party Project." *Canadian Journal of Political Science* 27, no. 2 (1994): 213–47.

"Le Canada dans le peau." *L'Actualité* 17, no. 11 (July 1992): 21–52.

Lederman, W.R., "The British Parliamentary System and Canadian Federalism." In R.M. Burns, ed., *One Country or Two?* 17–39. Montreal: McGill-Queen's University Press 1971.

Lee, H.P. "Emergency Powers in Malaysia." In F.A. Trindale and Lee, eds., *The Constitution of Malaysia: Further Perspectives and Developments*. 134–56. Petaling Jaya: Oxford University Press 1986.

Leistikow, Gunnar. "Co-operation between the Scandinavian Countries." In Henning Friis, ed., *Scandinavia: Between East and West*, 307–24. Ithaca: Cornell University Press 1950.

Lemco, Jonathan. *Political Stability in Federal Governments*. New York: Praeger 1991.

– "American Interests in Post-Sovereignty Quebec-Canada Relations: A View from Abroad." *Network* 2, no. 4 (April 1992): 13–15.

– *Turmoil in the Peaceable Kingdom: The Quebec Sovereignty Movement and Its Implications for Canada and the United States*. Toronto: University of Toronto Press. Forthcoming.

Leroy, Vély. "Les options monétaires d'un Québec souverain." In Québec, Assemblée nationale, Commission d'étude, *Les implications de la mise en oeuvre (deuxième partie)*, Exposés et études 4:289–326. Quebec 1992.

Leslie, Peter. "Equal to Equal: Economic Association and the Canadian Common Market." Discussion Paper no. 6. Kingston: Queen's University, Institute of Intergovernmental Relations 1979.

– *Federal State, National Economy*. Toronto: University of Toronto Press 1987.

– "Options for the Future of Canada: The Good, the Bad, and the Fantastic." In Ronald L. Watts and Douglas M. Brown, eds., *Options for a New Canada*, 122–40. Toronto: University of Toronto Press 1991.

– "The Fiscal Crisis of Canadian Federalism." In Leslie, Kenneth Norrie, and Irene K. Ip, *A Partnership in Trouble: Renegotiating Fiscal Federalism*, 1–86. Toronto: C.D. Howe Institute 1993.

Lindgren, Raymond E. *Norway-Sweden: Union, Disunion, and Scandinavian Integration*. Princeton: Princeton University Press 1959.

Lipsey, Richard G. "Comments on the Bélanger-Campeau Commission's Papers on Trade Relations." In Gordon Ritchie et al. *Broken Links*, Canada Round Series no. 4, 58–69. Toronto: C.D. Howe Institute 1991.

Lipsey, Richard G., Daniel Schwanen, and Ronald J. Wonnacott. *The NAFTA: What's In, What's Out, What's Next*. Toronto: C.D. Howe Institute 1994.

Livingston, W.S. "A Note on the Nature of Federalism." In Aaron Wildavsky, ed., *American Federalism in Perspective*, 33–47. Boston: Little Brown 1967.

Loungnarath, Vilaysoun. "A Comment on Hartt and de Mestral." In Stanley H. Hartt et al., *Tangled Web*, Canada Round Series no. 15, 60–70. Toronto: C.D. Howe Institute 1992.

Lucas, Robert F. "Comment." In Robin W. Boadway, Thomas J. Courchene, and Douglas D. Purvis, eds. *Economic Dimensions of Constitutional Change*, 2:433–44. Kingston: John Deutsch Institute 1991.

Lucas, R.F., and B. Reid. "The Choice of Efficient Monetary Arrangements in the Post Meech Lake Era." *Canadian Public Policy* 17, no. 4 (1991): 417–33.

Lukic, Reneo. "Twilight of the Federations in East Central Europe and the Soviet Union." *Journal of International Affairs* 45, no. 2 (1992): 575–98.

Lyon, Peter. "Separatism and Secession in the Malaysian Realm 1948–65." In W.H. Morris-Jones, ed., *Collected Seminar Papers on the Politics of Separatism*, Paper no. 19, 69–78. London: Institute of Commonwealth Studies, University of London 1976.

McCallum, John. "An Economic Union or a Free Trade Agreement: What Difference Does It Make?" In Stanley H. Hartt et al., *Tangled Web*, Canada Round Series no. 15, 54–9. Toronto: C.D. Howe Institute 1992.

– *Canada's Choice: Crisis of Capital or Renewed Federalism*. C.D. Howe Institute Benefactors Lecture, Toronto, 25 June 1992.

McCallum, John, and Chris Green. *Parting as Friends: The Economic Consequences for Quebec*. Canada Round Series no. 5. Toronto: C.D. Howe Institute 1991.

McDougall, John N. "North American Integration and Canadian Disunity." *Canadian Public Policy* 17, no. 4 (1991): 395–408.

Maclean's/CTV Poll. "Voices of Canada." *Maclean's*, 4 January 1993, 42–5.

– "How We Differ." *Maclean's*, 3 January 1994, 32–4.

Maclean's/Decima Poll. "Cross-Canada Opinions." *Maclean's*, 6 January 1992, 62–7.

– "In Search of Unity," *Maclean's*, 1 July 1994, 16–24.

McNaught, Kenneth., "A Ghost at the Banquet: Could Quebec Secede Peacefully?" In J.L. Granatstein and McNaught, eds., *"English Canada" Speaks Out*, 80–93. Toronto: Doubleday 1991.

McNeil, Kent. "Aboriginal Nations and Québec's Boundaries: Canada Couldn't Give What It Didn't Have." In Daniel Drache and Roberto Perin, eds., *Negotiating with a Sovereign Québec*, 107–23. Toronto: James Lorimer 1992.

McRoberts, Kenneth. *English Canada and Quebec: Avoiding the Issue*. North York: Robarts Centre for Canadian Studies 1991.

– "Protecting the Rights of Linguistic Minorities." In Daniel Drache and Roberto Perin, eds., *Negotiating with a Sovereign Québec*, 172–88. Toronto: James Lorimer 1992.

– "Disagreeing on Fundamentals: English Canada and Quebec." In McRoberts and Patrick J. Monahan, eds., *The Charlottetown Accord, the Referendum and the Future of Canada*, 249–63. Toronto: University of Toronto Press 1993.

McRoberts, Kenneth, and Patrick J. Monahan, eds. *The Charlottetown Accord, the Referendum, and the Future of Canada*. Toronto: University of Toronto Press 1993.

Manning, E. Preston. "Leadership for Changing Times." Address, Reform Party of Canada, Annual Assembly, Edmonton, 1989.

– "A New and Better Home for Canadians." Keynote address, Reform Party of Canada, Party Assembly, Ottawa, 15 October 1994.

Mansell, Robert L., and Ronald C. Schlenker. "A Regional Analysis of Fiscal Balances under Existing and Alternative Constitutional Arrangements." In Paul Boothe, ed., *Alberta and the Economics of Constitutional Change*, Western Studies in Economic Policy no. 3, 210–66. Edmonton: Western Centre for Economic Research 1992.

Martin, Peter. "Slovakia: Calculating the Cost of Independence." *RFE/RL Research Report*. (Munich), 20 March 1992, 33–38.

Martin, Pierre. "Association after Sovereignty? Canadian Views on Economic Association with a Sovereign Quebec." Manuscript, July 1993. Forthcoming in *Canadian Public Policy*.

Mason, John W. *The Dissolution of the Austro-Hungarian Empire, 1867–1918*. London: Longman 1985.

Maxwell, Judith, and Caroline Pestieau. *Economic Realities of Contemporary Confederation*. Montreal: C.D. Howe Research Institute 1980.

May, Arthur J. *The Hapsburg Monarchy 1867–1914*. Cambridge: Harvard University Press 1951.

May, Doug, and Dane Rowlands. "Atlantic Canada in Confederation: Uncharted Waters with Dangerous Shoals." In Norman Cameron et al., *From East and West*, Canada Round Series no. 6, 1–56. Toronto: C.D. Howe Institute 1991.

Means, Gordon P. *Malaysian Politics*, London: University of London Press 1970.

Monahan, Patrick J. *Meech Lake: The Inside Story*. Toronto: University of Toronto Press 1991.

– *Political and Economic Integration: The European Experience and Lessons for Canada*. Study no. 10. Background Studies of the York University Constitutional Reform Project. North York: York University Centre for Public Law and Public Policy 1992.

"The Sounds of Silence." In Kenneth McRoberts and Patrick J. Monahan, eds., *The Charlottetown Accord, the Referendum, and the Future of Canada*, 222–48. Toronto: University of Toronto Press 1993.

– "'Cooler Heads Shall Prevail": *Assessing the Costs and Consequences of Quebec Separation*." Unpublished manuscript (July 1994).

Monahan, Patrick, and Lynda Covello. *An Agenda for Constitutional Reform*. Final Report, York University Constitutional Reform Project. North York: York University Centre for Public Law and Public Policy 1992.

Morrison, Alex, ed. *Divided We Fall: The National Security Implications of Canadian Constitutional Issues*. Toronto: Canadian Institute of Strategic Studies 1991.

Morse, Bradford. "Comparative Assessments of Indigenous Peoples in Québec, Canada and Abroad." In Québec, Assemblée nationale, Commission d'étude, *Les implications de la mise en oeuvre (première partie)*, Exposés et études, 3:307–45. Quebec 1992.

Morton, Desmond. "The Canadian Security Dimension." in Alex Morrison, ed., *Divided We Fall*, 69–75. Toronto: Canadian Institute of Strategic Studies 1991.

– "Reflections on the Breakup of Canada, Conflict, and Self-Determination." In Stanley H. Hartt et al., *Tangled Web*, Canada Round Series no. 15, 86–98. Toronto: C.D. Howe Institute 1992.

Musil, Jiri. "Czechoslovakia in the Middle of Transition." *Daedalus* 121, no. 2 (1992): 175–95.

Nafziger, E. Wayne and William L. Richter "Biafra and Bangladesh: The Political Economy of Secessionist Conflict." *Journal of Peace Research* 13, no. 2 (1976): 91–109.

Nemni, Max. *Canada in Crisis and the Destructive Power of Myth*. Université Laval, Laboratoire d'études politiques et administratives. Cahier 92-10. November 1992.

Nordlinger, Eric A. *On the Autonomy of the Democratic State*. Cambridge: Harvard University Press 1981.

Norrie, Kenneth, Robin Boadway, and Lars Osberg. "The Constitution and the Social Contract." In Boadway, Thomas J. Courchene, and Douglas D. Purvis, *Economic Dimensions of Constitutional Change*, 1:225–53. Kingston: John Deutsch Institute 1991.

Obrman, Jan. "Civic Forum Surges to Impressive Victory in Elections." *Report on Eastern Europe* (Munich), 22 June 1990, 13–16.

– "Language Law Stirs Controversy in Slovakia." *Report on Eastern Europe* (Munich), 16 November 1990, 13–17.

– "Further Discussions on the Future of the Federation." *Report on Eastern Europe* (Munich) 20 September 1991, 6–10.
– "Czechoslovakia: Stage Set for Disintegration?" *RFE/RL Research Report* (Munich), 10 July 1992, 26–31.
– "Czechoslovakia's New Governments." *RFE/RL Research Report* (Munich), 17 July 1992, 1–8.
– "Slovakia Declares Sovereignty; President Havel Resigns." *RFE/RL Research Report* (Munich), 31 July 1992, 25–29.
– "Czechoslovakia: A Messy Divorce After All." *RFE/RL Research Report* (Munich), 16 October 1992, 1–5.
Olson, David B. "Dissolution of the State: Political Parties and the 1992 Election in Czechoslovakia." *Communist and Post-Communist Studies* 26 no. 3 (1993): 301–14.
Olson, Mancur. *The Rise and Decline of Nations.* New Haven: Yale University Press 1982.
Ongkili, James P. *Nation-building in Malaysia 1946–1974.* Singapore: Oxford University Press 1985.
Pang, Eng Fong, and Linda Lim. "Foreign Labour and Economic Development in Singapore." *International Migration Review* 16, no. 3 (fall 1982): 548–76.
Parti québécois. *La souveraineté: Pourquoi? Comment?* Montreal: Parti québécois 1990.
– *Programme du Parti québécois.* Montreal: Parti québécois 1991.
– *Le Québec dans un monde nouveau.* Montreal: VLB éditeur et le Parti québécois 1993.
Pehe, Jiri. "Czechoslovakia: An Abrupt Transition." *Report on Eastern Europe* (Munich), 5 January 1990, 11–14.
– "Growing Slovak Demands Seen as a Threat to Federation." *Report on Eastern Europe* (Munich), 22 March 1991, 1–10.
– "The State Treaty Between the Czech and the Slovak Republics." *Report on Eastern Europe* (Munich) 7 June 1991, 11–15.
– "Bid for Slovak Sovereignty Causes Political Upheaval." *Report on Eastern Europe* (Munich), 11 October 1991, 10–14.
– "Czechoslovakia's Changing Political Spectrum." *RFE/RL Research Report* (Munich), 31 January 1992, 1–7.
– "Czechoslovak Federal Assembly Adopts Electoral Law." *RFE/RL Research Report* (Munich), 14 February 1992, 27–30.
– "The New Slovak Government and Parliament." *RFE/RL Research Report* (Munich), 10 July 1992, 32–6.
– "Scenarios for Disintegration." *RFE/RL Research Report* (Munich), 31 July 1992, 30–3.
– "Czechs and Slovaks Prepare to Part." *RFE/RL Research Report* (Munich), 18 September 1992, 12–15.

- "The Referendum Controversy in Czechoslovakia." *RFE/RL Research Report* (Munich), 30 October 1992, 35–8.
- "Czechoslovak Parliament Votes to Dissolve Federation." *RFE/RL Research Report* (Munich), 4 December 1992, 1–5.

Pentland, Charles. "Association after Sovereignty?" In Richard Simeon, ed., *Must Canada Fail?* 223–42. Montreal: McGill-Queen's University Press 1977.

Pinard, Maurice. "The Dramatic Reemergence of the Quebec Independence Movement." *Journal of International Affairs* 45, no. 2 (1992): 471-97.
- "The Secessionist Option and Quebec Public Opinion, 1988–1993." *Opinion Canada* 2, no. 3 (June 1994): 1–5.

Progressive Conservative Party of Canada. *Resolution Guide.* General Meeting and National Policy Conference, Toronto, 6–10 August 1991.

Proulx, Pierre-Paul. "L'évolution de l'espace économique du Québec, la politique économique dans un monde de nationalismes et d'interdépendance, et les relations Québec-Ottawa." In Québec, Commission sur l'avenir, *Les avis des spécialistes,* Working Paper no. 4, 867–902. Quebec 1991.

Putnam, Robert D. "Diplomacy and Domestic Politics: The Logic of Two-Level Games." *International Organization* 42, no. 3 (summer 1988): 427–60.

Québec. *Québec-Canada: A New Deal.* Quebec: Éditeur officiel 1979.

Québec. Commission sur l'avenir politique et constitutionnel du Québec (Bélanger-Campeau Commission). *Report of the Commission on the Political and Constitutional Future of Quebec.* Quebec, March 1991.
- *Éléments d'analyse économique pertinents la révision du statut politique et constitutionnel du Québec.* Working Paper no. 1. Quebec 1991.
- *Éléments d'analyse institutionnelle, juridique et démolinguistique pertinents à la révision du statut politique et constitutionnel du Québec.* Working Paper no. 2, Quebec 1991.
- *Les avis des spécialistes invités à répondre aux huit questions posées par la Commission.* Working Paper no. 4. Quebec, 1991.
- Secrétariat de la Commission. "L'accès du Québec aux marchés extérieurs et à l'espace économique canadien." In Québec, Commission sur l'avenir, *Éléments d'analyse économique,* Working Paper no. 1, 19–54. Quebec 1991.
- Secrétariat de la Commission. "Analyse pro forma des finances publiques dans l'hypothèse de la souveraineté du Québec." In Québec, Commission sur l'avenir, *Éléments d'analyse économique,* Working Paper no. 1, 393–566. Quebec 1991.

Québec, Assemblée nationale. Commission d'étude des questions afférentes à l'accession du Québec à la souveraineté. *Draft Report.* Quebec, 1992.

– *Les attributs d'un Québec souverain*. Exposés et études, vol. 1, Quebec 1992.
– *Les implications de la mise en oeuvre de la souveraineté: Les aspects économiques et les finances publiques (première partie)*. Exposés et études, vol. 3, and *(deuxième partie)*, vol. 4. Quebec 1992.
– *Les options monétaires d'un Québec souverain*. Quebec 1992.
– *Les relations entre l'état et les nations autochtones*. Quebec 1992.
– *La succession d'états: Les relations internationales d'un Québec souverain*. Quebec 1992.
Québec, Ministère des finances. *1993–94 Budget: Budget Speech and Additional Information*. Quebec 1993.
Québec, National Assembly. *Bill 150: An Act Respecting the Process for Determining the Political and Constitutional Future of Québec*. Quebec: Quebec Official Publisher 1991.
Rawlyk, G.A. "The Maritimes and the Problem of the Secession of Quebec." In R.M. Burns, ed., One Country or Two? 205–30. Montreal: McGill University Press 1971.
Raynauld, André, with Jean-Pierre Vidal. "Les enjeux économiques de la souveraineté." Memoir submitted to the Conseil du Patronat du Québec, October 1990.
Reesor, Bayard. *The Canadian Constitution in Historical Perspective*. Scarborough: Prentice-Hall 1992.
Reform Party of Canada. *Blue Sheet: Principles, Policies & Election Platform*. Reform Party of Canada 1993.
Reid, Bradford, and Tracy Snoddon. "Redistribution under Alternative Constitutional Arrangements for Canada." In Paul Boothe, ed., *Alberta and the Economics of Constitutional Change*, Western Studies in Economic Policy no. 3, 65–110. Edmonton: Western Centre for Economic Research 1992.
Reid, Scott. *Canada Remapped: How the Partition of Quebec Will Reshape the Nation*. Vancouver: Pulp Press 1992.
Resnick, Philip. *Toward a Canada-Quebec Union*. Montreal: McGill-Queen's University Press 1991.
– *Thinking English Canada*. Toronto: Stoddart 1994.
Richards, Robert G. "The Canadian Constitution and International Economic Relations." In Douglas M. Brown and Murray G. Smith, eds., *Canadian Federalism: Meeting Global Economic Challenges*, 57–63. Kingston: Institute of Intergovernmental Relations 1991.
Ritchie, Gordon, et al. *Broken Links: Trade Relations after a Quebec Secession*. Canada Round Series no. 4. Toronto: C.D. Howe Institute 1991.
Robertson, Ian Ross. "The Atlantic Provinces and the Territorial Question." In J.L. Granatstein and Kenneth McNaught, eds., *"English Canada" Speaks Out*, 162–71. Toronto: Doubleday 1991.

Rousseau, Henri-Paul. "L'intégration politique est-elle nécessaire à l'intégration monétaire?" In Claude Montmarquette et al., *Économie du Québec et Choix Politiques*, 125–48. Montreal: Presses de l'Université du Québec 1979.

Royal Bank of Canada. *Unity or Disunity: An Economic Analysis of the Benefits and the Costs*. Montreal: Royal Bank 1992.

Russell, Peter H. "Towards a New Constitutional Process." In Ronald L. Watts and Douglas M. Brown, eds., *Options for a New Canada*, 140–56. Toronto: University of Toronto Press 1991.

– *Constitutional Odyssey: Can Canadians Become a Sovereign People?* Toronto: University of Toronto Press 1992.

– "The End of Mega Constitutional Politics in Canada?" In Kenneth McRoberts and Patrick J. Monahan, eds., *The Charlottetown Accord, the Referendum, and the Future of Canada*, 211–21. Toronto: University of Toronto Press 1993.

Saladin, Claudia. "Self-Determination, Minority Rights and Constitutional Accommodation: The Example of the Czech and Slovak Federal Republic." *Michigan Journal of International Law* 13, no. 1 (1991): 173–217.

Sancton, Andrew. "Eroding Representation-by-Population in the Canadian House of Commons: The Representation Act, 1985." *Canadian Journal of Political Science* 23, no. 3 (September 1990): 441–57.

Scarth, William M. "A Note on the Desirability of a Separate Quebec Currency." In David E.W. Laidler and William B.P. Robson, *Two Nations, One Money?* Canada Round Series no. 3, 65–76. Toronto: C.D. Howe Institute 1991.

Schroeder, Gertrude E. "On the Economic Viability of New Nation-States." *Journal of International Affairs* 45, no. 2 (1992): 549–74.

Schwartz, Herman. "Constitutional Developments in East Central Europe." *Journal of International Affairs* 45, no. 1 (1991): 71–89.

Scott, Stephen A. "Secession or Reform? Mechanisms and Directions of Constitutional Change in Canada." In A.R. Riggs and Tom Velk, eds., *Federalism in Peril*, 149–62. Vancouver: Fraser Institute 1992.

Simard, Pierre. "Compétition électorale et partage des pouvoirs dans un état fédéral." *Canadian Public Policy* 15, no. 4 (December 1991): 409–16.

Simeon, Richard, "Scenarios for Separation." In Richard Simeon, ed., *Must Canada Fail?* 189–203. Montreal: McGill-Queen's University Press 1977.

Simeon, Richard, and Mary Janigan, eds. *Toolkits and Building Blocks: Constructing a New Canada*. Toronto: C.D. Howe Institute 1991.

Simpson, Jeffrey. "The Referendum and Its Aftermath." In Kenneth McRoberts and Patrick J. Monahan, eds., *The Charlottetown Accord, the Referendum, and the Future of Canada*, 193–9. Toronto: University of Toronto Press 1993.

– *Faultlines: Struggling for a Canadian Vision*. Toronto: Harper Collins 1993.

Smiley, Donald. "As the Options Narrow: Notes on Post-November 15 Canada." *Journal of Canadian Studies* 12, no. 3 (July 1977): 3-7.
– "The Association Dimension of Sovereignty-Association: A Response to the Quebec White Paper." Discussion Paper no. 8. Kingston: Queen's University, Institute of Intergovernmental Relations 1980.
Smith, Miriam. "Québec-Canada Association: Divergent Paths to a Common Economic Agenda." In Daniel Drache and Roberto Perin, eds., *Negotiating with a Sovereign Québec*, 61–70. Toronto: James Lorimer 1992.
Smith, Murray G. "The Quebec Sovereignty Scenario: Implications for Canadian Trade Policies." In Robin W. Boadway, Thomas J. Courchene, and Douglas D. Purvis, eds. *Economic Dimensions of Constitutional Change*, 2:475–93. Kingston: John Deutsch Institute 1991.
Sniderman, Paul M., et al. "Political Culture and the Problem of Double Standards: Mass and Elite Attitudes toward Language Rights in the Canadian Charter of Rights and Freedoms." *Canadian Journal of Political Science* 22, no. 2 (1989): 259–84.
Soberman, Dan. "European Integration: Are There Lessons for Canada?" In Ronald L. Watts and Douglas M. Brown, eds., *Options for a New Canada*, 191–205. Toronto: University of Toronto Press 1991.
Solen, Erik. *The Nordic Council and Scandinavian Integration*. New York: Praeger 1977.
Spiro, Herbert J. "The Federation of Rhodesia and Nyasaland." In Thomas M. Franck, ed., *Why Federations Fail*, 37–89. New York: New York University Press 1968.
Statistics Canada. *Canada Yearbook 1990*. Cat. no. 11-202. Ottawa: Minister of Supply and Services.
– *Corporation Taxation Statistics 1987*. Cat. no. 61-208. Ottawa: Minister of Supply and Services 1990.
– *Daily*. Cat. no. 11-001E, 24 August 1993.
– *Exports: Merchandise Trade 1992*. Cat. no. 65-202. Ottawa: Minister of Industry, Science and Technology 1993.
– *Home Language and Mother Tongue*. 1991 Census. Cat. no. 93-317. Ottawa: Minister of Industry, Science, and Technology 1992.
– *Immigration and Citizenship*. 1991 Census. Cat. no. 93-316. Ottawa: Minister of Industry, Science, and Technology 1992.
– *Manufacturing Industries of Canada: National and Provincial Areas 1989*. Cat. no. 31-203. Ottawa: Minister of Industry, Science, and Technology 1992.
– *Monthly Survey of Manufacturing, March 1993*. Cat. no. 31-001. Ottawa: Minister of Industry, Science and Technology 1993.
– *Mother Tongue*. 1991 Census. Cat. no. 93-316. Ottawa: Minister of Industry, Science, and Technology 1992.

– *Postcensual Annual Estimates of Population By Marital Status, Age, Sex, and Components of Growth for Canada, Provinces, and Territories: June 1, 1993.* Cat. no. 91-210. Ottawa: Minister of Industry, Science, and Technology 1992.
– *Public and Private Investment in Canada: Intentions 1993.* Cat. no. 61-205. Ottawa: Minister of Supply and Services 1993.
– *Provincial Economic Accounts: Annual Estimates, 1981–1991.* Cat. no. 13-203. Ottawa: Minister of Industry, Science, and Technology 1992.
– *Summary of Canadian International Trade, December 1992.* Cat. no. 65-001. Ottawa: Minister of Industry, Science and Technology 1993.
Stein, Michael B. "Federal Political Systems and Federal Societies," *World Politics* 20 (1968): 721–47.
– "Canadian Constitutional Renewal, 1968-1981: A Case Study in Integrative Bargaining." Research Paper no. 27. Kingston: Institute of Intergovernmental Relations 1989.
Svec, Milan. "Czecholsovakia's Velvet Divorce." *Current History* 91, no. 568 (1992): 376–80.
Tapié, Victor-L. *The Rise and Fall of the Habsburg Monarchy,* trans. Stephen Hardman. New York: Praeger 1971.
Taylor, Charles. "Shared and Divergent Values." In Ronald L. Watts and Douglas M. Brown, eds., *Options for a New Canada, 53–76.* Toronto: University of Toronto Press 1991.
Thorburn, Hugh. "Disengagement." In Richard Simeon, ed., *Must Canada Fail?* 205–22. Montreal: McGill-Queen's University Press 1977.
Tihany, Leslie C. "The Austro-Hungarian Compromise, 1867–1918: A Half Century of Diagnosis; Fifty Years of Post-Mortem." *Central European History* 2, no. 2 (June 1969): 114-38.
Toy, Stewart, and Kathryn Leger. "Vive le Canada uni." *Financial Post Magazine* June 1992, 14–18.
Tremblay, Rodrigue. "Constitutional Political Economy and Trade Policies Between Quebec and Canada." In Gordon Ritchie et al., *Broken Links,* Canada Round Series no. 4, 70–81. Toronto: C.D. Howe Institute 1991.
Turp, Daniel. "Réponses aux questions posées par la commission sur l'avenir politique et constitutionnel du québec." In Québec, Commission sur l'avenir, *Les avis des spécialistes,* Working Paper no. 4, 1057–1116. Quebec 1991.
– "Le droit à la sécession: L'expression du principe démocratique." In Alain-G. Gagnon and François Rocher, eds., *Répliques aux détracteurs de la souveraineté du Quebec,* 49–68. Montreal: VLB éditeur 1992.
– "Quebec's Democratic Right to Self-Determination." In Stanley Hartt et al., *Tangled Web,* Canada Round Series no. 15, 99–124. Toronto: C.D. Howe Institute 1992.

Turpel, Mary Ellen. "Does the Road to Québec Sovereignty Run through Aboriginal Territory?" In Daniel Drache and Roberto Perin, eds., *Negotiating with a Sovereign Québec*, 93–106. Toronto: James Lorimer 1992.

– "The Charlottetown Discord and Aboriginal Peoples' Struggle for Fundamental Political Change." In Kenneth McRoberts and Patrick J. Monahan, eds., *The Charlottetown Accord, the Referendum, and the Future of Canada*, 117–51. Toronto: University of Toronto Press 1993.

Ulc, Otto. "The Bumpy Road of the Velvet Revolution." *Problems of Communism* 41 (May–June 1992): 19–33.

United States, FBIS (Foreign Broadcast Information Service). *Daily Report, East Europe*, 1990–93.

Usher, Dan. "The Design of a Government for an English Canadian Country." In Robin W. Boadway, Thomas J. Courchene, and Douglas D. Purvis, eds., *Economic Dimensions of Constitutional Change*, 1:91–116. Kingston: John Deutsch Institute 1991.

Vernon, Richard. "The Federal Citizen." In R.D. Olling and M.W. Westmacott, eds., *Perspectives on Canadian Federalism*, 3–15. Scarborough: Prentice-Hall 1988.

Vreeland, Nena, et al. *Area Handbook for Malaysia*. Washington: American University Foreign Area Studies 1970.

Watts, Ronald, L. *New Federations: Experiments in the Commonwealth*. Oxford: Clarendon Press 1966.

– "The Survival or Disintegration of Federations." In R.M. Burns, ed., *One Country or Two?* 41–72. Montreal: McGill-Queen's University Press 1971.

– "Canada's Constitutional Options: An Outline." In Watts and Douglas M. Brown, eds., *Options for a New Canada*, 15–30. Toronto: University of Toronto Press 1991.

– "Canada in Question, Again." *Queen's Quarterly* 99, no. 4 (1992): 793–804.

Watts, Ronald L., and Douglas M. Brown, eds. *Options for a New Canada*. Toronto: University of Toronto Press 1991.

Wendt, Franz. *Cooperation in the Nordic Countries: Achievements and Obstacles*. Stockholm: Almqvist & Wicksell 1981.

Whalley, John. "The Impact of Federal Policies on Interprovincial Activity." In Michael J. Trebilcock et al., *Federalism and the Canadian Economic Union*, 201–42. Toronto: University of Toronto Press and the Ontario Economic Council 1983.

Whitaker, Reg. "With or Without Quebec?" In J.L. Granatstein and Kenneth McNaught, eds., *"English Canada" Speaks Out*, 17–29. Toronto: Doubleday 1991.

– "Life after Separation." In Daniel Drache and Roberto Perin, eds., *Negotiating with a Sovereign Québec*, 71–81. Toronto: James Lorimer 1992.

- "The Dog That Never Barked: Who Killed Asymmetrical Federalism?" In Kenneth McRoberts and Patrick J. Monahan, eds., *The Charlottetown Accord, the Referendum, and the Future of Canada*, 107–114. Toronto: University of Toronto Press 1993.

Wightman, Gordon. "The Czechoslovak Parliamentary Elections of 1992." *Electoral Studies* 12, no. 1 (1993): 83–6.

Williams, Sharon A. *International Legal Effects of Secession by Quebec*. Study no. 3, Background Studies of the York University Constitutional Reform Project. North York: York University Centre for Public Law and Public Policy 1992.

Wittman, D. "Nations and States: Mergers and Acquisitions; Dissolutions and Divorce." *American Economic Review* 81, no. 2 (1991): 126–29.

Woehrling, José. "Les aspects juridiques de la rédefinition du statut politique et constitutionnel du Québec." In Quebec, Commission sur l'avenir, *Éléments d'analyse institutionnelle*, Working Paper no. 1, 1–110. Quebec 1991.

- "La protection des droits et libertés et le sort des minorités." In Alain-G. Gagnon and François Rocher, eds., *Répliques aux détracteurs de la souveraineté du Québec*, 131–67. VLB éditeur 1992.

Wonnacott, Ronald J. "Reconstructing North American Free Trade following Quebec's Separation: What Can Be Assumed?" In Gordon Ritchie et al., *Broken Links*, Canada Round Series no. 4, 20–44. Toronto: C.D. Howe Institute 1991.

Wood, John R. "Secession: A Comparative Analytical Framework." *Canadian Journal of Political Science* 14, no. 1 (1981): 107–34.

Young, Robert. "National Identification in English Canada: Implications for Quebec Independence." *Journal of Canadian Studies* 12, no. 3 (1977): 69–84.

- "Tectonic Policies and Political Competition." In Albert Breton et al., *The Competitive State*, 129–45. Dordrecht: Kluwer 1991.

- "Aboriginal Inherent Rights of Self-Government and the Constitutional Process." In Douglas Brown, ed., *Aboriginal Governments and Power Sharing in Canada*, 31–44. Kingston: Institute of Intergovernmental Relations 1992.

- "Le Canada hors Québec: Voudra-t-il coopérer avec un Québec souverain?" In Alain-G. Gagnon and François Rocher, eds., *Répliques aux détracteurs de la souveraineté du Quebec*: 392–407. VLB éditeur 1992.

- "Does Globalization Make an Independent Quebec More Viable?" In A.R. Riggs and Tom Velk, eds., *Federalism in Peril*, 121–34. Vancouver: Fraser Institute 1992.

- *The Breakup of Czechoslovakia*. Research Paper no. 32, Kingston: Institute of Intergovernmental Relations 1994.

- "The Political Economy of Secession: The Case of Quebec." *Constitutional Political Economy* 5, no. 2 (1994): 221–45.

- "What Is Good about Provincial Governments?" In Mark Charlton and Paul Barker, eds., *Crosscurrents*, 2d ed., 124–33. Scarborough: Nelson 1994.
- "How Do Peaceful Secessions Happen?" *Canadian Journal of Political Science* 27, no. 4 (1994). Forthcoming.
Young, Robert, Philippe Faucher, and André Blais. "The Concept of Province-building: A Critique." *Canadian Journal of Political Science* 17, no. 4 (1984): 783–818.

Index